The Russian revolution of 1917, like that of 1789 in France, remains
the subject of intense interest. The fundamental questions which have
divided historians over the last seventy years still stir fierce debate.
Was the Bolshevik victory preordained once the Tsarist régime was
overthrown in February? If not, was the only alternative a right-wing
dictatorship of the generals? Or given different leadership, could a
parliamentary democracy have established itself in Russia at that
time? And was the Stalinist dénouement encapsuled, immanent,
within Lenin's victory of October? The issue of alternatives, which
has always engaged Western historians, is now also a matter of great
public moment in a Soviet Union which once again finds itself, as in
1917, in a state of flux, facing an uncertain future.

In *Revolution in Russia: reassessments of 1917*, nineteen leading specialists re-examine the key issues and events of that crucial year.
Representing historians from different generations, countries and
schools of thought, they constitute a unique cross-section of Western
research. Some examine the unfolding crisis 'from below', describing
developments in specific localities or organisations, and some the
view as seen 'from above', exploring Lenin as leader of the Bolshevik
party and the emergent Soviet state. Others analyse the roles played
by the officer corps, industrialists, peasants, factory workers and the
soviets as well as the part of the press and the nationalities. And the
final section of the book deals with issues of historiography and
theory.

Never before in the West has so comprehensive a selection of original essays on 1917 been collected in one volume. *Revolution in Russia:
reassessments of 1917* will be essential reading for all students and specialists of twentieth-century Russian and Soviet history.

REVOLUTION IN RUSSIA:
REASSESSMENTS OF 1917

REVOLUTION
IN RUSSIA:
REASSESSMENTS OF 1917

EDITED BY
EDITH ROGOVIN FRANKEL
JONATHAN FRANKEL
BARUCH KNEI-PAZ

The Hebrew University of Jerusalem

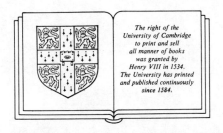

The right of the
University of Cambridge
to print and sell
all manner of books
was granted by
Henry VIII in 1534.
The University has printed
and published continuously
since 1584.

CAMBRIDGE UNIVERSITY PRESS

CAMBRIDGE

NEW YORK   PORT CHESTER

MELBOURNE   SYDNEY

Published by the Press Syndicate of the University of Cambridge
The Pitt Building, Trumpington Street, Cambridge CB2 1RP
40 West 20th Street, New York, NY 10011-4211, USA
10 Stamford Road, Oakleigh, Victoria 3166, Australia

Printed in Great Britain at the University Press, Cambridge

British Library cataloguing in publication data

Revolution in Russia: reassessments of 1917.
1. Russian Revolution, 1917
I. Frankel, Edith Rogovin II. Frankel, Jonathan
III. Knei-Paz, Baruch
947.0841

Library of Congress cataloguing in publication data

Revolution in Russia: reassessments of 1917 / edited by Edith Rogovin
Frankel, Jonathan Frankel, Baruch Knei-Paz.
p.   cm.

Essays first presented in preliminary form at a conference held in
Jerusalem in Jan. 1988 as a tribute to Israel Getzler.
Includes index.
ISBN 0 521 40523 8. – ISBN 0 521 40585 8 (pbk)
1. Soviet Union – History – Revolution, 1917–1921 – Congresses.
I. Frankel, Edith Rogovin. II. Frankel, Jonathan. III. Knei-Paz,
Baruch. IV. Getzler, Israel, 1920–
DK265.R396   1992
947.084'1 – dc20   90-22014   CIP
ISBN 0 521 40523 8 hardback
ISBN 0 521 40585 8 paperback

WV

For
ISRAEL GETZLER
from
his colleagues and friends

CONTENTS

ILLUSTRATIONS

FIGURES

LIST OF CONTRIBUTORS

EDWARD ACTON (University of Manchester) is the author of *Russia: The Present and the Past* and *Rethinking the Russian Revolution*.

JOHN CHANNON (University of London) is the co-editor of *Revolutionary Russia*.

INGEBORG FLEISCHHAUER (Bochum University) is the author of *Die Deutschen im Zarenreich* and *Der Pakt, Hitler, Stalin und die Initiative der deutschen Diplomatie, 1938–1939*.

EDITH ROGOVIN FRANKEL (The Hebrew University of Jerusalem) is the author of *Novy Mir: A Case Study in the Politics of Literature, 1952–1958* and editor of *The Soviet Germans: Past and Present*.

JONATHAN FRANKEL (The Hebrew University of Jerusalem) is the author of *Prophecy and Politics: Socialism, Nationalism and the Russian Jews, 1862–1917*, editor of *Vladimir Akimov on the Dilemmas of Russian Marxism, 1895–1903*, and co-editor of *Studies in Contemporary Jewry: An Annual*.

ZIVA GALILI (Rutgers University) is the author of *The Menshevik Leaders in the Russian Revolution: Social Realities and Political Strategies* and co-editor of *The Making of Three Russian Revolutionaries: Voices from the Menshevik Past*.

ISRAEL GETZLER (The Hebrew University of Jerusalem) is the author of *Martov: A Political Biography of a Russian Social Democrat* and *Kronstadt 1917–1921: The Fate of a Soviet Democracy*.

NEIL HARDING (University College of Swansea) is the author of *Lenin's Political Thought* (2 volumes), *Marxism in Russia* and *The State in Socialist Society*.

STEPHEN F. JONES (Mount Holyoke College) is the author of *Georgia: The First Social-Democratic Republic, 1918–21*.

JOHN KEEP (University of Toronto) is the author of *The Rise of Social Democracy in Russia; The Russian Revolution: A Study in Mass Mobilization*, and *Soldiers of the Tsar: Russian Army and Society, 1462–1874*.

BARUCH KNEI-PAZ (The Hebrew University of Jerusalem) is the author of *The Social and Political Thought of Leon Trotsky*.

DIANE P. KOENKER (University of Illinois at Urbana-Champaign) is the author of *Moscow Workers and the 1917 Revolution* and co-author of *Strikes and Revolution in Russia, 1917*.

DAVID LONGLEY (University of Aberdeen) is currently working on a history of the February Revolution.

DAVID MANDEL (Université du Québec à Montreal) is the author of *The Petrograd Workers and the Fall of the Old Regime: from the February Revolution to the July Days, 1917* and *Petrograd Workers and the Soviet Seizure of Power: from the July Days 1917 to July 1918*.

DONALD J. RALEIGH (University of North Carolina) is the author of *Soviet Studies in History since 1979, Revolution on the Volga: 1917 in Saratov* and *A Russian Civil War Diary: Alexis Babine in Saratov, 1917–1922*.

WILLIAM G. ROSENBERG (University of Michigan) is the author of *Liberals in the Russian Revolution* and co-author of *Transforming Russia and China* and *Strikes and Revolution in Russia, 1917*.

ROBERT SERVICE (University of London) is the author of *The Bolshevik Party in Revolution: A Study in Organizational Change, 1917–1923* and *Lenin: A Political Life*, volume I: *The Strength of Contradiction*, volume II: *Worlds in Collision*; and co-editor of *Revolutionary Russia*.

RONALD GRIGOR SUNY (University of Michigan) is the author of *The Baku Commune, 1917–1918, Armenia in the 20th Century* and *The Making of the Georgian Nation*.

REX A. WADE (George Mason University) is the author of *The Russian Search for Peace, February–October 1917, Red Guards and Workers' Militia in the Russian Revolution* and co-editor of *Politics and Society in Provincial Russia: Saratov, 1590–1917*.

ALLAN WILDMAN (Ohio State University) is the author of *The Making of a Workers Revolution: Russian Social Democracy, 1891–1903, The End of the Russian Imperial Army: The Old Army and The Soldiers Revolt (March–April, 1917)* and *The End of The Russian Imperial Army: The Road to Power and Peace*.

PREFACE

The essays collected here were first presented in preliminary form at a conference on the Russian revolution held in Jerusalem early in January 1988. The date, of course, was selected to fall as close as practicably possible to the seventieth anniversary of the revolution.

The participants were asked to present papers based on unpublished research and to focus on the period of just over one year which opened with the February revolution and concluded with the Brest-Litovsk treaty of April 1918. And, for the most part, the resultant essays now brought together in their final versions deal with specific issues of key importance in the Russian revolution. They subject developments in a given region, organisation or episode to the closest scrutiny, bringing under the microscope, as it were, the interaction of masses and élites; of social dynamics and leadership; of political action and ideology.

However, a few of the authors have chosen not to work from the particular to the general but rather to examine some of the more theoretical questions involved in a study of the revolution. This is true not only of the brief introduction and of the essays collected in the closing section ('1917 in retrospect: historiography and theory'), but also, for example, of Ronald G. Suny's comparative analysis of nationality, nationalism and class as factors in the revolutionary process.

The contributors belong to different generations, come from different countries and understand the history of the Russian revolution in very different ways. Some are primarily political, others primarily social, historians; some regard the Bolshevik enterprise with sympathy, others with the greatest antipathy. However, taken together, their essays do constitute a cross-section of the diverse ways in which the Russian revolution is perceived today by historians in the West.

If the liberalising trends currently prevailing in Russia persist, volumes of this kind assembled in the future will, of course, involve a free intermingling of Russian, East European and Western historians. When the conference met, the Soviet Union had in fact already entered a period of rapid change. As the book goes to press, the rate of that change has accelerated at a speed which few, if any, predicted.

What was then still the Soviet Bloc has, in the meantime, undergone a metamorphosis which can, without hesitation, be termed revolutionary. In the Soviet Union, too, the new course initiated by Mikhail Sergeevich Gorbachev has released social forces of extraordinary power which threaten to sweep away the existing régime and political structures. Many of those forces (although by no means all) have re-emerged as though little altered since 1917; it is as if the seventy years of Bolshevik rule had simply submerged them intact under a thick sheet of ice which is now melting away. And, again as in 1917, and indeed as during the entire period from 1917 to 1920, the ultimate outcome is a matter of the most intense speculation and of the gravest doubt.

In 1988, Israel Getzler retired from his professorial post in Russian history at the Hebrew University of Jerusalem which he had held with great distinction and dedication for close to twenty years. The idea of the conference was inspired by our foreknowledge of this fact and by our wish to find the most fitting way to express to him our deep respect, gratitude and friendship.

When we sent out the invitations, we let it be known discreetly that this was to be a conference not only on 1917 but also for Israel Getzler. We have no doubt that the most unusual response – almost everybody invited decided to come and found the necessary funding to do so – was to a very great extent a mark of tribute to Getzler who, ever since he published his biography of Martov in 1967, has been widely recognised as a leading historian of the Russian revolutionary movement. His more recent book on the role played by Kronstadt in the period 1917 to 1921 and his research on the soviets in the revolution have brought him into close contact with many of the historians working in this field.

This collection of essays is thus a tribute to him from his colleagues and friends. They are grateful to him for his wonderful vitality which has survived the vicissitudes of a lifetime (*inter alia*, the dangerous years spent first in Nazi Germany and then in Soviet Russia); for his integrity as a historian; for his loyalty; for his generosity in sharing his great knowledge of the sources; and for his ability to sustain, throughout, his steady but wry and by no means uncritical belief in his political credo – 'socialism with a human face'.

We wish to take this opportunity to thank the staff of the Marjorie Mayrock Center for Soviet and East European Research and of the Department of Russian and Slavonic Studies at the Hebrew University who worked so hard to make the conference the success which it was. In particular, special mention should be made of Shulamit Tsur, Naomi Kessler and Zehava Kelman who, as always, gave so unstintingly of their time and effort. This book was prepared for publication by the Marjorie Mayrock Center for Soviet and East European Research at the Hebrew University of Jerusalem.

We are grateful for the funding which has made this book possible, received from the Jay and Leonie Darwin Fund, the Leah Goldberg Fund for Russian Studies at the Hebrew University, the Israel Academy of Sciences, the Mayrock Fund, and the Israeli Association for Slavic and East European Studies.

Finally, great thanks are also due to David King who permitted us so generously to use photographs from his remarkable collection for this book.

EDITH ROGOVIN FRANKEL
JONATHAN FRANKEL
BARUCH KNEI-PAZ

GLOSSARY

aznaureba: (Georgian) nobility

chinovnik / chinovniki (pl.): government official (used pejoratively)

Comintern: the Communist (or Third) international; founded in March 1919 to unite the Communist movement on a worldwide basis

demokratiia: (lit.) democracy; used in the revolutionary movement to denote the Left and the working masses

desiatina / desiatiny (pl.): an area equal to approximately 2.7 acres

druzhina / druzhiny (pl.): used in 1917 to denote informal militia groups

dvorianstvo: gentry; nobility

dvornik / dvorniki (pl.): janitor; caretaker

genshtabist: an officer of the General Staff (*generalnyi shtab*)

guberniia: a province; a large-scale administrative unit of the Russian empire

hromada: (Ukrainian) community or assembly; a term favoured by Ukrainian populists (analogous to *mir* and *obshchina* in the terminology of the Russian *narodniki*)

intelligent / intelligenty (pl.): a member of the intelligentsia; in Tsarist Russia usually implied political commitment and oppositional leanings

Kadet: a member of the Constitutional Democratic (or People's Freedom) Party founded in 1905

komendatura / komendatury (pl.): headquarters of a commanding officer

Kornilovshchina: the attempted military coup led by General Konstantin Nikolaevich Kornilov in August 1917

krai: a region; in Soviet Russia, a very large administrative unit

kulak: a relatively rich peasant farmer (used pejoratively)

métayage: (French) share-cropping

mir: village community

muzhik: peasant

narodnik / narodniki (pl.): populist

oblast: an area; in Soviet Russia, an administrative unit

obshchestvo: society; in Tsarist Russia, usually implied society and public opinion as opposed to the régime; hence *obshchestvennyi*: non-governmental

obshchina: peasant commune or community; in large parts of Russia, re-divided land holdings periodically in accordance with family size; hence *obshchinnyi / obshchinnye*: communal

piaterka: numbered five; here, a five-man committee

pomeshchik/pomeshchiki (pl.): a land-owning nobleman or member of the gentry

praporshchik / praporshchiki (pl.): junior army officer

proizvol: arbitrary, despotic behaviour or rule

provizor / provizory (pl.): pharmacist

Rada: the quasi-parliamentary body established by the Ukrainian national movement in 1917, which became the sovereign parliament of the independent Ukraine in January 1918

skhod: meeting, assembly; in late Tsarist Russia, used to describe regular meetings of workers or peasants

sobranie / sobraniia (pl.): meeting, assembly

sovdepshchina: the soviet system and ethos (term derived from *sovety rabochikh deputatov*: soviets of workers' deputies)

starosta: village elder

starshina: a foreman; here, a volost foreman or elder

Stavka: military headquarters; often, specifically of the supreme command

tsentsovoe: politically privileged; a term used by the Left in order to describe in broad terms the middle and upper classes, in contrast to the *demokratiia*

tuzemets / tuzemtsy (pl.): native; indigenous inhabitant

uezd: local district, lower in administrative hierarchy than the *guberniia*

ukaz: a governmental edict or decree

volost / *volosti* (pl.): rural district, lower in the administrative hierarchy than the *uezd*, designed to handle peasant affairs

zemliachestvo: a mutual-support grouping formed initially by politicians or officials when working in the same locality

zemstvo: elected assemblies responsible for significant functions of self-government at the *uezd* and *guberniia* levels; established in 1864

zemskii nachalnik / nachalniki (pl.): government official in village districts who combined police, administrative and judicial functions

INTRODUCTION

I

1917: THE PROBLEM OF ALTERNATIVES

JONATHAN FRANKEL

THE revolution in Petrograd which overthrew the Romanov régime in February 1917 unleashed one of those great seismic upheavals which so drastically reshaped the history of the world during the twentieth century.

And like the other major revolutions of the modern era (the English in the seventeenth, the American and French in the eighteenth and the Chinese in the twentieth century) it has from the first been the object of the most intense interest and debate. The pivotal episodes, the political parties and leaders, the mass movements, the classes and nationalities caught up in the turmoil of the period, 1917 to 1920, have all been described and analysed in innumerable memoirs, biographies, surveys, monographs and articles. Moreover, as the Soviet archives continue to be opened up, and as the Russian state once again enters an era of rapid change, so the examination and re-examination of 1917 will become still more intense.

But while it is no doubt true that every generation sees the past in the light of the present and rewrites history accordingly, it is no less true that the basic questions endure even while the answers change.

The central issue which has always engaged the historians of 1917 is whether or not the ultimate outcome, the Bolshevik seizure and retention of power, was preordained. Given the history of the Russian state and society in general, and the conditions prevailing in Russia at the end of February 1917 in particular, was any other outcome possible? Should the Russian revolution be seen as working its way, like some Sophoclean drama, to its inexorable climax; or was it, rather, open-ended, determined ultimately by the interaction between great social forces on the one hand, and such contingent factors as individual judgement and leadership qualities on the other?

3

Surprisingly perhaps, the responses prompted by this question do not always divide neatly along party lines. Leon Trotsky, the true-believing Marxist, could, after all, maintain in his monumental history of the Russian revolution that the Bolshevik triumph in October might well have been impossible without Lenin in command to direct the decisive events.[1] And Mikhail Gorbachev in an article published in *Izvestiia* late in 1989 chose to justify the October revolution in terms not of inevitability but, rather, of 'counter-factual' historical analysis. 'Nowadays', he there wrote,

> as we attain a deeper understanding of what is essential in our own history, it becomes still more evident that the October revolution was not a mistake – after all, the only real alternative was not (as some would seek to have us believe even today) a bourgeois democratic republic, but rather anarchist chaos and bloody military dictatorship, the establishment of a reactionary régime opposed to the people.[2]

This interpretation of 1917 has long been held by many historians in the West who similarly have argued that, with the conditions prevailing in Russia in 1917, there was simply no chance of establishing there a parliamentary and pluralistic political system and that the basic choice was bound to reduce itself to that between either a socialist or a military dictatorship.[3] And many arguments can be marshalled in support of this hypothesis.

The Muscovite state had grown since the fourteenth century, after all, on strictly autocratic foundations; the period of mixed government and limited constitutionalism had been in existence for a mere eleven years by 1917. Tsarism had swung between its despotic, at times capriciously despotic, and its enlightened periods, but neither the occasional anarchic eruptions (the Time of Troubles, Razin, Pugachev) nor the revolutionary politics of the intelligentsia had threatened its survival until the early twentieth century.[4]

And when the revolutionary wave finally swept over Russia in 1905 it broke at last against the inner defences of the Tsarist system and had ebbed away by 1907. Many harsh facts had been revealed in that testing time. A deep gulf had been exposed dividing the liberal from the revolutionary socialist camps. Their united front did not survive the Tsarist manifesto of October 1905, the liberals choosing to participate in, and the socialists (for the most part) to boycott, the Duma elections of April 1906. Peasant violence and the spectre of a full-scale

Jacquerie had immeasurably strengthened ultra-conservative as opposed to constitutional sentiment among the land-owning nobility (reflected in the collapse of Kadet representation in the zemstvo assemblies).[5] Again, fear that the heterogeneous and far-flung empire could well shatter along national lines brought with it an upsurge of Great Russian nationalism not only within the ranks of the nobility but also within the urban middle class as demonstrated by the vacillations of the Octobrist and Kadet parties.[6]

Set against this background, it is hardly surprising that the armed forces, a few exceptional incidents apart, remained loyal to the régime enabling it to weather the storm – nor that Stolypin could rely during the years 1906–8 on widespread support for his political programme based on the defence of Tsarism (moderated by a much attenuated constitutionalism); of private property; of Russian nationalism and of empire.

Throughout the revolution of 1917 there was a deep-rooted belief not only on the right but also among many on the left, Lenin himself included,[7] that for good or for evil the only factors which ultimately could provide a bulwark against social revolution were Russian nationalism and the armed forces or, more specifically, the officer class. Miliukov, the Kadet leader, sought, in the early days of the revolution, to preserve the Romanov dynasty, albeit in the form of a fully constitutional monarchy, and later to rally support by his call for war until victory in proud defence of Russian imperial greatness. Kerensky undertook the June offensive on the assumption that only some dramatic military success could prevent the disintegration of both the army and the governmental coalition. And when word spread that the commander-in-chief of the army, General Kornilov, was about to stage a coup in August, many in the Kadet leadership (and no doubt in the party membership at large) were ready to greet him with open arms as the one strong man capable of saving the empire from its final slide into anarchy.

Such strategies, of course, failed utterly during 1917 itself, but they came into their own during the Civil War. Increasingly, the opposition to the Bolshevik régime became concentrated in the hands of the generals and the officer corps. By late 1918 the attempts made by some of the Socialist Revolutionaries, Mensheviks and liberals to turn the defence of the Constituent Assembly into a general rallying cry against the Communist régime had been brushed aside by the new military régimes of Kolchak and Denikin which preferred to fight in the name of 'Russia, one and indivisible'.

If the White armies which seemed to many observers (including the Bolshevik leaders themselves) so close to victory in October 1919 had, in fact, won the Civil War the result would then, in all probability, have been the establishment of a right-wing dictatorship in one form or another (with or without a monarchical restoration). The centre had failed to hold; in the chaos of the Civil War the basic choice, so the argument goes, which had been implicit in the 1917 revolution now became explicit: the Whites faced the Reds in their final titanic struggle.

And did not the experience of inter-war Europe totally confirm this hypothesis? In East-Central and Central Europe, the parliamentary régimes established after the First World War had all, with the single exception of Czechoslovakia, been swept away by the 1930s to be replaced by right-wing authoritarian régimes (whether of the radical-Right or the ultra-conservative varieties). And the civil war in Spain, a country like Russia on the periphery of Europe and comparable in many other ways, likewise ended up as a polarised struggle between the extremes of Left and Right, victory going in that case, of course, to the generals.

Nonetheless, however persuasive this line of thought may be, it is certainly not beyond question. First, it must be asked whether, in reality, the nationalist Right did constitute not merely an embryonic but a viable, real, alternative to the extreme Left in the circumstances prevailing in Russia in the months and years after February 1917. It can be argued that given the structure, both social and national, of the Russian state, the monarchist and conservative forces in general, and the officer stratum in particular, were at a hopeless disadvantage throughout.[8]

The peasantry still constituted the great majority of the population even in 1917. And the peasants, with their age-old conviction that the land of the nobility was theirs by right, could only regard the prospect of a White victory as truly disastrous. Stolypin's attempt to build up a strong and numerous proprietorial peasantry had only had a few years to take effect by 1914 and had in all probability served primarily to increase rural resentment against the *ancien régime*. Once the landed estates had been divided up finally after October 1917 the resistance to any threat of a return to the status quo ante was bound to be fierce — and this, surely, was the case despite all the terrible hatred aroused during the Civil War by the forcible expropriations of livestock, grain and every other form of food by the Communist régime.

Then, too, although the Russian empire was still not a highly developed country in economic terms, its industries tended towards the large scale and were heavily concentrated in areas of great strategic importance: Petrograd, Moscow and the Donbass–Krivoi Rog region of the Ukraine. As opinion polarised during the revolution and Civil War, the industrial working class rallied increasingly to the Bolshevik cause, ensuring their hold over the key industrial and urban centres of the country. The Red Army could thus count on a steady supply of weapons and ammunition, especially as the major arsenals of the (by then defunct) Tsarist army were likewise situated in heartland Russia.

Again, the members of the core population – the Great Russian national group – made up no more than half the population of the pre-1914 empire. The fierce Russian nationalism which developed as the primary cementing force within the White armies was enough to ensure that they would under no circumstances receive any major support from the subject nationalities which since 1917 had come to see independence as within their grasp. Here, too, the Bolsheviks succeeded, for the most part, in seizing the high ground as the lesser of the two evils.

Such deep-rooted structural causes apart, many contingent factors served to weight the scales in favour of Bolshevism. Thus, to take just one example, the officer corps, which had entered the war in 1914 as a professional and élitist stratum, had been decimated by 1917 and the newer recruits constituted a far more heterogeneous social grouping, politically fragmented. Tens of thousands of officers who had served in the Tsarist forces fought within the ranks of the Red Army during the Civil War, many coerced into so doing, but many others from choice.

The case for the idea that once the Tsarist régime had fallen nothing ultimately could stand in the way of full-scale social revolution was formulated in the by now famous memorandum drawn up early in 1914 by Durnovo who from his stance on the extreme Right (he was a bitter opponent of Stolypin whom he regarded as far too liberal) foresaw the future course of events with extraordinary prescience. 'In the event of defeat', he had there written, *inter alia*,

> the possibility of which in a struggle with a foe like Germany cannot be overlooked, social revolution in its most extreme form is inevitable.
>
> It will start with all disasters being attributed to the government. In the legislative institutions, a bitter campaign against the government will begin, which will result in revolutionary agitation throughout the country. There will immediately ensue

socialist slogans – which alone are capable of arousing and rallying the masses – first the complete re-apportionment of land and
then the re-apportionment of all valuables and property.

The defeated army, having lost its most dependable men during
the war, and carried away for the most part by the tide of the
general elemental desire of the peasant for land, will prove to be
too demoralised to serve as a bulwark of law and order. The
legislative institutions and the opposition intelligentsia parties,
having no real authority in the eyes of the people, will be powerless to stem the rising popular tide.[9]

The victories won in the period since 1945 by the indigenous forces
of the Left in marginally developed or still essentially agrarian
countries – China, Yugoslavia, Vietnam, Cuba, to name just the most
obvious – give force to the argument that in their eagerness to overturn
the foundations of traditional society, the mass of the people had to
find dictatorial leadership. Given such leadership, and *ceteris paribus*,
victory was assured. If Lenin and the Bolsheviks had not existed, they
would thus have had to be invented.[10]

When all such factors have been given their due weight, though, the
lingering doubt remains. Is it really so self-evident that a priori the
hope for a parliamentary régime in Russia in 1917 was doomed from
the start?

The argument based on history, on the nature of the Russian political culture, is in itself a matter of much controversy. There is an entire
school of thought, after all, which traces the growth of what it describes as an increasingly sturdy liberal tradition back as far as the
eighteenth century and which sees in the establishment of the Duma in
1906 not a new beginning but the culmination of a long process. The
so-called 'liberation of the nobility' (by the acts of 1762 and 1785); the
emancipation of the peasantry; the establishment of the *zemstva*; and
the creation of the independent judiciary, all formed, so the argument
goes, milestones on the road towards what could eventually have
become a *Rechtsstaat* and a fully fledged democratic system.[11] And this
gradual evolution at the political level was matched and underpinned
by far-reaching socio-economic change, by the growth of an industrial
and commercial middle class as well as by a vast expansion of the
educational system.[12] By 1914, in this view of things, the patrimonial
and autocratic political culture was in permanent retreat and a constitutional ethos – shared by liberals and the moderate wing of the

socialist camp alike – was striking deep roots in Russian consciousness.

Nor, it must be said, does the inter-war experience in Europe demonstrate as conclusively as at first appears that the cause of parliamentary democracy was bound to be swept aside in the Russia of 1917. Would not the constitutional régimes established throughout Central and East-Central Europe in the wake of the First World War have had a far greater chance of survival if a similar system of government had consolidated itself in Petrograd?

Beyond doubt, many factors contributed to the polarisation of opinion in Europe and to the destabilisation of the post-1918 order. The unprecedented loss of life and the catastrophic suffering caused by the First World War itself; the bitter hostility to the Paris peace settlements on the part of key states (Germany, Italy, Hungary) with the concomitant fears induced in neighbouring countries; and the economic crisis which followed the Wall Street crash of 1929, were clearly all of paramount importance.

But the existence of the Communist régime in Soviet Russia, imbued as it was with quasi-Messianic zeal, and the establishment of the Comintern to disseminate the message of socialist revolution across the world, certainly did much to increase the pervasive sense of impending collapse in which the extremes of both Left and Right could flourish, the one feeding on the hatred for the other. Seen in this light, then, the October revolution can be interpreted as not just a symptom of the weakness endemic to political pluralism when transplanted beyond the West, but also as itself a basic cause of that weakness in the Europe of the inter-war period.

But even if the Provisional Government and the liberal–labour bloc were then, perhaps, not condemned from the outset by macrocosmic forces, did they have even a hypothetical chance of grappling successfully with the immediate and utterly intractable problems facing them in 1917 itself? Could the Kerenskys, Chernovs and Tseretelis, the Lvovs, Nekrasovs and Tereshchenkos – or their equivalents – acting differently within the same objective parameters, have escaped the collective fate which overtook them? Could firmer and more far-sighted leaders have made qualitatively different choices and, in turn, would those choices have made an essential difference to the outcome?

Although, as already elaborated here, there are many reasons to answer in the negative, this is not an entirely clear-cut issue. So, for example, the repeated decisions to postpone the elections to the Constituent Assembly from the summer of 1917 until the late autumn very possibly constituted a decisive error. When the elections were finally held in November, they produced a major victory for the parties of moderation, specifically for the Party of the Socialist Revolutionaries. A few months earlier, moreover, the Menshevik and Social Revolutionary Parties would have been far less divided internally between their right and left ('internationalist') wings. And the Bolsheviks would have received much less than the approximately one-quarter of the total vote which they gained in the actual elections.[13]

A democratically elected government might well have felt strong enough to act with greater decision than a largely random conglomeration of politicians brought together on an avowedly provisional basis. In particular, a régime dominated by the Socialist Revolutionaries and answerable to a democratically elected Constituent Assembly could hardly have avoided action on the issue of land distribution to the same extent as the Provisional Government chose to do.

More important, the first government to be formed in Russia on the basis of universal suffrage would certainly have enjoyed far greater legitimacy than the succession of short-lived administrations which sought to rule between February and October 1917. And this fact, in turn, would have made it much more difficult to win support for a second revolution. Even as it was, Lenin found it no easy task to rally his own Central Committee behind his plans first for the seizure of power and then for the one-party dictatorship.

However, most historians are agreed that it was the intolerable burden of the never-ending First World War which brought down both the Tsarist and the Provisional Governments. And when it came to the issue of the war, the options open to the politicians of the Centre and moderate Left were very limited. Calls for a separate peace with Germany were held to be little short of treasonable in both the political world and on the street. It is no coincidence that the Bolsheviks denied with the greatest vigour, during 1917, that they were advocating any such idea. The establishment of a proletarian dictatorship in Russia, Lenin then argued, would force the imperialist powers to choose between a general, 'democratic' peace (without annexations, without indemnities) and a general wave of revolution throughout Europe. If all else failed, he declared, there might well be no choice but to fight a 'revolutionary war'.

Nonetheless there was no necessity for the Provisional Government to have launched its military offensive in June. Given the fact that the

German strategy in 1917 and 1918 involved a massive concentration of manpower on the Western front, hostilities could well have been kept to a minimum in the East, thus sparing both the army and the Provisional Government one of their greatest humiliations.[14] In order to gain time and to put more pressure on its allies to seek peace actively, a post-election (and hence more authoritative) government, rather than escalating the hostilities, could have threatened to open armistice talks with Germany and Austria–Hungary. It was the necessity to begin winding down the war effort in order to halt the headlong slide into chaos that constituted the strongest point in the case so vociferously advocated by such socialist 'internationalists' as Martov throughout 1917.

A parliamentary régime which thus survived into 1918 would presumably have avoided the Civil War which resulted, after all, from the Brest-Litovsk treaty. And by the end of that year the country would have found itself among the victorious powers. Under those totally changed circumstances, a parliamentary régime in Russia would surely have had a fighting chance of indefinite survival.

'Counter-factual' history can, of course, only advance hypotheses; it cannot finally prove them right or wrong. It can separate out the different factors at work but it cannot decide conclusively which were the independent and which the dependent variables; nor can it assess the relative weight to be assigned to them. But within every attempt to write empirical history, to describe the past *wie es eigentlich war*, the problem of possible alternatives will always be immanent.

In 1917, were the 'losers' faced by hopeless odds from the start? Or did they let their greatest opportunity slip through their fingers?

For that matter, though, who were the primary losers? Which force was it that represented the greatest threat to the Bolshevik challenge for power: the extreme Right; the forces grouped around the Provisional Government; or perhaps, as some suggest, the non-Bolshevik ('internationalist') Left?

Beyond this question there lies still another. In a world ever in flux, is not defeat ultimately implanted in the very act of victory – and vice versa?

NOTES

1 E.g. 'Lenin was not a demiurge of the revolutionary process ... he merely entered into a chain of objective historic forces. But he was a great link in that chain ... Is it possible, however, to say confidently that the party

without him would have found its road? We would by no means make bold to say that. The factor of time is decisive here, and it is difficult in retrospect to tell time historically. Dialectic materialism at any rate has nothing in common with fatalism ... The conditions of war and revolution ... would not allow the party a long period for fulfilling its mission. Thus it is by no means excluded that a disoriented and split party might have let slip the revolutionary opportunity for many years. The role of personality arises before us here on a truly gigantic scale' (L. Trotsky, *The History of the Russian Revolution*, vol. I (London, 1932), p. 341).

2 M. Gorbachev, 'Sotsialisticheskaia ideia i revoliutsionnaia perestroika', *Izvestiia*, 28 November 1989, p. 1.

3 E.g. J.P. Nettl's argument that, in the last resort, there was 'a choice between a White Tsarist restoration or the maintenance of Soviet power ... Nothing so clearly demonstrates the futility of any middle or reformist solution in pre-revolutionary Russia, and undermines Kerensky's claim that only an accident of history prevented him from establishing a legitimate government of moderation, as the way in which the latent polarity of Russian society came out inexorably into the open during these years' (J.P. Nettl, *The Soviet Achievement*, London, 1967, p. 65).

4 Richard Pipes, for example, has argued that given the 'relations between state and society in pre-1900 Russia ... none of the economic or social groups of the old regime was either able or willing to stand up to the crown and challenge its monopoly of political power. They were not able to do so because, by enforcing the patrimonial principle ... the crown prevented the formation of pockets of independent wealth or power. And they were not willing because, insofar as under this system the crown was ultimately the source of all material benefits, each group was strongly inclined to fawn on it' (R. Pipes, *Russia Under the Old Regime*, London, 1974, p. 249).

5 See, for example, Roberta T. Manning, *The Crisis of the Old Order in Russia: Gentry and Government* (Princeton, 1982), pp. 177 ff.; and L.H. Haimson (ed.), *The Politics of Rural Russia 1905–1914* (Bloomington, 1979).

6 E.g. R. Pipes, *Struve: Liberal on the Right 1905–1944* (Cambridge, Mass., 1980), pp. 88–97.

7 For Lenin's views on the dangers of what he termed the 'Kornilovites', see V.I. Lenin, 'Pismo k tovarishcham' (17/30 October 1917), *Polnoe sobranie sochinenii*, vol. XXXIV (Moscow, 1962), p. 406.

8 For a strongly stated expression of this viewpoint, see T. von Laue; e.g.: 'No dictatorship of the right could stem the tide of revolutionary spontaneity as embodied in the soviets ... [And] given its ideals, liberal democracy in Russia could never have been more than a transition phase. It would always have led to "Soviet democracy", to freedom of the "black people", which signified, under existing conditions, spontaneity carried to the point of anarchy. By the same logic, however, freedom was

bound to destroy itself ... Thus from November, 1917 onward, the
suppression of spontaneity began anew, slowly at first under Lenin,
furiously at last under Stalin' (T. von Laue, *Why Lenin? Why Stalin?: A
Reappraisal of the Russian Revolution 1900–1930*, New York, 1971, pp. 110,
120–1).

9 In G. Vernadsky, R.T. Fisher, Jr., A.D. Ferguson, A. Lossky and S.
Pushkarev (eds.), *A Source Book for Russian History from Early Times to 1917*,
vol. III (New Haven, 1972), p. 797. A complete translation of this document is to be found in C.A. Golder (ed.), *Documents of Russian History 1914–
1917* (Gloucester, Mass., 1964), pp. 3–23. It was first published in
Krasnaia nov, no. 10 (November–December), 1922.

10 On the interplay of political and social forces in modern revolutions see
e.g. T. Skocpol, *States and Social Revolutions: A Comparative Analysis of France,
Russia and China* (Cambridge, 1979).

11 Thus, Jacob Walkin argued, for example, that, 'Had there been no war,
there are grounds for believing that Russian society's growing maturity
and its new ways of action at the lowest levels would have forced the
central government to adjust its ways of acting at the top without a
revolution ... There can be no question that Russia was following the
other major European powers in moving from absolute monarchy to
constitutional democracy' (J. Walkin, *The Rise of Democracy in Pre-Revolutionary Russia: Political and Social Institutions Under the Last Three Czars*,
London, 1963, p. 179).

12 See Alexander Gerschenkron's view: 'From the point of view of the
industrial development of the country, war, revolution or the threat
thereof, may reasonably be seen as extraneous phenomena. In this sense,
it seems plausible to say that Russia on the eve of the war was well on the
way toward a Westernisation, or perhaps more precisely a Germanisa-
tion, of its industrial growth' (A. Gerschenkron, *Economic Backwardness in
Historical Perspective*, Cambridge, Mass., 1966, pp. 141–2). Arthur Mendel
has argued in similar vein that it was the First World War rather than
immanent socio-political forces which brought down the Tsarist régime.
He was clearly inclined to provide a negative reply to the question that he
posed about the Russian revolution: 'Would a political conflict of this
kind, likely to occur under conditions prevailing before the war, have
overthrown Tsarism?' (A. Mendel, 'Peasant and Worker on the Eve of
the First World War', *Slavic Review* 24 (1965), 32); this article was a
response to L. Haimson, 'Social Stability in Urban Russia, 1905–1917',
Slavic Review 23 (1964), pp. 619–42; 24 (1965), pp. 1–22.

13 On the elections held in 1917 at both the local and national levels see O.
Radkey, *The Election to the Russian Constituent Assembly of 1917* (Cambridge,
Mass., 1950).

14 See e.g. Louise E. Heena, *Russian Democracy's Fatal Blunder: The Summer
Offensive of 1917* (New York, 1987), p. 49.

Part 1

POLITICAL POWER
AND MASS ACTION

2

SOVIETS AS AGENTS OF DEMOCRATISATION

ISRAEL GETZLER

T HIS chapter is an attempt to draw some tentative conclusions from a larger study-in-progress of the political profiles and dynamics of the 1917 soviets. It concentrates particularly on Saratov – representative of the large majority of soviets – on the Bolshevik-dominated Krasnoiarsk; the Menshevik-dominated Tiflis; the radical-Left Kronstadt; and the self-consciously 'curial' or corporate Helsingfors Soviet where deputies were elected by and expected to represent such social groups as workers, soldiers, sailors and peasants regardless of their party political affiliations.

The main line of my argument is that during the period of the Provisional Government, the soviets became quasi-parliamentary bodies, intensively engaged in educating the masses in the practices of democratic elections, political pluralism and parliamentary procedures. And, turning outwards, they were also the foremost champions of municipal democratisation on the basis of universal suffrage, and of speedy elections to the Constituent Assembly.

Even for Lenin, returning to Russia in April 1917, the revolution had given the Russian people 'such unprecedented freedom as cannot be found in any nation of the world'.[1] The American radical, Albert Rhys Williams, went even further. What was to be marvelled at in the debates that he watched on his arrival in Petrograd in June 1917 was, he wrote, the manner in which the revolution had 'set the [masses] talking, so that Russia became a nation of one hundred million orators'.[2]

What I wish to suggest here is that, more than anything, it was the multi-party soviets that provided the forum for, and consolidated, that free and open debating society; that it was the soviets that, by working overtime on the elective principle, turned Russia into a society of voters *par excellence*.

17

Given the initiative they had shown and the leading role that socialist intellectuals and party activists had played in founding the soviets
and manning their executive committees and commissions, it was only
natural that the socialist parties, and particularly the Menshevik–
Socialist Revolutionary (SR) bloc, should dominate them. On the one
hand, that domination certainly encroached on and weakened the
participatory democracy of the rank-and-file workers and soldiers, and
eased out the 'curial' – or corporate – system by which soviet deputies
had originally been elected, divided and seated in sections representing workers, soldiers, sailors and peasants. But, on the other hand, the
cooption of representatives of competing socialist parties to the executive committees (more often than not with full voting rights) and the
division of the plenary assemblies into rival political 'fractions', to
which a self-consciously non-party fraction was often added, created
the mechanics of multi-party procedures and effective control over the
election of deputies and office-holders.

To my mind, as long as the multi-party system lasted, it was this
institutionalisation of political pluralism in the soviets which prevented their manipulation, as distinct from their domination, by one
particular party or interest group. And it was in this sense that, in the
absence of a national parliament – and with the delayed appearance of
democratised municipal and rural councils – the soviets became the
'parliaments' of the 'toiling people' to the exclusion of 'propertied'
elements and would not admit such 'bourgeois' organisations as
Kadets or feminists.[3]

By May–June 1917, with the intensive politicisation of the soviet
body politic, most soviet assemblies and their executives were already
divided into socialist party fractions and were busy drafting constitu-
tions and statutes governing their proceedings and activities, with
particular attention paid to elections. The stringent precautions, and
especially the prevalent enlistment of the multi-party system, to ensure
the proper supervision of the frequent election and re-election of
deputies, are particularly evident in the guidelines on procedures for
'partial elections' issued early in June 1917 to the district soviets of
Petrograd,[4] in the Moscow Soviet statutes of June 1917 on re-elections
and in the instructions governing elections drawn up in January 1918
by the Kronstadt Soviet.

While these elaborate procedures may not have been fully
implemented in practice, the contemporary complaints were not usually about the elections themselves, but rather about the preceding
agitation and the pressures for elections or re-elections.

1. The Petrograd Soviet of Workers' and Soldiers' Deputies in session, 1917.

The guidelines of the district soviets in Petrograd stipulated that an application to hold a re-election to replace a deputy could be lodged only at the request of at least one quarter of the electors in any given factory or army unit who had assembled for that purpose and drawn up a protocol of the meeting with a note of the numbers present. The district soviet would then elect an electoral commission consisting of one representative from its executive committee, one from the factory or army committee, and one representative from each socialist party organisation in the district. Seven days after the application had been lodged, the election would be held under the supervision of the electoral commission and in the presence of the outgoing deputy. The commission would then compile a protocol of the election and its outcome and forward it to the soviet's mandate (or verification) commission which would in turn confirm the election, provided that it was satisfied that the rules had been observed.[5]

The rules of the Moscow Soviet were not very different, although here the 'electoral colleges' were to include, in addition to the executive committee representative, one representative of each of the political 'fractions' of the district soviet. All 'electoral college' members were exhorted to refrain from electioneering and to secure full freedom of agitation to all political fractions. Elections were to be by secret ballot with the votes checked and counted by an elected commission of tellers, the winning candidate having to secure an absolute majority. Finally, the protocol was to be signed by the elected praesidium of the meeting, members of the factory or army unit, the tellers commission and the electoral college.[6]

The instructions of the Kronstadt Soviet authorised an election meeting only when 'the larger half of the "toilers' collective" [i.e. the factory or army unit assembly] would be present'. The 'political cells' and 'non-party group' of the toilers' collective were to put up lists of their candidates detailing their special qualifications. Each candidate was to be voted on separately in a first-past-the-post system. The elected praesidium of the meeting would give the winning candidate his mandate and inform the soviet. The new deputy, having presented his mandate to the soviet, would join his political fraction and give its secretary his address, professional qualifications and positions and the area of activity in which he was interested. The political fraction would keep a register of its deputies and their intellectual and technical skills.[7]

These elaborate procedures seem to have been disliked by the Moscow Bolsheviks, judging by E. Ignatov's complaint that the Menshevik-SR majority of the soviet had designed them 'to stall the spontaneous course of re-elections'.[8] Yet, from what is known of Kronstadt – where the Bolshevik activists Semen Roshal and Fedor Raskolnikov seem not to have relied on spontaneity but rather to have made the round of ships, workshops and army units agitating for re-elections[9] – and from complaints by the Mensheviks in the Moscow Soviet,[10] such strict precautions were very much needed.

Not for nothing did Lenin set such great store by 're-elections' when, in May, he rejoiced in the Bolshevik near-majority produced in the district soviet of Vasilevskii Ostrov.[11] But, apart from satisfying the watchful eyes of the rival political fractions in plenums and of the party cells in factories and army units, the soviet body politic had also to be reassured that elections were proper and fair. Thus, in addition to the general three-monthly elections to the soviets, the soviet electorate in workshops, factories, plants, commercial and public enterprises, army units and ships, was busy electing base committees and deputies to district and town soviets, and was thus asked time and again to make up its mind about the political profiles and qualifications of candidates.

As for some 200,000 or more soviet deputies, they were constantly kept busy voting on motions for the agenda, moving resolutions and amendments, speaking to the motion, and electing and being elected to executive committees and to the proliferating commissions, in short, receiving unprecedented on-the-job-training in what amounted to a massive education drive in the democratic process.

The Helsingfors Soviet, however, provides a major and telling exception to the general trend towards institutionalising the politicisation process by way of dividing the plenum into organised and recognised party fractions. In Helsingfors, the curial system was maintained, and soldiers, sailors and workers were represented and seated 'corporatively', with conscious disregard of their political views and affiliations. As its popular chairman, Sergei Garin, himself a marginal Bolshevik, claimed at the plenary session of 21 April, his work and that of the praesidium had been devoid of all 'party-mindedness' (*partiinost*). It was only that, he added, which would 'enable the praesidium of the revolutionary assembly to fulfil its duties'.[12]

That vaunting of above-partyism and the curial system of representation were challenged in the soviet plenum early in August by a group under the leadership of the sailor and deputy chairman of the executive committee, the SR Kolpakov, who, on 5 August, moved that the plenum be reorganised and divided into political party fractions and that the curial system be abolished.[13]

Although Kolpakov's motion was roundly defeated in the plenum by 213 to 72 votes, and unanimously rejected by the sailors' assembly later in the month,[14] his arguments in the plenum, and in his article in the newspaper of the soviet, *Izvestiia*, which preceded that session, are revealing.[15] The Helsingfors Soviet, Kolpakov urged, suffered chronically from political amorphousness, instability and inconsistency whenever it had to take important decisions. And that, he said, was due to the 'absence of party fractions, discipline and consistency'. Thus, he continued, on some issues there were 'as many opinions as deputies' and on any one particular issue some twenty speakers expressed the views that could have been presented by no more than two or three party spokesmen.

Party fractions, and especially those of the Bolsheviks, already existed in practice, Kolpakov argued, but they all lacked discipline, and deputies flitted all too easily from one fraction to the next. Were the plenum to be divided into party fractions, he continued, speakers would represent 'an entire trend', there would be less irresolution, and a permanent inter-fractional bureau could be set up to improve liaison between existing groups. Non-party deputies would, for their part, form a non-party fraction on a par with those of the parties themselves.

Moreover, the electors would thus know the political profile of any given deputy and they could find out from the local *Izvestiia* how the deputy had voted on any issue of importance to them.

In support of Kolpakov, L. Nikolin, a Menshevik, urged that as a result of the curial system the executive committee of the soviet, which had been elected and manned in accordance with the *professional* composition of the plenary assembly (soldiers, sailors and workers), did not faithfully reflect the *political* composition of the assembly. Yet the soviet, he urged, was above all a *political* organisation, and its executive committee should therefore be manned accordingly.[16]

Nikolin's complaint was taken up by the garrison committee at its meeting on 15 August. Here, the executive committee was accused of 'issuing decrees which often countermanded or changed the resolutions of the plenary session of the soviet, and without sufficient reason'. The garrison committee demanded nothing less than the re-election of the executive committee and its replacement by one that 'expressed the will of the soviet and implemented its decrees'.[17]

That the garrison committee had a point is borne out by the boast of the Bolshevik, Vladimir Antonov-Ovseenko, that, while only a mere 130 of the 535 deputies in the Helsingfors Soviet were Bolsheviks, 'in the executive committee almost one-half were ours'.[18]

Those who opposed the change-over to the 'fractional' system pointed to the political-organisational weakness of their soviet and argued that a deputy should represent the political views of all his base assembly electors. A deputy's mandate and instructions came from that electorate, they urged, and not from some political fraction in the soviet to which he happened to belong.[19]

What they wanted, apparently, was to preserve, as far as was possible, that direct democracy and unity that had initially characterised the soviets. Not for them those strife-ridden multi-party 'parliaments' that increasing politicisation had elsewhere made of the soviets. One 'above-party' sailor scourged the *partiinost* of 'Be-ki [Bolsheviks], Me-ki [Mensheviks], Es-ery [SRs]' thus:

> A plague on your programmes
> Your -isms and -ites,
> Your Be-ki and Me-ki, Es-ery and the like!
> They aren't made for us, they aren't worth a damn!
> A plague on your railing, your parties and strife,
> The people won't take it, the people will strike,
> They want you together! The cause is the thing![20]

The commitment to, and education for, the democratic process

2. Women demand equal rights; the banners read: 'The place of women is in the Constituent Assembly!' 'In unity lies strength!' 'The women citizens of free Russia demand the right to vote!'

demonstrated by the soviets was not confined to their own organisations, the membership of which (with the exception of Reval and Tula) was limited to 'toilers'.[21] On the contrary, together with the socialist parties, the soviets were the most active and consistent participants in the agitation for the 'democratisation' of town dumas and rural councils by way of elections based on the 'four-tailed' (universal, direct, equal and secret) franchise. They were, too, in the van of the campaign for speedy elections to the Constituent Assembly based on that same franchise.

For Saratov, Don Raleigh[22] has recorded the 'dogged determination' of the local soviet to 'reorganise local self-government on democratic foundations', with all political parties putting forward lists of candidates to be selected in accordance with the share each party had gained. That demand was adopted by the fourteen soviets which participated in the Saratov Provincial Congress of Soviets on 23 March 1917.[23]

When the town dumas of Kronstadt and Krasnoiarsk offered to coopt a sizeable group of soviet representatives, the local soviets rejected the offer out-of-hand, indignantly arguing that true 'democratisation' was possible only on the basis of the 'four-tailed' franchise.[24]

In Petrograd, a conference of representatives of all district soviets

held on 1 May 1917 urged all socialist parties to put up socialist bloc-
lists for district and city municipal elections and thus promote 'the
democratisation of urban self-government, something in which the
popular masses are vitally interested'.[25] Moreover, district soviets
backed and aided the election campaigns of all socialist parties. The
Bolshevik-dominated Kolomenskoe District Soviet, which on 16
August 1917 tried to have only the Bolshevik list endorsed, was the
exception.[26]

In Tiflis, the Georgian Mensheviks who dominated the soviet had
particularly good reasons to press for speedy 'four-tailed' elections to
the town duma if only to oust the largely Armenian bourgeoisie from
its stronghold there. But they also saw such democratic municipal
elections as 'an excellent preparatory school for the elections to the
Constituent Assembly' and that Assembly occupied a central place in
their revolutionary strategy. While acute major problems such as
labour relations, peasant demands for land and the explosive national
and religious conflicts were provisionally to be tackled by *ad hoc* agreements reached in 'arbitration chambers', their final and radical solutions would be left to the wider and authoritative forum of the
Constituent Assembly. In May they campaigned with special vigour
for its speedy convocation most probably because of their angry
opposition to the Petrograd Mensheviks' entry into the coalition
government formed on 5 May, in which the Kadets were the senior
partner.[27]

Indeed, as early as 29 April, Noi Zhordania, who was doing his best
to prevent the Petrograd comrades from joining the coalition government, urged that only a government issuing from the Constituent
Assembly would be treated as 'the master of the entire country, the
representative of the entire people'. The proposed coalition, he taunted, would be nothing more than 'some Provisional Government'.[28]

Thus almost the entire session of the Tiflis Soviet on 13 May was
concerned with speeding up elections to the Constituent Assembly.
Noi Ramishvili, the main speaker, fearful that the Provisional Government would continue dragging its feet, suggested linking immediate
elections to municipalities and rural councils to the preparation of the
elections to the Constituent Assembly, so that these could be held
within three months.[29] The Tiflis Soviet thus adopted a resolution that
Ramishvili moved demanding that the Provisional Government speed
up the democratisation of all organs of local government and appeal-
ing to soviets all over Russia to join the Tiflis Soviet in pressing for the
rapid convocation of the Constituent Assembly.[30]

3. Mass rally in Petrograd, in the early stages of the 1917 revolution; the banners read: 'Long live the democratic republic!' 'Land and liberty!' and 'Let's break with the old world: freedom!'

Indeed, all soviets were staunchly committed to the Constituent Assembly, and even tough Bolshevik-dominated soviets such as those of Krasnoiarsk and Eniseisk,[31] or radical soviets such as Kronstadt and Helsingfors, incessantly and emphatically urged its 'speediest convocation'.[32] The Bolshevik-dominated Ivanovo-Voznesensk Soviet (at its April conference) saw itself as a 'vestibule' to the Constituent Assembly (the Helsingfors Soviet used the term 'ante-chamber') and in Ivanovo-Voznesensk it was resolved that

> the activities of the soviet of workers' and soldiers' deputies shall cease once its tasks have been accomplished, but not before the Constituent Assembly has completed its work and a permanent legislative chamber has been set up. The functions and property of the soviet [after its liquidation – I.G.] will be handed over to local trade unions.[33]

Even when, in June, radical soviets such as those in Abo (Turku) and Helsingfors, both in Finland, appealed to the First Congress of Soviets, then convening in Petrograd, to assume power as an interim measure, they invariably invoked the Constituent Assembly.[34]

The Appeal of the Soviet of Deputies of the Army, Navy and Workers of Abo-Oland on 17 June is quaint, but telling:

> in the name of liberty and the existence of Russia, the Soviet of Abo ... implores the All-Russian Congress of Soviets ..., that

first Russian truly democratic parliament, to combine with the
All-Russian Congress of Peasants and – relying on us and on the
other representatives of the local democratic powers – to proclaim
together all over Russia: 'We are your people's parliament and we
take into our hands the entire state power of the country until the
convocation of the Constituent Assembly.'[35]

In the same vein, and throughout the entire period of the Provisional Government, the slogan of 'All Power to the Soviets' was – *pace*
Lenin's April theses, SR-Maximalists and Anarchists – neither anti-
parliamentarian, nor counterposed to slogans in support of the Constituent Assembly. Instead, it was generally understood, even by a
large majority of Bolsheviks, as directed above all against the Provisional Government and as a call for its replacement by a government
composed of the representatives of the soviets, until such time as the
Constituent Assembly should convene.[36] The latter was anyway expected to have a large majority of deputies representing the 'revolutionary
democracy', and to set up a broadly based socialist government – an
expectation strengthened again and again by the large socialist majorities returned in municipal elections.

Both the 'hard' Bolshevik, Ilia Mgeladze (Vardin), and the 'soft'
Bolshevik, Vladimir Miliutin, campaigned in Saratov in June 1917 for
'All Power to the Soviets' *and* 'the speedy convocation of the Constituent Assembly'. So, too, did Anatolii Lunacharsky who looked
forward to Russia's 'first parliament'. He thought that that body
would comprise all classes, including 'landowners and the *haute
bourgeoisie*', but he anticipated that the democratic classes and socialist
and semi-socialist parties would have an overwhelming majority, and
that the government would be firmly based on those elements.[37] Lenin
was even more sanguine. In a letter to Ivar Smilga, of 27 September
1917, he expected 'a bloc with the Left SRs' to give 'us firm state
power and a majority in the Constituent Assembly'.[38]

It was only after the October revolution, and particularly once the
November elections had given the SRs an absolute majority, that
Bolshevik spokesmen began to invest the slogan 'All Power to the
Soviets' with an anti-parliamentary meaning. 'Long Live Soviet
Power' thus became the counter-rallying cry to 'Long Live the Con-
stituent Assembly', while the latter, in reaction to the Bolshevik
seizure of power in the name of 'All Power to the Soviets', became 'All
Power to the Constituent Assembly'.[39]

As for the soviets, the October revolution marked their transformation from agents of democratisation into regional and local administrative organs of the centralised, one-party Soviet state.

That process began, at the local political level, with the attainment – by means fair, foul and terrorist – of Bolshevik majorities in the plenary assemblies of the soviets, and with the barring of all those not 'completely dedicated to Soviet power' from the newly established internal network of soviet administrative departments and from the soviet militias.[40] Soviets where Bolshevik majorities could not be achieved were simply disbanded.[41] That was at the local level.

At the summit, it was the All-Russian Central Executive Committee of Soviets (VTsIK), charged by the October revolution with controlling the government, the Council of People's Commissars (the CPC or Sovnarkom), which was now, by means of the vast Soviet network, used not to control but rather to extend the authority and centralising fiat of the government. That was the work of Iakov Sverdlov, the VTsIK chairman, who – in close collaboration with Lenin as chairman of the Sovnarkom – ensured that the governmental decrees and ordinances were passed by the VTsIK and that they were thus endowed with Soviet legitimacy when they were sent to provincial soviet executive committees for transmission to all local soviets. The unmistakable twofold message was:

> to make it the duty of all soviets to maintain their power firmly
> and energetically and to implement all the directives of the higher
> organisations of Soviet power speedily and unswervingly.[42]

To achieve that, Sverdlov had to reduce the 'Soviet Parliament' to nothing more than an 'administrative branch' (as Sukhanov put it) of the Sovnarkom. Using his position as the VTsIK chairman and his tight control over its praesidium and the large, disciplined and compliant Bolshevik majority in the plenary assembly, Sverdlov isolated the opposition and rendered it impotent.[43] So successful was he that, by early December 1917, Sukhanov had already written off the VTsIK as 'a sorry parody of a revolutionary parliament',[44] while for the Bolshevik, Martin Latsis-Zurabs, the VTsIK was not even a good rubber-stamp. Latsis campaigned vigorously in March and April 1918 for the VTsIK's abolition: with its 'idle, long-winded talk and its incapacity for productive work' the VTsIK merely held up the work of government, he claimed.[45] And he may have had a point: during the period 1917 to 1918, the Sovnarkom issued 474 decrees, the VTsIK a mere 62.[46]

The subsequent history of the VTsIK (until June 1918) was that of an unequal duel between its adroit and unyielding chairman and a vociferous but helpless opposition. On 14 June 1918 the climax came: to 'loud applause', a jubilant Bolshevik majority passed a decree excluding all Mensheviks and SRs ('right and centre') from the VTsIK.[47] 'All soviets' were asked to follow suit and 'remove the representatives of these fractions from their midst'.[48] With the expulsion of the Left SRs on 9 July 1918 (in the wake of the Left SR uprising), the soviets were to all intents and purposes one-party organisations (even when, from time to time, some prominent oppositionists such as Martov and Dan, and a few Anarchists and Maximalists, who supported the anti-White struggle, were readmitted). Moreover the VTsIK itself, as distinct from its praesidium, was not convened between 14 July 1918 and 1 February 1920.[49]

The political purge of the soviets was immediately complemented by a radical social purge from the soviets and by the brutal disenfranchisement ᴄᶠ all non-proletarian elements such as 'town and village bourgeois', 'kulaks and well-off peasants'.[50] As for the so-called 'between-classes intelligentsia' – there was no need to purge them. They, according to a report of April 1918, had already voted with their feet against the Bolshevised soviets and were being replaced by the 'common toiling people's ... own intelligentsia of workers and peasants'.[51]

At the administrative-institutional level, the drive towards the integration of the soviets into the administrative apparatus of the Soviet state began in earnest in April 1918. Under attack was the particularism, if not separatism, which had marked the early months of the Soviet régime when the spread and maintenance of Soviet power in the provinces, and the elimination of 'bourgeois' town dumas and rural councils, had been largely left to local and regional soviets. It was then that the 'Other-City Department' (*inogorodnyi otdel*) of the VTsIK (hitherto in charge of relations with provincial soviets) was transferred to the Department of Administration of the People's Commissariat of Internal Affairs (NKVD), headed by the notorious Latsis.[52] A centraliser *par excellence*, Latsis did his indefatigable best during the period April to June 1918 to cajole the soviets from the provincial (*guberniia*) to the rural district (*volost*) levels into setting up departments and sections of administration modelled on the Department of Administration of the NKVD and directly responsible to it.[53] A steady flow of imperious instructions and decrees from above and of reports from below would ensure that soviets at all levels would comply with and 'unswervingly' implement the policies of the Soviet state.

Both the language and the spirit of Latsis' injunctions were echoed on 10 May 1918 in a resolution of the Krasnoiarsk Soviet which defined its executive committee as 'the local organ of Soviet state power', subordinate to and implementing 'all the decrees of the central government and of the local soviet'.[54] It was therefore to be exclusively composed of such elective members as recognised the soviets as 'fully fledged organs of state power'. Indeed, when on 17 May 1918 a new executive committee was elected, it consisted – as prescribed by Latsis – of twenty-five members, twenty-four of whom were Bolsheviks, the other a Left SR.[55]

At the end of May 1918, the new draft constitution of the Krasnoiarsk Soviet was worked out: its six-point section on the functions and duties of the executive committee had three points (2, 5 and 6) which referred directly to the practical implementation of 'the decrees of the central government consonant with local conditions', while no less than four points of the six-point section on the praesidium (1, 2, 4 and 5) referred to its 'direct implementation of the decrees of the central government', to its 'relations with the central state power' and to its 'fullest surveillance of the implementation of the decrees of the central government by all institutions and citizens'.[56] The VTsIK was not even mentioned.

The new administrative structure of the soviets and its underlying principle were incorporated into the 'Sections on Soviets' (41–3) of the Soviet constitution of July 1918 (most likely drafted by Latsis himself), which defined the soviets as 'the local organs of the state' and listed as their first task 'the implementation of all the decrees of the relevant higher organs of the state'.[57]

When, in March 1919, the Eighth Party Congress postulated 'the complete dominance [of the Communist Party] in the state organisations of today – the soviets',[58] it already registered the complete *Gleichschaltung* of Russia's soviets, but it did not provide an adequate idea of their emasculation at the hands of the local 'extraordinary organs', such as Food Detachments (*Prodotriady*), the Poor Peasant Committees (*Kombedy*), a variety of army and party committees, and, notably, the all-powerful Chekas. By a decree of 26 September 1918, the Chekas were instructed that their sole obligation to the local soviet executive committees was to report Cheka activities to them – 'on demand' and after the event. The only exception to that was when the 'search, arrest or seizure' of members of the executive committee of the local soviet was at issue. Then, the Cheka had to seek the consent of the chairman or a representative of the executive committee.[59]

It was the Communist secretary of the Collegium of the NKVD,

Sergei I. Dukhovskii, who, in October 1918, sounded the warning that 'All Power to the Soviets' was turning into 'All Power to the Chekas'.[60] Small wonder that the principal political demand of Mensheviks, Left SRs, SR Maximalists, Kronstadt sailors and of many oppositionists ever since has been for freely elected soviets which would thus be restored to their original role as agents of democratisation.

NOTES

1 V.I. Lenin, *Polnoe sobranie sochinenii* (hereafter *PSS*), vol. xxxii (Moscow, 1962), p. 49.
2 A.R. Williams, *Through the Russian Revolution* (New York, 1920), p. 24.
3 *Krasnoiarskii sovet, mart 1917g.–iun 1918g., sbornik dokumentov* (Krasnoiarsk, 1960), pp. 121, 508–9; by late June 1917 when the Executive Committee of the All-Russian Congress of Peasant Deputies (estimated to represent some 17 million peasants) combined with the All-Russian Central Executive Committee of Soviets of Workers and Soldiers Deputies, the VTsIK (believed to represent more than 20 million workers and soldiers), they together made up the broadest representative body of Russia until mid November 1917 when some 44 million voted in the elections to the Constituent Assembly.
4 The instructions were probably issued by the Inter District Conference of Petrograd district soviets, on 2 June 1917, *Raionnye sovety Petrograda v 1917 godu*, vol. iii (Moscow and Leningrad, 1966), p. 265.
5 'Poriadok chastnykh vyborov', *Vpered* no. 5 (28 June 1917).
6 E. Ignatov, *Moskovskii sovet rabochikh deputatov v 1917 godu* (Moscow, 1925), pp. 71–2.
7 *Osnovnye organizatsii soveta rabochikh i soldatskikh deputatov* (Kronstadt, 1918), pp. 25–6.
8 Ignatov, *Moskovskii sovet*, p. 71.
9 *Izvestiia Kronshtadtskogo soveta*, no. 31 (26 April 1917).
10 Ignatov, *Moskovskii sovet*, pp. 60, 64.
11 Lenin, *Polnoe sobranie sochinenii*, vol. xxxii, p. 441.
12 *Izvestiia Gelsingforskogo soveta* no. 34 (26 April 1917).
13 Protocol no. 43 of general meeting of the Helsingfors Soviet, 5 August 1917, Sota-arkisto (Military Achives), Helsinki, Russian Collection 3220.
14 Protocol no. 65 of session of the Helsingfors Assembly of Sailors' Deputies, 26 August 1917, Sota-arkisto, Russian Collection 3221.
15 Kolpakov, 'O fraktsiiakh soveta deputatov', *Izvestiia Gelsingforskogo soveta* no. 114 (1 August 1917), no. 115 (2 August 1917).
16 L. Nikolin, 'Sovety i ikh vnutrennaia organizatsiia', *Izvestiia Gelsingforskogo soveta* no. 115 (2 August 1917).
17 Protocol no. 20 of general meeting of Helsingfors Garrison, 15 August 1917, Sota-arkisto, Russian Collection 3221.

18 V. Antonov-Ovseenko, *V semnadtsatom godu* (Moscow, 1933), p. 160.

19 Protocol no. 43 of general meeting of Helsingfors Soviet, 5 August 1917, Sota-arkisto, Russian Collection 3220.

20 E. Andring, 'Na zlobu dnia (Be-ki, Me-ki i Es-ery)', *Izvestiia Gelsingforskogo soveta* no. 78 (18 June 1917).

21 P.O. Gorin (ed.), *Organizatsiia i stroitelstvo sovetov RD v 1917 godu* (Moscow, 1928), p. 86.

22 Donald J. Raleigh, *Revolution on the Volga: 1917 in Saratov* (Ithaca and London, 1986), pp. 97, 106, 120–1.

23 *Saratovskii sovet rabochikh deputatov (1917–1918), sbornik dokumentov* (Moscow and Leningrad, 1931), pp. 66–7.

24 *Krasnoiarskii sovet*, pp. 57–8; Israel Getzler, *Kronstadt 1917–1921* (Cambridge, 1983), pp. 31–2.

25 *Raionnye sovety Petrograda v 1917 godu*, vol. III, p. 258.

26 *Raionnye sovety Petrograda*, vol. I (Moscow and Leningrad, 1964), p. 344.

27 *Borba* no. 2 (5 May 1917), Noi N. Zhordania, *Za dva goda* (Tiflis, 1919), pp. 5–6, 8. The Tiflis Soviet's protest against coalition 'stood out' as the only such telegram (out of twenty-six telegrams) received by the VTsIK which opposed coalition. In the same vein, after the coalition government was formed, the Tiflis Soviet sent a second telegram which declared that it would accord the new government 'the same conditional support that it had accorded the previous government', *Organizatsiia i stroitelstvo sovetov*, p. 196.

28 *Borba* no. 8 (14 May 1917).

29 *Borba* no. 11 (18 May 1917).

30 *Protokoly Zakavkazskikh revoliutsionnykh sovetskikh organizatsii* (Tiflis, 1920), p. 165.

31 *Krasnoiarskii sovet*, pp. 52–3, 207, 221; *Za vlast sovetov, sbornik dokumentov o borbe za vlast sovetov v Eniseiskoi gubernii* (Krasnoiarsk, 1957), pp. 148, 200; *Izvestiia Krasnoiarskogo soveta* no. 1 (14 March), no. 3 (17 March), no. 4 (18 March), no. 10 (25 March 1917).

32 *Izvestiia Gelsingforskogo soveta* no. 34 (26 April 1917).

33 M.K. Dianov and P.M. Eksempliarskii (eds.), *Ivanovo-Voznesenskii proletariat v borbe za vlast sovetov* (Ivanovo-Voznesensk, 1927), p. 36.

34 *Izvestiia Gelsingforskogo soveta* no. 92 (6 July 1917).

35 Ibid., no. 80 (21 June 1917).

36 N. Sukhanov, *Zapiski o revoliutsii*, vol. III (Berlin and Petersburg, 1922), pp. 59–60.

37 A. Lunacharsky, 'Klass, demokratiia, natsiia', *Vpered* no. 5 (28 June 1917), no. 7 (25 July 1917).

38 Lenin, *PSS*, vol. XXXIV (Moscow, 1962), p. 266.

39 The Appeal of the Executive Committee of the All-Russian Soviet of Peasant Deputies 'To All Peasants, Soldiers and Workers' which on 26 October 1917 had already protested at the seizure of power in Petrograd,

began and ended with the battle-cry 'All Power to the Constituent Assembly!', see S.A. Piontkovskii (ed.), *Sovety v Oktiabre, Sbornik dokumentov* (Moscow, 1928), pp. 33–4.

40 'Vsem Gubsovetam' (signed: 'Za Narkom Vnudel, Latsis'), *Vestnik Komissariata vnutrennykh del* (*Vestnik KVD*) no. 11 (24 April 1918), p. 1.

41 *Chetvertyi vserossiiskii sezd sovetov rabochikh, krestianskikh, soldatskikh i kazachikh deputatov:* stenograficheskii otchet (Moscow, 1919), pp. 433–4 (claimed by F. Dan), p. 436 (reluctantly admitted by Iurii Steklov).

42 Quoted in L.I. Egorova, 'Ob otnoshenii mestnykh sovetov k tsentralnoi sovetskoi vlasti v predkonstitutsionnyi period (oktiabr 1917–iul 1918 gg.)', *Uchennye zapiski Moskovskogo Gosudarstvennogo pedagogicheskogo instituta* no. 286 (Moscow, 1967), p. 88.

43 For a detailed examination of Sverdlov's role in the *Gleichschaltung* of the VTsIK see Charles Duval, 'Yakov M. Sverdlov and the All-Russian Central Executive Committee of Soviets (VTsIK): A Study in Bolshevik Consolidation of Power, October 1917–July 1918', *Soviet Studies 31*, no. 1 (January 1979), pp. 3–22.

44 *Novaia zhizn* (8 December 1917), quoted in John L.H. Keep (ed.), *The Debate on Soviet Power. Minutes of the All-Russian Central Executive of Soviets October 1917–January 1918* (Oxford 1979), p. 371.

45 M. Latsis, 'Ob apparate tsentralnoi vlasti', *Izvestiia* no. 63 (2 April 1918), no. 65 (4 April 1918); also Latsis, 'K voprosu o tsentralnoi vlasti', *Izvestiia* no. 67 (6 April 1918).

46 Walter Pietsch, *Revolution und Staat* (Cologne, 1969), p. 119n.

47 *Chetvertyi vserossiiskii sezd sovetov rabochikh, krestianskikh, soldatskikh i kazachikh deputatov* (Moscow, 1918), p. 439.

48 'Postanovlenie Vserossiiskogo tsentr. ispoln. kom. priniatoe na zasedanii 14 iunia 1918 g. v iskliuchenie soglashatelskikh partii', *Vestnik KVD* no. 17 (4 July 1918), p. 6.

49 Pietsch, *Revolution und Staat*, p. 119.

50 Cabled circular no. 7278 signed G. Petrovskii, 'O borbe s kulakami v sovetakh', *Vestnik KVD* nos. 18–19 (25 July 1918), p. 2; also 'O borbe s uchastiem kulakov v sovetakh', ibid., p. 22.

51 'Sovetskaia Rossiia (Dannye ankety)', *Vestnik KVD* no. 11 (24 April 1918), pp. 10–11; that 'replacement' appeared already in full force at the Fifth Congress of Soviets early in July 1918 where, as the late Charles Duval found, the large majority of Bolshevik deputies (651 out of 955) were young, barely educated and inexperienced newcomers. While the vast majority of Bolshevik deputies had joined the Communist Party only after the October revolution, 'three hundred and eighty of them had never even held a responsible position in a party organization', Charles Duval, 'Iakov M. Sverdlov and the Organization of the Russian Revolution 1885–1919', unpublished MS., p. 225.

52 *Vestnik KVD* no. 10 (15 April 1918), p. 4.

53 Circular 'Vsem Gubsovetam', *Vestnik KVD* no. 11 (24 April 1918), p. 1; circular no. 5066, 'Ob organizatsii Otdela Upravleniia', signed Latsis, *Vestnik KVD* no. 15–16 (June 1918), p. 2; for his eulogy of the centralised state as 'an apparatus of class coercion' see Latsis, 'Absurd federalizma', *Izvestiia* no. 60 (29 March 1918), no. 61 (30 March 1918), no. 62 (31 March 1918).

54 *Krasnoiarskii sovet, mart 1917 g.–iun 1918 g.*, p. 449.

55 Ibid., p. 455.

56 Ibid., pp. 461–2.

57 G.S. Gurvich, *Osnovy Sovetskoi Konstitutsii* (Moscow, 1921), pp. 165, 166–8.

58 *KPSS v rezoliutsiiakh i resheniiakh sezdov, konferentsii i plenumov Ts.K.*, vol. 1 (Moscow, 1954), p. 446; T.H. Rigby, *Lenin's Government: Sovnarkom 1917–1922* (Cambridge, 1979), pp. 180–1.

59. Prikaz no. 47, 26 September 1918, signed Peters, reprinted in Latsis (Sudrabs), *Chrezvychainye Komissii v borbe s kontr-revoliutsiei* (Moscow, 1921), p. 57; George Leggett, *The Cheka: Lenin's Political Police* (Oxford, 1981), p. 126.

60 S. Dukhovskii, ' "Chrezvychaiki" i "ispolkomy" ', *Vestnik KVD* no. 24 (28 October 1918), pp. 30–1, quoted in Pietsch, *Revolution und Staat*, pp. 95–6, also in Leggett, *The Cheka*, p. 128.

3

POLITICAL POWER IN
THE RUSSIAN REVOLUTION:
A CASE STUDY OF SARATOV

DONALD J. RALEIGH

A CENTRAL theme in any discussion of the dynamics of the revolutionary process is that of political power. In the case of the Russian revolution, an analysis of the problem of power must take into account the novel and ambivalent political arrangement known as dual power (*dvoevlastie*), 'the paradox of the February revolution', as Trotsky called it. The result of an agreement concluded on 2 March 1917, between the Temporary Committee of the State Duma and the Executive Committee of the Petrograd Soviet, dual power reflected the nearly simultaneous appearance of the Provisional Government headed by G. Lvov and the Petrograd Soviet. Although it acknowledged the legitimacy of the Provisional Government, the Petrograd Soviet commanded real power within Petrograd's working-class districts and garrison and before long in much of the country at large; the Provisional Government could not enact any significant legislation or make any important policy announcement without the soviet's endorsement. This unsatisfactory arrangement may have been the result of the balance of forces in Russia at the time, but it was not likely to bring about political or social stability.

Despite the significance of the question of power for the Russian revolution, Western historiography has devoted little attention to the nature of *dvoevlastie* in provincial Russia. The purpose of this essay is to help redress this imbalance by shedding light on revolutionary developments in the Russian heartland, in the provincial capital of Saratov. This chapter will analyse the nature of political power in a local setting and the changing social support various political factions enjoyed within the confusing institutional framework that surfaced haphazardly and spontaneously after the collapse of the autocracy. By concentrating on the institutional representation of political power (and to a much lesser extent on theoretical considerations and revolu-

4. Prince Georgii Evgenevich Lvov, Prime Minister of the Provisional Government (2 March–7 July 1917).

tionary tactics), I hope to shift the focus away from a discussion of why Russian liberalism failed, to what I believe to be a more central issue: why the radical wing of Russian socialism triumphed over the more moderate socialists who commanded such broad support in Saratov in the spring of 1917.

THE FEBRUARY REVOLUTION IN SARATOV

Before discussing the February revolution in Saratov a few words are in order about the revolutionary movement and socio-economic conditions there. Located in the eastern tip of the fertile Black-Earth zone, Saratov, by the beginning of the nineteenth century, had become a major centre of the processing and shipping of grain and agricultural products. Like many other Russian urban centres, it had registered dramatic population growth and progress in the wake of the booming industrial expansion in the 1890s and once again after 1910. By 1911 Saratov's population had expanded to 235,300, and it reached 242,425 in 1913, making it the eleventh largest city in the Russian empire. Saratov was a significant commercial and cultural centre, but was not a major industrial town; by 1914 only about 25,000 of its workers were classified as members of the industrial proletariat, employed in approximately 150 factories. The remaining part of the working class consisted of large numbers of artisan employees, dock hands, domestics and unskilled workers.

The First World War greatly altered Saratov's social make-up, creating conditions that left a clear imprint on the events of 1917. Roughly 25 per cent of the indigenous work force was conscripted. Polish and Latvian workers evacuated from the front as well as other refugees, including students from Kiev university, soon flooded the city. By early 1916 an estimated 41,000 refugees made up the second largest social group in town. Moreover, after Kazan, Saratov housed the most important garrison in the Kazan Military District. In 1917 the local garrison fluctuated in size between 30,000 and 70,000 soldiers.

Saratov's revolutionary past was to cast a heavy shadow over 1917 as well. Local conditions reflecting the overall political health of the country had created a favourable climate for the development of a unique radical tradition in Saratov. The plight of the rural masses, in particular, brought about by acute land shortage and overpopulation, had exalted the peasant in the eyes of the local intelligentsia. Saratov province emerged as a hotbed of Russian populism in the late nineteenth century and remained so throughout the revolutionary period. A constant influx of political exiles into the city contributed to the development and diversification of the radical movement, and by the second half of the 1890s Marxist circles had taken root in town. Further, the robust activities of Saratov's zemstvos (organs of local government) made the province a centre of Russian liberalism. A

much-acclaimed characteristic of the local opposition movement was
the liberal–radical alliance and tradition of cooperation between
moderates and extremists that had come to prevail by the turn of the
century.

The vicissitudes of the Saratov revolutionary movement (and of
liberal politics) after 1905 follow the pattern for the country at large
etched out in the historical literature: police repression between 1907
and 1910; a rise in working-class activism beginning in 1910 and
coming into its own in 1912; confusion in the socialist movement
caused by the war; and growing economic unrest during the war itself
that resulted in a revival of the strike movement by the autumn of 1915
and a rejuvenation of revolutionary activities. By early 1916, however,
police infiltration of the underground movement led to a spate of
arrests, preventing worker activists and the intelligentsia from forging
a united front. On the eve of the February revolution a small group of
Social Democratic worker activists, in cooperation with other elements
of the opposition, sought to restore ties via medical funds with metal-
workers, lumberyard workers, Latvian workers and other strata of the
working class. In the meantime, the economic and social strains of two
and a half years of war had created deep anxieties among the
townspeople. Food shortages coincided with an energy and transportation crisis that forced factories to close.

Although the pressing problems and discontent linked with the war
contributed immensely to a deepening critical sentiment within
Saratov society, it was the broad legacy of the past quarter century
that determined political relationships after February. The cumulative
success over the previous generation of the revolutionary and liberal
parties, which had politicised society and weakened the autocracy
through their implacable criticism of the régime, helps explain the
reaction of society to the events of February. In few countries, I would
imagine, was widespread belief in the likelihood of some sort of revolutionary explosion as widely held as in early twentieth-century Russia.[1]

The February revolution dealt a death blow to centralised state
authority, making all power relationships largely voluntary. It also
inaugurated the direct participation in politics by the heretofore disenfranchised Russian masses. In Saratov, as elsewhere, the revolution
unfolded without detailed directives from the capital and in a few days
a new political apparatus arose locally. Unable to keep news of revolutionary developments in Petrograd from the town population, the
Saratov Governor, S.D. Tverskoi, could not prevent city duma leaders
from meeting with representatives from the War Industries Commit-

tee, university administration, City Cooperative Board, garrison command and other such public organisations, including the workers' club *Maiak* (Lighthouse), which charged Bolsheviks M.I. Vasilev (Vasilev-Iuzhin), V.P. Miliutin, and a tailor named Stepanov to represent Saratov's workers at the duma meeting. By the evening of 2 March the election of a workers' soviet and the formation of a military committee in the garrison, as well as the arrest of more than 300 Tsarist officials by soldiers and workers, prompted the duma to create a Public Executive Committee (*Obshchestvennyi ispolnitelnyi komitet*) (hereafter PEC) empowered to serve as an impartial government and to work with the army 'for a decisive victory over the enemy'. The PEC included six representatives from the duma, five from the soviet, three from the city's organisation of lawyers, one from the zemstvo and one from the cooperatives. A lawyer and former State Duma deputy, the Kadet A.A. Tokarskii, was appointed chairman of the PEC and the Popular Socialist, N.I. Semenov, active in the War Industries Committee, was named provincial commissar.[2]

In Saratov and elsewhere in the provinces the alignment of political forces differed from the situation in the capital where, with the exception of A.F. Kerensky, soviet leaders did not join the government. An examination of the February revolution in other provincial towns reveals that elsewhere, too, besides soviets, variously titled PECs were set up by city dumas, zemstvos, representatives of War Industries Committees, cooperatives and industrial enterprises, and by revolutionary activists, soldiers, officers and workers. What is striking about these new executive committees is that the majority of soviets not only cooperated closely with them but took part in them *and sometimes even formed them*, creating broadly representative coalition organs. Local conditions and experiences in each case determined the specific strength of the *tsenzovoe obshchestvo*, the 'census' or propertied strata of society, the privileged classes of the old régime, *vis-à-vis* the elements of the so-called 'democracy' which, broadly speaking, represented all political groups to the left of the Kadets. In a few cases, such as in Khabarovsk and Nikolaevsk, Bolsheviks headed the local public executive committees.

The significance of the development described above lay in the coalition itself, and in the numerical strength of the socialist parties. My research suggests that what happened in Saratov was common: because it contained heavy representation from the soviet and other popular bodies from the beginning, the Saratov Public Executive Committee immediately began to yield to pressures from the garrison

and soviet. Western historical literature has largely ignored this particular turn of events, while most Soviet historians criticise Bolshevik
participation in public executive committees. A striking exception is
V.I. Startsev, who acknowledged that 'only in Petrograd, the capital of
the government, was, perhaps no coalition organ of local power, such
as a committee of public safety or a committee of public organisations,
created'.[3]

THE NATURE OF DUAL POWER

Throughout March the Saratov Soviet was in almost constant session,
creating numerous committees and generating considerable political
power. Within a week of the formation of the soviet, 60 per cent of the
city's industrial enterprises had already elected deputies to it. The
soviet consisted of a workers' and soldiers' section; *intelligenty* and
professionals predominated in the workers' section, and SRs and other
populists in the soldiers' section. By May the soviet had increased in
size to 532 members – 322 workers and 210 soldiers. As was often the
case in provincial Russia, one's length of service in the underground
and overall prestige commanded more respect at this time than one's
party affiliation. Despite the small number of Bolsheviks in town, they
occupied six of the nine seats on the soviet's ruling board, the
praesidium, primarily because of the party's success in organising
workers during the war and because some well-known leaders such as
Miliutin and Vasilev were on hand.[4]

By the end of March, as the Saratov Soviet and military committee
hammered out an agreement to merge and the soviet established control over the duma, political power in Saratov appeared to be moving
towards dual power shared between the soviet and the PEC. But at
this point the overriding strength of the socialist parties within the
PEC compelled political developments to follow a logic of their own.
By late spring 1917 the PEC quietly faded away, its leadership undermined from the start by the inclusion in it of socialists and representatives from the Saratov Soviet. It bears repeating that the soviets were
not perceived by their leaders as an alternative form of government,
but as organs for watching over the bourgeoisie and for defending the
gains of the revolution. Many socialists considered the February
revolution 'bourgeois' and hence did not look upon the soviets as the
focus of political power. Moreover, at the end of March the Petrograd
Soviet instructed local soviets to work in conjunction with other
organisations, and under no circumstances to assume governmental

functions. Be that as it may, in Saratov a small number of socialist activists dominated the soviet, provided leadership for the 'non-bourgeois' political parties, edited their respective party newspapers, participated in the PEC and gained control over the city duma.

When these same few individuals began to ignore the PEC, it simply stopped meeting. In effect, a situation bordering on the single power (*edinovlastie*) of the local soviet was taking shape regardless of any theoretical notions about the nature of the revolution or directives from Petrograd. By the late spring of 1917, the real question of political power in Saratov concerned not so much the transfer of power to the soviet as the outcome of the intra-soviet party fighting – barely felt in March, but quite noticeable by April.

How did this happen? Two developments in April profoundly affected Saratov politics. The first was Lenin's return to Russia and the Bolshevik party's eventual adoption of his April theses which, above all, advocated an immediate struggle for the transfer of power to the soviets. The other development was the April crisis that brought about the collapse of the Provisional Government and its replacement by the first coalition government on 5 May, which included representatives from the socialist parties, with the notable exception of the Bolsheviks. Besides Kerensky, five other socialists accepted cabinet portfolios. Even though dissatisfaction with the stance of the previous government on the war had led to its downfall, the first coalition government, while paying lip-service to the Petrograd Soviet's peace declarations, also failed to take any serious measures towards securing peace. In the following months the Bolshevik refusal to serve in a government with the bourgeoisie and their increasingly vocal support for Lenin's theses contributed to the drawing of hard party and class lines in political institutions everywhere in the country.[5]

This was true in Saratov, where the adoption of Lenin's April theses and the public reaction to the April crisis greatly undermined the concept of coalition government along the Volga. In Saratov local socialists consolidated their position at the expense of the liberal parties and the Right, which were too weak to pick up the reins of power in the spring of 1917; at the same time, however, a split developed between moderate and radical socialists. As a result of elections to the soviet in late May and its merger with the military committee, moderates came to dominate the council. Having joined the non-socialist parties in a coalition government at the national level, the moderate socialists sought to make the local organs of government work too. They argued against soviet power, maintaining that rule by the councils of workers and soldiers, as class institutions, would strengthen centrifugal tendencies and that the prosecution of the war required unity. Such attitudes affected their relationship to the local soviet and they now sought to curb its energies. The ambiguous behaviour of their leaders confused many workers and soldiers, led to their dissatisfaction with the political status quo and tied the fate of the soviets to the Bolsheviks and other radical elements.

The rapid collapse of the organs of the Provisional Government at the local level and the administrative paralysis resulting from the weakness of the PECs, I would argue, must be emphasised in any assessment of the unfolding of the revolution in provincial Russia because the inherent incongruities of coalition were exposed earlier in the provinces than in Petrograd. In Saratov the soviet stepped into the political vacuum and soon generated tremendous political power. Apart from merging with the military committee, the soviet dealt a psychological death-blow to the city duma by forcing the mayor's resignation and new elections. Until these were held, early in July, many members stopped attending the infrequent meetings, which were usually cancelled anyway for lack of a quorum.[6]

At the same time, the soviet won the upper hand over the PEC. Composed of representatives of all major parties, the PEC experienced increasing difficulty in reaching a consensus on pressing business, especially in its dealings with the soviet. During April the PEC became the Provincial Public Executive Committee (PPEC). Then, at the end of May, when poor health induced the provincial commissar (as governors were now called), Semenov, to retire, a five-member collegium representing the major political parties replaced him. The Saratov Bolshevik committee, however, refused to take part in the coalition collegium, a decision that mirrored the degree to which Lenin's policy of non-support for the national coalition government had taken hold at the local level. The withdrawal of the Saratov Bolsheviks from the PEC marked the end of their willingness to cooperate with the non-socialist elements and the beginning of their as yet restrained advocacy of an all-socialist government.

As it turned out, the PPEC merely functioned as an extension of the soviet anyway. The new collegium included the Menshevik, D.A. Topuridze; the SR, A.A. Minin (both of whom sat on the soviet's Executive Committee); the Popular Socialist, N.I. Maksimovich from the military committee; and the Kadet, A.M. Kogan. Referring to the 'chronic crisis' of the new coalition governorship, the local Bolshevik newspaper *Sotsial-Demokrat* (*The Social Democrat*) reported that 'members of the committee rarely attend' and 'are little interested in their business'.[7] P.A. Lebedev, a leading Saratov Bolshevik, penned an editorial on the 'death of the Provincial [Public] Executive Committee'.[8] Semenov, now retired, lamented that the PEC and Commissariat 'are not ruling organs but madhouses'.[9] *Saratovskii vestnik* (the *Saratov Herald*) noted the repeated failure of the PPEC to assemble a quorum. By the end of June, the committee's collapse was broadly recognised. The editors of *Saratovskii vestnik* complained that 'at the last meeting of the [Public] Executive Committee the need to confer on the committee greater authority in the eyes of the population and greater capacity for work was discussed . . . This question arose in connection with the fact that lately power not only in the city but throughout the province *has actually passed to the soviet of workers' and soldiers' deputies*, since the [Public] Executive Committee has not met for three weeks now' (my italics – DR).[10] For all practical purposes, then, by late spring 1917 local power, diffuse as it was, rested in the hands of the Saratov Soviet.

How representative were developments in Saratov? An examination of the alignment of political forces in the Volga provinces shows that the situation in Saratov was common. At the district level in Saratov province, for instance, soviets had emerged as sovereign organs. According to the assistant provincial commissar of Kazan, 'public organisations show no noticeable activity, and even the Committee of Public Safety is dying out'. From Mokshan in Penza province officials reported that 'local authorities are powerless, local *uezd* [district] committees are powerless. Local organs are idle.' The Buguruslan Soviet in Samara province at its very first meeting discussed disbanding the town's PEC, 'which is becoming well known for its inactivity'.

Tsaritsyn soon acquired the reputation of a provincial Kronstadt because by the end of April the soviet was recognised as the ruling organ in town. After falling under the leadership of Bolshevik and Left SR radicals, the soviet found itself under attack in the national non-socialist press. Reacting to a resolution passed by the city soviet in early June calling for a transfer of power to the soviets, the provincial commissar of Astrakhan appealed to the Provisional Government for help. In Glazovo (Viatka province) an executive committee of soviets of peasants', workers' and soldiers' deputies declared itself the ruling organ and demanded the liquidation of the PEC installed after the February revolution. The Nikolaev Soviet in Samara province on 16 June declared itself the highest political authority in the *uezd* and appointed its own district commissar. Soviets in Samara, Penza and Syzran routinely replaced governmental organs during crises.[11]

The initiative soon passed to the soviets not only in the Volga region. In his study of the Bolsheviks in Siberia, Russell E. Snow described how leaders of soviets entered PECs and even controlled them, and how the soviets became the *de facto* authorities in central Siberia during late spring. According to Snow, 'the Krasnoiarsk Soviet was the ruling authority in Eniseisk *guberniia* from the outset'. In Tomsk and Novonikolaevsk, to take two slightly different examples reminiscent of the situation in Saratov, the leading members of the soviets and PECs 'were the same men'. Examining the situation in Latvia, Andrew Ezergailis concluded that

> one peculiarity of the revolution in Latvia was that there was no counterpart for the *dual power* which, according to Lenin, existed in Russia. In the beginning there were as many as seven different councils claiming broad governing powers, but as the weeks went by, a process of elimination set in. By June the councils were in the hands of the Bolsheviks.

Ronald G. Suny, in recent essays on the revolution in Tiflis and Baku, concluded that 'soviet power existed except in name'.[12] A.I. Lepeshkin observed that 'soviets in this period often exercised effective control over the activities of the organs of state administration in the provinces and directed institutions of local government'.[13] G.A. Trukan in his study of the October revolution in central Russia noted that 'the state apparatus in the provinces was more disorganised than in Petrograd. State authority here turned out to be weaker and the pressure of the democratic forces more powerful.'[14]

In fact, at the Bolshevik April Conference some provincial delegates expressed more optimistic views of the role of local soviets and Bolshevik committees than their Petrograd comrades, prompting even Lenin to conclude that

> in a number of local centres . . . the role of the soviets has turned out to be especially important. Single power [*edinovlastie*] has been created. The bourgeoisie has been disarmed entirely and has been reduced to complete subordination; wages have been raised, the workday has been shortened without a drop in production; food supplies have been guaranteed, control over production and distribution has gotten under way; all of the old authorities have been replaced.[15]

Documenting the extent to which soviets throughout Russia found themselves in the unexpected role of administrative organs is one thing; explaining *how* the soviets came to amass such power is another.

To a certain extent, there is certainly a straight line of development between the first soviets of 1905, the first freely elected workers' mass organisations, and the revolutionary councils of 1917. As Oskar Anweiler put it, 'The instant revival [of the soviets] . . . expressed a living memory of the revolutionary role of the soviets of 1905 and proved that these organisations could adapt instantly to widespread needs in a new revolutionary rising.'[16]

However, despite its many merits, Anweiler's pioneering work does not adequately explain the vitality of the soviets during 1917. My own research suggests that it was not so much the concept of soviets *per se* as the implicit recognition among workers and soldiers of the need for some sort of institution that would articulate their revolutionary energies and project their sheer numerical strength that gave rise to the formation of soviets and the myriad of other mass organisations. (Again and again in Russia during 1917, the socialist parties *combined* captured large majorities of the popular vote in elections to city dumas, food-supply assemblies and the Constituent Assembly. In the July duma elections in Saratov, for instance, the socialist parties captured 82.3 per cent of the popular vote; and they won approximately the same percentage of the electorate in elections to the Constituent Assembly in Saratov province in November.)[17]

The power of the soviets had other sources as well. The very revolutionary origin of these councils, chosen in free elections, made them instantly popular, for elections were deemed essential as a bulwark against privilege. Despite the lack of uniformity among the soviets throughout Russia they remained the most constant, regular form of local government and political life. Another reason for the leading position of the Saratov Soviet was that it developed independently of the political parties and initially remained neutral towards partisan politics. Further, the revolution had given rise to expectations that many problems facing the people could be resolved in a short time; the soviet's apparent success in dealing with the threat to public order and with dwindling food supplies seemed to justify such expectations, at least in the period immediately after February. Concrete steps taken by the soviet to democratise all organs of local government and to improve the economic situation of its constituency (in the battle over the introduction of an eight-hour work-day, to cite one example) likewise justified its claim to speak for the previously disenfranchised. This was particularly the case in view of the collapse of local organs of the Provisional Government, a development that turned the soviets into governing bodies in which the economic and political struggles were fused. Not surprisingly, the soviets before long became political battlegrounds. The radicalisation of the soviets reflected the radicalisation of the masses.

The Saratov Soviet and other local soviets also emerged as popular institutions because the immediate experience of revolution itself forged new values and expectations (shaped, to be sure, by the alienation of the socialist intelligentsia from the old state structure). Richard Stites, in his stimulating essay on iconoclastic currents in the Russian revolution, argues convincingly that revolutionaries realised the extent to which 'signs and symbols – and the very act of revising them – are able to mobilize certain sentiments of devotion and loyalty, and to evoke political and social dreams'.[18] Surprisingly enough, however, Stites ignores the soviets, the political representation of revolutionary iconoclasm, whose very existence was symbolic of the political ritual of reversal which had taken place when the masses were brought into politics. In this regard we can learn as well from studies of the French revolution. In her investigation of how politics were transformed in the heat of conflict during the French revolution, Lynn Hunt argues that 'the structure of the polity changed under the impact of increasing political participation and popular mobilisation; political language, political ritual, and political organisation all took on new forms and meanings'.[19]

My study of Saratov would certainly bear this out. As a marketplace for revolutionary ideas, the soviet served as a distribution point for revolutionary language (the 'privileged bourgeoisie' and the 'revolutionary democracy'); for revolutionary imagery (counterrevolutionary forces conspiring, always conspiring, to arrest the deepening of the revolution); and for revolutionary symbols (red bunting and ribbons, workers' caps and soldiers' greatcoats). What one did for a living, what one wore, what one ate, and where one lived, now took on new significance. The soviet undertook the renaming of streets; it removed Tsarist monuments and erected revolutionary ones (to N.G. Chernyshevskii, for example, who was born in Saratov province); it presided over revolutionary celebrations and rituals (such as May Day).

Social polarisation made language an expression of power, too. The unprecedented proliferation of revolutionary party newspapers whose circulations quickly surpassed that of the established press; the mass printings of party programmes and pamphlets written in a popular style; and the public singing of revolutionary songs served both to demonstrate and to bolster power. Faith in the regenerative power of revolution likewise made it easier to break with tradition. Anthropologists and sociologists maintain that political authority requires some sort of 'cultural frame' with a 'centre' commanding sacred status. In Saratov it was the soviet that gave those formerly excluded from the corridors of power their sense of place in society, 'the place where culture, society, and politics come together'.[20]

SOCIAL REVOLUTION

Elsewhere I have argued that the unprecedented level of mass participation in all aspects of public affairs created an environment in which various social groups worked towards their own diverse priorities.[21] For the ruling circles and Western-oriented political leaders of the country, the revolution had swept away all of the frustrating impediments that had made a scandal of the war effort. To ordinary citizens, however, the revolution had created conditions which appeared to promise a better life. The deeply rooted feelings of injustice and suspicion towards the old order soon carried over to those in the post-February administration who sought to curb popular initiative and reform. In Saratov the so-called 'democratic' elements (the socialists) succeeded in democratising the dumas and zemstvos as well as in establishing their own class organs, which amassed considerable power. Among the overlapping network of popular organisations created in the first half of 1917, those elected directly by the people mobilised the most authority: factory committees and soviets, soldier committees, volost and village executive committees. All these lower-level bodies tried to establish some means of control over factory administrators, officers and estate owners, just as the Petrograd Soviet had served as watchman over the 'middle-class' government and its institutions before the formation of the first coalition government in May. The practices of the popular institutions often had little in common with Western notions of representative political democracy. The common people may not have understood this concept at all, or viewed it with suspicion.

Social polarisation complicated the tactical dilemma of the moderate socialists who entered the government in May. Many Saratov SR and Menshevik leaders had rightly feared that joining with the Kadets and other non-socialist parties would compromise their party programmes and beliefs. This was particularly true of the SRs, who were enormously influential in Saratov province. While the fate of some SRs became linked to that of the coalition government, others who were more directly involved with the peasantry at the lower levels under-took to carry out programmes advocated by the party even before 1905. The more moderate leaders of the party were hard put to deal with 'our Bolsheviks', as they called their impatient comrades. Mean-while, the Bolsheviks' call for a soviet régime and their rejection of the first coalition government set up in May sharply distinguished their programme from that of the other parties. Their growing anti-war stand also came to separate them from the majority socialists. By late June the illusion of socialist solidarity had been shattered, and the moderate socialists sought to apply the brakes to a social revolution that threatened to speed past them.

The July Days in Petrograd further complicated the question of political power in provincial Russia. Affected by the leftward march of society in neighbouring Tsaritsyn and by what they believed to be a premature and dangerous clamour for an all-socialist government, moderate socialists in Saratov as in other provincial towns now strove to revive the authority of the city dumas. In a sense, a resurgence of the Saratov Duma, elected in the aftermath of the July crisis when Bolshevik fortunes were at their lowest, could be seen as to their advantage, for it was a representative rather than a class organ and the Bolsheviks made up only 12 per cent of its membership. Restoring the authority of the duma also appealed to some moderate socialist leaders' belief that cooperation with the bourgeoisie was essential. Besides, the Provisional Government had instructed local communi-ties to re-elect dumas to replace PECs.

The moderate socialist leaders, however, did not foresee that the class-oriented soviet would continue to muster more authority than a democratically elected duma, and that the working class and soldiers in Saratov were beginning to listen more attentively to what the Bol-sheviks had to say. An examination of the city duma's efforts to govern in the summer of 1917 reveals how close Russia had come to civil war and also exposes the seriousness of the administrative crisis facing the country at large. The moderate socialists who controlled the duma could not decide with whom to ally themselves – the liberals or the Left socialists. Mutual suspicion of Bolshevik tactics was not enough to unite the moderate socialists and liberals. All in all, the duma accomplished virtually nothing. A survey of other administrative organs reveals an equal degree of inefficacy. At a meeting of a provin-cial congress of *uezd* commissars at the end of July, delegates reported on their inability to maintain order in the face of the social revolution erupting in the countryside.[22] In Petrovsk, Pokrovsk and Nikolaevsk no one wanted to assume the office of district commissar, which remained temporarily vacant.[23]

Early in August Tokarskii, a member of the PPEC, wrote that

> because of illness I was unable to attend any meetings of the committee for a month. Resuming my duties after my recovery, I discovered that the committee had not met in the course of the month due to its members' absence ... Moreover, for the entire period there was not even one gathering of the Praesidium.

Tokarskii rebuked the new provincial commissar, the Menshevik Topuridze, for not convening the PPEC and for eventually doing so only after he had *'conferred with the praesidium of the soviet of workers' deputies and received directives there'* (italics mine – DR). In view of the influence that the soviet had over the PPEC and of its members' realisation 'that its role was spent', Tokarskii submitted his resignation.[24] Again, the situation in Saratov resembled that in neighbouring towns and probably was widespread throughout much of Russia. Calling for the State Duma to establish stable power in the country, M.V. Rodzianko, former president of the State Duma, wrote in the central Kadet newspaper *Rech* that

> new representatives of the government in the provincial and *uezd* centres are completely dependent on local party and class organisations, which authoritatively dictate their will to them. Judicial authorities are inactive. Committees and soviets under various names, and of various and often self-willed origin, which constantly change their membership, rule locally. They know neither their rights nor their responsibilities. Deprived of government guidance and not restrained by anyone, they believe they possess total state authority.[25]

When compared with the ineffectual city duma and the largely ignored PPEC, the soviet remained the only viable authority in the city. But this should not cloud the fact that a real paradox had emerged, for workers and soldiers were growing indifferent to the soviet as well. Plenums were called less frequently and decision-making was left to the executive bodies – a phenomenon that appears to have been common in much of urban Russia at the time. The reason for the indifference towards the soviet may well have been that the advances of the revolution were coming to a halt partly because of the visible deterioration of the economy. The growing apathy of the working class towards the soviet worried some moderates, who expressed reservations about their own backing for the liberal elements. One

Menshevik observed 'that workers ... are no longer taking it [the soviet] into consideration ... in part because of the impassioned factional bickering'.[26] All in all, by the summer of 1917 it is clear that the impulse towards localism in the immediate aftermath of February, followed by an emerging organisational malaise, had actually contributed to a further breakdown of the state apparatus and of law and order in general. As the year progressed, the atomisation of political forms underlined the need for a return to a state of normality and to an administrative order that would make things work again.

More than anything else, the attempt by the political Right to seize state power during the Kornilov affair at the end of August, and the blatant snubbing of popular organs by the military authorities in neighbouring Tsaritsyn, radicalised politics along the Volga. The workers and soldiers in Saratov responded to Kornilov as if they themselves were fighting surrogate Kornilovs, and in this respect the effort at a conservative restoration in the summer of 1917 served as a dress rehearsal for October. The Bolsheviks in the city now capitalised on the fact that new elections to the soviet had given them a majority. To the dismay of the burghers of Saratov, armed local workers were prepared to fight against counter-revolutionaries, while Bolshevik slogans were enthusiastically echoed in the garrison. Compromised by their support of the coalition government, the local SR and Menshevik organisations split apart as the more left-wing members sided with the Bolsheviks against further coalition with propertied Russia and as the centrist elements refused to repudiate the policies they had pursued since February, perhaps still hoping that civil war could be staved off.

Moreover, in the wake of the Kornilov affair the peasant movement entered its most radical phase. The rural now converged with the urban revolution as the Russian army disintegrated. Up and down the Volga and across the eastern tip of Russia's Black-Earth zone, workers' soviets, soldiers' soviets, PECs and party organisations called for a transfer of power to the Petrograd Soviet nationally and to soviets and other democratically elected bodies locally. The mood of provincial Russia had a synergistic effect on Lenin and other Bolshevik militants and helped convince them that the country was ripe for a transfer of power to the soviets.[27]

CONCLUSION

In this chapter I have sought to explain why urban provincial Russia came to back revolutionary extremists by the autumn of 1917. Admittedly, the rich diversity of the revolutionary experience makes such analysis risky; nonetheless, despite the obvious pitfalls of such an endeavour, I think it time to hazard some tentative generalisations.

Crippling the centralised state structure, the February revolution removed all the impediments that had excluded the Russian masses from the political life of the country; now an array of other factors led to the events of October. The view of many socialists that Russia was not ready for social revolution undermined their party programmes after February: in Saratov it caused them to abandon the legitimacy of the popular organs set up in 1917, particularly the soviets, and it eventually led to a rupture between party leaders and the rank and file, who accepted the Bolshevik call for an all-soviet government.

Although riddled with problems, the Bolshevik party offered a consistently plebeian programme to the Russian people, and rode to power atop self-legitimised popular organs – soviets, factory committees, trade unions, Red Guard detachments, soldiers' committees and the rest. As elsewhere in Russia the Bolshevik tactical platform of land, peace and bread, and the slogan 'All Power to the Soviets' appealed increasingly to common people, whose expectations had often soared to unreasonable levels while their economic situation deteriorated. The Bolsheviks' combination of tactical flexibility with a militant class interpretation of Russian political life (in the inclusive Russian sense of all the upper and middle classes pitted against the rest) proved successful in a fluid setting characterised by economic ruin, growing anarchism and a tottering structure of voluntary authority relationships. The October revolution was the triumph of all those radical groups that had broken with the camp supporting continued coalition with the bourgeoisie.

Two broad political conflicts actually took place in 1917. The first involved the competition between Russian socialism and Russian liberalism. It found expression in the system of dual power that surfaced after February (and it may well have ended when the initiative passed to the soviets in much of provincial Russia early in the year). The second involved the competition between radical socialism and moderate socialism. It found expression in the battle over whether or not an all-socialist government could rule Russia. To understand the dynamics of the move towards what might be called a crude class solution to the question of the political future posed by the February revolution, it is necessary to give due weight to the impact of popular attitudes in Saratov towards political power and towards the new plebeian institutions formed after the fall of the autocracy. For the first time since 1905, the people were brought into politics; what is most striking about their behaviour is the degree to which it had been shaped by crudely formulated socialist ideas and rhetoric during the preceding generation. This conclusion, I would argue, is bound to cast doubt on whether a democratic representative government could have been viable in Russia at that time.

The unresolved question of Russia's political future acquired an institutionalised form in the compromise system of dual power embodied in the Provisional Government and the Petrograd Soviet, which soon spoke out on behalf of the popular organs newly established throughout the country. When translated into a provincial setting, the dual authority fashioned in Petrograd took on a new shape. The weakness of Russian liberalism was much more apparent in Saratov and throughout much of provincial Russia in general, where as early as April political power had already been concentrated in the hands of local soviets.

Lenin's return to Russia in that month and the collapse of the Provisional Government in the wake of the Miliukov affair pushed the Mensheviks and SRs into a coalition with the liberals. Now only the Bolsheviks maintained that Russia could move immediately to establish a socialist government without the participation of the propertied elements. Insisting that his party should not support the Provisional Government, Lenin lobbied for a transfer of power to the soviets; this turned out to be one of the most important tactical positions taken by a political party in 1917. The leaders of the moderate socialists, seeking to prevent social and civil war, saw their historical mission as that of harmonising the discordant political voices raised throughout the country. Entering the coalition ministry, they believed that they were saving war-torn Russia from a counter-revolutionary restoration and from the demagogic appeals of the Bolsheviks. In retrospect, however, the cooption of the moderate socialists into the government blurred the meaning of dual power at both the national and the local level and failed to resolve the differences they had with Russian liberalism. More important, it forced many moderate leaders eventually to reject their own revolutionary programmes.

The efforts to suppress Bolshevism in July, followed by the failure of a military restoration in August, shattered the hopes for a liberal or peaceful outcome. Force failed to curb the revolutionary tide and the disintegration of state power; instead the threat of counter-revolution revitalised the soviets, whose deputies across much of Russia now elected Bolshevik and other leftist representatives. Isolated from the lower classes, the liberals remained politically vulnerable. Dissensions sapped the strength of the moderate socialist parties. In the popular view the Bolsheviks became inseparably associated with soviet power, whereas the moderate socialists, clinging stubbornly to coalition with the bourgeoisie and to their belief in the righteousness of a revolutionary war against the Central Powers, lost credibility.

Although they faced determined opposition from moderate leaders, the Saratov Bolsheviks controlled the soviet's executive bodies from September.[28] Throughout that month, workers and soldiers passed resolutions demanding a transfer of power to the soviets, the dissolution of the State Duma and the arming of workers. Across Russia people expected a promulgation of soviet power at the upcoming Second Congress of Soviets; others feared a Bolshevik coup in the name of the soviets still earlier. In either case, the strength of the Bolsheviks and other leftist groups within the context of the soviets was manifest. The Bolsheviks won the bid for power in Saratov because they stood for Soviet power and in this respect enjoyed institutional legitimacy.

And, even though the Bolsheviks' coming to power before the Second Congress meant that the party's leaders may have been willing to break with the concept of soviet democracy, they could not risk destroying the powerful image of the soviets as revolutionary organs – even while they were being transmogrified into pillars of state power during the tortuous years of the Civil War.

NOTES

1 The above description of Saratov and summary of the revolutionary movement are drawn from my *Revolution on the Volga: 1917 in Saratov* (Ithaca, 1986), pp. 1–74.

2 Ibid., pp. 75–85.

3 V.I. Startsev, *Vnutrenniaia politika Vremennogo Pravitelstva pervogo sostava* (Leningrad, 1980), p. 198.

4 Raleigh, *Revolution on the Volga*, pp. 104–10.

5 I detail the impact of Lenin's April theses and the Miliukov affair at the local level in ch. 3 of *Revolution on the Volga*.

6 See *Sotsial-Demokrat* no. 21 (2 June 1917), p. 1 and no. 27 (11 June 1917), p. 3; *Izvestiia Saratovskoi gorodskoi dumy* (Saratov, 1917), pp. 101–2, 112–13, 127; *Proletarii Povolzhia* no. 5 (22 April 1917), pp. 3–4, no. 6 (26 April, 1917), p. 3; *Saratovskii vestnik* no. 87 (22 April 1917), p. 3.

7 *Sotsial-Demokrat* no. 25 (9 June 1917), p. 3.

8 *Saratovskii vestnik* no. 127 (11 June 1917), p. 4.

9 I.I. Mints *et al.*, *Oktiabr v Povolzhe* (Saratov, 1967), p. 102.

10 *Saratovskii vestnik* no. 138 (28 June 1917), p. 3. A similar assessment appears in *Saratovskii listok* no. 136 (24 June 1917), p. 3.

11 The examples cited above can be found in R.K. Valeev, 'Krizis mestnykh organov Vremmenogo Pravitelstva letom i oseniu 1917 goda (Po materialam Povolzhia)', in *Oktiabr v Povolzhe i Priurale (Istochniki i voprosy istoriografii)* (Kazan, 1972), pp. 120–1; Donald J. Raleigh, 'Revolutionary Politics in Provincial Russia: The Tsaritsyn "Republic" in 1917', *Slavic Review* 40 (1981), 198–202; Mints, *Oktiabr v Povolzhe*, p. 99: A.I. Lepeshkin, *Mestnye organy vlasti sovetskogo gosudarstva (1917–1920 gg.)* (Moscow, 1957), p. 89.

12 Russell Snow, *The Bolsheviks in Siberia, 1917–1918* (Rutherford, 1977), pp. 69–70, 97, 106, 108; Andrew Ezergailis, *The 1917 Revolution in Latvia* (Boulder, 1974), pp. 16–18; Ronald G. Suny, 'Nationalism and Social Class in the Russian Revolution: The Cases of Baku and Tiflis', in *Transcaucasia, Nationalism, and Social Change: Essays in the History of Armenia, Azerbaijan, and Georgia*, ed. R.G. Suny (Ann Arbor, 1983), pp. 246, 250. For further evidence see 'Obzor polozheniia Rossii za tri mesiatsa', *Krasnyi arkhiv* 2, no. 15 (1926), pp. 30–60.

13 Lepeshkin, *Mestnye organy vlasti*, pp. 99–100.

14 G.A. Trukan, *Oktiabr v tsentralnoi Rossii* (Moscow, 1967), p. 53.

15 A.I. Razgon, 'O sostave sovetov Nizhnego Povolzhia v marte-aprele 1917 g.', in *Sovety i soiuz rabochego klassa i krestianstva v Oktiabrskoi revoliutsii* (Moscow, 1964), p. 107.

16 Oskar Anweiler, *The Soviets: The Russian Workers, Peasants, and Soldiers Councils, 1905–1921*, translated by Ruth Hein (New York, 1974), p. 64.

17 For the results of the July duma elections see *Saratovskii vestnik* no. 152 (12 July 1917), p. 1, and no. 159 (20 July), p. 2. Results of elections in Saratov province to the Constituent Assembly can be found in *Saratovskaia zemskaia nedelia* no. 1 (5/18 February 1918), p. 17.

18 Richard Stites, 'Iconoclastic Currents in the Russian Revolution: Destroying and Preserving the Past', in Abbott Gleason, Peter Kenez and Richard Stites (eds.), *Bolshevik Culture: Experiment and Order in the Russian Revolution* (Bloomington, 1985), p. 2.

19 Lynn Hunt, *Politics, Culture, and Class in the French Revolution* (Berkeley and Los Angeles, 1984), p. 2.

20 Cited in ibid., p. 87.

21 See my *Revolution on the Volga*, pp. 149–90.

22 *Proletarii Povolzhia* no. 47 (29 July 1917), p. 4.

23 Valeev, 'Krizis mestnykh organov', p. 129.

24 *Saratovskii vestnik* no. 173 (5 August 1917), p. 3.

25 Akademiia nauk SSSR, Institut istorii, *Revoliutsionnoe dvizhenie v Rossii v iule 1917 g.: Iulskii krizis*, ed. D.A. Chugaev (Moscow, 1959), pp. 318–19.

26 *Izvestiia Saratovskogo soveta* no. 70 (8 August 1917), p. 2.

27 See my *Revolution on the Volga*, pp. 225–61.

28 For the results of the elections to the Saratov Soviet held in September see V.P. Antonov-Saratovskii, *Pod stiagom proletarskoi borby: Otryvki iz vospominanii o rabote v Saratove* (Moscow and Leningrad, 1925), p. 145.

4

THE RED GUARDS:
SPONTANEITY AND THE OCTOBER
REVOLUTION

REX A. WADE

JOHN REED, in his classic description of the taking of the Winter Palace, described how

> in the light that streamed out of all the Winter Palace windows, I could see that the first two or three hundred men were Red Guards with only a few scattered soldiers. Over the barricade of firewood we clambered, and leaping down inside gave a triumphant shout as we stumbled on a heap of rifles thrown down by the yunkers [military cadets] who had stood there.[1]

Less dramatically but with more overview, Nikolai Podvoiskii, who as leader of the Bolshevik Military Organisation was concerned primarily with mobilising the garrison, wrote later that

> the Red Guard was brought to fighting readiness earlier than the regiments. It occupied the most important strategic points. It took over the defence of Smolny . . . [and] the guarding of factories and public buildings.[2]

Yet, the Bolshevik leaders had so underestimated these armed workers' forces that, in assessing their potential sources of support only a few days earlier, on 15 October, the Bolshevik Petersburg committee made a ridiculously low assessment of their size and readiness,[3] while they are virtually absent from the writings of Lenin. Who, then, were the Red Guards?* What role did they play in 1917, especially in the October revolution? Why did the Bolshevik Party leadership, which

---

* Workers' armed bands in 1917 were called by various terms, workers' militia and Red Guard being the most common. Workers' guards, factory militia, fighting *druzhina* and other terms were used also. Generally, the term 'workers' militia' was used most commonly in early 1917, while Red Guard (which had a more militant connotation) became more common later; usage here reflects that. In referring to specific organisations, however, their actual name is used.

later relied so heavily upon them, underestimate them as late as October and why have historians since then also underestimated them?

Part of the answer to these questions lies in the special role of the workers' armed bands as representative of the phenomenon of spontaneity and popular self-assertion which swept Russia in 1917. The Red Guards played an important role in 1917, especially in the October revolution, and hence merit study on that ground alone. Yet, they also are a valuable vehicle for studying another aspect of the revolution: the role of spontaneity, local leadership, self-organisation and self-assertive action, and the relationship between these lower-level activists and workers and the higher party officials. The Red Guards are especially useful for studying these themes because the central political party leadership made little effort to control them – although local leaders, both in the districts of Petrograd and in provincial cities, did try somewhat harder – and so the Guards had more opportunity to develop according to their own views of the revolution than did organisations such as trade unions or factory committees. Yet, at the same time that they vigorously defended their autonomy they also sensed a need for broader organisation and leadership and made repeated efforts in that direction. In this respect they were typical of the bewildering array of new and self-formed organisations – political, economic, cultural, geographic, large, small – which sprang up across Russia in 1917. This broader self-organising, self-activating characteristic of Russian society in 1917, this enormous spontaneity, and what it meant for the course of the revolution was a phenomenon which any political leadership had to confront.†

The workers' armed bands arose out of, and continued to represent, the tremendous drive for self-assertion, the spontaneity, that characterised the Russian population after the February revolution. Their initial formation came in response to and was part of the events of that revolution. The original urge seems to have come from below and to have been resisted at first by higher-level leaders. For example, even as

† Perhaps a word needs to be said about spontaneity and self-organisation as they are used here. There is an older historical controversy about the adequacy of 'spontaneity' as translation of the Russian *stikhiinost* and about the latter in contrast to 'consciousness'. That is not our concern here; we are using spontaneity in its English sense in order to examine behaviour during the revolution. We are especially interested in the means by which and extent to which armed workers' bands came into being, defined their own roles, established their own organisational structures and leadership, and took political and armed action spontaneously, on their own volition, with few or no outside directives.

workers were demanding arms, a meeting of Bolshevik leaders on 26 February in Petrograd rejected a proposal to arm the workers and this decision was reaffirmed on 27 February by Alexander Shliapnikov, probably the leading Bolshevik then in the city.[4] Even so, workers – and others – pressed ahead, forming the first armed bands towards the evening of 27 February.[5] Late that night the first meeting of the Petrograd Soviet approved the formation of factory-based militias, but did little to implement it.[6]

Nonetheless, word of that resolution probably encouraged workers to form armed bands, but more by providing a sense of legitimacy and confidence than by determining whether or how they were formed or what they did. Even Bolshevik memoirists – usually quick to attribute all actions to party guidance and initiative – stress the self-directing nature of the early armed bands, 'not waiting for the call of leaders or parties', and at most claim the influence of earlier party schooling of the proletariat.[7] Throughout the first few days of the revolution examples abound of the self-formed militias, created either at a factory or other institution or under the leadership of some vigorous individual. Some were student or multi-class in composition, but only the worker and factory-based groups proved to have permanence beyond the first weeks of the revolution.[8] A similar phenomenon was to be seen throughout the country in the larger cities – and some smaller ones – as word of the revolution in Petrograd reached them. Workers, and often students and other citizens as well, took to the streets in self-organised armed bands before their self-proclaimed leaders – busy organising city soviets and 'public committees' – took notice, much less action.[9]

With the revolution secure within a matter of days, the question of the future of these armed bands arose. Spontaneity now became a matter of self-organisation rather than a sudden burst of activity, and thus the whole question of spontaneity versus leadership and direction from above emerges more sharply, as does the question of the role to be played by these armed bands in the new Russia. The problem in the spring centred around at least two related issues: the attitude of higher leaders – soviet, government, party – towards the workers' militias and Red Guards, and the struggle of the latter for organisation and survival within the complex, fluid situation created by revolutionary Russia, by the hostility or indifference towards them from outside and above and by their own mixed feelings about their role, independence and relationship to 'higher' bodies.

What of party and political attitudes? Although arming all the people had been a longstanding plank in the platforms of the socialist parties, they had no clear position on what role, if any, should be assigned to the kind of armed bands that appeared during and after the February revolution. Nor did they quickly develop one. It was difficult to oppose such clearly proletarian organisations, but equally difficult to conceptualise what function they might serve over the long run in the revolution or how they might be organised. Moreover, there was some discomfort among high party leaders about them and their self-assertiveness. This ambivalence, the difficulty of working out a role – if any – for them, and the sheer pressure of time and events, all contributed to inactivity in providing leadership or guidance.

The Bolsheviks were the most supportive. During March they began, mostly through *Pravda* articles by Vladimir Bonch-Bruevich and Vladimir Nevskii, but also in some party meetings, to call for a permanent, autonomous, revolutionary, class-oriented armed force. The article by Bonch-Bruevich, on 18 March, contained the first printed use of the term Red Guard in 1917, although it harked back to a Finnish group in the revolution of 1905. However, these expressions of support were usually made within the context of the call to arm all the people and rarely showed any firm concept of a role for the existing militias. Similarly, the party leadership limited itself to articles and resolutions and did not provide them with concrete help. The Bolshevik Military Organisation saw the organisation of armed workers' units as one of its tasks, but in fact it did not do so and instead concentrated on the soldiers.[10]

Other parties took a quite different attitude. The Mensheviks, in their sole statement on the subject in March, an article in the *Rabochaia gazeta* of 8 March, accepted the value of a civil guard in maintaining public order, but did not go on to work out any role for armed workers' bands. Indeed, they even questioned the need for an 'armed people', given the existence of the revolutionary army. The tone of impending social conflict and the consequent plea to arm the workers, which permeated the articles of Nevskii and Bonch-Bruevich, were therefore absent. The Socialist Revolutionary (SR) newspaper, *Delo naroda*, did not even raise the matter of the workers' militias. This foreshadowed a basic dilemma for the Mensheviks and Socialist Revolutionaries (SRs): throughout 1917 they were bedevilled by difficulties when opposing a workers' movement, yet they feared the anarchistic, extremist element and possible Bolshevik influence within that movement. They were also constrained by their concern with the maintenance of public order. The non-socialist parties and newspapers actually had a somewhat clearer, if negative, picture of the role of these armed units; they viewed them with alarm either as a danger to society, or as transitory bodies which would soon give way to a new civic police force.

Leadership, then, especially in the struggle for organisation and survival, would have to come from individuals in the factory or the local district, from the lower-level leaders of the revolution, and not from higher party officials. Such leadership did emerge, and with it a change of focus. March had been a period of initial formation in response to the February revolution. April saw the beginnings of a new concern with sustained self-organisation and with building larger district and city-wide structures. The problem became how to make the militias permanent, to find a function for them in the new society. One such role evolved in practice as workers' militias staked out effective control of portions of the city, attempting to provide them with basic security; although always tenuous, a *de facto* territorial division took place between them and the City Militia (police). This fact necessitated some larger organisation and direction, which were provided sometimes by the district soviet but more often by self-created and self-directed 'workers' militia commissariats' at the subdistrict or district level.

In the process some of their leaders began to debate the role of the workers' militias, and especially the extent to which they were there to maintain order or were, rather, more overtly political, functioning to advance workers' political and economic interests (an issue never resolved, but increasingly tilted towards the political role). In the process a cadre of leaders began to appear, men who were active in the workers' militias and other local political and workers' organisations, and who gradually developed theories about, and experience with armed workers' organisations. These individuals, more politically aware than the average worker and often with the experience of political exile or jail behind them, developed the idea of the armed workers as an important force in the revolution, articulated the need for organisation and undertook to turn these ideas into reality in 1917. They also provided the point of contact between the self-created and largely independent worker organisations and the more aloof party organisations. They were often frustrated both by their parties' attitudes and by the local orientation of most workers' militias, which tended jealously to preserve their autonomy from any higher authority, certainly any authority outside the factory. There emerged, then, a mixture of a very local – factory – orientation with some still hazy concepts of a larger role which required better and broader organisation and leadership.

The first clash between these lower-level militia leaders eager to build stronger organisations and the hostile or indifferent higher party leadership came in April. The initiative came from leaders of the Printers' Union Fighting Detachment and other local militia leaders. Under the leadership of N. Rostov, a Menshevik activist working with the printers' detachment, they convened a meeting of delegates from across the city and attempted to weld together a strong, city-wide, workers' guard. They also posed the question of the long-term role of the armed workers. However, even though lower-level Mensheviks were actively involved (the executive commission set up at the first meeting had three Mensheviks and two Bolsheviks), the Menshevik and SR parties and the Petrograd Soviet leadership strongly condemned the effort. They labelled it 'unnecessary and harmful' and ordered their party members to cease involvement: their opposition was sufficient to put an end to the project.[11] Although the Bolshevik press did defend it *post facto*,[12] neither the Bolshevik Central Committee nor the Petrograd committee took any steps to assist the project. These events set a pattern which proved to be characteristic of party attitudes and action until September.

Such attitudes rechannelled rather than stopped efforts at organisation. On 29 April the Bolshevik-led Vyborg District Soviet approved regulations for a district-wide workers' guard organisation; in May a meeting in the Peterhof district formed a district Red Guard; and similar initiatives were taken elsewhere.[13] Efforts by the City Militia Administration and by factory managements to abolish the militias merely reinforced their sense of mission and encouraged them to seek better organisation. Individual factories defended their Red Guard units vigorously, and in May and June some militia leaders undertook the creation of a new city-wide network. They set up an 'initiative group' which included some recently returned political exiles, who probably provided it with a more confident and politically oriented leadership. However, for the most part, the lead seems to have come from a broad spectrum of party and non-party Red Guard members prominent at the factory level. The initiative group managed to convene a 'Conference of the Petrograd People's Militia' on 27 May. Its call for a broadly based workers' militia, whose members would be recommended by factory committees, trade unions or political parties, met with considerable response at workers' meetings, and led to the formation of a Council of the Petrograd People's Militia on 3 June.[14]

The Council had a more leftist and more Bolshevik character than the organising group formed in April: some half of the eleven members were Bolsheviks; the one SR known to be involved was distinctly a Left SR; the chairman, F.P. Neliubin, was either non-party or an anarchist.[15] Direct party support seems to have continued to be minor, mostly taking the form of editorials and resolutions. Although *Pravda* reiterated the principle of a universal militia with all citizens being armed ('If Miliukov wants a *Berdanka* [rifle] let one be given to him too'), and although Lenin's first writings after learning of the revolution (the 'Letters from Afar'), as well as his 'April theses' and draft for a party programme, had referred to arming the proletariat or to universal armed service,[16] there is little evidence that Lenin or other top party leaders paid much attention to the existing workers' armed bands or gave much thought to what to do with this type of organisation. What attention this question drew from Bolshevik spokesmen came from a few second-level leaders such as Nevskii or Bonch-Bruevich, and still more from third-level leaders such as Vasilev, the Vyborg District Soviet leaders and people such as the *piaterka* leaders Pavlov, Iurkin and the Trifonov brothers (see below). It was these lower-level Bolshevik leaders, men working in the factory committees, district party committees, district soviets and trade unions, who recognised the need for these organisations. The importance of individual and local initiative was even greater for those members of the SR or Menshevik parties who played an active role in the armed bands, since their party leaders generally opposed them.

The Council of the Petrograd People's Militia struggled throughout June to provide leadership and organisation for the many workers' militias and Red Guards, but with only limited success. The intensely local nature of the workers' armed bands, combined as it was with the hostility of the Petrograd Soviet, the Provisional Government and employers, was more than it could overcome. In the aftermath of the July Days, the Council was suppressed as a consequence of its participation and that of workers' militias, in the street demonstrations.

This was, however, only a temporary setback. Although the newspapers of the time and intelligentsia memoirists and writers afterwards made much of the conservative reaction in July and August, the story at the lower levels was quite different and shows their views to have been exaggerated. Indeed, even before July ended the worker and soldier masses resumed their leftward shift. This is graphically reflected in the Bolshevik and left-wing coalition victories in the district soviets of Petrograd in late July and August,[17] and in developments among the Red Guards.

Immediately after the July Days workers' militia and Red Guard units saw a loss of membership, came under intense pressure from factory management and were sometimes broken up. However, by the second half of July they had begun to recover and to reassert themselves, as demonstrated by the renewed movement towards a more openly political role for the Red Guard and by renewed efforts at organisation-building. In July and early August there were efforts to build stronger district-level organisations in the Vyborg, Narva and Nevskii districts. Moreover, there was once again an attempt to build a city-wide Red Guard structure and staff.

On 2 August Red Guard leaders from twelve or thirteen districts of Petrograd convened a conference. Statements at the meeting showed clearly that the initiative for the conference came from local Red Guard leaders, but also that they were mostly Bolsheviks. The higher party organs – the Petersburg committee and the Central Committee – had no role. Valentin Trifonov, a Bolshevik, commented at the conference that 'the Bolsheviks have not thus far occupied themselves with the question' of the workers' armed units, a statement seconded by other speakers. One speaker from the Vyborg district, a Bolshevik stronghold, stated that it was 'time for the Bolshevik organisations to wake up'. They did not: when the Petersburg committee was asked (between 5 and 8 August) to send a representative to help, it declined.

The organisers, left on their own, pushed ahead anyway, and throughout August a *piaterka* worked to hammer out both an organisational structure and broad principles for a 'workers' guard'. It is interesting to note in this context, and in contrast to earlier efforts in April and in May–June, that the organising group set up by the conference, the *piaterka*, included four and later five Bolsheviks as against only one other – anarchist – member.[18] Before they could put their plans into effect, however, the Kornilov affair dramatically altered the situation within which they were working. However, it did not change the fact that the main impetus continued to come from below, and that the work of the *piaterka* and of earlier similar groups would bear fruit during and after the October revolution.

The Kornilov affair provides another opportunity to explore the layers of Red Guard organisational activity in 1917. When General Kornilov launched his drive on Petrograd the Soviet Central Executive Committee formed a 'Committee for the People's Struggle Against

Counter-revolution', which called for groups of workers to be armed under the direction of the district soviets and the Interdistrict Conference of Soviets. This was as close as any central soviet or governmental body had come to sanctioning the pre-existing armed bands. The actual leadership, however, even then immediately devolved on the districts, with the Interdistrict Conference providing some city-wide coordination. On 28 August the latter decided upon an organisational structure for the workers' *druzhiny*, focusing on the district level. Many district soviets responded to this initiative, taking an active role in organising Red Guards, *druzhiny* and militia and in establishing district command centres. In some districts they were provided with backing by other worker organisations such as councils of factory committees.

Thus, the Kornilov thrust provided district-level organisation with a new impetus partly in response to the events themselves, partly in response to the call from the Interdistrict Conference and the soviet Committee for the People's Struggle Against Counter-revolution.[19] Even so, the main organisation and direction took place, as before, at the factory level. There was an immense outpouring of activity, the formation of new, and the expansion of old, detachments. No doubt calls from the soviet and the political parties encouraged this development, but often both factory resolutions calling for formation of armed units and their actual formation or mobilisation predated any action by these higher organs.[20]

Although soviet endorsement faded with the threat from Kornilov, the Bolshevik party central organs now demonstrated more interest and even took a small role in efforts to organise the Red Guard, although this did not change the essential nature of the relationship between the Red Guard and the party. The Military Organisation now, for the first time, turned its attention to them. On 6 September it issued in its newspaper, *Soldat*, detailed instructions for organising and training 'workers' *druzhiny*'. However, it did not pursue the organisational aspects of its plan, but instead devoted its efforts to training workers in the use of arms, and even that initiative soon lapsed. The Petersburg committee in late September and early October discussed the importance of the Red Guard and of arming all the people, but itself did nothing. The Central Committee gave this issue even less attention. The party newspapers did give it considerable space at that time, but again without discernible results.[21]

It was symptomatic that both newspaper articles and party resolutions still tended to discuss the Red Guard and arming the workers in

5. Distribution of political propaganda, 1917.

conjunction with the idea of arming all the people. This fact suggests
that the higher party leadership still had little concept of what role
armed workers' units might play and that their thinking had not
evolved much under the impact of the actual events of the revolution.
With their thinking still at the pre-revolutionary theoretical stage
which focused on the arming of all the people, they could not provide
significant leadership or direction for the organisation of the armed
units which the workers were forming at the factories, or even for the
efforts of lower-level leaders to build a larger and broader organisational framework.

The efforts at organisation thus continued to bubble up from below.
In mid September a group of '12 commandants and 12 commissars of
the workers' militia' invited themselves into a meeting on the militias
sponsored by the Petrograd Soviet, the government, and some other
organisations, and effectively took control of it. They attempted to
establish a city-wide organisation, with a 'central *Komendatura*' and a
structure of district *komendatury*. Little is known of the work of the
Komendatura in September, but it does seem to have had some lasting
impact at the district level in building the Red Guard organisations.
An ongoing leadership had probably emerged by then, for it appears
that some of the *piaterka* leaders of August were active in this new
effort.[22] There is some evidence of a similar continuity at the district

level, suggesting that by September a hard core of Red Guard activists had begun to consolidate itself.

Whether as a result of efforts from the Central *Komendatura* or as a result of local efforts, the most strikingly new feature of late September and early October was the development of more meaningful district-wide organisations and command staffs. At this level a real leadership cadre, strong enough to sustain a city-wide structure, could emerge. The most notable example in this respect was that of the Vyborg district where, despite its radicalism and repeated earlier efforts, no central Red Guard organisation or leadership had hitherto been created. The district soviet now made a new effort, convening a conference on 7 October. This meeting drew up a set of rules for the Red Guard, including provisions for an organisational structure to reach from the factory to the district and thence to an as yet non-existent city Red Guard staff subordinate to the Petrograd Soviet. The latter provision presumably reflected the Bolshevik take-over of the Petrograd Soviet, since the old soviet leadership had been hostile to the Red Guard.

The newly established Red Guard staff of the Vyborg district immediately set to work, attempting to establish closer ties with the factory units, provide instructors, obtain arms and generally strengthen and improve the fighting ability of the guard. It was the most active and effective militia or Red Guard organisation yet established in the city above the factory level. Its members would play an important role in convening a city-wide conference later in October.[23]

Vyborg was not an isolated case. At about the same time, a joint conference of the Narva and Peterhof districts adopted a set of regulations and established a staff. The dissimilarity of the rules suggests that they were worked out independently of Vyborg. Other areas, including some of the most important working-class quarters, also developed district-wide organisations at this time, usually closely linked or subordinate to the district soviet.[24]

These efforts finally met with support from above and the efforts at the lower and higher levels began to merge. The Bolshevik victory in the Petrograd Soviet in late September, resulting in the replacement of the Mensheviks–SRs by a new leadership under Leon Trotsky, opened up new opportunities. The soviet created a Department for the Workers' Guard, chaired by Konstantin Iurenev. A meeting which he held with some of the long-time leaders from the districts resulted in a decision to strengthen the central *Komendatura*; it was now to consist of Iurenev, four members of the old *piaterka* – Valentin Trifonov, Evgenii

Trifonov, Vladimir Pavlov and A.A. Iurkin – and A.K. Skorokhodov, a Bolshevik and Red Guard activist in the Petrogradskii district. The revitalised central *Komendatura* worked to strengthen the Red Guards, and together with the soviet's Department for the Workers' Guard (they were really two variations of the same leadership group), undertook to convene a city-wide conference of Red Guard representatives to be elected by all the units in the city.

The meeting convened on 22 October, against the background of rumours of a Bolshevik coup; the confrontation between the Provisional Government and the Bolshevik-led Petrograd Soviet over control of the garrison; the arrival of delegates for the forthcoming Second All-Russian Congress of Soviets, and the general tensions of the last week before the October revolution. Now, on the eve of the October revolution, they worked out an elaborate city-wide structure for the Red Guard, headed by a general staff (which military-sounding term provoked vigorous debate).[25] Although its plans could hardly be put into effect before the day of the revolution, a central command group was thus established which could provide some leadership for the Red Guards later, one moreover that was staffed by men who had already had several months of experience in working with those units.

While the city conference was thus putting together the plans for a general staff of the Red Guard, individual units at factories and some of the district and subdistrict organisations were reacting to the increasingly tense situation in the city on the eve of the October revolution. On 22 and 23 October many units went on the alert, staying under arms at their factories or otherwise increasing their readiness to react to whatever 'counter-revolutionary' threats might appear. As early as 21 October the Vyborg district Red Guard staff ordered the Guard of the Petrograd Cartridge Factory – and presumably others as well – to be on the alert all day on 22 October, the 'Day of the Petrograd Soviet', to guard against counter-revolutionary activity. On 23 October it sent another order to all units to maintain readiness.

Numerous memoir accounts, even allowing for a certain embellishment, make it clear that the various Red Guard units reacted to the tensions in the city by preparing for the 'defence of the revolution'. A worker at the Vulkan Factory wrote that, in response to the Vyborg district staff-order,

> The bolts of rifles clicked. In the yard of the factory they fitted the trucks with sheet armour and mounted machine guns. The factory ceased to be a factory and became an armed camp.[26]

6. Red Guards and pro-Bolshevik soldiers, 1917.

Although it is tempting to see a connection between these activities and the newly formed general staff, they appear to have been a local factory and district response to the heightened tensions in the city, preparations to defend the gains of the revolution.[27]

Thus, when Kerensky's ill-considered moves against the Bolsheviks on 24 October provided the long-anticipated 'counter-revolution', the Red Guards quickly sprang into action. The mobilisation of the Red Guard and its share in the confused struggle for control of the key points of the city on 24–25 October seems to have come mostly from local initiative, from individual units or from factory, district or sub-district leaders reacting to news and events. There is very little evidence that either the Military Revolutionary Committee (MRC)‡ or the General Staff of the Red Guard played any significant role in mobilising or directing the actions of the Red Guard, even though the latter played a central, perhaps decisive, part in the struggle for 'soviet

‡ The Military Revolutionary Committee was created in October as an agency of the Petrograd Soviet. It quickly took on a major role, becoming the primary soviet instrument in the struggle for control of the garrison on 21–23 October, then in organising resistance on 24 October to what was seen initially as an attack by Kerensky, and then in directing the final stages of the seizure of power on 25–26 October.

power' and the success of what came to be known as the October revolution. Their role is best indicated by a brief sketch of their actions during the October revolution.

The Red Guards were active – together with soldiers – in the seizure of many of the more important points in the city as well as in guarding factories and policing the streets. Red Guards made up most of the force which gradually assembled to protect the Smolny Institute, headquarters of the MRC, the Soviet and the Bolshevik party. They played a key part in securing control of the bridges, which was essential if free movement were to be maintained from Vyborg and other working-class districts on the right side of the river across to the government districts on the left bank. Similarly, they were active in occupying the railway stations, which would be the entry points for any troops from outside the city responding to the government's calls for help. Control of the bridges and stations was especially important in the early stages of the struggle on 24 October. Red Guards as well as soldiers were involved in the struggles all over the city for control of the utility and other important public buildings.

Moreover, they seem to have played a decisive role in confronting what was possibly the government's most likely source of armed support within Petrograd, the cadets of the various military academies. Whether by chance or design, Red Guards rather than soldiers were used for this difficult task, perhaps because of a fear that the soldiers might either come under the sway of officers at the schools or else vent their anger on the young cadets. Finally, Red Guards were of major importance in the encirclement and eventual capture of the Winter Palace. They increased their role in the siege on the 25th, replacing or supplementing army units. Some brought their own medical units with them in anticipation of fighting. Leaders of the siege were relieved to see the arrival of Red Guards, since they had little confidence in the reliability of their soldiers (many units had declared 'neutrality'), and it appears that the Red Guards stiffened morale and resolution.[28]

How important were the Red Guards in the October revolution in Petrograd? No precise answer can be given for we are, after all, dealing with a confused and chaotic event, in which armed groups fought, and often bluffed, each other for control of key buildings and places, with little and largely ineffectual central direction. Moreover, soldiers and workers frequently acted together, making it more difficult to assess their respective roles (although even there workers seem often to have played a leadership role, as illustrated by John Reed's comment that patrols of soldiers were 'invariably' commanded by a Red Guard).[29]

7. Women's Battalion; members of this unit were among the last defenders of the Winter Palace against the Bolshevik uprising (24–25 October 1917).

Nonetheless, some conclusions are possible. For one, the confused situation in which they operated put a premium on local initiative and self-assertiveness, which were very much characteristics of the Red Guard units. Moreover, while the garrison soldiers outnumbered the Red Guards, only a small proportion of the garrison, ill-disciplined and not inclined towards fighting, took part. By contrast, virtually every Red Guard unit estimated to be in existence on the eve of the October revolution, as well as many other workers with weapons, participated. In addition, the Red Guards not only provided actual armed support for the revolution, they provided vital encouragement, given their strong and unwavering support for soviet power, to those troops who did participate. There were no 'neutral' Red Guard units, no detachments which the Bolshevik leaders in Smolny feared might support the government. The garrison was huge but unreliable and the fickleness of army units during the July Days as well as the role of the army in suppressing revolt in 1905 were fresh in everyone's mind. The traditional emphasis upon the garrison in historical accounts is a reflection of the anxiety felt by the Bolshevik leadership about the support of the soldiers – an anxiety amply mirrored in the records of the MRC. Concomitantly, the role of the armed workers, which was much greater than that usually attributed to them in historical accounts, especially in the West, has been played down.

The misassessment by the Bolshevik leadership and the MRC of the potential of the Red Guards is one of the peculiar features of the October revolution, although it is at least partially explicable. The Bolshevik leadership devoted extensive efforts in October to assessing their sources of support, yet completely underestimated the size, determination and potential of the armed workers. Why? In answer, most weight should be given to the fact that the Bolsheviks, although the party most attuned to the popular mood, did not fully understand the dynamics of popular, self-directed, organisations and activity. The local, factory-based nature of the Red Guards and the absence of a central leadership confused them and led the Bolshevik leaders to underestimate both their size and potential. The fact that they were not under Bolshevik Party control, even though radical and ardently committed to 'soviet power', probably contributed to that same assessment. Moreover, it must also be noted that the top leaders had given little attention to the workers' militias throughout 1917. Although theory based the party on worker support, the top leaders failed to grasp the potential of such self-formed organisations, and completely overlooked the importance of armed workers not under their direct command. It was left to lower-level activists, increasingly but not only Bolsheviks, to recognise the potential of the Red Guards and to act on it. Given their underestimation of the militias, the preoccupation of the Bolshevik leaders with the garrison is the more understandable.

As mentioned above, the tendency to neglect the Red Guards in the accounts of the October revolution has been reinforced by the role and records of the MRC. The origins of the MRC as an agency designed to control the garrison were reflected in its actions during the October revolution: its orders were directed almost entirely to the army units. Historians, focusing extensively on the MRC, have thus naturally emphasised the role of the garrison at the expense of the workers. This tendency has, in turn, reinforced traditional interpretations emphasising central Bolshevik direction of a carefully planned and executed revolution.

The Red Guards played a role in the October revolution in the provinces similar to that in Petrograd, although the wide range of conditions and power relationships found in the various cities of the Russian empire meant that there were considerable differences in detail. The nature of the Bolshevik revolution locally depended upon a host of conditions: the political make-up of the local soviet; the social composition of the community; the size and attitude of the garrison; the vigour of local political leaders and nationality issues. In most instances, however, the Red Guard played an important role. In some cities the local soviet, already under Bolshevik control, was able to declare Soviet power immediately on receiving the news from Petrograd, and used Red Guards and soldiers to take over key points quickly and with little opposition. In those places where fighting occurred, the Red Guard played an important role, which as in Petrograd exceeded its size relative to whatever army garrison existed (excepting front cities).

Typical of cities where the transfer of power took a few days and involved a confrontation and shooting was Saratov, where the actions of the Red Guard were decisive. They organised and strengthened their forces during a period of political manoeuvring from 26–28 October, and took control of the main buildings of the city. In the final confrontation with local opponents at the city duma building on 28–29 October, the Red Guard was particularly important. The evidence suggests that, despite the large garrison, Red Guards made up half or more of the besieging force of about 3,000, and testimony – including that of military leaders – suggests that they were especially determined and enjoyed higher morale than the soldiers involved.[30]

Their role was equally important in cities where the struggle took longer and more fighting took place; Moscow is the great example, and worth examining in detail because of its importance. Only a small part of the garrison played an active part, whereas the Red Guard numbered 8,500 at the time the revolution began and reached nearly 30,000 armed men by the time it ended. Even though they were poorly trained and most spent the period guarding factories or undertaking similar tasks, the numerical preponderance of the Red Guard proved critical in a situation in which, as in Petrograd, overawing opponents was usually the key to gaining control of contested points. Again, as in Petrograd, local initiative, a strong point of Red Guard and other worker leaders, was of crucial importance. Moreover, whatever their training, the Red Guards in Moscow were committed to the success of the uprising, which they equated with defence of the revolution against counter-revolutionary provocations. They were prominent in the denunciation of efforts to establish a truce on 2 November. Several thousand of them were members of Red Guard units from nearby industrial settlements who were sufficiently committed to make the

8. Kronstadt sailors (October 1917).

trek to Moscow; and they were willing to fight if necessary – their casualties in the fighting ran into hundreds.[31]

In yet a third type of 'October revolution' in the provinces – those cases in which the seizure of power extended over several weeks – the Red Guards also played a key role. In Kharkov, for example, they were crucial in the gradual takeover of the city and in warding off both Ukrainian nationalist, and Russian, anti-Soviet forces. They were associated with support for Soviet power, and translated that into support for the Bolsheviks during the political struggle in November when the two came to be seen as one and the same thing. Moreover, their strength grew during November, while that of the garrison, and especially of the pro-Bolshevik units, melted away in self-demobilisation.[32] A similar development took place in other cities where the revolution took a long time to complete.

CONCLUSION

Across Russia, the Red Guard played an important part in the revolution generally and in October in particular, a role that has been underestimated for several reasons. First, once the October revolution in Petrograd forced the issue of 'Soviet power', then such a small and committed group could and did play a role out of all proportion to its numbers, especially when armed. Second, in most cases only a small number of people were actively involved in the local struggle for power in October and November, and thus the role of a group such as the Red Guard was magnified. Third, in most instances (except in front areas), only a small part of the local garrison took part, thus making the Red Guard, as the only other significant armed force, the more important. Fourth, since there was usually a common desire to avoid bloodshed, the ability to overawe opponents, which entailed enthusiasm and commitment as well as numbers and arms, was especially important in determining the outcome of many confrontations; the Red Guard had those characteristics more than almost any group and few of their opponents were willing to risk death for a generally discredited régime.

Paradoxically, the Red Guards' success in the October revolution marked the beginning of their end. During and immediately after the revolution, the Red Guard provided essential armed support for the Bolshevik government: serving as a police and security force of sorts, mounting expeditionary units to fight opponents of Soviet power in the provinces, and providing an important kernel in the formation of the new Red Army. Indeed, one of the first decrees of the new régime, on 28 October, was that all soviets of workers' and soldiers' deputies form workers' militias, to be provided with government weapons by both civilian and military authorities.[33] Yet, they were ill-suited to function indefinitely in these roles. The essential characteristics of the Red Guard included their voluntary, self-formed and self-directed nature, their local – usually factory – orientation, their hostile attitude towards established authority, their volatile membership. They saw themselves as workers volunteering for short-term actions (they responded better to immediate crises than to more sustained activity) in order to defend or advance *their* revolution, which might or might not be the same as that of the Bolshevik leaders. These were not the traits that the government needed in its new army or security forces.

Yet the Bolshevik leadership, motivated by emotional, ideological and practical factors felt compelled to seek a key role for the workers. This fact led to heated debates in the winter of 1917–18 on the question of how to form a reliable armed force loyal to the new régime and how to integrate the armed workers therein. In these debates the old ideas of arming all the people and of universal military or militia service still exercised a powerful attraction. Nonetheless, although the régime made extensive use of the Red Guards in the new army and of Red Guard leaders in its command, necessity pushed it towards a more traditional army structure.

Finally on 10 June 1918 the Fifth All-Russian Congress of Soviets abolished the Red Guard and similar self-formed and autonomous armed bands, declaring that 'the period of casual formations, of self-willed detachments, of amateurish construction, must be considered as over'.[34] The era of expansive spontaneity and self-formation of organisations by the people of Russia, introduced by the February revolution was coming to an end. The very traits which made the Red Guards so effective in helping to destroy the old order in Russia and to make the October revolution rendered them obsolete under the new régime only a few months later, a fate which in time was to overtake most of the new popular organisations created in 1917.

NOTES

1 John Reed, *Ten Days that Shook the World* (New York, 1919), p. 99.
2 N.I. Podvoiskii, *Krasnaia gvardiia v Oktiabrskie dni (Leningrad i Moskva)* (Moscow and Leningrad, 1927), p. 27.
3 *Pervyi legalnyi Peterburgskii komitet bolshevikov v 1917 godu: Sbornik materialov i protokolov* (Moscow and Leningrad, 1927), pp. 307–19, for an example of the discussions and miscalculations.
4 A.G. Shliapnikov, *Semnadtsatyi god* (Moscow, 1923), vol. 1, p. 109; E.N. Burdzhalov, *Vtoraia russkaia revoliutsiia: Vosstanie v Petrograde* (Moscow, 1967), pp. 152–4.
5 See for example the account of A.S. Gundorov, 'Za Nevskoi zastavoi', *V ogne revoliutsionnykh boev (Raionny Petrograda v dvukh revoliutsiiakh 1917 g.)* (Moscow, 1967), pp. 317–20, and that of M. Rafes, 'Moi vospominaniia', *Byloe* no. 19 (1922), p. 187.
6 *Izvestiia* 28 February and 1 March 1917; Shliapnikov, *Semnadtsatyi god*, vol. 1, pp. 125–6; A.P. Peshekhonov, 'Pervye nedeli (Iz vospominaniia o revoliutsii)', *Na chuzhoi storone* no. 1 (1923), 211; N.N. Sukhanov, *Zapiski o revoliutsii* (Berlin, St Petersburg and Moscow, 1922), vol. 1, p. 155.
7 G.P. Georgievskii, *Ocherki po istorii Krasnoi gvardii* (Moscow, 1919), p. 65; V. Malakhovskii, *Iz istorii Krasnoi gvardii. Krasnogvardeitsy Vyborgskogo raiona, 1917 g.* (Leningrad, 1925), p. 10.
8 See Rex A. Wade, *Red Guards and Workers' Militias in the Russian Revolution* (Stanford, 1984), pp. 44–57.
9 Ibid., pp. 210–17, 243–7, 275.
10 *Pravda* 17 March and 18 March 1917 (articles by Nevskii and Bonch-Bruevich); *Izvestiia* 19 March and 29 March 1917 (articles by Nevskii); *Pervyi legalnyi*, pp. 8, 10, 36, 71–8 *passim*; N.I. Podvoiskii, 'Voennaia

organizatsiia TsK RSDRP(b) i voenno-revoliutsionnyi komitet 1917 g.',
Krasnaia letopis no. 6 (1923), 64–5.

11 N. Rostov (Kogan), 'Vozniknovenie Krasnoi gvardii', *Krasnaia nov* 2, no.
2 (1927), 168–80; M.L. Lure, *Petrogradskaia Krasnaia gvardiia (fevral 1917–
fevral 1918)* (Leningrad, 1938), pp. 29–31; 'Pervoe sobranie po organizatsii Krasnoi gvardii (17 aprelia 1917 g.)', *Istoricheskii arkhiv* no. 6 (1961),
178–9; E. Pinezhskii, *Krasnaia gvardiia. Ocherk istorii piterskoi Krasnoi gvardii
1917 g.*, 2nd edn (Moscow, 1933), pp. 22–3, 154–5; *Izvestiia* 28 April 1917;
Rabochaia gazeta, 29 April and 5 May 1917; *Rech* 29 April 1917.

12 *Pravda* 5 May 1917: e.g. the article by Shliapnikov ('Belinin').

13 *Raionnye sovety Petrograda 1917 godu*, vol. 1 (Moscow and Leningrad, 1965),
pp. 135–6; M.A. Voitsekhovskii, 'Rozhdenie Krasnoi gvardii', *Narvskaia
zastava v 1917 godu, v vospominaniiakh i dokumentakh* (Leningrad, 1960),
p. 112.

14 A. Vasilev, 'Moe uchastie v Krasnoi gvardii i Oktiabrskoi revoliutsii',
Katorga i ssylka nos. 11–12 (1932), 101–2; V.I. Startsev, *Ocherki po istorii
petrogradskoi Krasnoi gvardii i rabochei militsii (mart 1917–aprel 1918)* (Moscow
and Leningrad, 1965), pp. 72–5; E.F. Erykalov, 'Krasnaia gvardiia
Petrograda v period podgotovki Velikoi Oktiabrskoi sotsialisticheskoi
revoliutsii', *Istoricheskie zapiski* 47 (1954), 74–5; *Raionnye sovety*, vol. 1, pp.
199–200. Vasilev, who is the main source for the origins of this project, is
very vague about who the organisers were (other than himself), and since
he normally is quick to claim Bolshevik leadership the absence of such a
claim here indicates that the leadership was politically broadly based
rather than Bolshevik.

15 Vasilev, 'Moe uchastie', pp. 102–4; Startsev, *Ocherki*, pp. 82–3.

16 V.I. Lenin, *Collected Works*, vol. xxiii (Moscow, 1964), pp. 287–329 *passim*,
and vol. xxiv (Moscow, 1964), pp. 23–70.

17 Rex A. Wade, 'The *Rajonnye Sovety* of Petrograd: The Role of Local
Political Bodies in the Russian Revolution', *Jahrbücher für Geschichte
Osteuropas* 20, no. 2 (1972), 226–40.

18 The records of the *piaterka* are reprinted in Startsev, *Ocherki*, pp. 294–9.

19 *Raionnye sovety*, vol. 1, pp. 224–7; vol. ii, p. 252; vol. iii, pp. 254–5, 292–7;
Rabochii 30 August and 31 August 1917; *Izvestiia* 29 August, 1 September
and 5 September 1917; Lure, *Petrogradskaia Krasnaia gvardiia*, p. 78; Startsev, *Ocherki* p. 155; S.M. Korchagin, 'Razgrom generalskoi avantiury',
Narvskaia zastava v 1917 godu, p. 162; P.O. Gorin (ed.), *Organizatsiia i
stroitelstvo sovetov rabochikh i soldatskikh deputatov v 1917 godu. Sbornik dokumentov* (Moscow, 1928), pp. 359–60.

20 *Rabochii* 30 August 1917; *Izvestiia* 31 August 1917; 'Iz istorii Krasnoi
gvardii Petrograda', *Istoricheskii arkhiv* no. 5 (1957), 133; *Moskovskaia
zastava v 1917; stati i vospominaniia* (Leningrad, 1959), p. 158; M.D.
Rozanov, *Obukhovtsy. Istoriia zavoda 'Bolshevik' 1863–1938* (Leningrad,
1938), p. 391.

21 *Pervyi legalnyi Peterburgskii komitet*, pp. 285–7; Pinezhskii, *Krasnaia gvardiia*, 1st edn, p. 50; *Protokoly Tsentralnogo komiteta RSDRP(b): Avgust 1917–fevral 1918* (Moscow, 1958), p. 53.

22 *Soldat* 25 September 1917; Pinezhskii, *Krasnaia gvardiia*, 2nd edn, pp. 49–51; M. Fleer, 'Rabochaia Krasnaia gvardiia v Fevralskuiu revoliutsiiu', *Krasnaia letopis* no. 1 (16) (1926), 36–7.

23 Malakhovsky, *Iz istorii*, pp. 16, 20–1, 48–50; *Soldat* 13 October 1917; Startsev, *Ocherki*, pp. 178–80; *Oktiabrskoe vooruzhennoe vosstanie v Petrograde: Dokumenty i materialy* (Moscow, 1957), pp. 203–4, 209–10.

24 Lure, *Petrogradskaia Krasnaia gvardiia*, pp. 112–13; Startsev, *Ocherki*, p. 182; *Raionnye sovety*, vol. III, p. 120; S.I. Tsukerman, 'Petrogradskii raionnyi sovet rabochikh i soldatskikh deputatov v 1917 godu', *Krasnaia letopis* no. 3 (1932), p. 59.

25 Pinezhskii, *Krasnaia gvardiia*, 1st edn, pp. 46–7, 2nd edn, pp. 57–62, 65–70; Startsev, *Ocherki*, pp. 167, 184–5: Malakhovskii, *Iz istorii*, pp. 16–17; A. Chechkovsky, 'Krasnaia gvardiia Moskovskoi zastavy', *Moskovskaia zastava 1917 g.* (Leningrad, 1959), p. 167.

26 Account of F.A. Ugarov, quoted by Tsukerman, 'Petrogradskii raionnyi sovet', p. 64.

27 Lure, *Petrogradskaia Krasnaia gvardiia*, pp. 112, 116, 122–3: Tsukerman, 'Petrogradskii raionnyi sovet', no. 3, p. 64; Podvoiskii, *Krasnaia gvardiia*, p. 53; B. Shabalin, 'Ot fevralia – k Oktiabriu (Iz istorii Zavoda 'Treugolnik', nyne 'Krasnyi Treugolnik')', *Bastiony revoliutsii. Sbornik materialov iz istorii leningradskikh zavodov v 1917 godu* (Leningrad, 1957), p. 296; *Velikaia Oktiabrskaia sotsialisticheskaia revoliutsiia: Oktiabrskoe vooruzhennoe vosstanie v Petrograde. Dokumenty i materialy* (Moscow, 1957), p. 229.

28 Wade, *Red Guards*, pp. 196–206.

29 Reed, *Ten Days that Shook the World*, p. 99.

30 See Wade, *Red Guards*, pp. 231–8, 305–10.

31 A picture of Red Guard involvement in the October revolution in Moscow is possible only by sifting large numbers of memoir and historical accounts of the revolution in the various districts of the city. An extensive and valuable account is in the memoir–history by one of the Moscow leaders, Ia. Peche, *Krasnaia gvardiia v Moskve v boiakh za Oktiabr* (Moscow, 1929), pp. 50–159. See also Wade, *Red Guards*, pp. 307–9 and Diane Koenker, *Moscow Workers and the 1917 Revolution* (Princeton, 1981), pp. 332–42.

32 Wade, *Red Guards*, pp. 260–74.

33 *Izvestiia* 30 October 1917. On the Red Guard after October see in particular M.A. Molodtsygin, 'Krasnaia gvardiia posle Oktiabria', *Voprosy istorii* no. 10 (1980), 25–43, and Wade, *Red Guards*, pp. 311–32.

34 Cited in Molodtsygin, 'Krasnaia gvardiia', p. 42.

5

OFFICERS OF THE GENERAL STAFF
AND THE KORNILOV MOVEMENT

ALLAN WILDMAN

IN the historiography and classical accounts of 1917 the Kornilov
affair appears sometimes as a pathetic or comic interlude,
sometimes as the only viable alternative to Bolshevism, sometimes as a
bargain between Kerensky and Kornilov which broke down because of
meddling intermediaries or Kerensky's failure of will, sometimes as a
straightforward contest between the dichotomised social and political
forces of the revolution. Variants are to be encountered in both
Western and Soviet historiography. Since the appearance of serious
new research on the Russian revolution, above all the works of
Rabinowitch and Rosenberg, the political significance of the affair has
come more sharply into focus and can no longer be relegated to the
status of a side show.[1]

Clearly Kornilov's plans rode the crest of a broad political revival of
the Centre and Right in the wake of the July Days and the collapse of
the June offensive, a revival that reached its climax in the adulation
accorded to Kornilov at his appearance at the Moscow State Conference in mid August.[2] Even the Kadets pinned their hopes on
Kornilov to shore up a floundering Provisional Government, in their
view a captive of the soviet-oriented elements, and if that required
military action, many were prepared to look the other way. Based on
numerous public and private declarations of support, Kornilov had
every reason to believe that he spoke for the 'nation' (or at least its
'healthy' parts), and that he would face very little resistance to his
efforts to occupy the capital and 'clean out the Bolsheviks', who in his
mind included the soviets and several members of the Provisional
Government. Revolutions generate not only social paranoia, but illusions of power; political calculations seldom correspond to political
realities.

The question I would like to address is pivotal to historiographical conceptions of the Kornilov episode, namely, what in fact was Kornilov's base of support among the officer corps at the front upon which the success of his venture presumably would depend? Misconceptions abound in the scholarly literature and my own researches should help to clear some of them up. To speak of officers or the 'officer corps', or 'Tsarist officers' as if they behaved monolithically according to a professional code, or according to monarchist sympathies, or rigidly followed the chain of command and therefore 'naturally' belonged in the Kornilov camp, would be a gross misconception. In fact there were deep and longstanding cleavages within the pre-war professional officer corps, between aristocratic guards and plebeian general staff types (with considerable overlap), between products of the cadet corps and the junker schools, between the rapidly promotable privileged officers and the morass of impoverished lieutenants and captains frozen in provincial assignments, and finally between the career professionals and the student volunteers who constituted the reserve officers to be mobilised in wartime; second, the war brought in an entirely new levy of 'mobilised civilians', products of the speeded-up training schools, some 172,000 of them, who imported their civilian experiences, attitudes and education into the officer corps, considerably diluting the professional element. Finally, the war itself brought a vast sifting-out process, carrying off countless numbers, battle-hardening others and rapidly elevating a select few.

The revolution was a monumental new challenge to the survival instinct of front-line officers as they faced a tumultuous soldier mass with no guidelines from above; each officer, high or low, had to devise his own way to cope as best he could. A good many officers, mainly senior commanders of regiments and divisions, were arrested by their men and accused of various counter-revolutionary crimes. Few were dealt with violently; more were simply removed from command for their own safety, sent to the rear and given indefinite leave. They tended to accumulate in Petrograd or other urban centres, where they joined various officer and patriotic organisations and were ripe material for the Kornilov movement; those few who were actively involved performed ludicrously during the crisis. Officers who remained in command were obliged to accept soldiers' committees and other revolutionary innovations, and had no way of enforcing their orders other than by persuasion. In fact, most officers relied heavily on their committees – with relative degrees of enthusiasm – to get essential tasks done. Officer demagoguery, professions of loyalty to the revolution and inflated rhetoric to curry the favour of soldiers and committees were not at all uncommon, and sometimes lower officers were deliberately used as lightning conductors by senior commanders seeking to extricate themselves from difficult situations. No one formula can possibly capture the infinite variety of situations differentiating one unit from another along the front.[3]

Similarly one cannot simply dichotomise officers and soldiers, as if there were an absolute barrier between them in terms of social composition, commitments and values. True, most infantry soldiers as opposed to those in the rear technical services were peasant by background; but so were the 'non-coms' and a large proportion of the junior officers, products of the wartime schools for *praporshchiki* (non-promotable second lieutenants), as Peter Kenez has pointed out.[4] Moreover, many wartime officers and classified ranks of the rear technical services were drawn from the large class of student intelligentsia, carrying the freight of revolutionary traditions or easily subject to radicalisation in the context of the revolution. (A good share of the doctors and veterinarians in the non-commissioned classified ranks were professionally educated Jews, who were excluded by law from obtaining commissions.)

Those who took the initiative in collaborating with soldiers in the formation of committees during the month of March usually came from these strata. Officer-socialists supplied or shared the leadership of every 'soldiers'' committee from the regimental level up, especially the influential army committees. They staffed the committee structure throughout 1917 as loyal extensions of the soviet leadership and once elected tended to stay put. They were not only distinguished from the soldier mass by social background, literacy and political articulateness, but were also in the main very pro-war, patriotic and committed to the restoration of the fighting capacity of the army, and therefore soon became an indispensable prop to command authority. Though they presumed to represent the soldier mass to the institutions of authority, they in fact represented a separate social–institutional layer in the shifting front landscape. In May they became strong partisans of the coalition government and the People's War Minister, Kerensky, and literally threw themselves into the task of preparing for the June offensive which soon alienated them from their constituency.[5]

The soldiers for their part had been deeply stirred by March events and strongly identified with the revolution as they understood it. They viewed the soldiers' committees as their own particular fulcrum of power, and expected from them guardianship over the gains of the revolution. Marc Ferro has portrayed the peasant soldier mass as

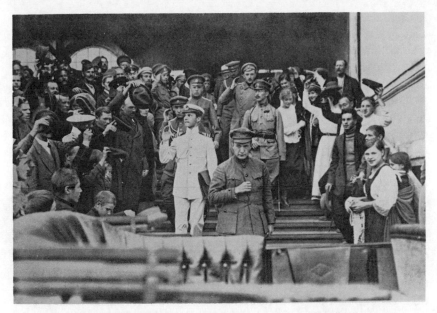

9. Aleksandr Fedorovich Kerensky, successively Minister of Justice, Minister of War and Prime Minister in the Provisional Government, seen here at the Moscow State Conference, August 1917.

strongly patriotic, defencist and revolutionary; this portrait must be seriously qualified so far as the front soldiers are concerned.[6] True, in March, however hostile to their officers, they took pains to secure the defences of the front and made their own improvisations. At the same time the revolution deeply stirred their longing for peace, which in their minds was closely linked to other expectations of the revolution, above all their entitlement to the land. Basically the revolution to them was an overturn of authority and social ascendancy, what I have characterised elsewhere as an 'inversion'. Their loyalties shifted from the Provisional Government to the soviet when they came to perceive in the latter the democratic-representational principle and the champion of 'no annexations and no indemnities'. When German intelligence promoted a truce and widespread fraternisation in April, the front soldiers welcomed these steps as proof that the 'international socialists' were about to make peace, and therefore normal observance of military routine no longer made any sense.

When the soviet leadership in Petrograd and its supporters in the higher committees at the front shifted towards defencism and the higher committees at the front shifted towards defencism and the renewal of active operations in May, the soldiers were deeply disillusioned, and attuned themselves to Bolshevik agitation which reached the front via newspapers and marching companies on a massive scale in early June. The committee element at the front, having come out for the idea of an offensive at a series of army and front congresses in May, now lost ground to the legions of 'Bolshevik' agitators, very few of whom were actually active members of that party. Now the democratic institutions not only stood for the revival of the pointless war, but the restoration of officer authority and observance of military discipline (obedience to orders 'without discussion').

Heavy doses of persuasion by touring members of the Soviet Executive Committee, by British and French socialists, by the new 'commissars' of the Provisional Government (chosen generally from right-wing defencist socialists) and by Kerensky himself did manage to launch the summer offensive on the southwestern front, but after a short burst of effort it collapsed miserably in a sea of mutinies and mass refusals to obey orders; on the northern and western fronts it did not even get off the ground. Shortly thereafter came the German breakthrough at Tarnopol and the panicky retreat of the armies on the southwestern front; in their wake came severe repressive measures, the round-up of Bolshevik agitators and the restoration of the death penalty.

The disenchantment of the soldiers with revolutionary verities was profound. They were aware that the command and the bourgeois press had branded them as cowards and traitors, that the soviet leadership had acquiesced in the restoration of the death penalty, and that commissars and committees collaborated, even supervised punitive actions. Since Kerensky's name, now as Minister-President, became attached to all these developments, for some he now became synonymous with betrayal of the revolution.

Far more quickly than their committeemen, the soldiers grasped the symbolism of the appointment of Kornilov as Commander-in-Chief. Already as commander of the Eighth Army and during a brief tenure on the southwestern front he had publicly attached his name to invocation of the death penalty before it had become law, and thus had become the darling of the right-wing press. The soldiers sensed the marked shift in mood of many of their officers who took their cue from Kornilov's pronouncements, reasserted their authority, ignored or bullied committees, and no longer observed revolutionary etiquette (again addressing soldiers with the demeaning *ty*). Still, it would be a mistake to view the soldiers as utterly cowed by the repressions.

10. Lavr Georgievich Kornilov (left), Commander-in-Chief of the Russian Army, summer 1917.

Rather, the situation should be gauged as one of rough balance, with a tacit agreement between soldiers and lower officers not to push matters to a confrontation. The soldiers welcomed the respite from active operations and wished to provide no new occasions for being branded cowards and traitors, and therefore went through the motions of obeying orders and observing military routines, whereas the officers conveniently looked the other way at the countless manifestations of passive defiance. When the officers pushed too hard to 'restore order', violent confrontations did occur, and some of the most vicious lynchings of senior officers took place in August (in addition to the famous one of Commissar Linde). Officers tended to vent their frustrations on the committees whom the soldiers no longer defended, secretly vexed at the committees' misplaced defence of officers' authority during the offensive and the repressions.[7]

Such generally was the setting on the eve of the Kornilov Affair. Given the heterogeneity of the officer corps, how does one gauge their support for Kornilov at the front? One cannot look for them among the great mass of wartime, non-professional officers in lower commands. If they were not drawn from the intelligentsia, they tended to be totally apolitical. Throughout most of 1917, faced with impossible pressures both from their superiors and their men, without real enforcement powers, they were haunted by a sense of isolation and vulnerability, and seldom were they in a position to express their real feelings openly. Though many may have taken temporary heart at the tough new laws of July they quickly became aware that little use could be made of them without provoking new confrontations and upheavals. It is doubtful whether many of them followed political events in the capital with any care and if they did it would have been imprudent to have expressed any open sympathy for the Kornilov circle or the Union of Officers. They were more likely to have been concerned lest the soldiers held them accountable for the trumpetings of Kornilov's devotees, but for the most part the record of their true feelings is simply silent. Strong identification with the political cause of Kornilov, or what one might call the Kornilov 'code' based on his well-advertised 'programme' was restricted to a fairly small cohort of senior commanders and staff officers, the activist element consisting almost exclusively of colonels of the general staff. I shall try to define here the type of officer who shared Kornilov's code of values even before he became their symbol.[8]

First of all, it would be very misleading to characterise Kornilov's supporters simply as 'counter-revolutionary' and monarchist. To be sure, many who sympathised with Kornilov, like the Generals Denikin, Alekseev and Wrangel, preferred a monarchy to a republic as a form of government, but in most cases the officers involved, if they were at all politically self-conscious, tended towards the concept of a constitutional monarchy or *Rechtsstaat*, not necessarily tied to the discredited dynasty.[9] Unreconstructed monarchists, particularly guardsmen such as Akintievksii and Krasnov, were sometimes attracted to

the Kornilov venture, but few were at the centre of the conspiracy and
some even looked rather askance at the men of plebeian origin visible
in its leadership.[10]

In general, all the chief conspirators, plebeian and aristocratic, were
with very few exceptions graduates of the Nicholas Academy of the
general staff (collectively known as *genshtabisty*) and proudly wore
black velvet and silver aiguillettes. The Generals Wrangel, Erdeli and
Gerua were guardsmen to be sure, but associated with the general staff
as well. They were first and foremost educated military professionals
who viewed the war and affairs of state in the context of their hierarch-
ically ordered world in which discipline and subordination to authority were seen as the essential ingredients of successful performance.
The more catholic accepted the world of statecraft as a legitimate
counterpart to their own world, but others, like Kornilov, measured
statesmen solely by the soldier's rulebook. Officers in both categories
saw the messy intrusion of 'politics' – whether of the court, of
Rasputin's protégés, of the Duma or still more of democratic institutions and political parties – as prompted by ambition, selfishness or
extraneous party or class interests, rather than by lofty patriotism; the
purity of their own motives was as readily assumed as the narrow
partisanship of civilian politicians. The goal of military men in becoming politically involved was to put an end to the influence of egocentric
politics on the affairs of state and the conduct of the war.

Revolutionary politics were objectionable in several ways: first, they
intruded democratic representational organs into the army itself, con-
travening the axiom of unitary command; second, they taught the
soldiers to become preoccupied with the politics of the rear rather than
with the business of fighting; and finally, they preyed on the civilian
government which, itself riven by party interests, was too weak and
cowardly to resist. If the politicians in the government could not keep
the revolutionary forces in check and provide the front army with the
sinews of war, the military itself would have to take matters in hand
and purge the government of noxious, unpatriotic elements. Long
before Kornilov, the acting Commander-in-Chief, M.V. Alekseev, at
the Supreme Headquarters (Stavka) contemplated military intervention, but was dissuaded by his fellow generals.[11] Similar thoughts on
other occasions stirred in the minds of Generals Denikin and Gurko,
and of the commander of the Black Sea Fleet Admiral Kolchak.

Whether written by plebeians or elitists from the guards, the self-
justifications put forward by Kornilov's supporters in diaries and
memoirs were on the whole little different. Thus to General Gerua, a

graduate of the Corps of Pages and the Nicholas Academy, Kornilov
was a 'sombre and forthright Cossack' who understood that to win the
war Russia 'must manifest an iron discipline, not only in the army, but
in the entire rear' and that 'only a single military authority was capable of tightening up the dissolute revolutionary rear', while to the
plebeian Denikin, from the general staff, Kornilov was 'courageous,
stern, decisive, totally independent, ready to take on any responsibility
and overcome any obstacles'.[12] Baron Wrangel, a much-decorated
cavalry officer in the guards and a familiar figure at court, but like
Gerua a talented Academy graduate, claims to have discovered in
April the formula that was to become the basis of the Kornilov
movement:

> Neither in the government nor in the surrounding social circles
> was there a man capable of putting a stop to the political deterio-
> ration. One had to look for such a man in the army, among the
> very few popular leaders. Such a leader with the army behind him
> could compel obedience from the country, particularly if he dis-
> played the requisite will-power in backing up his demands with
> bayonets. Reckoning with the circumstances of the times, the
> name of such a leader had to have a 'democratic' ring.[13]

Wrangel was one of those casualties of the March events at the front
mentioned above who found himself stranded in the capital with little
to do but engage in political fantasies. Having ruled himself out as too
aristocratic, his choice first fell on General Lechitskii, former commander of the Ninth Army on the Rumanian front and another March
casualty. Still, Lechitskii was an able general of some charisma and of
plebeian origin who for the latter reason had not been elevated to
general staff rank in spite of an outstanding record at the Nicholas
Academy (Denikin for a time had suffered a similar fate). When
Lechitskii declined the honour, Wrangel claims that his election fell on
Kornilov, then chief of the Petrograd military district and tested in
daily encounters with the democratic elements. When Kornilov
resigned over his humiliation during the April Days, Wrangel writes
that they remained in touch through an adjutant Prince Shuvalov
(Kornilov was reassigned to command the Eighth Army).[14]

Wrangel may have exaggerated his prescience in the above account,
and in any event the possibilities for a successful coup at the time were
very remote. Most commanders on active duty in the first months of
the revolution were fully engaged in coping with the immediate problems of turbulence in their units. Kornilov, as commander of the
Petrograd district, dealt with the revolutionary forces day by day and

had worked out practical methods of co-existence. He carried out such unpleasant assignments as the formal arrest of the imperial couple (otherwise the soviet would have taken the task upon itself), and on occasion exercised his powers of verbal persuasion. The Generals Denikin, Lukomskii, Gurko, Dragomirov and others who argued against the soldiers' committees so eloquently in July were promoting them in various ways in March to maintain a semblance of military order.[15] Those like Lechitskii and Kaledin who refused to compromise were soon deprived of their commands. To have promoted anything like the Kornilov programme in March, in other words, would have been suicidal and most commanders thought in terms of guiding and utilising, rather than abolishing, the committees.

Nevertheless, there was one important exception, in which a number of future Kornilov supporters including Wrangel were involved, that sheds considerable light on the forces at work. In the winter of 1916–17, as the result of extensive regrouping to stabilise the Rumanian front, an exceptionally large number of cavalry units were stationed in the reserve near Kishinev and formed into the Third Cavalry Corps under Count Keller. The commanders of individual units sound almost like a roll call of the future Kornilov movement: Wrangel, commander of the Nerchinskii Regiment; Krymov, of the Ussuriiskii Cossack Division; Polovtsev, of the Caucasus Native Division; and Mannerheim, of the Twelfth Cavalry. All were aristocratic cavalry guardsmen, but at the same time graduates of the Nicholas Academy.

Inactive during the winter, their company was rife with rumours of the Rasputin affair and several of them made the trip to Petrograd in search of political news. Krymov, as is well known, was particularly outspoken against the Tsar and offered his cavalry division to Rodzianko, the president of the Duma, in order to remove Nicholas by force, but he was turned down. Only Count Keller was upset over the abdication when it occurred, and most shared the attitude of Colonel N. V. Shinkarenko-Brusilov, the chief source for this episode, who held that they were well rid of the weak Nicholas and that patriotic statesmen like Rodzianko, Guchkov and Miliukov could be counted on to guide the country to victory.[16] Krymov, the most political figure in the group and a personal friend of Guchkov, returned from the capital on 2 or 3 March in a very optimistic mood.

But the optimism collapsed when Orders nos. 1, 2 and 3 came over the wires of the command network, the latter co-signed by General Potapov on behalf of the military commission of the State Duma with

the note that it had Guchkov's endorsement. Shortly thereafter came
Guchkov's own Order no. 114 which drastically altered, in their view,
the established system within the army (abolishing the old titles and
ty, and ascribing to soldiers the same political rights as civilians).[17]
Wrangel was dispatched on an unsuccessful mission to Petrograd in
order to persuade Guchkov to reverse his pernicious order; shortly
thereafter, Guchkov summoned Krymov again and Wrangel returned.
The result of this travelling back and forth was that the cavalry
generals became acutely aware of the upheaval in the capital and of
the dangerous influence enjoyed by the soviet and by revolutionary
elements. The commanders resolved collectively to pack up their divisions and head for the capital to 'send the *sovdepshchina* to the devil'
(*sovdepshchina* being the pejorative term for Soviet-oriented elements).
The political logic seemed quite simple to Shinkarenko-Brusilov: the
Provisional Government was a captive of the soviet; revolutionary
agitation would soon flood the army bringing about its ruin; the Provisional Government was helpless because it lacked a military force; and
the cavalry officers had eight well-armed, well-disciplined divisions
under their command ('Not a bad fist', comments Shinkarenko).

It never occurred to them for a minute that their devoted
cavalrymen would fail to follow them. A few days later, Count Keller
was removed from command by his Orenburg Cossacks for expressing
his loyalty to Nicholas. With Wrangel's return the plot became
serious, and the plan was to take the occasion of the ceremonial oath of
allegiance to the Provisional Government in order to appeal directly to
the soldiers to defend the new government against the soviet.
Shinkarenko's fate was typical. Pointing to the red banners carried by
some of the cavalrymen, he declared: 'Throw those red rags away,
they aren't going to keep out the Germans. Obey only the Provisional
Government!' The procedure was then to get the cavalrymen to sign
up as 'volunteers' for the expedition to the capital. Some signed, but
when the machine-gunners flatly refused, many asked to have their
signatures removed. 'My failure was complete', Shinkarenko con-
fessed, and within an hour he resigned his command.[18] Wrangel in his
memoirs is reticent about the mode of his own removal, but
Shinkarenko claims he was nearly lynched by his men. Wrangel and
Shinkarenko joined the pool of unassigned officers in Petrograd.

Krymov had not been a party to this affair, having already departed
for Petrograd, but Denikin encountered him there and cites him as
exclaiming:

How can you carry on under these conditions, when the government can't take a step without the *Sovdep* [soviet] and the
unbridled soldiery? I [Krymov] offered to clear out Petrograd in
two days with one division, of course, not without casualties ...
But Guchkov won't agree and Lvov holds his head and wails
'Lord help us, it would cause such an upheaval!'[19]

He was especially incensed that a clique of general-staff colonels, some
of them his friends from Academy days, were acting as Guchkov's
closest advisers and were architects of a policy of compromise and
collaboration with the soviet. They had drafted the ordinance on
soldiers' committees at the front and had advised Guchkov on the
framing of Order no. 114 and on the establishment of the Polivanov
commission on military reform. Among them was his close friend and
colleague from the Third Cavalry Corps, Colonel P.A. Polovtsev, who,
stranded in the capital by the revolution, was now Guchkov's right-
hand man.[20]

Krymov accused Polovtsev of treachery, but was confounded when
informed that the cavalrymen of the Third Corps were demonstrating
with red flags on the streets of Kishinev; he allowed himself to be
swayed by Guchkov's plan to temporise with the soviet while commis-
sioning a Cossack general-staff officer, General N.N. Khagondokov, to
recruit support among the various Cossack hosts to combat the revolutionary elements in return for recognition of their historic rights to
autonomy.[21] Whatever the precise instructions Krymov received from
Guchkov, they are not documented and were rendered moot by Guchkov's resignation at the end of April, but he was given command of the
Third Cavalry Corps, replacing Keller, and there are brief allusions to
his recruiting activities among the unassigned officers of the Kiev
military district.[22] Kornilov seems to have been aware of Krymov's
orientation, as he confidently summoned him to the Stavka in mid
August and made the transfer of the Third Cavalry Corps to the
Petrograd district the centre-piece of his plans.[23]

The above episode illustrates the ambiguity of attitudes within the
class of military professionals in working out a suitable strategy to deal
with the revolution. If a handful of cavalrymen and officers of the
general staff revealed 'Kornilovist' tendencies in March, they were
more than offset by those willing to collaborate with the democratic
forces in order to work out some sort of viable system. A good many
senior officers were involved in the politics of military 'reform', but it
would be very difficult to distinguish them from future Kornilov sup-

porters by sociological type. In the former category Academy graduates, guardsmen, cavalrymen, fighting generals, desk-bound staff
officers, plebeians and aristocrats of the court were also well represented. The Generals Verkhovskii, Brusilov, Parskii, Kvetsinskii,
Polivanov and Radko-Dmitriev, all of them enjoying a reputation as
'democratic generals' and reformers, covered the same social spectrum
as the Generals Krymov, Romanovskii, Gerua, Denikin, Kornilov,
Lukomskii and Selivachev, the most inveterate Kornilovites. The
same is true of the activist colonels on either side: Pronin, Lebedev,
Sidorin, Desemeter and other members of the Union of Officers at the
Stavka differed little in their background from the 'Young Turks' –
that is, those general staff officers denounced by Krymov who
engineered the political settlement in Petrograd and followed in the
wake of Guchkov and Kerensky – Polovtsev, Tugan-Baranovskii
(Kerensky's brother-in-law), Bagratuni, Iakubovich, Balabin and
Gushchin. In both camps they were almost exclusively members of the
general staff 'corporation'.

In some cases within the democratic cohort, as with Brusilov and
Polovtsev, the pose was manifestly contrived, a mere strategy of
survival or careerism. The majority, however, sought amidst the chaos
of revolution to create a workable system that would keep the army,
and therefore the nation, intact, capable of defending the interests of
the new democratic state. They were more flexible in the instruments
and stratagems they were prepared to employ, but were just as committed as their counterparts in the Kornilov camp – and for much the
same reasons – to the prosecution of the war, to the interests of the
state and to the orderly functioning of society, which they viewed as an
indissoluble whole.

Unlike the proto-Kornilovists they were much more inclined to view
the injustices of the old order as the chief cause of the revolutionary
chaos, and were more or less sincerely convinced that the democratic
impulses of the masses could be harnessed for the reconstruction of a
new order. Their rejection of the idea of rigid discipline enforced by
draconic punishments undoubtedly led them to naïve illusions that
'conscious discipline' and participatory soldier-citizenship were
adequate substitutes, but certainly the accusations that they were
motivated by careerism or by slavish subservience to democratic icons
were grossly unfair. Professionalism and deep patriotism of a sort
different, but perhaps kindred to that of the Kornilov school, was at
the core of their activity. Like their opponents they sometimes became
embroiled in comical ventures that could not possibly succeed; and

they, too, were motivated by calculations ranging from the unworthy
to the high-minded and manifestly sincere.

Unfortunately very few personal records of generals and officers of
this second type have been left to posterity, and one full record, by
Polovtsev, was that of a cynic of the first magnitude, at heart in
sympathy with the opposite camp; most of the democratic camp either
did not survive the Civil War or made their careers in the Red Army.
General Verkhovskii, one of the latter, nevertheless published an
uncensored diary in 1918 that is a relatively untarnished monument to
the outlook of this particular type of officer. Excluded from the Corps
of Pages for his sympathies with the revolutionary movement, he still
served in the Russo–Japanese War with distinction and eventually
entered and graduated from the Nicholas Academy. His wartime
entries reveal him as at once a well-educated military analyst and a
mystical nationalist, keenly distressed over the Russian soldier's lack
of cultured patriotism. Of Germany he said:

> Her chief superiority is in her spiritual culture, manifested in the
> broad patriotic education and upbringing of her people. More
> than any other nation on earth she has reconciled the conflicting
> principles of independence and discipline.

The Russian people, though good-hearted and ready for enormous
sacrifices, were by contrast 'dark, beaten down and uninstructed'. The
soldier-*muzhik*'s interests 'seldom go beyond his native village' and 'the
grand idea of the motherland is alien to him'. However, Verkhovskii
blamed the ruling circles for this state of affairs, whose selfishness he
described in the most unflattering terms; equal blame was heaped on
'our intelligentsia' which rejected patriotism and equated the idea of
the fatherland with the hated autocratic system.[24]

Thus Verkhovskii imported into 1917 his own version of mystical
Populism – a democratic vision of a 'nation in arms'. It is not surprising that he was one of the chief architects of the committee system, first
in the Black Sea Fleet, then in Petrograd, and finally at the Stavka. 'In
committees', he claimed,

> the Russian people has become transformed . . . In working out
> practical tasks with officer representatives they have become our
> friends and colleagues, championing the idea of the state to the
> masses.[25]

All the more crushing was the collapse of authority suffered by
Kolchak, whom he never ceased to idolise, and the perversion, as he

saw it, of the committee system into an organ of popular phobias binding the command hand and foot. In July, as chief of the Moscow military district, he enlisted the support of the soviet and other democratic organisations to ensure that the garrisons kept up a steady supply of replacements to the front, but when these efforts broke down he was obliged to conduct a series of repressive actions in Riazan, Tver, Tula and Kharkov. His mood throughout 1917 vacillated between elation and despair, but he never gave up his efforts to make the democratic institutions work, and when the Kornilov crisis came he was the first to offer his services to the Provisional Government.

The above orientations are easy enough to document with regard to senior officers, but one cannot safely project them to the officer corps as a whole. Although there were a good many officers in democratic and other organisations, for the most part they did not claim to be representing the officers' 'corporation'. Soldiers were very suspicious of efforts to organise officers separately and officer activists in committees usually deferred to this sentiment. Though the ratio of officers to soldiers in the committee structure was usually fixed at 1:4 or 1:8, once elected, they went to great lengths to allay any suspicions that they represented the interests of officers rather than soldiers, and soldier deputies usually accepted them without prejudice as colleagues.[26] In May, however, two officer congresses were held almost simultaneously at the Stavka and in Petrograd respectively, the former called by a group of staff officers at the Stavka identifying themselves as a 'Union of Officers' whose aim was declared to be purely 'professional' rather than political, and the latter by an 'officers' soviet' in Petrograd whose goal was to bring officers formally into the soviet structure which was already the practice in the garrisons of Moscow, Kiev and elsewhere, but not yet in Petrograd or nation-wide. The claim of each of these congresses to represent the true front-line officers must be treated with scepticism, as, despite the formalities of elections, they both reflected the efforts of highly politicised staff officers in Petrograd and at the Stavka respectively to mobilise support for their positions.

The form of the invitations and the process of selection led to strikingly different results: the Stavka congress, far from being apolitical, was in fact a calculated counter-mobilisation directed against the soviet and a milestone on the road to the Kornilov affair; while the Petrograd congress turned out to be a total political fiasco, revealing how divided officers were among themselves and how unrealistic was the idea of linking them as a body to the soviet. Although not an objective measure of officer attitudes, the two congresses demonstrate how untenable it is to view the officer corps monolithically.

The promoters of the Petrograd congress, which met for nearly three weeks (8–27 May), were a general staff colonel, S.E. Gushchin, and a staff captain, Vrzhosek, who, if not directly associated with the general staff clique of 'Young Turks' who now gathered around Kerensky at least had close links to them.[27] Vrzhosek informed the congress that his group of officers during the critical first days of the revolution had worked closely with both the soviet and the Temporary Committee of the Duma. When on 2 March most officers, still fearing to return to their units, assembled in the Hall of the Army and Navy at Rodzianko's request, this group persuaded them to declare their support for the new government and on no account to allow the return of the Romanovs, since the soldiers had already made their determination known. During the month of March the group also organised the officers' soviet and cultivated the goodwill of the defencist wing of the Soviet Executive Committee.

The congress had been chosen according to a formula broader and more precise than that applied by its rival: two officer deputies were to be *elected* from each infantry division, one each from cavalry units and corps staffs, three from each of the thirteen armies, two from each front and two from the Stavka, with adjusted distributions for garrisons. Most armies, except the Sixth (Rumanian front), were well represented, averaging twenty-seven deputies each. The Petrograd garrison was over-represented, having 169 deputies out of the total of 748, but 68 per cent were in fact directly from the front. By rank only the generals were poorly represented, only eight attending the congress; colonels comprised 18 per cent of the total; captains 25 per cent; lieutenants, another 25 per cent; *praporshchiki*, 20 per cent; and special classifications (doctors, *chinovniki*, priests), 12 per cent.

Thus neither the senior ranks nor the politicised lower ranks predominated, and the colonels and captains tended to monopolise the debates. A surprising number of the middle-ranking officers who had arrived from the front declared pro-soviet sentiments. Captain Glukharov of the 24th Infantry Division, for example, declared that the government should be responsible to the soviet because it represented 90 per cent of the people, while Colonel Rybalko of the 188th Division on the Rumanian front credited the soviet with 'avoiding civil war' during the April Days by clearing the streets, and he blamed Miliukov and the Kadets for precipitating the crisis. On the

other hand, Captain Khitrovo of the Second Guards Cavalry Division
spoke for a vociferous minority in denouncing Order no. 1 and dual
power. (Khitrovo was in fact an activist in the Union of Officers in the
Special Army and later a Kornilov supporter.)

The debates and resolutions put to the assembly, which followed the
standard soviet format with regard to the issues of power, war and
peace and social policy, illustrate how deeply divided the assembly
was on matters of basic principle. Support for both the Provisional
Government and the soviet (albeit without the phrase 'insofar as'),
received 262 votes from the assembly, whereas the alternative resolution, on 'undivided power' for the Provisional Government alone,
received 242 (with 77 abstentions). However, when the time came to
vote on the soviet peace formula at a less well attended session, 210
voted in favour and only 69 against (an alternative resolution supporting Miliukov's policy received only 8 votes), and a resolution calling
on the Constituent Assembly to transfer all land to the peasants was
passed without a dissenting vote![28]

The congress revealed that the most thoughtful officers were still
feeling their way politically and were not irrevocably aligned into
camps. To most the problem of power and related issues were to be
resolved pragmatically from the standpoint of how it affected their
relations with their soldiers and how best to revive and strengthen the
army at the front. To a slim majority at this congress, it seemed that
the most expeditious route was to enlist the support of the soviet in
order to normalise front discipline, but for most this cooperation was
contingent on discarding the idea of 'control' over the Provisional
Government and on providing it with undivided authority. Delegates
revealed only a vague understanding of the political orientation of the
soviet, and the chief argument in its favour was that it commanded the
loyalty of the soldiers. The project collapsed on 19 May, however,
when the Soviet Executive Committee, declaring that 'chauvinist
resolutions' were being debated, recalled its representatives.

Professor Katkov has provided us with a detailed description of the
Stavka congress, and there is no need to duplicate it here.[29] It was
distinguished chiefly by the swift approval of the positions and the
statute worked out in advance by the Union of Officers, and by
passionate speeches from the Generals Alekseev and Denikin
(Quartermaster-General at the time). Alekseev's speech was essentially a stirring appeal to patriotism laced with sarcastic references to
the 'utopian peace schemes' of the soviet and the divisive appeal to
class hatred. Denikin primarily defended the honour of officers against

what he saw as slander and violence emanating from pro-soviet circles. Alekseev was removed from office by Kerensky while the congress was in session and replaced by Brusilov, which was interpreted by the assembly as an act of spite by the offended soviet and of cowardly subservience by the government. The speeches were printed in large numbers and distributed through the staff apparatus by the Union of Officers.[30]

Although it may be surprising that the results of the two congresses could be so different, it should be noted that the Union of Officers enjoyed the protection of the Stavka and circulated its programme together with the invitation to the congress via the staff communications network.[31] Though it did not explicitly condemn the soviet, it declared its exclusive loyalty to the Provisional Government and employed the coded phrases, 'complete victory' over the enemy and 'faithfulness to the Allies', which aligned it with Miliukov's note to the Allies of 18 April. Despite the disclaimers, the political orientation of the sponsors was made clear in the programme of the Union which included points on 'elevating the moral and political level of the officers' in preparation for elections to the Constituent Assembly and on mounting a 'struggle against attempts to usurp the power which the people has vested in the Provisional Government'. The intent to mobilise the officer corps as a body against the soviets and the soldiers' committees became evident both in the highly centralised structure of the Union which vested nearly dictatorial powers in a 'Chief Committee' charged with disciplining member bodies and also in the announced call to ostracise formally those officers whose actions were deemed to be undermining the strength of the army.

The effort of the Union of Officers to mobilise the officer corps politically was as little successful as that of the Petrograd congress. With the appointment of Brusilov, it lost the sponsorship of the Stavka and consequently the generous access to staff communications. It also failed utterly in constructing the strong organisational network envisaged, yet it provoked a vigorous counter-campaign by the soldiers' committees and in particular by the activist officers in those committees. Except for a number of negative references in the committee press there is little record of the Union's activities in May and June. The best evidence of its organisational difficulties is reflected in its organ, *Vestnik glavnogo komiteta Soiuza ofitserov*, four issues of which appeared in June and July. The statute had called for 'sections' in each army and corps headquarters and 'sub-sections' or cells in each branch of the staff organisation (revealing that staffs were meant to form the skeletal structure); however, they were obliged to answer inquiries whether subsections could cut across staff units since it was difficult to find the statutory minimum of eight members for a single cell in many units. Though the journal claimed a circulation of 15,000, this probably reflected the generous subsidy from 'non-military organisations' rather than a devoted readership.[32]

Some senior commanders, such as General Fedotov of the Second Army, encouraged recruitment among their staffs, but in the Third Army a 'congress' of officers decided to support the Petrograd effort rather than that of the Union of Officers, since it was more 'democratic'. General Tsiurikov of the Sixth Army forbade the formation of any officer organisations whatsoever, on the grounds that this was in conflict with the committee structure.[33] It seems improbable, therefore, that the Union of Officers either influenced or represented the sentiments of the vast majority of officers; but that it 'premobilised' a network of staff officers of a certain type that fed into the Kornilov movement there can be no doubt.

When Kornilov surfaced with his 'programme' for renewal of the army in July, the *Vestnik* proclaimed its immediate support. In fact, the Union's Chief Committee became the conduit for Kornilov's contacts with the many patriotic officer groups in the rear (the Knights of St George, the Military League, the League for the Salvation of Russia) which were generously funded by a civilian 'Republican Centre' and by Guchkov's League for the Economic Regeneration of Russia, the chief financier of which was the industrial magnate, A.N. Putilov.[34]

Kornilov's plan depended exclusively on the successful occupation of Petrograd by Krymov's Third Cavalry Corps, which was to be coordinated with a 'Bolshevik rising' orchestrated by the officer organisations in Petrograd. Krymov's expedition collapsed when the trainloads of his cavalrymen were intercepted by Soviet agitators, some of the latter Don Cossacks and Caucasian tribesmen (who could speak the language of many among the troops). The officer plotters in Petrograd were drinking up Putilov's generously supplied funds at the Villa Rode at the time set for action. Kornilov did think he had secured Kerensky's cooperation through Savinkov and V.N. Lvov, and was persuaded that Kerensky would come cowering to him for protection. However, when Kerensky announced his removal by telegram on 27 August, Kornilov was so surprised that he became seriously ill and behaved totally irrationally, requesting his staff voluntarily to follow him in suicide.[35]

He had no special strategy for the front, as he assumed that his subordinate commanders would approve of his action, and Denikin seems to have been the only front commander to have been informed in advance. The Chief of Staff, Lukomskii, took charge from the distraught Kornilov. When Kerensky ordered him to assume Kornilov's post until a replacement could be named, Lukomskii flatly refused, declaring that Kornilov's removal signified an unwillingness on the part of the Provisional Government to carry out the measures agreed to with Kornilov and could only result in civil war. This telegram was circulated to the front commanders, four out of five of whom sent their own telegrams to Kerensky urging him not to remove Kornilov, though only Denikin's was couched in a tone of open defiance of the Provisional Government. These telegrams were sent as a package down the chain of command with the order to close down all communications, military and civilian, including radio, the intention being to prevent Kerensky's messages from getting through.

Nothing illustrates the futility of the military conspiracy better than the total failure of the pro-Kornilov commanders to control communications. Telegraph operators and orderlies immediately alerted soldiers in staff units and near-by garrisons; committeemen demanded access to the telegraph and, if refused, called on improvised units of soldiers to occupy the premises; many officers in charge of communications ignored the order, realising its futility. In no time, massive forces were arrayed against those commanders who were now manifestly guilty of complicity in Kornilov's rebellion.

The fate of Kornilov's bastion on the southwestern front is typical. In the Special Army commanded by General Erdeli, Kerensky's telegram declaring Kornilov a traitor was picked up by radio before controls could be imposed. A clerk informed a member of the army committee who alerted all staff units and then demanded access to the staff telegraph (normally granted on 'official' committee business), but was blocked by an officer. Rather than risk confrontation, the army committeeman persuaded another communications officer to pass on his messages and was thus able to alert lower and higher committees of the situation. When he demanded that General Erdeli reverse his orders, the latter refused, whereupon the committeeman informed a nearby garrison unit which raised a scratch force to arrest Erdeli. There was no armed unit to come to Erdeli's defence, and the committee named his successor.[36] The same pattern developed with minor variations at the headquarters of the Eleventh and Seventh Armies, except that the commissar intervened in the former case to rescue the commander once he had declared his submission to the Provisional Government.

Denikin's situation was equally hopeless. His field police which maintained security at headquarters had long been 'spying for the front committee' and reported all suspicious moves by the staff officers. Denikin ordered out a company of his personal guard of Orenburg Cossacks on the morning of the 28th, claiming he was threatened by a 'gang of Bolsheviks'. They were intercepted by another cavalry unit and two armoured cars loaded with men who shouted: 'Your officers are backing the old régime!' The Cossacks passed on in good order, but their faith in their commander was shaken, and their unit committee called a session to discuss the situation. At headquarters they were met by a colonel speaking in the name of the southwestern front committee who demanded to see their orders. The Cossack unit melted into a 'meeting' which adopted a resolution condemning their commander for leading them against the Provisional Government. Denikin took no further action in his own defence, and that afternoon a huge procession of the local garrison and staff units surrounded his headquarters while the commissar solemnly undertook the arrest.[37] In other words, there was not the faintest chance of serious military resistance even by staff officers loyal to their commander. Most lower officers readily sided with their men.

On other fronts there was even less of a show of resistance. When Baluev and Shcherbachev, commanders of the western and Rumanian fronts respectively, learned of Kornilov's open defiance of the Provisional Government (proclaimed in an intemperate manifesto, composed by his crafty mentor in politics, Zavoiko, but in his name), they retracted their earlier declarations of support and now sided with the government. Klembovskii, commander of the northern front, sympathised with Kornilov, but when he realised that resistance was futile, he disguised himself as a soldier and fled. Nearly all other army commanders on the northern and western fronts (Parskii, Danilov, Tsykovich) sided with the Provisional Government from the very outset.

Thus, in the final analysis, when the test came Kornilov's supporters at the front were reduced to a mere handful, and not all of them behaved very heroically. Of course, there were doubtless many officers who sympathised with Kornilov and would have welcomed his success, but out of prudence did not reveal themselves. That, however, reflected their essential lack of power despite the widely advertised

11. This and the following cartoons (13 and 16) come from *Bich*
(*The Whip*) no. 30, August 1917, the satirical weekly edited by
Aleksandr Amfiteatrov.

A Human Barricade
Everything changes: it used to be 'Comrades, forward!' But
now, when A.F. Kerensky calls on the army to fight the enemy,
he has to shout 'Comrades, backward!'

repressive measures of July and August. The soldiers had remained
quiescent then because they no longer believed in their own committees. Now the committees and commissars took the initiative in arrest-
ing Kornilovite officers and taking charge of headquarters. For the
first and last time in 1917 committees, commissars and soldiers acted
in unison to defend the revolution, and the result was an impressive
display of power.

The soldiers felt that their innermost promptings had finally been vindicated. They, however, did not discriminate between the real and suspected Kornilovites and continued to subject officers to arrest and abuse, so that the committees were obliged to turn round and once again defend the officers. Kerensky put an end to his own reputation at the front by ordering the peremptory dismantling of all those *ad hoc* measures of control over headquarters and communications with which the soldiers were convinced they had just saved the revolution.

In their view, the Kornilovite officers were the most visible representatives of an authority structure that they had presumed over-turned by the revolution. In the coming weeks they were able to validate this claim by their own actions. The Bolshevik coup in Petrograd was to them the 'soviet revolution' which they had long awaited, as it expressed their own claims to power. The Kornilov affair brought out the essential powerlessness of the officers at the front, and whether they sympathised with Kornilov or not did not make much difference. In fact, the hard-core support for Kornilov was exceedingly slight and revealed itself only among a certain section of the general-staff officers.

NOTES

1 See Alexander Rabinowitch, *The Bolsheviks Come to Power: The Revolution of 1917 in Petrograd* (New York, 1976), chs. 3 and 4; and William Rosenberg, *Liberals in the Russian Revolution: The Constitutional Democratic Party, 1917–1921* (Princeton, 1974), ch. 6.

2 George Katkov provides a very detailed and useful treatment of Kornilov's efforts made through Boris Savinkov, Kerensky's Assistant Minister of Defence and promoter of an alliance between Kornilov and Kerensky, to persuade Kerensky to adopt his 'programme', which included extending the death penalty to the rear; the restoration of the officers' disciplinary authority; and the sharp curtailment of the soldiers' committees. The final outcome was the 'misunderstanding'. He mentions obliquely the conspiratorial activities of Kornilov and his supporters, but minimises or ignores crucial facts indicating that Kornilov intended to dictate a political settlement, Kerensky or no, and was prepared to use military force from the outset. See his *The Kornilov Affair: Kerensky and the Break-up of the Russian Army* (London and New York, 1980).

3 All the above points are developed in my book *The End of the Russian Imperial Army: The Old Army and the Soldiers' Revolt (March–April, 1917)* (Princeton, 1980). Because of space constraints, I was unable to use material in my possession from the Nicolaevsky Archive at the Hoover Institution on officer organisations in the rear.

4 See his 'A Profile of the Pre-Revolutionary Officer Corps', *California Slavic Studies* 7 (1973), 147.

5 Points developed in ch. 7 of *The End of the Russian Imperial Army* (1980).

6 See 'The Russian Soldier in 1917', *Slavic Review* 30 (1971), 483–512.

7 My views on soldiers during the summer of 1917 are developed in the sequel to the above cited work, *The End of the Russian Imperial Army: The Road to Soviet Power and Peace* (Princeton, 1987), especially pp. 141–7. For the theme of the confrontation between committees and officers, see ch. 5.

8 The above points on officers are developed in part in *The End of the Russian Imperial Army*, but much of the material profiling general staff officers elaborated below was not included in my book due to constraints of space and appears here for the first time.

9 Anton Denikin's views are expressed repeatedly in his voluminous writings, but see his *Ocherki russkoi smuty*, 5 vols. (Paris and Berlin, 1921–6), vol. I, part 1, ch. 3 which deals specifically with his views on monarchy and the dynasty. Wrangel's ideas must be inferred from his narrative in *Vospominaniia generala P.N. Vrangelia* (Frankfurt, 1969) which is cited below. One can infer Alekseev's position from his behaviour during the abdication crisis. See Wildman, *The Old Army*, pp. 202–15.

10 General N.N. Akintievskii has left a manuscript narrative in English at the Hoover Institution. P.N. Krasnov narrates his 1917 experiences in 'Na vnutrennom fronte', *Arkhiv russkoi revoliutsii* I (1922), 97–190, but his outlook and not uncritical fondness for monarchy comes out best in his remarkable novel–memoir, *From the Double Eagle to the Red Flag* (New York, 1928).

11 See Wildman, *The Old Army*, p. 213 and *The Road to Soviet Power*, p. 18. In the first instance it was his alarm over the February revolution when he discovered that Rodzianko and Guchkov were under heavy pressure from the revolutionary forces, and in the latter his reaction during the April Days to Kerensky's proclamation of the Declaration of the Rights of Soldiers. Alekseev's strong interventionist sentiments come out in a series of letters to Minister-President Lvov in July, published as 'Iz dnevnika gen. M.V. Alekseeva' in *Russkii istoricheskii arkhiv* (Prague, 1929).

12 B.V. Gerua, *Vospominaniia o moei zhizni*, 2 vols. (Paris, 1969), vol. II, p. 209 and Denikin, *Ocherki*, vol. I, part 2, p. 192.

13 *Vospominaniia Vrangelia*, p. 32.

14 See ibid., pp. 20–9.

15 See Wildman, *The Old Army*, ch. 7.

16 The entire story is told in his manuscript memoirs at the Hoover Institution, pp. 295–310. Wrangel alludes to some of the same events, though far less frankly, in his *Vospominaniia*, pp. 20–9.

17 On the story behind these orders, see Wildman, *The Old Army*, pp. 182–92 and 231–4.

18 Colonel N.V. Shinkarenko–Brusilov, MS., Hoover Institution for War, Revolution and Peace, Stanford, California, p. 301.

19 *Ocherki*, vol. I, part 2, p. 73.

20 See Polovtsev's account, which is the chief source for these events, *Dni zatmeniia* (Paris, n.d.), pp. 39–45.

21 Guchkov's own account in *Poslednie novosti* (23 September 1936) is boastful and not reliable, but fortunately we have Khagondokov's own frank account in his manuscript memoirs at the Archive of Russian and Eastern European Culture (Bakhmeteff Archive) at Columbia University. See pp. 775ff.

22 For Krymov's recruiting activities that leave no doubt as to his purpose, see B.P. Aprelev's manuscript diary at the Columbia Russian Archive.

23 The most reliable inside account of Kornilov's plans is that of his Chief of Staff, General A.S. Lukomskii, *Vospominaniia* (Berlin, 1922), pp. 228–40.

24 *Na golgofe (iz pokhodnogo dnevnika 1914–1918 gg.)* (Petrograd, 1918), p. 8 (entry date is 1 August 1914). Verkhovskii's autobiography *Na trudnom perevale* (Moscow, 1959) has been heavily edited and reflects his altered perspective as a Soviet officer, though in some respects it is remarkably frank. Katkov has a particularly negative judgement of Verkhovskii which I regard as unjustified. See his *The Kornilov Affair*, pp. 198–9.

25 Verkhovskii, *Na golgote*, p. 11.

26 See Wildman, *The Old Army*, chs. 7 and 8.

27 The account below is based on the published record *Stenograficheskii otchet zasedanii Vserossiiskogo sezda ofitserskikh deputatov armii i flota v Petrograde s 8 do 27 maia 1917 goda* (Petrograd, 1917). Gushchin was known to Gerua as an outstanding general staff officer before the war (*Vospominaniia*, vol. 1, p. 232); he graduated from the Academy in 1910 and was elevated to the general staff in 1912.

28 For individual points, see *Stenograficheskii otchet*, pp. 63–5, 135, 141, 167 and *passim*.

29 See Katkov, *The Kornilov Affair*, pp. 14–19. See also Denikin, *Ocherki*, vol. I, part 2, pp. 108–10 and Lukomskii, *Vospominaniia*, pp. 154–6.

30 The latter point is confirmed in the archive of the Third Grenadier Division, Eleventh Army, southwestern front, Tsentralnyi gosudarstvennyi voenno-istoricheskii arkhiv (TsGVIA), f. 2326, op. 4, d. 4, 1. 228. The author has followed the way representatives were chosen for the Stavka and Petrograd congresses in a number of archives of military units and has made a more lengthy analysis than is presented here.

31 The full text of these documents was published, for example, in the staff organ of the Special Army, *Vestnik osoboi armii* on 22 April. For the fact that a mimeographed version was in circulation in the Third Grenadier Division, see TsGVIA, f. 2326, op. 4, d. 4, 11. 87–8.

32 See the issue for 22 June, where outside contributions of 33,500 roubles are mentioned. Most certainly a large contribution came from A.I. Putilov, an industrialist whom Guchkov recruited for his League for the Economic Regeneration of Russia. See below, note 34.

33 Information from archival records TsGVIA, f. 2327, op. 4, d. 1, 11.

241ff., *Golos tretei armii* (25 April) and *Izvestiia Vybornykh Osoboi Armii* (7 May).

34 A leaflet distributed in August through the staff network recounting the history of the Union of Officers is quite frank about these contacts. See the archive of the Fourth Siberian Corps (Sixth Army, Rumanian front), TsGVIA, f. 2282, op. 6, d. 3, 11. 61–2. On the civilian organisations see Rosenberg, pp. 205–12 and accounts by such participants as Finisov, Putilov and others in *The Russian Provisional Government 1917. Documents*, edited by A. Kerensky and R. P. Browder, 3 vols. (Stanford, 1961): vol. III, pp. 1527–43. For the menagerie of right-wing and monarchist officer organisations from their perspective, see F. Vinberg, *V plenu u obezian. Zapiski kontr-revoliutsionera* (Kiev, 1918).

35 This last point is reliably reported by a close eye-witness, a young general staff captain who operated the teletype at the Stavka: D.N. Tikhobrazov in a manuscript memoir, 'V stavke posle revoliutsii', p. 96, deposited at the Columbia Russian Archive. Other points are covered in my own account in *The Road to Soviet Power*, ch. 6.

36 The above is taken from materials in the archive of R.R. Raupach at the Columbia University Russian Archive on which my own account in *The Road To Soviet Power* is based. Raupach was a member of the Shablovskii commission which investigated the Kornilov affair and collected documentary materials and depositions at the front from witnesses. He was actually a party to the Kornilov conspiracy unknown to Kerensky and made sure that the results did not incriminate Kornilov. The documentary materials, however, he maintained in his possession and he managed somehow to bring them to Finland, later depositing them in the Columbia Archive.

37 The above is based mainly on materials from the Raupach Archive, but see also Denikin's own vivid account in *Ocherki*, vol. I, part 2, pp. 217ff.

Part 2

PEASANTS, WORKERS AND BOURGEOISIE

6

THE PEASANTRY IN THE REVOLUTIONS OF 1917

JOHN CHANNON

The peasantry itself is the true autocrat of Russia.
V. Chernov, in April 1917

INTRODUCTION

B<small>Y</small> 1914, Russia was still essentially a peasant country. Although much progress had been made within the agricultural sector, a far-from-harmonious situation prevailed in the countryside on the eve of the war. In 1905 peasant revolution came to Russia, carried via communal and other local organisations. Despite Stolypin's efforts to undermine the institution of the peasant commune, it was this structure that once again provided the organisational momentum for agrarian revolution in 1917.

Considering its significance, relatively little study has been made in the West of this peasant revolution. This fact partly reflects the general lack of specialised peasant studies, notwithstanding several more recent works on both the revolution and agriculture which include sections on the peasantry between 1917 and 1921,[1] and partly it is the result of the longstanding bias in Western literature towards the urban revolution.[2] Yet this should not lead us to assume that Soviet scholars have similarly ignored the peasantry. On the contrary, regional and local studies of the agrarian revolution abound, covering virtually all areas of the USSR.[3] In recent years, Western scholars have also begun serious study of the peasantry, largely as a consequence of the upsurge of interest in 'peasant studies' in the 1960s and 1970s. In practice this was the effect of development studies feeding back into history, namely, the realisation that study of contemporary rural societies and the revolutionary changes to which they have frequently been subject can teach us much about the Russian agrarian revolution and the subsequent post-revolutionary rural transformation.[4]

It is our aim in this chapter to examine, on the basis of both Western and Soviet sources, the current state-of-debate on the peasant revolutions of 1917. The chapter comprises four main sections: the peasant movement from February to October 1917; the peasant organisations during the years 1917–18; land revolution and land reform; and an analysis of peasant behaviour in the revolution.

THE PEASANT MOVEMENT (FEBRUARY TO OCTOBER 1917)

Numerous studies have attempted documentation of the so-called peasant or agrarian movement of 1917, frequently producing typologies of peasant unrest or disturbances, by type of activity, by month and by region. Although useful in comparing the number of such disturbances with those of rural revolution during 1905–6, as well as during the entire period 1857 to 1917, we should be aware of the limitations of such a methodology. There is no consensus among Soviet scholars as to what constitutes a 'disturbance', and this term can cover anything from a non-violent to an exceedingly violent action, and from an isolated individual act to one of mass participation.[5] However, more detailed research in regional and local archives has enabled Soviet scholars in recent years to increase their estimates of the number of such disturbances deemed to have occurred during the period. Thus, the most recent Soviet scholar to examine the issue has concluded that there were 16,298 peasant disturbances between February and October 1917, a figure higher than estimates suggested during the previous decades and well in excess of the figures accepted earlier.[6] Doubtless future investigations in local archives will push this figure even higher, though it will not necessarily become more meaningful unless more sophisticated typologies are devised and Soviet scholars agree to adhere to a commonly accepted methodology.

What then were the main forms of peasant unrest in 1917 according to this recent research? The most detailed list has been drawn up by Maliavskii who, adopting the methodology of Kostrikin from some years earlier, has noted the following: (i) seizure of land, means of cultivation, livestock and foodstuffs (with ten sub-divisions); (ii) curtailment of the proprietary rights of landowners and forestry owners (nine sub-divisions); (iii) anti-kulak uprisings and the struggle with the Stolypin separators (nine sub-divisions) – and, curiously, it is under this heading that we find 'black repartition'; (iv) the agricultural workers' movement (eight sub-divisions); (v) peasant terror (five sub-divisions); (vi) the struggle against governmental punitive actions (three sub-divisions).[7]

As work proceeds, however, our understanding of the dynamics of

such peasant activities also becomes clearer. The majority of disturbances occurred in European Russia even though only one-third or so of
its fifty constituent provinces has actually been researched. Within
European Russia, the Central Black-Earth region together with the
Middle Volga accounted for most of the disturbances (half of all
disturbances according to Owen, though with different proportions for
different months) as well as some of the most violent clashes. The
monthly pattern of unrest has also been subject to modification.
Recent work reveals an increase in disturbances from March to June
while July was subject to strong provincial fluctuations: some provinces noted an increase in disturbances in June, others a decrease.
Furthermore, contrary to Provisional Government data, Soviet
historians now argue for a rise in disturbances from mid August until
the Bolshevik revolution thus denying the claim for a fall in September, as previously thought. In general, mid July to mid August
experienced a brief fall-off in disturbances, after which came a strong
upsurge during September and October.[8]

Western scholars have recently reiterated the idea that peasant
unrest followed a traditional rural pattern, ebbing and flowing in
accordance with the seasonal agrarian cycle. In general, unrest
increased in slacker times, and decreased during busy agricultural
periods.[9] Similarly, despite regional variations, peasants everywhere
were united in putting forward demands for more land but the type of
land they demanded tended to differ in accordance with such factors
as a region's agricultural specialisation. Thus in the Central Black-
Earth region and the mainly agricultural areas, peasants were chiefly
concerned with arable land. Increasing demands for non-peasant
ploughland were witnessed in March, immediately prior to the spring
sowing and in September before the winter sowing. In the Central
Industrial region, on the other hand, where dairying and livestock
production were more important, peasant demands for meadows and
pasture land were greatest, while in the more northerly forest areas
where wood was vital not just to the domestic economy (for building
homes and outbuildings and as fuel) but also to the peasant economy
(for crafts and trades), peasants were primarily concerned with non-
peasant woods and forests. Attempts to prohibit timber cutting on
privately owned and government forests were evident in other regions
of the country too, a re-assertion of timber rights recalling the days of
serfdom.[10]

Between April and June peasants attempted to increase their potential sown area by bringing into cultivation land which was unused but

which remained in the possession of *pomeshchiki*. Although large numbers of peasants had been called up between 1914 and 1917, severe rural underemployment had meant little reduction in the land area used by peasants since there were still sufficient hands left in the countryside to work the land. Why, then, were peasants so keen to seize this unused arable land? During the war *pomeshchiki* had set rent levels so high that peasants began to refuse to lease land, thus leaving it empty. By 1917 the area leased by peasants from *pomeshchiki* had fallen dramatically from the pre-war level.[11] It is often argued in the literature that peasants benefited in real terms from the fall in rents due to an increase in grain prices, but while the area sown by peasants remained the same, the proportion of the crops marketed declined. Furthermore, because of the shortage of manufactured goods and inflation, peasants saw little purpose in marketing grain or hoarding (increasingly worthless) roubles.[12] Under such conditions there was no incentive to rent *pomeshchik* land (especially at prices considered by peasants to be exorbitant). The main decline in renting came in the later war years, with only a small decrease being registered in 1914–15.

Renting, moreover, affected various socio-economic groups of peasants differently. Clearly many were subsistence producers or dependent on the purchase of grain and did not benefit from the increase in market prices, notwithstanding regional differences.[13] Peasants also refused to lease land, as formerly, through métayage (sharecropping) and in this case an even higher percentage of land was left unused. Leaving this land idle clearly meant a loss of income for *pomeshchiki* though their persistence in sticking to rent levels appears to have been prompted by the fact that the land was mortgaged (or re-mortgaged) to the Land Bank.[14] Landowners were evidently thinking in the short term, expecting the disturbances to be only a temporary phenomenon that would cease with action by the Provisional Government. That the government was prepared to use force to oppose infringements further incensed peasants.[15] In most cases, moreover, when *pomeshchiki* reported to the Provisional Government that peasants were seizing arable land, they omitted to mention that the land was lying unused.

The most recent Western attempt at a new taxonomy of peasant unrest between February and October is that of Holubnychy, based on his study of the agrarian revolution in the Ukraine. He compares it with the situation in central Russia and notes some interesting similarities and differences. According to his calculations, the seizure and confiscation of arable land with its subsequent distribution (either free or for sale or lease at reduced prices by the new 'owners') comprised 41 per cent of all 'actions' in the Ukraine but only 28.1 per cent in the remainder of Russia.[16] He also calculated that the take-over of land and property followed by their immediate partition between the peasants was more frequent than in the remainder of Russia by a ratio of about two to one. The *hromada* in the Ukraine and the mir in Russia both evidently gained ground, and regions not strongly communal before 1917 became more so during 1917 and after.

Other features of the agrarian revolution in the Ukraine were more indicative of its agricultural specialisation. Clearly the seizure and partition of land sown with industrial crops, such as beet and tobacco, were important to Ukrainian peasants, while wood was crucial to the peasant economy. Demands linked to large-scale capitalist estates were noticeable, too, though not perhaps on the scale that one might have expected. Coercion of landlords to pay higher wages to hired hands (3.6 per cent in the Ukraine as against 0.6 per cent in the rest of Russia) was linked to the development of commercial agriculture there, as was the Luddite phenomenon of machine smashing on estates in conditions of rural over-population and shortage of work.

Nationalism was also a factor that many historians expected to find surfacing during the Ukrainian agrarian revolution of 1917. Some indications of nationalist aspirations might be noted, such as the expropriation of non-Ukrainian landowners, though female landowners were subject to greater attack, which was, perhaps, just a sign that peasants were simply hitting out at the weakest. A stronger link with nationalism was to be found in the way that the Ukrainian Socialist Revolutionaries (SRs) linked independence to the land issue.[17] That nationalist aspirations and the quest for political autonomy did not assume central importance for the Ukrainian peasantry should come as no surprise. As I have noted elsewhere, several Western historians have argued that agrarian issues were more important to Ukrainian peasants than demands for national autonomy and cultural freedom and, as such, it was on the basis of land policy that peasants would judge the performances of the various governments between 1917 and 1921. To succeed, therefore, a government would have to satisfy the economic demands of the rural majority.

Regional variations in the agrarian movement in accordance with different types of agricultural development are also confirmed by the study of the revolution in the Latvian countryside by Andrew Ezergailis.[18] In Latvia, as in central Russia, an important part was

played by the conflict within the peasantry, between the landless and
the proprietary peasants, the so-called 'grey barons'. Other factors
bore greater similarity to the Ukraine. The disputes, for instance,
between peasant wage-labourers and estate owners in the Ukraine and
Latvia (see, for example, the strikes of 'farmhands') would benefit
from further study; on the other hand, nationalism was clearly an
important factor of conflict between the landless Latvian peasantry
and the predominantly German landowners. The 1905 revolution and
the subsequent repression did much to exacerbate this conflict as did
the upsurge of anti-German sentiment during the war. 'External' factors also had a significant bearing on the seasonal pattern of unrest in
Latvia and on the course of the agrarian revolution. After increasing in
momentum in the summer, the peasant movement abated after the fall
of Riga but saw a further upsurge after the October revolution. The
agrarian revolution, however, could not be completed during 1918, as
in central Russia, because the Brest-Litovsk treaty left Latvia in German hands, further intensifying peasant–landowner conflict.

PEASANT ORGANISATIONS AND RURAL REVOLUTION, 1917–1918

Much has been learned in recent years about the way peasants
organised the revolution in the countryside. We have studies of how
peasants, through communal and volost gatherings, committees and
soviets, operated in 1917 and after; how they took over non-peasant
estates, guarded them and then shared out the property; we have a
rough idea of the number of estates confiscated (with inventories of
their stock and property) in a few provinces at the centre of European
Russia; and we know that much of this process occurred before the
majority of peasant volost organisations adopted the appellation
'soviets'.[19] The Soviet breakthrough came in 1984 with the publication
of an article by Kabanov. Since the issues for debate are determined
by the dominant theoretical framework, a change in the latter brought
with it a changed focus of attention. Interest has moved away from
issues of differentiation within the peasantry and the second (intra-
peasant) revolution in the countryside (in the summer of 1918), to a
consideration of how the peasantry organised itself in revolution and
how types of unrest differed according to regional and local agrarian
differences.

Recent Soviet historians (such as Maliavskii and Kabanov) have
come to a viewpoint shared by contemporary Western historians that

'the peasantry in 1917 created its own organisations'.[20] Yet the increasing self-determination of volost and village assemblies in 1917 had been noted long before. After February a multiplicity of 'spontaneously acting' executive committees had sprung up in the countryside, while by July volost committees were ubiquitous. Such self-determination of affairs at the local level was strengthened by the fact that links between the volosts and the district (*uezd*) were weak in most provinces (also undermining military attempts to control matters from Petrograd). It was this local authority that the Provisional Government was to challenge. It knew from the experience of 1905–7 that peasant solidarity could only act to strengthen the volost. By early April, volost committee resolutions showed that the machinery of volost control was 'clearly in full operation'. The supremacy of volost committees was 'undoubted in April' while a 'new sense of communal rights appeared in the countryside'. In fact the peasant gathering (*skhod*), the legal meeting of the mir, was 'now asserting its local sovereignty'. The village and volost committees were the old peasant assemblies and outsiders were not generally welcomed.[21]

These volost and village peasant committees (some later named soviets) generally appeared with the abolition of the post of volost elder (*starshina*). The volost was finally freed from 'government control' *de jure* with the abolition of the land captains in September, though in practice this frequently occurred earlier (see p. 114 below). The variety of forms assumed by the lower-level rural administration (in the names adopted, in particular) in 1917 was clearly accepted at the time, as shown by the following statement from April: 'All forms are possible in relation to organs of local self-administration, as long as they do not contradict general democratic principles'. In fact, village committees were often no different from village soviets, save in name alone. (Similarly volost organisations might be called soviets or committees.) One Soviet writer in an exemplary piece of linguistic contortionism, claimed that the 'majority of village soviets named themselves village committees'.[22] The questionnaires sent out by the Moscow oblast Executive Committee in the spring of 1918 contained questions on Soviet construction in the countryside, sometimes talking of a village soviet (Q. 57) and at other times of a village committee (Qs. 58–62).[23] As with the volost, the village committee/soviet took the place of those rural authorities whose powers had now declined or been abolished. In early 1917 peasants often arrested the *zemstva nachalniki*, the village policemen, and the guards. They might also replace the village and volost administration and then form new authorities, village and volost committees. Yet this village committee/soviet was clearly a communal organisation, too, as is illustrated in instructions from the volost soviet to the village committees. In one instance the obligations placed on the committees included: defending the interests of the commune (*obshchestvo*); observing arrangements of the commune (*obshchestvo*); and exacting taxes and other collections.[24]

Thus, whatever appellation was adopted, the village organisation was a communal one, there to defend community interests. Yet not all those in authority were replaced. The village elder (*starosta*) for instance, was usually included in the committee, especially if he had the trust of his fellow villagers, while examples abound where the president of the village committee (the community organisation) and the village elder were one and the same person. When taking over an estate, villagers were often led by the elder, thus providing one explanation of how village elders became village soviet presidents.

The composition of these peasant organisations frequently differed from those of the pre-revolutionary period. The peasant soviets or committees were organs of self-administration but the nature of elections to these organisations reflected not just communal principles but an increasing democratisation of communal arrangements. This trend was clearly witnessed in the changing composition of the gathering, no longer restricted to household representatives. A meeting of all the peasants occurred in practice, an ear even being given to agitators, soldiers (especially those from the front), workers and, occasionally, other outsiders. (The gathering might expand to take account of those individuals registered with the community although this did not necessarily mean that outsiders were included.) But the gathering did enable contact between peasants and representatives from government and the army. The latter would explain their points to the *skhod*, the members of which would listen, decide and then pass a resolution to that effect. These meetings (variously termed *skhody*, *sobraniia* or *mitingy*) occurred frequently, and would discuss general political questions. Since the *skhod* was not an organ of government it tended not to discuss economic issues, such as the division of land or the apportionment of dues.[25]

Arrangements for elections were made in the community and these occurred either in the gathering or by open vote. The elections not only comprised all those who were traditionally included in the gathering, that is, the heads of households, but might also be broadened to include the majority of adult members of a community and even, on occasion, those not registered with it. Volost soviets were selected from communal representatives elected on a universal (*vseobshchii*) basis, all members having equal electoral rights. Volost and village soviets were elected from all communities on the basis of one representative per one hundred adult members. If communities had less than a hundred members either the same rule was nonetheless applied or they were obliged to unite with the nearest community. In the Middle Volga area, volost soviets were set up 'as a rule' by the volost peasant congresses although volost congresses were also called volost gatherings. Despite the diversity of forms, maintains Kabanov, 'it is clear that there was a swift broadening in the composition of the gathering'.[26] In Tver province, situated in the Central Industrial region, these volost gatherings were also known as *skhody*, since such a meeting (*sobranie*) of peasants from all the constituent villages elected the volost soviets, usually by open vote.[27] Yet there were clearly regional variations. In the majority of cases in Petrograd province, for instance, volost soviets were elected on the assumption that there were universal and equal electoral rights, though in some instances elections were restricted to so-called 'toilers'.[28]

From the Second Congress of Soviets of the Western oblast, on 13 April 1918, we learn that village soviets were elected from all toilers in the village who had reached eighteen years of age. The communal soviets (*obshchinnye sovety*) were elected by the 'gathering of all toilers in a given *obshchestvo*'. The communal principle, moreover, could deprive those not registered with the community (such as doctors, agronomists, refugees, urban dwellers) of the right to vote. Whereas the village soviet replaced its 'village *skhod* of electors and the village administration', the communal soviet replaced its 'communal administration and the former village elder'.[29] This democratisation was subject to regional and local variations, while the elections of village soviets might be more democratic than the communal ones. According to some historians, volost soviets were, in practice, elected exclusively by the village gatherings.[30]

Sometimes commune and village boundaries coincided, whereas in other villages there were two, three or even more communes. In the latter case there could be several communal soviets (*obshchinnye* or *obshchestvennye sovety*). And it was not unknown for a village gathering to elect a communal soviet. On being set up some volost soviets saw it as their responsibility to 'embark immediately on organising within the volost, communal and village soviets'.[31] In general, the communal principle prevailed in determining how soviets were constructed in the early years of the revolution (1917–18), though a change took place from early 1920 following the re-election of volost soviets in 1919: villages which had had several communes in 1917–18 and thus elected several soviets, could now elect only one soviet, albeit one elected from the entire population.[32]

Yet the establishment of soviets clearly did not undermine the authority of the village gathering, as often hitherto believed. Fenomenov shows that the village soviet (the president and members) had the right to conduct 'current administration' – without having to convoke a gathering – but for decisions concerning the apportionment of taxes, and the distribution of other obligations the gathering would be convoked, with the agreement of fellow-villagers, just as in former times. All officials arriving from the volost on fiscal business had to take their requests to the gathering, not to the village soviet.[33] The strength of the commune was also seen elsewhere. Peasants were not concerned with resolutions which issued from the centre and passed through the district land department. In their opinion, 'power in the localities' came from their own resolutions. Neither did the revolution shake the basis of village life, the authority of the village gathering. In fact, the weakness of the centre facilitated the consolidation of local power, based in the community, the village and the volost. A meeting of volost representatives from Elatomsk district in Tambov province in spring 1918 reported that each village considered that it had the right to resolve all questions itself, while in Novgorod province a joint sitting of the district and town soviets in April 1918 noted that 'volosts are separated from the towns'. An analogous process was noted in Saratov province.[34]

Paralleling these peasant organisations were the organisations set up by the Provisional Government in the volosts: the land and food committees and the volost *zemstva*. As Owen noted, the food and land committees 'found little support locally, save where their personnel either coincided with, or was locally controlled by, the cantonal (volost) or village executive committees'.[35] The food and land committees were 'definitely unpopular' since they impeded the self-determination of the village. These committees had been given the task of preserving private landownership while through the agencies of such committees the government was seen as the 'perpetual extractor of food supplies'. And the fact that Chernov became Minister of Agriculture early in May did little or nothing to lessen the growing unpopularity of the Provisional Government. Fifty per cent of volost land committees were created during May and June 1917 and not until the beginning of August were they functioning in the majority of

12. Viktor Mikhailovich Chernov, SR leader, and Minister of Agriculture in the first and second coalition governments.

volosts of European Russia.[36] Thus for much of early 1917 peasant committees, organised in the villages, communities and volosts, enjoyed virtually unchallenged control of rural affairs.

The food committees, according to Maliavskii, were the most undemocratic, rarely being involved in 'guiding' peasant actions: 'between March and June, peasant actions were guided by volost

Тънь Распутинъ.—Передаю тебѣ, товарищъ Викторъ, крестьянство мое, селянство мое, шарлатанство мое, окаянство мое... Ну, а чего прочаго,—ищи самъ! ты парень дошлый!

13. Handing over the Inheritance
The ghost of Rasputin says to Viktor Chernov: 'I hereby hand over to you, comrade Viktor, my peasants, my villagers, my charlatanry, my sinful life – as for the rest, find it yourself! You're a cunning so-and-so!'

executive committees'.[37] The volost *zemstva* 'evoked no enthusiasm among the villagers'; elections to the *zemstva* were disrupted in September, while peasants seemed uninterested in talk of the Constituent Assembly.[38] In fact the food question proved to be the main source of conflict between the Provisional Government and the peasantry and the food and fuel crisis brought to the surface the fundamental contradictions between governmental policy and peasant aspirations.

(There was an important difference between the pre- and post-October periods: although food and fuel supplies were still threatened after October, land divisions were now sanctioned and openly supported.) This threat to food and fuel supplies led to military force being used against the peasantry in the pre-October period; the grain monopoly met opposition everywhere.[39]

THE PEASANTS, LAND REVOLUTION AND LAND REFORM

Land and freedom were the two key issues in the history of peasant demands, both springing from serfdom and continuing after the disappointment with the Emancipation. Neither of these issues was addressed satisfactorily by the Tsarist government before 1914, though this is not to say that there would have been an agrarian revolution had the First World War not taken place. However, neither is it correct to assume that agrarian unrest was merely sparked off by the February revolution. Although Western economic historians now speak of improving living standards in the countryside in the decades prior to 1914, there is no a priori reason to assume that peasant dissatisfaction had been assuaged. In fact improving, no less than falling, standards of living could just as easily have led to unrest, if the recipients perceived a mismatch between expectations and reality. Contrary to common belief, moreover, the years immediately preceding 1914 were not peaceful ones in the Russian countryside: peasants had lost interest in the Duma as early as 1908, just at the time when the Stolypin reform was being debated; maybe 60 per cent of those who had migrated to Siberia had returned to European Russia by 1911; peasants who had borrowed from the Peasant Land Bank were increasingly being drawn further into debt; the famine of 1911 was accompanied by rumours, which spread throughout the empire, of a 'new uprising on the anniversary of the Emancipation'; the late summer and early autumn of 1912 witnessed 'disorders' and rumours of the division of non-peasant lands in some villages; while the years 1910 to 1914 witnessed 17,000 recorded agrarian disturbances in European Russia.[40]

At the heart of this unrest was the peasant desire for a more just and equal distribution of land. The history of such demands has been well documented elsewhere, but the cornerstone of the peasant notion of 'black repartition' was hostility to private ownership and, as its corollary, support for a strong community. Peasants turned against private ownership of land and property in 1917, sometimes justifying their acts as necessary to save Russia. How should we view such acts? No longer could these have been seen in terms of the myth of the 'good and just Tsar' to whom peasants owed allegiance, though they might well have been perceived as patriotic acts. After all, most soldiers are now generally considered to have remained 'patriotic' until later in 1917. Or was the pseudo-legal expropriation of all private rights by the village community no more than a thinly veiled attempt to legitimise what was understood to be an illegal act?[41] Private property contradicted peasant notions of right and justice, as seen in the idea of 'black repartition' and in peasant customary law and justice. In general private ownership vanished *de facto* before it was abolished *de jure*.

Local peasant organisations executed the land revolution which occurred principally within the volost and the community. Some boundaries were redrawn though many remained the same. The registration of non-peasant estates (taking inventories and so on) was carried out by peasant committees, as was the division of land and other property.[42] The parcelling-out was frequently determined by former traditions and practices. A 'black repartition' or total redistribution of all land occurred rarely and mainly only within the Central Agricultural region. This had seemingly little to do with the revolutionary aspirations of the poor peasants or with Bolshevik influence, despite the endless claims to the contrary in earlier Soviet studies. In a traditionally strong communal area it had more to do with the rational response of the community to a swift and dramatic increase in the man-to-land ratio, as a consequence of the large number of people pouring into the countryside from urban areas.

It has also been claimed that such redivisions were due to the influence of outsiders such as the armed urban detachments. The role of the community and volost in land redivision has been the subject of a special investigation with particular reference to the central areas of European Russia, and tentative steps have been made towards a comparative study of the Ukraine.[43] It appears that the conflicts which developed in the countryside over the distribution of land and property were dealt with largely at local level by the mir and the volost, in accordance with traditional practices, although new agencies for resolving land disputes (the conflict commissions) were also utilised. In general, conflicts were not serious (though this may indicate a less radical transformation of agrarian relations within communities and volosts than formerly thought) and they did not become a major issue between the Bolsheviks and the peasantry.

The community was the chief vehicle of the peasant land revolution.

In central Russia the community had remained strong, possessing an economic and social rationale for its activities. The Stolypin reforms had done little in these regions to undermine its influence. In areas where the non-redivisional community had operated before 1917 – often termed 'non-communal' areas – there was a different rationale for the apparent upsurge in communal activity during and after 1917. There the commune assumed more the function of the mir in earlier Russian history and in Siberia in the nineteenth and twentieth centuries. It provided a safer haven from the prey of outsiders and guaranteed a better chance of subsistence in times of revolution and civil war than isolated private farmsteads.[44] It also re-activated the communal processes for redistribution of land and property which in these regions had long remained dormant. Thus, in the former areas, the continuation of communal practices proved beneficial in terms of the new political realities; and in the latter, these same realities, as well as the demands of economic survival, made for a resurgence of community.

The peasant notion of 'black repartition' also embraced the idea that all who were prepared to till the land themselves had a right to a share of land on which to work for their own (and their families') livelihood. This concept could include former landowners (*pomeshchiki*) and local clergy. Whether it did so in practice depended very much on the local circumstances.[45] Just as the previous paragraphs suggested little evidence of overt class struggle within the peasantry, so we also need to modify our picture of the nature of conflict between landowners and peasants. It was a far more muted affair than is usually imagined and its subtleties leave much to be explored.

A further problem concerns the role played in the revolution by various socio-economic categories of peasants. Playing down the conflict within the peasantry and taking account of the levelling process, historians in recent decades have frequently emphasised the role of the middle peasants in the revolution of 1917–18. Yet attention has also been directed to the role of rural wage-labourers, particularly in regions where large capitalistic estates employed sizeable numbers of peasant workers. The studies of Latvia and the Ukraine in 1905 by Ezergailis and Edelman respectively suggest that interesting comparisons with regard to this issue can now be made with 1917.[46]

The peasants were implementing their own radical agrarian reform during the revolution. By early 1918 peasants in different regions were expressing their own desires for different types of land use. Even peasants who continued communal farming were not averse to change, where conditions permitted, revealing a willingness to adopt improved methods of cultivation such as the multi-field or broad-strip systems. The main problem seemed to be not peasant unwillingness but practical difficulties such as the complex situation regarding land use, lack of cash, or paucity of technical assistance. Yet peasant notions of land reform did not necessarily correspond with those of the agricultural specialists and the types of land reorganisation that the specialists preferred could only be implemented by imposing them on peasants. However, not only such specialists as land surveyors and agronomists but also the SRs and later the Bolsheviks tried to advance their own ideas about land reform.[47]

The October revolution for Lenin was based on the assumption of a quid pro quo with the peasantry: the Bolsheviks sanctioned land seizures while the peasantry would hand over grain to the cities and the army. And this policy was seen in the context of Bolshevik expectations of an international proletarian revolution which would lend support to ailing Russia. The disappointment of revolutionary expectations and the virtual separation of town from country by October, reinforced by the lack of Bolshevik organisation in the countryside, produced a very different reality. The peasantry began to retreat into rural autarky. The continuing food and fuel crisis in the towns and the flood of migrants to the villages further strengthened this trend. The peasantry continued to subsist within their mirs and volosts. As in the period of the Provisional Government, grain remained within the volost boundaries. The Brest-Litovsk settlement served to worsen the food situation. Just as the Provisional Government had resorted to force before October (and the Tsarist authorities before February) so now the Bolsheviks, after several months of experimentation with a policy of goods-exchange (interspersed with shows of strength), turned to all-out compulsion. The justification, that it was a 'kulak strike' and that the poor peasants required assistance in order to make their revolution against wealthier neighbours, made a nonsense of rural reality (an increase in the middle peasantry) and of Lenin's prognostications (that it would take a lengthy period of capitalist development before there could be a second revolution in the countryside). It was the food issue that was to rupture Bolshevik–peasant relations in the wake of October.[48]

14. Abram Rafaelovich Gots, prominent SR leader in 1917 and a
leading supporter of the principle of coalition government.

PEASANT BEHAVIOUR AND THE RURAL REVOLUTION

The behaviour of the peasantry in the revolution has also been questioned recently, raising anew such questions as to whether peasant
actions were in the main organised or disorganised, violent or non-
violent. In many respects analysis of such behaviour has come full
circle, returning to the views of some Western scholars in the twenties
and thirties, who detected a rationale behind such peasant activities,
though not within the contemporary 'peasant' paradigm.

The now-hackneyed Soviet view of a spontaneous peasant move-ment, organised through the leadership of the working class and the Bolshevik party, has been gradually eroded over the last few decades, reaching its zenith in 1984 in an article by V.V. Kabanov.[49] It is now acknowledged that peasants were capable of organising their own affairs in an orderly and rational way. Owen, in the West, some forty years earlier, had similarly noted the tendency to associate 'organisa-tion' in the peasant movement with 'outside parties'. In his case study of the Central Black-Earth and Middle Volga regions, he noted that at the beginning of 1917 the SRs claimed to lead the movement in the countryside but, by the end of the year, 'it is questionable whether any existing party "led" them at all'. In general, outsiders were not welcome, whether political parties, teachers (and especially female ones) or others. When peasants sought knowledge about the revolu-tion, they preferred soldiers to teach them.[50] This resistance to out-siders was a grim reminder of the strength of the divide between town and country that still persisted despite decades of development.

In general, for Owen, the peasant revolution was a 'relatively calm affair'. 'Few of the squires lost their lives during the March to October period', there was no Pugachevshchina (in the sense of the 'slaughter of the old rural arbiters'). Notwithstanding the quaintly archaic terminology, Owen seems to have been right. In general, the revolu-tion witnessed the relatively bloodless expulsion of all types of land-owner.[51] Peasants would inform the estate manager of their intention to assume control while the volost assembly might resolve to expel the staff from a local estate. The problems at the centre of the country were insufficient land and rural overpopulation and it was these fac-tors, together with grievances against especially harsh landowners, that led there to more violent, destructive acts. After all, half of all disturbances registered by the militia were in the Central Black-Earth and Middle Volga regions. Instances of violence characterised a minority of disturbances, though violence increased between July and September.

When it did occur, it was often linked to problems of immediate urgency – in September, for example, food-supply problems led to the dispatch of troops. In the Central Agricultural provinces increased peasant unrest was due to the absence of sugar, white flour and butter. This case again provides a clear indication that the food question (which first emerged in 1916) was a major source of such conflict. Much of the violence was also linked to the raiding of 'alcohol stores', yet the Provisional Government was not prepared to destroy such commercially valuable stores in order to reduce vandalism and destruction. Soldiers on leave were often responsible for leading peasants in pillage, due to military indiscipline and agrarian upheavals. The mix of alcohol and mutinous soldiers added fuel to the flames. An 'alarming feature' of the indiscipline among troops was the ease with which they could secure alcohol. Wine and vodka were demanded by troops from alcohol stores on landowners' estates, while no measures were taken against illicit distilling, a phenomenon said to be 'endemic' in Kazan province and elsewhere by October.[52]

Due in large part to the increase in comparative studies of peasant revolutions (and work on the peasantry in the French revolution especially), social and economic historians of the Russian revolution have become more sophisticated in their approaches to the Russian peasantry. Such phrases as the 'dark masses, illiterate and uncultured, wantonly engaging in acts of violence and destruction', are no longer acceptable as characterisations of the agrarian revolution. Neither were they, of course, in much earlier Western historiography (such as Owen's) which lacked the more sophisticated methodology and interpretation of today, but still revealed a sound basic understanding of the mechanics of peasant society and of what propelled it towards revolution. Soviet historians in recent years have also displayed a readiness to acknowledge that the peasantry was itself capable of making and creating its own revolution, as well as providing the organisations to carry it through the revolutionary period and beyond.[53]

There is clearly an emerging consensus among writers, Western and Soviet, that the peasant movement was organised mainly by the peasants themselves, that it was in large part not wantonly destructive, nor characterised by bloodshed. In one sense this is a logical extension of the so-called 'moral economists'' view that there is an economic and social rationale to peasant farming and communal life, while peasant activities during 1917 and 1918 are seen as a fuller expression of those that developed during 1905 and 1906.[54]

This picture also accords with recent attempts to understand peasant behaviour in terms of *mentalités*. Richard Stites for one has questioned the traditional view which juxtaposes 'rural (spontaneous) vandalism' to 'urban (conscious) iconoclasm'. He doubts the accuracy of two assumptions implicit in many studies of the rural revolution in 1917. Did the Russian peasant possess only a vandalistic mentality? Does 'wilful ignorant destruction' accurately describe Russian peasant behaviour in the rural revolutions of 1905–6 and 1917–18? 'No pattern

of a single vandalistic *mentalité* could be discerned', he declares, but
rather a combination of envy (directed towards visibly larger land
holdings or equipment); hatred (towards the supposed arrogance and
indifference of the rich); self-interest (in the destruction of premises
and the burning of landlords' records, to prevent the latter re-
establishing themselves, and the burning of prisons to prevent
reprisals); and symbolism (through the destruction of the emblems of
peasants' former subjection, such as manor houses, and other features
of an alien landlord life, such as valuable works of art). Peasant
vandalism, asserts Stites, usually refers to the physical destruction of
things. Yet this should not be seen as 'visceral, irrational and unplanned'. It had a symbolic significance too. Just as the burning of rental
documents in France in 1789 showed that phenomenal devastation
could result from 'cool reason', so peasant struggles in Russia and
elsewhere were 'always marked by iconoclasm'.

Peasant actions in Russia during 1917 and 1918 possessed just such
a rationale. Take, for instance, the damage done to railway stations
and telegraph lines. These steps prevented military reprisals in the
former case, while both activities had the effect of disrupting links with
urban areas. Other outsiders or intruders also suffered. Schools were
set ablaze and sometimes the homes of teachers. The involvement of
entire villages and communities in destroying orchards, barns and
houses provided anonymity and collective responsibility and could
make it harder to find culprits and more difficult to punish them. All
this leads Stites to propose two types of activity: that typical of a
'looting consciousness' and that arising from a 'burning consciousness'. The former, he believes, more accurately describes peasant
actions in 1917. When occupying manor houses, for example, peasants
took what they needed and destroyed the rest. This should be
perceived not as senseless vandalism but as shrewd peasant behaviour,
aimed at preventing the return of the landlord. It was more usual,
claims Stites, to find manor houses burnt when townsmen were
present.[55] Whether this is true can only be determined by further
detailed studies of the revolution in the countryside during 1917 and
1918.

CONCLUSION

Thus, whether the forms of unrest were 'indirect' or 'direct' they
possessed a rationale, however parochial and inward-looking this may
have been. As Teodor Shanin has recently emphasised for 1905–6, the

peasant revolution was carried out fundamentally at the local level, within peasant communities and villages, and uniting those settlements which comprised the volost. Communities made decisions and passed resolutions at their traditional meetings and, beyond the villages and communities, at the volost gatherings. The experience of 1905–6 was clearly paralleled in 1917–18, even though in the latter period such gatherings often assumed different names. It is this aspect of the peasant revolution that tells us so much about how far the process of modernisation had advanced in Russia by 1914.

The multitude of autonomous organisations that sprang up and flourished in the countryside in the course of 1917 shows that peasants were as capable as workers, soldiers and sailors of organising their own affairs. After all, they had had experience of such activity in previous years and now that outside constraints (government authorities and officials) were removed they could expand the parameters of their activity. And, of course, links between 'peasants in uniform' as well as 'peasant-workers' with those back in the villages must not be underestimated especially in a rural society where large numbers were still illiterate, where an oral culture predominated and where information, whether about local or national events, was relayed through rumour, counter-rumour and personal interpretation or misinterpretation.

NOTES

1 A more detailed discussion of the historiography may be found in John Channon, 'The Peasantry in the Revolutions of 1917', paper presented to the conference on 'The Revolutions of 1917: 70 Years After', The Hebrew University of Jerusalem, Israel, January 1988. For general studies of the revolution see J.L.H. Keep, *The Russian Revolution* (London, 1976) and Marc Ferro, *The October Revolution. A Social History* (London, 1985); for agriculture, see D. Atkinson, *The End of the Russian Land Commune, 1905–1930* (Stanford, 1983) and Teodor Shanin, *The Awkward Class* (Oxford, 1971).

2 This bias is discussed in John Keep, 'The Agrarian Revolution of 1917–1918 in Soviet Historiography', *The Russian Review* 36, no. 1 (1977), 405–23. The paucity of specialised studies of the peasantry became evident, for example, at a conference at Essex University (England) on the theme of Social Groups and the Bolsheviks in the Early Months of Soviet Power, held in 1984, when there was only one contribution on the peasantry.

3 Regional and local case studies of the agrarian revolution abound in the USSR, covering virtually all areas of the country. Although by no means exhaustive, many of these case studies are listed by tri-decennial periodis-

ation in J. Channon, ' "Peasant Revolution" and "Land Reform": Land Redistribution in European Russia, October 1917–1920', unpublished PhD thesis, University of Birmingham, England, 1983, vol. 1, Introduction.

4 A good example would be the works of Teodor Shanin but see also the works of the 'moral economists' such as Jerome Blum and James C. Scott. See also in a different context the attempts at testing the theories of the Russian agrarian Marxists with respect to contemporary developing societies (for example, T. Shanin, 'Measuring Peasant Capitalism: The Operationalisation of Concepts of Political Economy: Russia's 1920s – India's 1970s' in E.J. Hobsbawm, W. Kula, A. Mitra, K.N. Raj and I. Sachs (eds.), *Peasants in History: Essays in Honour of Daniel Thorner* (Oxford, 1980).

5 For recent discussion of this problem see Roberta Thompson Manning, *The Crisis of the Old Order in Russia: Gentry and Government* (Princeton, 1982), pp. 444–5, n. 13. The point is also assessed in Maureen Perrie, 'The Peasant Movement in 1917', in R. Service (ed.), *Society and Politics in the Russian Revolution* (Macmillan, 1992).

6 A.D. Maliavskii, *Krestianskoe dvizhenie v Rossii v 1917g., mart–oktiabr* (Moscow, 1981), p. 58.

7 Ibid., p. 58; Perrie, 'The Peasant Movement'. This was, of course, only one way in which 'black repartition' occurred and the usage here is explained by Maliavskii's own interpretation of the term.

8 Maliavskii, *Krestianskoe dvizhenie*, p. 59; L. Owen, 'The Russian Agrarian Revolution of 1917: ii', *The Slavonic and East European Review* 12 (1933–4), 368–86.

9 The most recent such Western interpretation may be found in Graeme Gill, *Peasants and Government in the Russian Revolution* (London, 1979) and 'The Mainsprings of Peasant Action in 1917', *Soviet Studies* 30, no. 1 (1978), 63–86.

10 Owen, 'The Russian Agrarian Revolution', pp. 370, 377.

11 Maliavskii, *Krestianskoe dvizhenie*, pp. 69, 71. Before the First World War peasants leased 24 million *desiatiny* of arable land from *pomeshchiki* but by February 1917 this had fallen to 17 million. All land rented fell during the same period from 32 to 25 million *desiatiny*.

12 On the eve of the war it cost on average 13.72 roubles, to rent one *desiatina* in European Russia. This had fallen to 12.51 roubles in 1916 (Maliavskii, *Krestianskoe dvizhenie*, p. 70). According to Keep, rents accounted for one-third of each *desiatina* harvested in 1913 but only one-tenth in 1916 (*The Russian Revolution*, 1976). For other estimates see also S.M. Dubrovskii, *Stolypinskaia zemelnaia reforma* (Moscow, 1963). For an early estimate of the 'real cost' of goods due to inflation see M. Farbman, *Bolshevism in Retreat* (London, 1923).

13 For a discussion of the effects on the 'consuming' and 'producing' peasants see Lars T. Lih, 'Bread and Authority in Russia: Food Supply

and Revolutionary Politics, 1914–1921', PhD dissertation, University of Princeton, 1981.

14 Maliavskii, *Krestianskoe dvizhenie*, pp. 69, 71. For an estimate of the loss of income to *pomeshchiki* see A.M. Anfimov, *Rossiiskaia derevnia v gody pervoi mirovoi voiny (1914–fevral 1917)*, (Moscow, 1962), p. 71.

15 For use of force against peasants, land committees, etc. see, for example, Maliavskii, *Krestianskoe dvizhenie*, pp. 21–35, 244–8; *Krestianskoe dvizhenie v 1917 godu, Dokumenty i materialy* (Moscow and Leningrad, 1927), pp. 154, 416–21, 427; *Revoliutsionnaia borba krestian Kazanskoi gubernii nakanune Oktiabria, Sbornik dokumentov* (Kazan, 1958), pp. 43–50, 68, 417, 431–4, 441.

16 Vsevolod Holubnychy, 'The 1917 Agrarian Revolution in the Ukraine' in I.S. Koropeckyi (ed.), *Soviet Regional Economics: Selected Works of Vsevolod Holubnychy* (Edmonton, 1982). 'Seizure of estate land' accounted for 20.8 per cent of all actions between March and October, according to Shestakov's estimate in 1927.

17 This is discussed in John Channon, 'Peasants and Land Reform in the Ukraine in the Early 1920s', paper presented to the Thirteenth Conference of the Study Group on the Russian Revolution, Exeter College, Oxford, January 1987. Some writers have taken a different view of peasants' national consciousness. For a recent example see Steven Guthier, 'The Popular Base of Ukrainian Nationalism in 1917', *Slavic Review* 38 (1979), 30–47. Dittmar Dahlmann takes issue with this view, however, in the light of his work on the Makhno movement (see his 'Anarchism and the Makhno Movement' in *Sbornik. Study Group on the Russian Revolution*, no. 11, 1985, 4–25), while Robert Edelman in his recent study of the peasantry in the right-bank Ukraine during the revolution of 1905–6 found little evidence of nationalist sentiments (see *Proletarian Peasants. The Revolution of 1905 in Russia's South West*, Ithaca, 1987, esp. pp. 100–1, 109).

18 Andrew Ezergailis, *The 1917 Revolution in Latvia* (Boulder, 1974), pp. 14–15, 152, 199, 200, 203.

19 Soviet historians have recently been arguing that the confiscation of estates occurred largely before the construction of volost soviets (i.e. for them the organs of power in the countryside) and thus through the land committees. (See *Leninskii dekret o zemle v deistvii*, Moscow, 1979, for an example of such views.) Only in the last few years has it been possible to acknowledge that the peasants themselves were capable of executing such coordinated acts. Hence the significance of the works by V.V. Kabanov and (to a lesser extent) Maliavskii.

20 Maliavskii, *Krestianskoe dvizhenie*, p. 60, for example; V.V. Kabanov, 'Oktiabrskaia revoliutsiia: krestianskaia obshchina', *Istoricheskie zapiski* 100 (1984), 100–50.

21 Owen, 'The Russian Agrarian Revolution of 1917', *Slavonic and East European Review* 12 (1933), 157, 160, 162–3, and 'The Russian Agrarian

Revolution: Part II', 370, 372, 373, 375; Shanin, *Russia 1905–07. Revolution as a Moment of Truth* (London, 1987); Keep, *The Russian Revolution*; Gill, *Peasants and Government*. Though see below, n. 50.

22 Kabanov, 'Oktiabrskaia revoliutsiia', pp. 107–8; V.V. Grishaev, *Stroitelstvo sovetov v derevne* (Moscow, 1967).

23 These are located in the Central State Archive of the National Economy (TsGANKh), fond 478 in Moscow.

24 Maliavskii, *Krestianskoe dvizhenie*, p. 10; Kabanov, 'Oktiabrskaia revoliutsiia', p. 107. The terminological use of *obshchina* is significant here.

25 M.Ia. Fenomenov, *Sovremennaia derevnia* (Leningrad, 1925), pp. 28, 115; Kabanov, 'Oktiabrskaia revoliutsiia', *Istoricheskie azpiski* III (1984), pp. 107–8.

26 Ibid., pp. 108–9.

27 Ibid., p. 109.

28 V.M. Gubareva, *Razvertyvanie sotsialisticheskoi revoliutsii v derevne v 1918 g.* (Leningrad, 1957).

29 A.A. Piontkovskii (ed.), *Sovety v oktiabre* (Moscow, 1928), pp. 312–33; Kabanov, 'Oktiabrskaia revoliutsiia', p. 110.

30 Ibid., p. 109; Grishaev, *Stroitelstvo sovetov*.

31 Kabanov, 'Oktiabrskaia revoliutsiia', pp. 109–10.

32 Ibid., p. 110; see also the chapter by O. Figes on the peasant revolution in the Middle Volga during 1917–18 ('The Russian Peasant Community in the Agrarian Revolution, 1917–18') in R. Bartlett (ed.), *Land Commune and Peasant Community in Russia* (London, 1990).

33 Fenomenov, *Sovremennaia derevnia*.

34 Kabanov, 'Oktiabrskaia revoliutsiia', p. 111.

35 Owen had claimed that it was the inability of the Provisional Government to provide leadership of these local committees that led to the downfall of Kerensky and Chernov in October ('The Russian Agrarian Revolution of 1917', p. 163).

36 Maliavskii, *Krestianskoe dvizhenie*, pp. 59, 63–4; Owen, 'The Russian Agrarian Revolution of 1917: II', p. 379.

37 Maliavskii, *Krestianskoe dvizhenie*, pp. 63, 70.

38 Owen, 'The Russian Agrarian Revolution of 1917: Part II', pp. 373, 384.

39 John Channon, 'The Bolsheviks and the Peasantry: the Land Question during the First Eight Months of Soviet Rule', *Slavonic and East European Review* 66 (1988), 593–624.

40 E. Vinogradoff, 'The Russian Peasantry and the Elections to the Fourth State Duma', in Leopold H. Haimson (ed.), *The Politics of Rural Russia, 1905–14* (Indiana, 1979); Esther Kingston-Mann, 'A Strategy for Marxist Bourgeois Revolution: Lenin and the Peasantry, 1907–16', *Journal of Peasant Studies* 7 (1979–80), 147; Anfimov, *Rossiiskaia derevnia*, p. 174; Dubrovskii, *Stolypinskaia zemelnaia reforma*, p. 531.

41 Owen, 'The Russian Agrarian Revolution of 1917: Part II', pp. 371, 374.

Those who argue for patriotism seem to equate it with the lack of any significant desertion until late 1917 (see M. Ferro, *The Russian Revolution of February 1917*, Routledge, 1972; N. Stone, *The Eastern Front, 1914–17*, London, 1975, for two such examples).

42 For details see Channon, 'Peasant Revolution'; Keep, *The Russian Revolution*; Gill, *Peasants and Government*. Further evidence is provided in the research of O. Figes on the Middle Volga region in 1917–18 (see 'The Russian Peasant Community', in Bartlett (ed.), *Land Commune and Peasant Russia, Civil War; the Volga Countryside in Revolution, 1917–1921*, Oxford, 1989).

43 Channon, 'The Bolsheviks'; Channon, 'Peasant Revolution'; Channon, 'Peasants and Land Reform'; Figes, 'The Russian Peasant Community' and *Peasant Russia, Civil War*.

44 Kaufman, writing in Russia before 1914, believed that the development of the Siberian commune provided a mirror for viewing the emergence of the mir west of the Urals.

45 For examples of former landowners remaining in the countryside after 1917 see Channon, 'Tsarist Landowners after the Revolution: Former Pomeshchiki in Rural Russia During NEP', *Soviet Studies* 39 (1987), 575–98; Figès, *Peasant Russia, Civl War*, pp. 132–5.

46 Edelman, *Proletarian Peasants*.

47 John Channon, ' "Land Revolution" and "Land Reform": the Case of the Peasantry in the Central Black-Earth Region, 1917–24', in L. Edmondson and P. Waldron (eds.), *Russian Economic and Social History: Essays in Honour of Olga Crisp* (London, forthcoming).

48 Discussed in more detail in Channon, 'The Bolsheviks'.

49 Kabanov, 'Oktiabrskaia revoliutsiia'.

50 Owen, 'The Russian Agrarian Revolution of 1917', p. 162 and 'The Russian Agrarian Revolution: Part II', pp. 373–4, 376; Shanin, *Russia 1905–07*.

51 Owen, 'The Russian Agrarian Revolution: Part II', p. 376; Channon, 'Tsarist Landowners'.

52 Owen, 'The Russian Agrarian Revolution of 1917', pp. 159, 164 and 'The Russian Agrarian Revolution: Part II', pp. 369–71, 374, 376, 378, 380–2, 384–5; A.K. Wildman, *The End of the Russian Imperial Army: the Old Army and the Soldiers' Revolt (March–April 1917)* (Princeton, 1980).

53 Kabanov is the most recent example but the works by Kostrikin and Kravchuk should also be noted and one should never forget the monumental endeavours of V.P. Danilov.

54 E. Vinogradoff, 'Household and Systemic Insurance Mechanisms Among the Peasants of Central Russia', paper presented to the First Annual Meeting of the Social Science History Association, Philadelphia, October 1975. I am grateful to Professor Vinogradoff for permitting me to cite from this paper. The most recent study of 1905–7 is by Shanin,

Russia 1905–07 but see also Manning, *The Crisis of the Old Order* and Maureen Perrie, 'The Russian Peasant Movement of 1905–1907: its Social Composition and Revolutionary Significance', *Past and Present* 57 (1972), 123–55.

55 Richard Stites, 'Iconoclastic Currents in the Russian Revolution: Destroying and Preserving the Past', in Abbott Gleason, Peter Kenez and Richard Stites (eds.), *Bolshevik Culture* (Bloomington, 1985), esp. pp. 2–6.

7

PERCEPTIONS AND REALITIES OF LABOUR PROTEST, MARCH TO OCTOBER 1917

DIANE P. KOENKER
AND WILLIAM G. ROSENBERG

PERCEPTIONS OF STRIKES AND THE REVOLUTIONARY PROCESS

IN revolutionary Russia, strikes constituted the largest, most wide-spread, most universal manifestation of labour protest. Over the eight-month span from 3 March to 25 October 1917 no less than 2.4 million workers went on strike to press claims for better wages, better working conditions, changes in work rules, dignified personal relations, and, more rarely, political change.[1] To say that the overwhelming number of strikers advanced economic, wage-related demands, and to say that the largest numbers of strikers and the largest strikes occurred in the autumn of 1917 is to highlight two important characteristics of strikes in 1917, but also to illustrate the complex and contradictory messages that the strike record conveyed to contemporaries and continues to convey to historians. On the one hand, 'economic strikes' are associated with economism, reformism, moderation. On the other hand, an acceleration of strike activism in 1917, at a time when political events focused on the question of state power itself, suggests an intimate link between labour protest and politics, between strikes and the political dimensions of revolutionary change.

To be sure, patterns of strike frequencies have universally been read as objective indices of labour unrest: peaks in strike activism are assumed to measure political mobilisation and, often, political opposition.[2] When one disaggregates this form of labour activism, however, it is quite clear that strikes also possess 'lives' of their own: together with broader social, economic and political patterns, they reflect local histories, particular grievances, different processes of decision-making and diverse enterprise cultures. To understand the relationship of strike activism to the revolutionary process as a whole, it is therefore

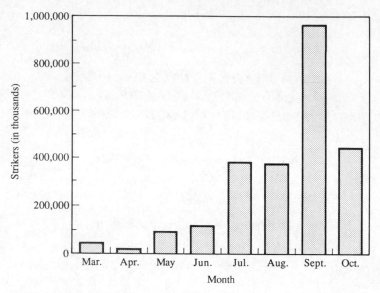

Figure 1 Strikers in Russia in 1917, by month in which the strikes began

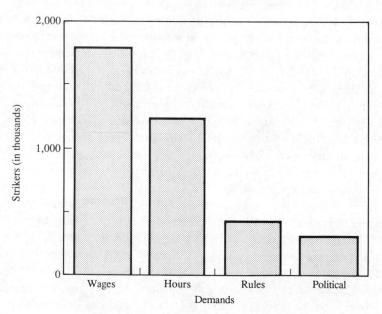

Figure 2 Strikers and issues in 1917

essential to appreciate the inner logic of strikes as well as their aggregate contours.

When this is done, strikes become much more than objective indices of broader trends. They signify formative experiences for all their participants that in various ways influence subsequent relations to unfolding events. The act of striking itself affects the ways strikers come to think about management, political institutions, or the way their enterprises are organised. In revolutionary situations like that in Russia during 1917, concepts like 'democracy' (or 'Bolshevism') become contextualised, taking on particular meanings often unrelated to broader (and especially official) discourse. Furthermore, strikes influence perceptions about the nature of labour protest, the possibilities of mediation and the roles of democratic institutions, elements or parties. So doing, they help define an understanding of political possibilities. In revolutionary Russia, how strikes were reported and perceived, in fact, may well have contributed as much to the determinant processes of political and social polarisation as their objective features – who struck, in what numbers, when and where.

The complex issue of perceptions and representations thus demands our attention, particularly as it concerns strikes, but also in terms of the broader context of revolutionary change. On the one hand, we need to explore the way in which workers and the labour press thought and wrote about strikes, and attempt to discern the ways in which this may have influenced worker activism; on the other, we must examine management perceptions of striking workers, at least insofar as they were reflected in the public organs of what one can roughly label the trade-industrial 'bourgeoisie', and attempt to discern the ways in which these public images themselves may have contributed to the changing climate of labour–management relations.

The question of perceptions and representations is complicated by the fact that all social groups in revolutionary Russia had, in effect, multiple and often competitive identities, stemming from their professions, locations, social backgrounds, self-conceptions and even their ideas about the nature of the Russian state. Tensions existed between one's role as a patriotic citizen, for example, and as an industrialist or businessman concerned about profits; as a peasant from a village in Poltava concerned about getting a share of the land, and as a loom operator in a Moscow textile mill worried about staying employed. Whether one or another identity played a dominant or passive role in shaping both perceptions and activist behaviour obviously depended on political and social circumstances, as well as the arena in which group aspirations were played out. Russia's workers in particular entered the revolutionary period not only with a sense of themselves as members of a single estate or class, but also as members of smaller but highly significant aggregates: trades or crafts, particular factories, even workshops within plants. At the same time, the February revolution enabled workers to identify with an even larger collective, the body politic of all Russia, a community of which the revolution had made all working people, at last, participants on an equal basis with those who formerly enjoyed special privilege.

If the experience of going out on strike itself helped to overcome sectional divisions and produced broader class identifications, the perspective offered by strike reporting, as we hope to demonstrate, went beyond this class mobilisation, to affirm the parity of the working class within the larger society and ultimately to convey a sense that this class, in default of other social groups, had become obligated to dominate society. The very periodisation of revolutionary change can therefore be set, at least in part, in terms of moments when the balance between sectional, class and national identities shifted, the moment when one or another of these multi-layered identities became, in effect, the dominant impulse underlying social action and political behaviour.

Industrialists and businessmen in Russia experienced a similar competition of identities. Textile manufacturers, oilmen and other entrepreneurs were simultaneously part of local communities with their own rich and individual traditions, and members of broader collectives, increasingly aggregated in 1917 into associations like the Petrograd and Moscow Societies of Factory and Mill Owners and the Council of Congresses of Industry and Trade. In some ways the Moscow merchants and manufacturers, closely tied to the Old Believer communities, were as different socially from Petrograd industrialists and bankers as they were from their own employees, even though the politics of revolutionary change increasingly forced them into common stereotypical categories and identities.[3] Like workers, manufacturers and industrialists thus felt the strength at various times of particularistic and class identities, while also feeling themselves connected to broader national interests and the country as a whole.

The strike movement played an important role in the evolution of both class formations and social identities during 1917 in several ways. For many workers, the very act of participating in strikes was a means of identifying with a broader collective based firmly on the relationship to the means of production. To be a 'worker' took on important social and political meaning, even if one worked as a waiter in a Petrograd café or a cab driver in Piatigorsk. At the same time, since strikes always required some form of response from management, they also necessarily helped define its identities as well, encouraging organisational alliances among owners and managers and a clearer sense of class positions. In moments of conflict, particularistic qualities tended to be blurred. Very different kinds of workers with quite diverse values, outlooks and political commitments tended to look the same from across the barricades, and so did the 'bourgeoisie'.

In addition, the various ways in which different newspapers, reflecting the perspectives and biases of particular political or social groups, represented strikes and strikers, also affected social formations and outlooks. We think it likely, in fact, that strike reporting and especially the ways contending groups were represented may, perhaps as much as activism itself, have played a paramount part in shaping social attitudes in 1917, influencing the ways in which those on both sides of the labour–management divide developed their sense of themselves, their place in the broader society and hence their relationship to unfolding events.

The tasks of this chapter are thus severalfold. First, we want to explore how strikes were represented in the principal sources of information in 1917, and how the public face of strikes compared to the private goals of both workers and employers. We want to ask as well whether strikes were represented similarly in the principal sources of information, whether different reading publics, in other words, were treated to different pictures of strikes. From this vantage point we might then return to the question of social identities, even if only briefly, and try to understand more fully the consequences of the strike experience, both reported and 'real', for the course of revolution in 1917 as well as for subsequent historical understanding.

STRIKE REPORTING AND THE READING PUBLIC IN 1917

Let us begin with some general observations about the patterns of strike reporting in the major Petrograd and Moscow daily newspapers. While one must be extremely cautious about over-generalisation, particularly in terms of the way in which different patterns of reporting may have reflected deliberate efforts to shape the news, it is apparent from even a cursory review that the strike movement was reflected quite differently in different newspapers, and that the conservative ('right'), moderate liberal, moderate socialist and radical ('left') press regarded strikes and strikers in a great variety of ways.[4]

Of particular interest, first, is the almost studied indifference, at least in the early weeks of the revolution, of the 'bourgeois' press in general to strikes and to the labour movement as a whole. With the end of the February revolution, *Rech*, *Russkie vedomosti*, *Birzhevye vedomosti*, *Russkaia volia*, and other comparable newspapers concentrated their reporting almost entirely on activities of the Provisional Government and the soviets. One finds virtually no strike reports whatsoever, for example, in such major newspapers as *Rech*, *Russkie vedomosti* and *Russkaia volia* from approximately the second week of March until after the April crisis. Such reports as appeared in the moderate liberal press were almost entirely in 'boulevard' newspapers such as *Trudovaia kopeika*, whose readership among the constituents of the liberal parties was at best uncertain.[5]

It is impossible to know precisely the reasons for this apparent indifference. There were probably several, ranging from the judgement of editors about their readers' interests to limits on the type of assignments reporters could readily undertake. But in general it seems evident that in these early weeks, at least, strikes were not especially notable events for those with liberal or conservative viewpoints, and there seemed to be no particular concern about the development of the labour movement more generally. At least through the early months of the revolutionary period, the focus of the non-socialist press was on 'political' events, defined rather narrowly.

There was almost no reporting in the right or liberal press, for example, of the Petrograd laundry strike, which began on 1 May and to which *Pravda*, *Rabochaia gazeta*, *Novaia zhizn* and other socialist papers devoted such attention. On 3 May *Russkaia volia* did carry a long article on 'The Tasks of the Citizen-Woman', lauding the 'important roles' women 'had long fulfilled' in bringing up children as mothers and educators, and suggesting that the time had now come for society at large to take some responsibility for these vital functions so that women themselves could become more socially active, and fulfil their civic duties as electors and representatives in local government, even the Constituent Assembly.[6] Nonetheless, the laundresses were virtually ignored (a report on 25 May merely indicating that some owners had offered concessions which the workers refused).[7] Early strikes in Petrograd and Moscow by coopers, wood craftsmen working in industrial shops, leather workers and even metallists, also remained largely unnoticed in the liberal press, although the latter strike (in

May) did receive some attention because of its potential impact on the country's defence effort.[8]

On the other hand, the liberal and right-wing press did pay considerable attention to strikes outside the capitals. Many provincial conflicts, such as those among the Odessa cabmen or the Baku oil-workers, were conveyed to the capital by the Russian Telegraph Agency, and while their reports tended to be terse and factual, they did serve to inform the readers of the scope of labour conflict throughout the empire.

Over time, what emerged as of primary importance to the liberal press, as one might expect, were the ways in which strikes and other forms of labour protest were infringing on management prerogatives, generally reported as 'rights'; strikes which appeared to have a strong impact on the economy as a whole; strikes which potentially affected government activities, such as those of paper workers and printers which threatened to delay elections; and strikes involving direct government intervention, which increased as the year progressed.

One of the earliest strikes to gain the attention of the *Birzhevye vedomosti*, for example, was that of the foremen at Treugolnik Rubber in Petrograd who walked out on 23 June at the insistence of rank-and-file workers to protest at the dismissal two days earlier of some twenty female foremen.[9] This assault on the prerogatives of foremen and management also captured the attention of the Kadet paper, *Rech*, which published a letter to the editor about the situation on 21 June and followed subsequent events closely. What is particularly interesting about the reporting in *Rech* is that the developing conflict at the huge Sormovo works in Nizhnyi Novgorod, which directly threatened military production, was almost entirely ignored. While *Novaia zhizn*, *Vpered*, and other socialist papers took up the story in the third week of June, substantive accounts did not appear in the liberal papers until early July, when they emphasised the mediating role of the Ministry of Labour.[10]

Further, *Russkoe slovo* in reporting on the strike of Moscow doormen and janitors (*dvorniki*) in early June emphasised that only some 20 per cent of the *dvorniki* actually wanted a strike, but the remaining 80 per cent had been 'terrorised' into submission, and now would not even let home-owners sweep their own sidewalks.[11] When Moscow envelope makers went on strike in late May, *Russkoe slovo* worried whether this would prevent the proper distribution of ballots for the city duma election.[12] Increasingly, *Rech*, *Birzhevye vedomosti*, *Russkie vedomosti* and the liberal press in general followed the activities of the Ministry of

Labour as it involved itself in settling strikes throughout the summer and autumn, reiterating the importance of settlements to the 'national interest'. Occasionally there were serious errors in reporting as the liberal press emphasised the plight of management in strikes: *Russkoe slovo* indicating wrongly that tobacco plant owners had offered their workers an 80 per cent wage increase in August, for example, but that workers were 'holding out' for 120 per cent.[13] At other times there were noticeable errors of omission, such as the failure to indicate that Moscow rubber workers were striking in August because management refused to take the dispute to arbitration, or to report the strike at the Nobel works near Petrograd which broke out in May when management simply refused to respond to worker demands.[14]

These almost predictable biases and concerns were certainly not absent from strike reports in the moderate socialist press, but the approach to strikes in newspapers like *Rabochaia gazeta*, *Novaia zhizn* and the official press of the Moscow and Petrograd Soviets was still quite different. Strikes here were newsworthy events, just as were the formation of trade unions and factory committees, and the development of other major components of the labour movement as a whole. Understandably, the moderate socialist press focused on the material difficulties of the workers and tended to report strike demands extensively. Both liberal and socialist reports tended to emphasise the primacy of wage demands: these constituted the great majority of specific claims. But the liberal and conservative press noted relatively more frequently demands about challenges to managerial authority: the eight-hour and six-hour workdays, and changes in management personnel. The socialist press was more likely to report issues involving workers' rights: trade unions and factory committees; rehiring fired workers; specific questions of remuneration such as rate-setting and forms of payment. And whereas the liberal press gave attention to the government, socialist reporters concentrated on the activities of mediation commissions and the soviets.

Even more significant than these variations in content was the sheer abundance of strike reporting in the moderate socialist press, particularly in Menshevik newspapers and in the non-partisan organs of the two soviets. Although our figures on individual strike reports represent an approximation of the actual volume of reports rather than an exact count, our calculations indicate that the Menshevik press and the soviet organs each published over 400 strike reports between March and October. Socialist Revolutionary newspapers carried at least another 260 reports, and the left-wing Menshevik papers another 150 at a minimum. The Bolshevik press also produced over 260 reports, whereas the moderate liberal press accounted for somewhere in the neighbourhood of 220 reports, and the conservative press only around 50.[15] While the length of these reports varied, and we cannot systematically distinguish between the terse one-line reports of the telegraph agency and the lengthy detailed reports that would appear in the course of long strikes, there is no doubt that the moderate socialist press dominated the field of strike reporting, and that the perspective generated by their reports must have reached a broad number of readers.

Moreover, the moderate socialist press tended to play an important *functional* role in strikes, particularly early in the year. Strike reports frequently carried appeals for funds or boycotts, and often gave information about where meetings would be held and under whose auspices. They served as well as vehicles for trade unionists, emphasising the need for organisation, and at times even decrying the degrees of 'isolation' and 'spontaneity' in strike actions. And particularly in the summer and autumn, *Vlast naroda*, *Edinstvo*, *Delo naroda*, *Rabochaia gazeta*, and especially *Izvestiia* in both Moscow and Petrograd tended to focus attention on the efforts of trade unionists and of soviet functionaries to settle strikes and return workers to their jobs. When more than 50,000 Baku oil-workers walked out in September, for example, the Right SR newspaper *Volia naroda* considered their action 'completely incomprehensible' in view of the imminent arrival in Baku of a special government commission to deal with the matter headed by the Deputy Minister of Labour, Gvozdov.[16] Like the liberal press, *Volia naroda* worried about the 'extreme dangers to the nation' from a shortage of fuel. In the same vein, while *Rabochaia gazeta* reported the appeal of striking Petrograd druggists for funds in July, and *Den* emphasised ongoing mediation efforts in its accounts, *Edinstvo* reported that the union board and strike committee both were urging employee pharmacists to return to work, having received written confirmation of the owners' intention to accept the results of arbitration.[17]

There seems little question, in sum, that the moderate socialist press, deliberately or not, represented the interests of organised labour to its membership and to the public at large, just as the moderate liberal press both reflected and represented the interests of the state, and to some extent, those of management as well. 'Representation' here, moreover, is the important word, since the views of liberal and socialist leaders alike about strikes were necessarily shaped by these reports. Thus the relative indifference of the liberal press to the work-

15. The first All-Russian Congress of Factory Committees
(Petrograd, 30 May to 3 June 1917).

ers' demands undoubtedly reinforced the tendency to see strikes as
essentially reckless and even conspiratorial in origin. Certainly
without full reporting, the logic of strike protests tended to be lost, and
the sense of worker unreasonableness exaggerated. At the same time, a
better informed readership of the socialist press undoubtedly understood more fully the dimensions of social conflict unfolding in the
factories as well as its political implications. If strike reporting thus
contributed to the increasingly anti-labour views of liberals and the
right, it also sharpened the awareness among moderate socialists in
the soviet of the difficulties of labour organisation, and of the danger to
their ideals of the increasing intransigence of their bourgeois partners
in industrial relations.

For example, the presence of violence in strikes posed critical problems for those seeking to minimise the political conflict between labour
and management. Overall in 1917, violent behaviour by strikers was
not widespread, and much of the violence that received attention in
the press was not connected with strikes. But not all readers were
exposed to the same representations of violence. Only the socialist
press, for example, mentioned repressive action against workers. Violence, of course, to socialists was a sign of the immaturity of the labour
movement, and we would expect socialists to minimise the attention
paid to it, to demonstrate their maturity both to outsiders and to new
cadres within the movement. Conversely, we would expect the capital-

ist press to emphasise violence in order to prove the immaturity of the labour movement and its unfitness to govern. Generally, the incidence of reports of violence conforms to expectations: the Bolsheviks mentioned violent actions least often, the right-wing press the most frequently, with the moderate socialists and moderate liberals falling in the middle.[18] Interestingly, most reports of violence came early in the year, before the July Days. Only the moderate socialist press paid greater attention to violence in the months after July, a position perhaps consistent with the fear among the socialist 'coalitionists' of unbridled radicalism.

In general, though, that section of the press reflected a remarkably benign view of labour relations overall: moderate socialists tended to stress success as well as successful cooperation between labour and management. They also emphasised the organisational characteristics of strikes, and, more than other types of newspapers, described many subjective characteristics: the serious, peaceful, or spirited determination of strikers to wage battle with the bourgeoisie. The very dualism of the Menshevik position in 1917 is reflected in their strike reporting: the proletariat was engaged in class struggle with the bourgeoisie and should hone all its weapons in this struggle, but at the same time, the proletariat had also to exist in a bourgeois society in which their 'class enemies' were dominant. We see in the patterns of such reporting the belief that strikes were a major element of class struggle in bourgeois society, through which labour could improve its position collectively and individually. Yet there is nothing in these reports to indicate that these same strikes might serve to topple the bourgeois order. In fact, as presented, the strike movement in Russia – orderly, organised, widespread – constituted proof that a period of bourgeois economic and social relations could benefit workers and the nation alike. Strikes in the perspective of the moderate socialist editorial boards were thus very much an element of 'ordinary' or 'routine' bourgeois social relations.[19]

Not so for the Bolsheviks. Several interesting features of their strike reporting stand out. Unlike the liberal press, Bolshevik newspapers quickly began to report on the strike movement as soon as the old régime fell. Particularly in May, the pages of *Pravda* were full of long and attentive reports about strikes among Petrograd woodworkers, sales clerks, dyers and laundresses. But the interest of the Bolshevik press in strikes (or its ability to report them) waned significantly after July. The repressive measures of the Kerensky government provide some explanation of this decline: *Pravda* was unable to come out during much of July, and when it resumed it was limited to just two pages.[20] However, the Moscow Bolshevik paper, *Sotsial-Demokrat*, which did not suffer such repression, also reduced its strike reporting anyway. Once the Sixth (Bolshevik) Congress in early August had adopted a policy of discouraging strikes, which the party felt only drew energy away from the revolutionary goal of a proletarian government, Bolshevik editors quite naturally would not want to draw attention to the continuing persistence of the strike phenomenon.

We should also note here that the Bolshevik press concentrated its attention largely on strikes in the two capitals. One obvious explanation for this focus was the absence of Russian Telegraph Agency (RTA) reports in the Bolshevik press, reports which added to the strike coverage of the moderate newspapers. It is unclear whether the lack of provincial coverage was due to editorial preference; an inability to afford the RTA news service; or the unwillingness of the RTA to provide such service; but the net result was that readers of the Bolshevik press drew their conclusions about the strike movement largely from the capital cities alone.

In addition to this geographic selectivity, the Bolshevik press tended much less than the moderate socialist press to report the presence of outside mediation; their strike movement thus may have *appeared* to be the self-reliant product of workers themselves.[21] Reports of the final outcome also diverged in interesting ways: the Bolshevik press was least likely to report success, most likely to report compromise and failure. By this selectivity in what they reported, were Bolshevik editors sending a message to readers that strikes were inexpedient? Such a picture of labour relations might well have heightened a sense of class struggle among the readers of the radical left-wing press.

We must not impute too much ideological motivation to overworked editors. What is so interesting about the reports in *Pravda* in particular, but also in *Sotsial-Demokrat*, *Proletarii* and *Rabochii put* is not any particular degree of partisanship or distortion, but the very attentiveness of Bolshevik reporters to all strikes, and especially those of clerks, salespeople and other service-sector employees whom one does not usually identify as among the proletarian constituents of the party. *Pravda* covered the strike of the Petrograd laundry workers in detail, for example, giving far more attention to the efforts of women workers to organise and coordinate their efforts than any other paper. Its reports paid particular attention to the activities of the 'yellow' union organised by employers to break the strike, and sounded frequent warnings about this and other 'false inducements' to reach a settlement.[22] The strike of shop assistants at Gostinnyi Dvor received similar treatment, as did that of the fishmonger employees and other food workers at the Apraksin market complex.[23]

Not surprisingly, Bolshevik press reports frequently represented the mood of strikers as 'firm' or 'resolute', published appeals for solidarity and aid, and represented owners as 'yielding' or 'about to yield'.[24] Reports also tended to focus on the attacks made by other papers against striking workers; frequently reported evidence of speculation among managers and factory owners; and decried rather consistently the ways in which industrialists and businessmen were organising themselves to resist labour demands. But what distinguished Bolshevik strike reports was not so much the obvious class bias, but rather the apparent recognition that activist behaviour by generally 'dormant' workers like shop assistants and women laundry employees was itself a matter of real political import, worthy of extensive reporting largely one suspects as an example to others. (This was a characteristic, too, of reporting in the moderate socialist press which reported extensively, if not intensively, on strikes among non-industrial workers, particularly in service, trade, communications and transport.)

Thus socialist editors of all persuasions appeared to portray class struggle, as illustrated by the strike movement, in the broadest possible terms, encouraging diverse segments of the labour force to abandon their narrow interests and to identify with a working class that transcended the limits of manufacturing industries. The very identification of shop assistants with leather workers, laundresses with metal-workers, could not help but suggest a broad commonality of interest and an aggregate workers' 'class', legitimately entitled on these grounds to share in determining the political future of Russia. In these circumstances, the competitive identity of 'citizen' – and the corresponding importance of national as opposed to sectarian interests (tenuous enough to begin with) – was seriously compromised, whatever the social realities; and the liberal values, on which Provisional Government authority was based, were likewise weakened.

STRIKE REPORTING: TWO CASE STUDIES

The interplay of strike reporting and its possible effect on the different readerships can be seen from another perspective when specific strikes are examined in detail. We have selected for elaboration two well-reported cases, for which extensive accounts appeared in both the socialist and liberal press. We have also chosen strikes by workers not employed in factories or major industries, the better to illustrate, we think, the ways in which the strike experience itself served to consolidate broader class affiliations and identities.

Approximately 350 workers in Petrograd dye and dry-cleaning works and some 150 sales people in affiliated retail shops began a strike on 12 May that would prove to be one of the longest of the revolutionary period. Many were women. The strikers demanded a minimum wage of four roubles a day for women and five for men, goals which, if achieved, would also put an end to piece rates, an important gain in terms of extending their control over the pace of work. According to one account, these wage levels were worked out in discussions between the Petrograd Soviet and the Petrograd Society of Factory and Mill Owners.[25] They also demanded salaries of 150 and 175 roubles a month for those who worked in the retail trade.

The strike was coordinated by a newly organised union of chemical workers and led by a central strike committee, which appealed early to the Ministry of Labour for assistance. The latter attempted without success to persuade the owners' association to submit the case to arbitration. The firm of Danziger and Golaevskii agreed, as did a number of smaller establishments, and the strike here was settled quickly, raising hopes for a city-wide agreement. But the largest plants, led by Peklie, held out. It was not until just before the October revolution that these enterprises finally announced their desire to settle and agreed to negotiate with the union an end to the strike.

Three aspects of the way this long strike was reported are of interest. First, the strike caused a considerable inconvenience to many residents of Petrograd who had left their clothes and other goods for colouring, cleaning and repair. *Rabochaia gazeta*, *Izvestiia* and other newspapers generally representing moderate socialist viewpoints indicated, however, that workers in some establishments, particularly the large Danziger works, were arranging to have goods returned. In contrast, *Russkaia volia* reported not the strike issues nor the nature of the conflict itself, but the 'significant number' of suits in local magistrates' courts for the return of (or compensation for) lost goods. In its account, all the efforts of the owners of the plants to return goods had been blocked by workers, who remained adamant that 'no work be allowed until the satisfaction of their demands'.[26]

In fact, many firms had hired strike-breakers, an issue which very much concerned union leaders as the dispute continued. *Rabochaia gazeta* even published a list of strike-breakers' names as a way of ostracising them from the labour community, while other newspapers emphasised that no 'real' workers were going back to work, despite various inducements by management. (In the case of Peklie, this included an attempt to allow employees to buy stock in the firm, even offering to advance the fifty roubles each share would cost, if only they would call off the strike.)[27] Management also secured the cooperation of the militia, which protected the strike-breakers and reportedly arrested some strikers. At the same time, the moderate press repeatedly described the dispute as peaceful, and workers as firm and unanimous in their commitment. There were no reports of violence.

At the outset of the strike, *Pravda* alone reported a major split in worker ranks between those who demanded that the enterprises be seized and taken over by their employees, and those who thought this was a mistake because of the 'danger of such an isolated action'.[28] In contrast, *Rabochaia gazeta* sought to emphasise the resistance of the managers, who sent spurious representatives to bargain, who falsely accused workers of stealing the goods left for repair, who threatened strikers with weapons to force them to return to work.[29] Towards mid July, rumours that plants had been seized must have surfaced again, for the editors of *Rabochaia gazeta* took pains to reassure readers that no such steps had occurred or were planned, that the dyers and dry-cleaners, in other words, were not political extremists despite their prolonged strike. At the same time, the moderate socialist papers published appeals for contributions, and listed the names of enterprises from which the workers had sent funds, clearly stressing the solidarity of these employees with their comrades in other industries. Reports here also emphasised the hardships suffered by the striking workers as a result of weeks and months without wages, thus suggesting that this small group of underpaid men and women represented the many workers who expected the revolution finally to bring some degree of material betterment and well-being.

The strike of Petrograd pharmacy workers in October was one of the most contentious work stoppages of 1917. It affected all but a handful of pharmacies located in hospitals and clinics, causing serious hardship. 'Who is to blame?' became a central question as the strike continued. It was not settled until several weeks after the Bolsheviks came to power.

The central issue was wages, although an important subsidiary question concerned the role of unions in hiring. Earlier, in April, conflict between pharmacists and their employees developed into a five-hour strike when owners refused to abide by a decision of the conciliation board on hours, wages and firing procedures. Pharmacy clerks struck reluctantly, 'not with easy hearts', while the Petrograd Soviet explicitly blamed the owners for the hardships the strike would create for the urban population.[30] *Pravda* as well as *Rabochaia gazeta* rushed to the defence of the strikers, in response to 'insinuations' directed against the pharmacy clerks printed in the boulevard paper, *Petrogradskii listok*.[31] (The 'insinuations' were unspecified, but as pharmacy clerks tended to be Jewish, the attack of the boulevard press may have been of an antisemitic nature.) The April strike produced a settlement favourable to the clerks, but the agreement failed to protect pharmacy workers from the ravages of inflation and the enmity of their employers, who for their part drew closer together in a highly active employers' association.

During the third week of September a general union meeting of the workers approved a new salary schedule worked out by the union contract commission. The new salaries ranged from 100 roubles a month for minors under the age of sixteen to 300–50 roubles for assistant pharmacists and 425 roubles for highly skilled pharmacists (*provizory*). The delegates approved the new scale reluctantly, since it still left them behind other professional groups, and submitted it to the Society of Pharmacy Owners on 18 September.

The society rejected it after a week's deliberation, claiming that it would cause 'financial ruin'. Shortly afterwards, both sides were brought together by the Assistant Minister for Internal Affairs, Bogutskii, who sought a rapid settlement in the interests of the city's health and welfare. When the Society of Pharmacy Owners categorically rejected any suggestion that salaries be increased, soviet spokesmen and city duma representatives quickly pressed for additional mediation efforts, raising the possibility of 'municipalising' the pharmacies if necessary. Additional mediation efforts under the offices of the Ministry of Labour and the Petrograd Soviet also failed, however, and the strike began on 3 October.

At first the union agreed to staff some forty pharmacies in order to permit emergency prescriptions to be filled. Pharmacy owners also tried to staff their own shops themselves or with family members. An anxious public, at first inconvenienced, soon reacted to the resulting shortage of available medicine. The issue was taken up at various levels of municipal and state government, and in both the district and city soviets.

Pharmacists blamed the Society of Pharmacy Owners for both the strike and the shortage of medicine. According to reports in the moderate socialist press, the society threatened to withhold supplies of medicine from any pharmacy that yielded to the strikers' demands.[32] Representatives of the society accused pickets of preventing customers from entering those shops that had managed to remain open.[33] The most serious conflict was over who was responsible for limiting the dispensing of necessary medicines. Union spokesmen insisted that the owners of the shops still functioning were guilty of deliberate sabotage, by sending *all* urgent prescriptions to the union-sanctioned public pharmacies, overloading them and thus creating a public furore. The owners insisted that it was the pharmacy workers who were responsible for the shortages.

Violent incidents intensified the conflict (including an armed attack on a pharmacy worker by a shop owner), and the union announced that it could not staff even emergency pharmacies since its members could not be protected. More important, government and soviet representatives both began to discuss municipalising (or nationalising) the pharmacies, placing a cloud of 'socialisation' over the whole dispute. For pharmacy owners in mid October, refusing to yield seemed to represent the entire effort of 'bourgeois' society to hold back the socialist tide. For pharmacy workers, who tried to absolve themselves from the blame for causing the population to suffer, the tactics of the owners seemed to reflect the unacceptable callousness of this same 'bourgeois' society towards the needs of ordinary Russians.

The biases involved in reporting this strike were neither especially surprising nor particularly distorting. The issue of who controlled the right to hire and fire workers was consistently mentioned by both sides as the most controversial of the strike demands. By autumn, this issue had become bitterly contested in a number of strikes. It had come to symbolise the primacy of the capitalist system in which employers disposed at their will of the commodity of labour. The liberal press, predictably, emphasised the fiscal problems of management, repeating that pharmacy owners faced 'financial ruin', the same term used by the Society of Owners itself. *Rech* took pains to point out in October that municipalisation of the shops would place them under military administration (the plan of the city duma), thus making the pharmacy workers 'military personnel'.

While the liberal press emphasised that the *strikers'* excesses were being reported to the city health authorities because they interfered with the dispensing of medicines, *Vpered* and especially *Novaia zhizn* emphasised the hostility of shop owners. The revolver attack, for example, was apparently not reported outside the socialist press. It was also on the left that the reports appeared about shop owners ignoring essential prescriptions in favour of non-essential ones as a way of aggravating tension.

For readers of *Rech* and *Birzhevye vedomosti*, this important strike was represented as the result of the employees pressing their own interests regardless of the degree of suffering they might inflict, but the implied danger was as much 'socialisation' by government decree as victory for the workers themselves. Taken together with a simultaneous movement in Moscow calling on the soviet to sequester those leather factories which rejected strike demands, one can readily understand how readers of the liberal press might have concluded that workers and government were both about to destroy the system of private property. For those reading *Den*, *Rabochaia gazeta*, *Edinstvo* and *Delo naroda*, on the other hand, the strike (or 'lockout', as *Rabochaia gazeta* described it on 17 October), was a clear indication that the rights of private ownership infringed the public welfare and that radical new solutions were needed.

WHO IS TO BLAME? PUBLIC CONSCIOUSNESS AND PUBLIC RELATIONS

The biases of the press in 1917 represent a complex interplay of interest and public relations. Three sets of interests served as the focus of strike reporting. The national and public interest was made paramount in the official point of view as illustrated in the strike of the pharmacy workers. Since this was the one strong bond that might have contained class antagonisms, editors of the moderate socialist press may have deliberately stressed the importance of mediation and the involvement of government agencies in the mediation process. On the other hand, strikes involved deep-seated class-related conflicts, and often harmed the public. When they did so, each side blamed the other for the broader injury. Newspapers associated with the contending groups did not need to distort the facts of strikes to make their case, and by and large they did not. Simply by representing their cause as a just one, they supported their side and deliberately or not, helped to undermine belief in the unified national interest they may have wanted to uphold.

At the same time, since strikes themselves syncretised the revolutionary experience of workers and constituted an important aspect of democratic labour–management negotiations, it is important to ask what this form of labour protest really meant, in fact, to its participants and opponents? Before the revolution, the costs of striking were the risk of repression (dismissal, arrest, exile, conscription) as well as the temporary loss of wages. The benefits, particularly in political-demonstrative strikes, were less tangible: expressing political views, challenging authority, memorialising past victims of the struggle, securing new allies by publicly risking repression and economic sacrifice. Generally, however, from the point of view of socialists and labour activists, strikes before the revolution were viewed positively; the revolutionary heritage signified that any salvo of solidarity fired against the Tsarist enemy was a heroic act.

With the fall of Tsarism the moral valuation of strikes became more complicated. Workers and their representatives, now much more a vital part of Russian society, were also more responsible for maintaining social order and securing effective social support. Democratic rights entailed democratic responsibilities. Like everything else, the cost of strikes consequently escalated in 1917: a work stoppage was seen to harm not the Tsar or even individual capitalist profiteers, but the entire economy, now ostensibly under democratic control. A dual valuation of strikes and their consequences thus emerged in the process of the February revolution. For many members of the 'democracy', workers and intellectual revolutionaries alike, strikes in 1917 could be seen as negative, harmful phenomena, or at best, as a costly but necessary tactic. Strikes stopped production, harmed the war effort in general, and endangered the safety of ordinary peasant-soldiers in particular. Halts in production contributed to economic shortages that rippled through the entire economy, disrupting transport and agriculture as well as manufacture; ultimately they harmed workers. As a result, workers and capitalists had common interests; and these constituted an important basis of support for the régime of dual power, for the consensus that the new order included a 'bourgeois democratic' system of industrial relations, in which workers and the labour movement were equal but not dominant partners.

But there existed side by side with this negative assessment an important legacy of the past. Even while curtailing production, strikes also symbolised the freedom which workers had won with the February revolution, and for some the withdrawal of labour was justified under any circumstances because it both demonstrated and strengthened the autonomy, cohesion and hence the interests of an aggregated working class. This view was expressed by a Bolshevik trade-union activist in June, who said, 'On the basis of the experience which we have had in the course of three years of war – as the basis of all that we see, we have come to the conclusion, that the single serious revolutionary method is the strike.'[34]

Both positive and negative views of strikes found expression in 1917, but the negative view seemed to dominate in the months after the fall of the Tsar. A new moral valuation can be observed in the rhetoric of a wide range of contemporary activists, an ethic that perceived the deliberate withdrawal of labour as harmful, improper, inefficacious, a form of leverage and protest to be used as seldom as possible and only under the most extreme conditions. This point of view was crystallised, for example, in the programmatic statements of the trade-union movement. At the All-Russian Conference of Trade Unions in June, almost all the activists, regardless of political party, coalesced in their views of the strike movement. First, the strike as a weapon was a sacrosanct *symbol* of the trade-union and labour movement; it symbolised the revolutionary heritage of the Russian workers, their readiness to confront capital. Second, the strike was seen as an important agitational and organisational tool. Third, however, nearly all speakers agreed that the strike should be used carefully and selectively.[35] 'Under the present critical conditions', argued Lozovskii, who would become leader of the trade-union movement after October, 'when the fate of the Russian revolution depends upon skilful, organised, unswerving and mobilised [*splochennye*] assaults by workers – at this time, for every strike, for every assault, we must be governed by the principle, "measure thy cloth seven times, since thou canst cut it only once".'[36] Strikes were to be the weapon of last resort, after peaceful methods of conflict resolution (those that did not involve the cessation of work) had failed.

The majority view of the trade-union movement on the moral inutility of strikes reflected the prevailing Menshevik conception of industrial relations in 1917, at least among the defencists. A number of leading Mensheviks, both in and out of government institutions, placed great faith in the principle of arbitration as a way of avoiding work stoppages, something they felt both workers and management wished to achieve.[37] 'In any case', argued the Menshevik, Koltsov, 'any strike, any successful action, in the final analysis is settled by peaceful negotiation. In well-known cases trade unions have found it advantageous to conclude a peaceful agreement at the start, before a strike begins.'[38] When arbitration failed to ameliorate labour unrest, Mensheviks turned to another means of resolving conflicts without resorting to work stoppages, that of government intervention and the regulation of the economy.[39]

Regulation, or *kontrol*, as an alternative to isolated and individual work stoppages, was also central to Lenin's vision of industrial relations in 1917 and, by extension, to the perspective of the Bolshevik party leadership as a whole. One looks in vain in Lenin's writings in 1917 for any positive assessment of strikes as a revolutionary tool. Despite his earlier enthusiasm about the revolutionary significance of strike waves in 1905, Lenin apparently discounted the strike tactic in 1917, as he seems to have discounted every aspect of industrial relations, be it negotiations, arbitration boards or strikes. Strikes against the *government* – railway and postal strikes in September – interested Lenin, and he certainly understood strikes on the whole as indicators of generalised worker discontent (of which he wrote frequently in 1917); but he assigned no positive role to strikes as a means of reconciling the conflicting goals of labour and management, and unless strikes were well organised and effective, they could also fragment radical energies and commitments.

For Lenin and many other Bolsheviks, these goals could not be reconciled; economic security for the workers could not be gained by bargaining, but only by regulation of the economic apparatus by a proletarian government. Hence the workers were urged not to allow themselves to be provoked into laying down their tools: 'The proletariat should not succumb to the provocations of the bourgeoisie, who very much desire at the present time to incite workers to a premature fight.'[40] Far better in the view of many Bolsheviks that workers *seize* factories rather than shut them down, and create a basis in action for taking the revolution forward.

The value of production and the importance of work itself was also a common theme running through both Menshevik and Bolshevik views about strikes, a theme which echoed in numerous assessments of the grassroots movement for workers' control.[41] Bolshevik warnings against workers being provoked into strikes were, in part, rooted in concern about worker welfare, and the fear that strikes would weaken the workers themselves by denying them wages and isolating them from their allies in the army and elsewhere. Many Mensheviks, on the other hand, urged workers to seek peaceful arbitration because damage to the economy jeopardised the stability of the new revolutionary order and only paved the way for extremists on the right or the left. The Bolsheviks and the moderate socialists thus differed not on the unsuitability of work stoppages, but on the alternatives to them.

Understanding that many activists and rank-and-file workers agreed that work stoppages were morally reprehensible, we can recognise that an essential element in strike reporting was to justify to a broader public the necessity, the unavoidability, of laying down tools. And in most cases this meant placing the blame for this anti-social act on the capitalists. The striking pharmacy employees embarked on their walkout 'not with easy hearts . . . They applied all their strength to end the dispute by peaceful means . . . It was not the employees but the proprietors who refused to submit to the decisions of a [conciliation] chamber, when they saw it would go against them.'[42] Similarly the appeal of the striking paper workers:

> Comrades and Citizens! The irresponsibility of the capitalists, and our difficult hopeless conditions, the complete indifference of entrepreneurs to the ever-growing high cost of living, so difficult for workers, and the impossibility of obtaining an improvement in our economic situation by other more peaceful methods without the introduction of a strike – have forced us, workers in paper-manufacturing factories, to this ultimate method of struggle.[43]

The Petrograd print workers likewise instructed their union to make it clear to the public that their strike could have been avoided without the provocation of the owners' association, and that the workers were not the guilty party.[44] Strikers repeatedly stressed that the immediate cause of strikes was action by management: refusing to meet demands, dismissing individual workers or their elected representatives, refusing to negotiate, reneging on previous agreements. Whether from conviction or in order to appeal for public understanding and support, workers were thus blaming the capitalists themselves for violating the conventions of bourgeois industrial relations.

The same line was to be found not only in specific strike reports, which usually emanated from the pens of the local trade-union organisers, but also in more general discussions. For example, *Rabochaia gazeta*, the leading Menshevik paper, published an editorial about the coming economic catastrophe on 19 May under the heading, 'Who Is To Blame?'. If, as the liberal minister Konovalov argued, it was workers' excessive demands that were causing economic dislocation, then the solution was government wage and price regulation, not the spiralling cycle of strikes. But if the government failed to impose such regulation, the editorial implied, how could the workers be blamed for seeking to keep up with the cost of living? The following day *Rabochaia gazeta* became even more pointed: industrialists 'had declared war' on the workers. Owners themselves were waging 'Italian strikes' – refusing to repair factories, or to renew the reserves of oil and other raw materials. The paper implied that workers were being forced to strike in order to exert any pressure at all. Industrialists then castigated the strikers for 'excessive wage demands', shutting down their plants, and blaming the workers as a whole for the growing economic crisis.[45]

Indeed, the overall tenor of these reports was to emphasise how reasonable, moderate and public spirited the behaviour of the workers was. Hence, the appeals to comrades *and* citizens, the apologetic tone in which many strike reports were couched. Strikers were represented as Russians, as citizens of the republic, not just as a special and distinct class. But ominously, the very shifting of blame, the assignment of guilt to other parties – owners and industrialists – exemplified and ultimately intensified the underlying antagonistic nature of industrial relations in 1917.

Both the ways in which strikes were reported, then, and the strike process itself clearly served to consolidate the workers, on the one hand, and the businessmen and industrialists, on the other, into broader and more powerful class aggregates – classes which were defined in large measure primarily by their opposition to one another, their conflictual interactions. The continued appeals of both groups to some vague and uncommitted public suggests that those who spoke did not perceive society exclusively in class terms. But the language of these appeals and the lessons to be learned from the subtle but consistent variations in strike reporting clearly helped to consolidate class formation and intensify class conflict. The act of striking in 1917 thus came not only to reflect deepening processes of social polarisation, but, especially in the way strikes were represented and perceived, helped to create and consolidate those cleavages.

NOTES

1 This is a minimum estimate based on our own collation of the strike reports in contemporary newspapers, published document collections and unpublished archives. A complete discussion of the data and our methodology may be found in our book, *Strikes and Revolution in Russia, 1917* (Princeton, 1989).

2 Edward Shorter and Charles Tilly, *Strikes in France, 1830–1968* (Cambridge, 1974); James E. Cronin, *Industrial Conflict in Modern Britain* (London, 1979); P.K. Edwards, *Strikes in the United States, 1881–1974* (Oxford, 1981).

3 See Alfred J. Rieber, *Merchants and Entrepreneurs in Imperial Russia* (Chapel Hill, 1982), esp. ch. 9.

4 We include among conservative or 'right-wing' newspapers *Russkaia volia* and *Utro Rossii*: among 'moderate liberal': *Rech, Birzhevye vedomosti, Russkie vedomosti, Torgovo-promyshlennaia gazeta, Russkoe slovo* and the so-called 'boulevard' press; among 'moderate socialist' papers, the press of the Menshevik, Socialist Revolutionary and Popular Socialist parties, as well as publications of the soviets: *Rabochaia gazeta, Den, Vpered, Delo naroda, Trud, Zemlia i volia* (Petrograd and Moscow), *Volia naroda, Novaia zhizn, Proletarii* (Moscow), *Vlast naroda, Vpered, Edinstvo, Narodnoe slovo, Izvestiia petrogradskogo soveta rabochikh deputatov, Izvestiia moskovskogo soveta rabochikh deputatov* (Hereafter *Isvestiia MSRD*); on the 'Left' the Bolshevik press: *Pravda, Proletarii, Rabochii put* (Petrograd) and *Sotsial-Demokrat* (Moscow). We include the Menshevik-Internationalist press (*Novaia zhizn, Proletarii* (Moscow)) with the moderate socialists because on issues of labour relations their line was generally conciliatory, like that of the mainstream Mensheviks.

5 On the 'kopeck' press, see Jeffrey Brooks, *When Russia Learned To Read: Literacy and Popular Literature, 1861–1917* (Princeton, 1985), ch. 4, and Jeffrey Brooks, 'The Breakdown in Production and Distribution of Printed Material, 1917–1927', in Abbott Gleason, Peter Kenez and Richard Stites (eds.), *Bolshevik Culture* (Bloomington, 1985), pp. 151–74.

6 *Russkaia volia* (3 May 1917).

7 *Russkaia volia* (25 May 1917).

8 See e.g. *Russkie vedomosti* (24 May 1917).

9 *Birzhevye vedomosti* (24, 25 June and esp. 28 June 1917).

10 Compare e.g. *Rech* (21–28 June 1917); *Birzhevye vedomosti* (2 July 1917); *Vpered* (22 June 1917 *et seq.*); *Novaia zhizn* (23 June 1917 *et seq.*).

11 *Russkoe slovo* (4 June 1917).

12 Ibid. (4 June 1917).

13 Ibid. (5 August 1917). The actual figures were 15 per cent increase offered versus 43 per cent demanded. See *Izvestiia MSRD* (6 August 1917).

14 See *Novaia zhizn* (13 May 1917); *Delo naroda* (13 May 1917).

15 Strike reports were collected from each of the newspapers cited in note 4 above, and each strike record includes the source and its political or institutional affiliation. But in cases where two different sources provided identical information (which sometimes happened when the common source of the strike report was a factory or trade-union communication), only one source was recorded. We assume therefore that our counts are somewhat underestimated, but not by much, and that the relative proportions indicated here are reasonably accurate.

16 *Volia naroda* (29 September 1917).

17 *Edinstvo* (19 July 1917).

18 The frequencies are low but progress precisely according to expectations. Violence is mentioned in 1.9 per cent of Bolshevik reports (and three of these five cite violence against workers), 2.7 per cent of moderate socialist reports (two of thirty-six cite violence against workers), 3.2 per cent of moderate liberal reports, and 4.1 per cent of right-wing press reports.

19 For a further elaboration of the notion of 'routine' bourgeois social relations, see William G. Rosenberg and Diane P. Koenker, 'The Limits of Formal Protest: Worker Activism and Social Polarisation in Petrograd and Moscow, March to October, 1917', *American Historical Review* (April 1987), 296–326.

20 Peter Kenez, *The Birth of the Propaganda State: Soviet Methods of Mass Mobilization, 1917–1929* (Cambridge, 1985), pp. 34–5.

21 Some 12 per cent of all strike reports in the moderate socialist press, and 11 per cent of liberal reports included mention of the presence of government or conciliation board mediation; the Bolsheviks included such information less than half as frequently, in only 5 per cent of their reports.

22 *Pravda* had long accounts, for example, in its issues of 20, 23, 25, 27, 29, 30 May and 1, 3, 8 and 13 June, as well as other, less lengthy reports. See also the comments on this strike and the role in it of Alexandra Kollontai in N. Sukhanov, *Zapiski o revoliutsii*, vol. IV (Berlin, 1922), pp. 143–4.

23 See e.g. *Pravda* (1, 2, 7, 8–13 June 1917).

24 See e.g. *Pravda*'s report on the Petrograd coopers' strike on 11 July 1917, among many others.

25 *Novaia zhizn* (20 July 1917).

26 *Russkaia volia* (6 August 1917).

27 *Rabochaia gazeta* (28 September 1917).

28 *Pravda* (13 June 1917).

29 *Rabochaia gazeta* (15 June 1917).

30 Ibid. (25 April 1917).

31 *Pravda* (9 May 1917) (new style); see also *Novaia zhizn* (25 and 26 April 1917).

32 *Delo naroda* (10 October 1917).

33 *Rabochaia gazeta* (7 October 1917).

34 A.M. Bakhutov, in *Tretiia Vserossiiskaia konferentsiia professionalnykh soiuzov, 1917*, edited by Diane Koenker (Millwood, 1982), p. 253.

35 See the speeches of D.A. Koltsov, in *Tretii Vserossiiskaia konferentsiia professionalnykh soiuzov*, pp. 243–4, and of Lozovskii, pp. 255–6.

36 Ibid., p. 256.

37 Ziva Galili y Garcia, *The Menshevik Leaders of the Petrograd Soviet: Social Realities and Political Strategies, February–October 1917* (Princeton, 1989).

38 *Tretiia Vserossiiskaia*, p. 245.

39 Galili y Garcia, *The Menshevik Leaders*, ch. 5.

40 *Protokoly Shestogo sezda RSDRP(b). Avgust 1917 g.* (Moscow, 1934), p. 233. The alignment of opinion on the issue of strikes at the Sixth Congress,

which Lenin did not attend, is extremely interesting. Miliutin, a trade unionist who would later resign from the Central Committee to protest at the party's refusal to share power after October, argued in favour of utilising the strike wave to further politicise and radicalise the workers (pp. 147–8). Osinskii, later to become a member of the Workers' Opposition, countered that the current economic situation meant strikes could too easily lead to lockouts and that they should not be encouraged (p. 153). The Congress adopted a resolution based on Osinskii's position, but when someone suggested a change in the wording, from 'premature fight' (*boi*) to 'premature action' (*vystuplenie*), Stalin, as chairman, ruled that the latter wording would be too restrictive and could be interpreted as discouraging all demonstrations and strikes (pp. 233–4).

41 This may come as a surprise to the numerous commentators who have described the Russian worker as supremely lazy; although, on the other hand, the gap between official values and reality in the labour movement was undoubtedly wide. Nonetheless, our goal here is to explain official reporting in terms of these official values which were expounded in order to provide models for workers to follow. In any case, a study of the 'work ethic' in Russian working-class consciousness, before and after 1917, might provide some interesting perspectives.

42 *Rabochaia gazeta* (25 April 1917), pp. 2–3.

43 Ibid. (20 September 1917).

44 Ibid. (15 August 1917).

45 Ibid. (20 May 1917).

8

OCTOBER IN THE IVANOVO-KINESHMA
INDUSTRIAL REGION

DAVID MANDEL

THE Ivanovo-Kineshma textile region was located 250 kilometres
northeast of Moscow. It embraced the three southeastern districts
of Kostroma province and the three north-central districts of Vladimir
province. In 1917, approximately 150,000 factory workers were
employed in the region, 93 per cent of these in the cotton industry.[1]

The region's workers were known for their militancy and almost
exclusive allegiance to Bolshevism. This they displayed on numerous
occasions in elections – to the State Duma before the war; and to the
soviets, factory committees, trade unions, local governments and the
Constituent Assembly in 1917.[2] Not even among the skilled metal-
workers of Petrograd's 'red Vyborg' district, did the Bolsheviks enjoy
such unshakable hegemony.

Such radicalism was unusual in Russia's textile industry, in which
the workers were characterised by a low literacy rate, low wages and
skills, a predominance of women and significant ties with the land.[3]
But other traits, peculiar to the workers of the Ivanovo-Kineshma
region, fostered a strong class-consciousness and opposition to the
propertied classes and their political parties.

According to the industrial census of 1918, an average of 825 workers worked in each of the region's factories, as opposed to 388 in
Petrograd and 176 in Moscow. This was the highest concentration in
the whole of Russia.[4] Socially, these workers were a remarkably homogeneous group: almost all were unskilled, low-paid textile workers,
recruited from the local and adjacent districts. A significant proportion owned land (36 per cent according to the 1918 census), but one-
third were at least second-generation factory workers, and almost two-
thirds had been employed in factory work since before the war. Even
among those who owned land, factory wages were the main source of
income. Many workers clung to their villages although the rural

157

economy there had all but died, because housing at the mills was scarce.[5]

But it was especially the combination of these traits with one other – the extreme polarisation of local society – that accounts for Bolshevik strength. Typical of the region were the 'mill villages', settlements of an urban character that had grown up in the villages surrounding the mills. Sereda, a town of 16,659 inhabitants, which as early as the eighteenth century had been known as a prosperous trading village, was the site of three large textile mills employing 12,000 workers. For three-quarters of these, Sereda was the sole and permanent place of residence. Ivanovo-Voznesensk, the largest town in the region, was itself, in fact, only the largest 'mill village', one that had grown into a city of 85,000 inhabitants.[6] Virtually absent here was the intermediate social stratum, the so-called 'third element' that consisted of employees of local government and members of the liberal professions. Educated society here, what little there was of it, was closely tied to capital, both economically and politically, and so hostile to the labour movement. This had always been the case, even during the 1905 revolution. As for socialist intellectuals who might venture in from the outside, they were easily picked out in this homogeneous social milieu and soon arrested.[7]

The mill owners were for the most part descendants of local peasants. They lived in the region (but usually had second homes in Moscow) and until the revolution held the reins of local power firmly in their hands. 'Nowhere have I seen so naked and blatant a contrast between misery and luxury', recalled a Bolshevik visitor to Ivanovo in 1907. 'Without any camouflage, without any intermediate strata, the two sides stood facing each other: labour and capital. It was more than clear why we Bolsheviks, though we had scarcely any organisation, did not have any competition from the Mensheviks or SRs.'[8]

In contrast to the situation in the capitals, the workers here did not immediately perceive the October revolution and the transfer of power in the capital as a watershed. The first collective agreement signed here did not include 25 October in the list of holidays, although the 'Day of the Revolution', 27 February, figured prominently.[9]

In part, this was because the workers in this region had already held *de facto* power since well before October. In almost all the industrial centres, the Bolsheviks had long since won majorities in the soviets, and the soviets controlled the only armed forces – the garrisons and the Red Guards.[10] In a number of places, following elections by universal suffrage to the organs of local self-government (dumas and zemstvos) towards the beginning of September, the Bolsheviks won power *de jure* also. In Ivanovo-Voznesensk, they received 56.5 per cent of the vote. They also won majorities in elections in the city and district of Shuia, the district of Iurevets, the town of Rodniki, as well as in many smaller rural districts (*volosti*). In other local governments, the Bolsheviks formed large minorities.[11]

The Provisional Government was without influence in the region. A meeting of the Society of Factory and Mills Owners in October discussed reports of workers' organisations' requisitioning food, stopping the shipment of goods and even replacing managerial personnel. The society took note of the widespread régime of 'seizures, violence and arbitrariness that is encouraged by the powerlessness of the central and local legal authorities'.[12]

But the transfer of power in Petrograd was also not perceived as a watershed because it had little immediate practical relevance to the workers' most urgent concern – a living wage. Their economic situation was desperate. Wages here had always been among the lowest in Russia and the raises won following the February revolution had long since been eaten up by inflation. But although the workers held effective political power, there was no way they could use it to wring a living wage out of mill owners who would rather shut their mills than make concessions – unless the workers were prepared to accept the eventuality of managing the mills themselves. In October, they were still not ready to face this.

As for the owners, they were fast losing their interest in production. By the beginning of September, twelve large mills employing 30,000 workers had been shut, and the number of unemployed was growing daily.[13] The owners cited shortages of fuel and materials, but the workers accused them of malicious negligence, and their own organisations moved in to fill the void left by management. Swift action by the Ivanovo-Voznesensk Soviet, for example, had allowed the town's mills, in danger of closing, to quadruple their fuel supply. Commenting on the situation, the executive of the soviet noted:

> It has reached the point where the entire region's production is being stopped, while wagons and tankers stand idle on sidings for months at a time awaiting repairs that should take no more than a few days. This shows the industrialists' desire to disorganise production, and, by stopping the mills, to crush the entire organisation of our democracy.[14]

Nor was this opinion limited to the workers' organisations. The Factory Conference of the Moscow Industrial Region, a governmental body, pointed to the 'deliberate refusal of the owners of industrial enterprises to pursue production in the factories and mills, even when the Factory Conference established the possibility of doing so'.[15]

For these reasons, the October revolution in the Ivanovo-Kineshma region took the form of a general strike for a minimum wage tied to the cost of living. During the strike the workers did indeed seize the mills – not to run them, but to prevent sabotage by the owners. The news of the October insurrection in Petrograd was greeted with enthusiasm by the region's workers. They themselves began calling for action of this kind soon after the February revolution. The Teikovo Soviet of Workers' Deputies (representing the 6,000 workers of the Karetnikova Mill) passed such a resolution on 24 April, two months before the workers' section of the Petrograd Soviet, in response to the note of the Foreign Minister, Miliukov, to the allies expressing the Provisional Government's intention to honour the annexationist treaties signed by the Tsar. The workers' deputies vowed by their 'fraternal blood to come out to aid the Petrograd and Moscow Soviets at their first call'.[16] The soviets and the other workers' organisations of Ivanovo-Voznesensk and all other industrial centres soon followed suit.[17]

Here there was none of the *attentisme* that characterised broad segments of the working class in Petrograd on the eve of the insurrection. Largely because of this mood in the capital, the Bolshevik leaders (though not Lenin) linked the coming insurrection to the Soviet Congress and spoke of it as a defensive measure to defend the Congress against an inevitable attack by the Provisional Government, that would not passively accept a vote by the Congress to take power.[18] In contrast, workers' resolutions in the Ivanovo-Kineshma region in the weeks preceding the October revolution rarely mentioned the Soviet Congress at all when they demanded soviet power 'at once'.[19] The mood here was one of impatience, with workers accusing the Bolsheviks of indecision.[20] Shortly before October, the Bolshevik, I.V. Beliaev, reporting to the Kineshma Soviet on his recent trip to Petrograd, concluded: 'History calls on us to take power . . . Are we ready?' 'We have been ready for a long time now', retorted someone from the hall, 'but we don't know why they are still asleep in the centre.'[21]

The hesitation in October in Petrograd was deeply influenced by the experience of the July Days that had ended in bloodshed and the onset of political reaction. The Ivanovo-Kineshma region had had its July

Days too (during which the Ivanovo Soviet seized key institutions), but they had been entirely peaceful and left the local political situation unchanged. As in the capital, the local Bolsheviks were accused by non-soviet organisations (united in the Executive Committee of Public Organisations) of attempting to seize power. The executive of the Ivanovo Soviet, to clear its name, even agreed to cooperate in an inquiry into the events. But this was firmly vetoed by the general assembly of soviet delegates, who affirmed that they were responsible solely to the Central Executive Committee of Soviets in Petrograd and owed no one apologies. The assembly then proceeded to elect a new executive.[22] More important, perhaps, the workers here did not share their Petrograd comrades' fear of political isolation from moderate socialists and democratic intelligentsia that would inevitably result from the soviet seizure of power. Workers in the Ivanovo-Kineshma region had no experience of cooperation with these elements and so could scarcely fear their alienation.

Frunze, chairman of the Shuia Soviet and municipal government, summed up the pre-October mood in the following manner:

> The mood everywhere, especially among the workers and soldiers, was strongly revolutionary. The soviets felt their strength and acted in the consciousness of the absolute inevitability of the final transfer of power to the toilers in the whole republic. Everyone lived in the expectation of a signal from the centre. But as time passed and it did not come, the movement here and in the entire Vladimir province soon began to overflow its banks.[23]

Besides the threat of counter-revolution, the continuing war, and the threat to production posed by the deepening economic dislocation, it was especially the deterioration of the food situation in September and October that was driving the movement 'over its banks'. On 4 September, a meeting of the workers of the F. Garelin Mill in Ivanovo demanded that the government send grain at once, 'since we workers are on the eve of a hungry death and no longer have the strength to work for lack of food'.[24] The local paper reported cases of workers falling on the road from exhaustion.[25] On 8 September, the Ivanovo-Voznesensk food authority informed the government that the city's population was starving and the mills would soon have to stop, unless fifty wagons of grain arrived in the next few days.[26]

On 20 and 21 September, the Ivanovo Soviet heard reports from the mills. The delegates described the workers' distress, their discontent with the soviet and the food authority, and warned that the workers' desperation was pushing them into the streets.[27] In an effort to channel this discontent, the soviet decided to call a demonstration for 23 September under the slogans 'All power to the Soviets' and 'Peace, Bread and Jobs'. In its resolution, the soviet took note of the spontaneous movement that was being provoked by hunger, low wages and the general economic disorganisation that was leading to the closure of the mills. It accused the owners of not taking measures to maintain productivity and of refusing to deal with the workers' organisations, and concluded with the observation that the solution to all these local problems was linked to the general situation in the country, and that could not be improved until the soviet replaced the present form of government.[28]

Demonstrations took place in all the industrial centres of the region. At meetings, the workers were told that the economic crisis could not be seriously tackled until the war ended and the bourgeoisie was removed from power. In Ivanovo, after the meetings, the workers gathered before the duma, where they greeted the new Bolshevik mayor and executive. But the food situation did not improve, and still nothing happened in Petrograd. On 2 October, several women workers of the N. Garelina Mill went to the mill committee to demand bread. Soon the whole mill was gathered in the yard. Some speakers criticised the Food Authority, mill committee and other public organisations, calling for 'active operations' against the authority. In the meantime, other workers had summoned representatives of the soviet executive and the Food Authority, who with great difficulty persuaded the workers to go back to work.[29] Such incidents were frequent. On 3 October, the executive of the Ivanovo Soviet noted that 'the situation has become so tense that it is impossible to guarantee order'. As an emergency measure, it decided to authorise searches where there was some evidence of hoarding. Again it telegraphed Petrograd for food, but also began its own negotiations with the railway for help in shipping cloth, to be traded with other regions for food.[30]

The next day, delegates from the Ivanovo mills met to discuss the food crisis. The town's two big grain merchants, Latyshev and Kurazhev, had also been invited. The workers expressed their frustration by letting Latyshev chair the meeting. When the soviet representative told them that there was no hope of obtaining flour in the next few days, the meeting exploded with anger directed at the soviet and mill committees. Seeing an opening, the merchants offered to organise food distribution, if they were freed from the tutelage of the various committees. But other speakers took the floor and eventually turned the mood around, explaining, once again, that the root cause of the crisis was the war and the policies of the Provisional Government. The meeting then elected a new praesidium and voted a series of concrete measures, including the organisation of a special collective, consisting of two delegates from each mill, within the Food Authority, whose task it would be to keep the workers informed and to send people to the points of collection to see the difficulties themselves. The meeting concluded with the vow 'to struggle against ignorance and to defend with might and main our workers' organisations'.[31]

This sort of incident was to become common over the next three years of chronic food crisis. The Bolsheviks' ability to retain worker support, shaky though it often became, was remarkable. Yet the workers had not come originally in 1917 to support soviet power and the Bolsheviks because of hunger, ·and hunger in itself was not, apparently, a sufficient cause for the workers to abandon them. Reports at a Bolshevik conference in the Kineshma district in late September all confirmed the strength of Bolshevik influence, while noting that party 'work had been more intense before the food crisis – the food crisis distracts the masses'.[32] The delegate from Teikovo to the conference of soviets of the Shuia district, reported that 'the soviet has always been equal to the situation, and the workers believe in its strength. But the food crisis complicates the soviet's work.' From Kokhma: 'The soviet's situation is stable, but its work comes up against the same wall: the food and economic crisis.' And Zimenki: 'The soviet is the leader and sole authority in the area. But the food question is acute.'[33]

It was in these circumstances that the Ivanovo-Kenishma Regional Union of Textile Workers prepared to present its demands to the mill owners. This was the culmination of a process initiated in April that, it was hoped, would lead to a region-wide collective agreement based upon the principle of a minimum living wage tied to the cost of living, a principle that reflected the interests of this basically unskilled, homogeneous work force.

The region had witnessed a massive economic strike movement on the eve of the February revolution. But it yielded little for the workers, and immediately after returning to their mills following the revolutionary days, they presented their wage demands to the management. The owners, having been suddenly deprived of the support of the Tsarist state, were generally in a conciliatory mood. But the concessions were unequal across the region, and a regional conference of soviets was called on 4–6 April to decide on a common set of demands. These included the eight-hour day, a wage rise and a single payment equal to 20 per cent of the total wage paid between Easter 1916 and Easter 1917. A meeting between the workers' and owners' delegates in Moscow on 10–12 May ended in a deadlock over the modalities of introducing the eight-hour day and over the size of the wage package – the owners' offer was 35–40 per cent below the workers' demand. When the owners declared that they would implement their offer unilaterally, the workers' side walked out. At a meeting afterwards, they decided to allow the owners to go ahead (thus doubling the basic wage), but not to yield on the workers' demands. But since the workers were not yet organised and economic dislocation threatened the very existence of the mills, they would first set up a regional union and ensure that the mills were adequately supplied before joining battle. The workers at the mills, when presented with this plan, endorsed it fully.[34]

The regional union was officially founded at a delegates' conference on 10–12 June. By that time, about a third of the work-force had been organised. The conference decided to continue the organisational campaign and to collect data from the mills on the movement of prices and wages since the start of the war, as well as on the workers' budgets. These data were to be the basis for calculating the minimum living wage.[35] The survey, concluded in August, found that wages had risen 300–600 per cent since the start of the war, while prices had shot up 600 to 1,200 per cent. The minimum subsistence wage for *both men and women* (something that broke with the owners' traditional practice) was calculated at 7.53 roubles a day. This was based upon a budget that allocated 52 per cent for food, 27 per cent for clothing and foot-wear, and 21 per cent for hygiene, culture, tobacco and other extras.

The delegates' conference on 12–15 August discussed these demands and noted that the atmosphere was heavy with the threat of a mass strike, and that the workers were eager for it. All agreed, however, that the struggle would be much harder than in the spring, since the owners had recovered from their initial shock. They were better organised than the workers and felt confident, hurling chal-lenges at the workers: refusing now to pay for idle time due to stop-pages and ignoring the factory committees. The conference gave the executive a strike mandate, after which the demands were taken back to the mills for approval or amendment. The rank and file strongly supported the union's position and, with a few exceptions, heeded its calls to refrain from isolated strikes.[36] On 11–12 October, a joint conference of union delegates and representatives of the soviets and

16. Love at Close Quarters
The worker says to the bourgeois intellectual: 'See how tenderly
I love you! There's no need for any words.'

councils of factory committees decided to present the demands on 13
October, giving the owners until the 18th to respond. In the eventuality of a negative reply, an (all-male) strike committee was elected.[37]

Besides wages, the other main demands were an eight-hour day (six
hours on the eve of holidays); four weeks' pregnancy leave and six
weeks' maternity leave; two weeks' annual paid vacation; owner-
financed and worker-managed medical care; cultural facilities,
crèches, kindergartens and playgrounds; an end to fines and searches;
payment for idle time; hiring and firing only with union agreement;

and access to information on fuel and raw-material supplies. There was also a long list of demands concerning health and safety conditions, housing, washing facilities and limits to the number of machines tended by various types of worker.[38]

No reply came on 18 October and the union issued its Order no. 1 to begin the strike on the 21st. The mood in the mills was militant and eager.[39] A similar textile strike in Moscow was called off in view of the impending transfer of power, and in Petrograd strikes in general had been rare since the late summer for the same reason.[40] But the question of power presented itself differently here: in practice, it had already been settled. It was characteristic that Order no. 1 did not even make a passing reference to the issue of power. Rather, it gave a history of the economic conflict leading to the strike and set out the goals. All of these, too, were economic. But the local workers did not accept the liberal distinction between the economic and political when it came to their basic rights. And a living wage was regarded as fundamental.[41]

The owners had apparently sent a reply by post on 16 October, but for reasons that are unclear, it only arrived on 25 October. However, on the 19th, the union did receive a telegram from the owners asking for a reply to their letter. Since this had not been received, the union decided to proceed with the strike. When, on the 21st, a second copy of the owners' letter finally arrived, proposing to meet in Moscow in an arbitration committee with equal representation from both sides, the union executive replied by telegram: 'We can start talks in Ivanovo, if you accept our subsistence minimum of seven and a half roubles.'[42]

The union issued the following declaration to the citizens of the region:

> The victims of need are taking action to improve their lot: better wages, living, sanitary and technical conditions of work ... In some mills the workers' wages are at the starvation level ... It is not surprising then that the workers, prodded by the bony hand of hunger, went to the capitalists for a raise. But this remained a voice calling in the wilderness. 'The workers have gone too far. They are ruining industry.' This was heard from all sides. The petty-bourgeois philistine also opposed the workers. He thought they were seeking paradise on earth ... We want to live like people. We can no longer live never eating and drinking our fill, dressing in rags, without boots, so that the capitalists can dress in silk and velvet, wear gold, eat sweetly, sleep a lot and make merry. We are asking for what we need, without which a person does not live but beats like a fish on the ice ... From this table [a worker's budget], you can see clearly how modest our demands are ... We

> are staking our existence and we will fight our merciless opponent
> with all the means the organised workers have at their disposal.
> We believe firmly that any reasonable person will understand that
> we have no other way out, that we have a right to take this
> action.[43]

As expected, the workers, even in the farthest backwaters of the
region, responded enthusiastically. Their reaction also showed clearly
the political underpinning of this economic strike. In this connection,
it is worth noting that, on the eve of the strike, the Ivanovo Soviet
established a Red Guard command, consisting of a member of its
executive, the commander of the Red Guard, and one representative of
each of the socialist parties. It declared that henceforth all soviets in
the province of Vladimir were 'in a state of open warfare with the
Provisional Government'. They were to regulate the life of their localities on their own authority, 'adhering strictly to the interests of the
toiling masses'.[44] In fact, this declaration merely formalised the existing state of affairs in the industrial centres and it therefore had no
noticeable effect.

In Ivanovo, the mills came to a stop at 10 a.m. on 23 October. The
workers formed into columns behind red banners and, singing revolutionary songs, marched to the central square. The banners bore mostly
economic demands, but some demanded 'All Power to the Soviets' and
'Down with the Provisional Government'. In the town of Shuia with
its large garrison, soldiers, in full battledress, also took part in the
demonstration. Addressing the crowd, Frunze told it that the Provisional Government was incapable of dealing with the fast approaching
economic calamity. Nor was it capable of adopting decisive policies in
the interests of the popular classes. The only hope in the coming crisis
was to transfer power to the soviets in the centre and in the localities.[45]

At once, the strike committees took control of the mills, setting up
armed pickets at the gates. No one and nothing could enter or leave
without written authorisation of the factory committee.[46] As was their
custom in times of serious unrest, most owners had already retreated
to Moscow. But those who remained found themselves subject to a
'state of siege', their homes guarded by armed workers, who demanded passes from the owners and their family members when they
wanted to leave the area. In the village of Vakhromeevo, about seventeen kilometres from Ivanovo, the workers carried matters rather far.
The owner ran out of food and wanted to slaughter a cow, but the
factory committee refused permission, seeing that the cow was part of
the mill's inventory and was therefore the property of the entire work-

ing class. Matters were soon set straight by a member of the union executive, who was passing through. But at the Garelin Mill, the owner's wife became hysterical, when the mill committee refused to give her access to the factory cashbox.[47]

On 23 October, the Society of Mill Owners of the Shuia region decided to post announcements informing the workers of their readiness to raise wages and negotiate, hoping to undermine support for the union. But it wisely decided not to post the declaration of the Moscow-centred Union of United Industry, which threatened to fire all workers not reporting for work within three days. It was felt that this might 'irritate the masses'.[48] The non-socialist press, giving full vent to its imagination, reported on the anarchy in the mills and claimed that the strike had taken the workers by surprise. They accused the union of needlessly disrupting production and causing the ruin of the industry. The union replied with a call 'to boycott the bourgeois press'. All this had little effect on the workers' resolve.[49]

On 24 October, the Minister of Labour invited the union to come to Petrograd to discuss ways of resolving the conflict. The union replied that since the strike was in the Ivanovo-Kineshma region, it would make more sense for the minister to come there.[50] In any case, the Provisional Government was overthrown the next day. According to Frunze, the transfer of power in the capital went almost unnoticed here. 'It was accepted as something completely self-evident and inevitable.'[51] 'In a city such as Ivanovo-Voznesensk', recalled V. Kuznetsov, the Ivanovo Soviet's first chairman, 'we had nothing to overthrow ... We contacted Shuia, Kineshma, Teikovo and other worker settlements. Everywhere – quiet, calm, restraint. February and October were two such quiet months – it was surprising.'[52] The only active resistance in the industrial centres came from the state employees, and this was a minor affair.

The Ivanovo Soviet was in session on 25 October, when D. Furmanov (then an SR Maximalist) reported the news, received by telephone, that the Provisional Government had been overthrown. According to the protocols, 'this news provoked a storm of applause and shouts of joy'. In view of the excitement, a recess was proposed, during which the party factions could discuss their positions. Upon reconvening, a joint proposal of the executive and the majority Bolshevik fraction called for the formation of a Provisional Revolutionary Command, consisting of five people with full powers to maintain order. The five were elected unanimously. The soviet empowered the command to monitor all conversations and telegrams at the telephone exchange and telegraph. The post and telegraph employees responded with a strike.[53]

On the evening of 27 October, the soviet called a meeting of public organisations to decide on a more permanent body to replace the Revolutionary Command. Present were the executive of the soviet, the duma executive, and the praesidia of the four socialist parties as well as of the railway and regimental committees. The Mensheviks and Bolsheviks each proposed resolutions. The Mensheviks condemned the defunct Provisional Government, a coalition of moderate socialists and liberals, but called for the formation of a new government on the basis of 'broad revolutionary strata of the people'. They specifically ruled out a government responsible solely to the soviets, which represented only the workers and soldiers (the soldiers being over-whelmingly peasants), as ruinous, given the country's political and economic backwardness. Such a government would lead to the political isolation of the working class and the ruin of the revolution. As for the local government, the initiative in organising it should fall to the city duma (elected by all classes of the population) and to the regimental committee.

The Bolshevik resolution was short: support the struggle of the Petrograd workers and soldiers for a 'homogeneous government of socialist democracy' (i.e. without liberals or other representatives of the propertied classes) in the form of the soviets of workers', soldiers' and peasant deputies. This resolution won by twenty votes against five with three abstentions. The Socialist Revolutionaries (SRs) did not participate in the vote, and the Mensheviks walked out immediately afterwards. Neither party sent representatives to the new General Command of Revolutionary Organisations which replaced the Provisional Revolutionary General Command. This new body was to consist of two delegates from the soviet executive and one from the SRs, Mensheviks, Bolsheviks, Maximalists, duma executive, railway committee and regimental committee.[54] As in Petrograd, the rejection by the moderate socialists of the coalition proposal was based upon their outright rejection of any government responsible solely or mainly to the soviets.

This stand sealed their fate with the workers in October, who, for their part, were not prepared to yield on the issue of soviet power. The workers of the Ivanovo-Kineshma region greeted with enthusiasm the news of the formation of a soviet government in Petrograd.[55] The delegate from Ivanovo to the Moscow Regional Bureau of the Bolshevik Central Committee reported at the time that 'the mood of the workers and soldiers is excellent. During the insurrection in Moscow, they pleaded to be sent to aid the [Moscow] Military-Revolutionary Committee.'[56]

G. Korolev, a leader of the textile union, recalled that when the news of fighting in Moscow reached Ivanovo, the union was 'literally besieged with requests and demands to be sent to Moscow to aid the workers there'.[57] The Moscow Soviet suggested that Ivanovo wait. But in Shuia, with the region's largest garrison, the soviet, with Ivanovo's agreement, sent an armed force of 900 workers and soldiers, which was seen off at the railway station by a huge crowd. By the time the force reached Moscow, it had gathered some 1,100 additional men. Arriving on the outskirts of the city in full battledress, they were at first taken for troops sent by Kerensky from the front against the soviet. All the more demoralising was the effect when the anti-soviet forces realised that these were hostile men.[58]

This was only a part of the influx of revolutionary forces, especially workers, from the provincial industrial centres around Moscow. According to A. Pireiko, an instructor for the Moscow Province Soviet, 'without the participation of the workers of the regional industrial centres, the victory on the barricades in Moscow would scarcely have been possible'.[59]

Support for the Soviet Government was strong not only in the mills, but among all strata of the working class. In Kineshma, an administrative centre, where the soviet, despite its Bolshevik majority, did not take power in October, the printers, generally a moderate element, refused to type-set the paper of the Revolutionary Committee (a non-soviet organisation that continued to support the overthrown Provisional Government) without the soviet's written approval.[60] The strike called by Vikzhel, the executive committee of the Railway Union, which was trying to force the socialist parties into a coalition government not responsible to the soviets, was roundly condemned by the railway workers in the town. Their delegates' council on 1 November voted unanimously to support fully the Soviet Government.[61]

The issue of a coalition government with the moderate socialists that temporarily split the national Bolshevik leadership had little impact here. The local workers, like those all over Russia, did want socialist unity in order to meet the dangers facing the revolution, but that unity had to be based upon the soviets, political bodies that represented only the popular classes. There could be no return, in whatever modified form, to a coalition with representatives of the propertied classes. After the moderate socialists refused the offer by the Ivanovo Soviet to join the General Command of Revolutionary Organisations, the soviet, on 4 November, resolved that the 'defencists' (the Right Mensheviks and SRs) could not be allowed in the General Command 'because they did not adhere to the uprising of the workers and soldiers'.[62]

The soviet took the same position on the question of the national government. When it first discussed this on 1 November, the position of the moderate socialists against Soviet power was not yet clear. The soviet passed the following resolution:

> Russia is now going through a period of acute class struggle, civil war. It was not the workers, nor the soldiers and peasants who began the bloodshed. The blood that is being shed in the streets of Petrograd and Moscow falls on the head of the overthrown Provisional Government and the parties and groups that support it.
>
> At this moment, when a new *Kornilovshchina* has arisen, all socialist parties must rally to form a united socialist front. Those parties that refuse this and seek coalitions with various committees of public salvation consisting of Kornilovite elements thereby cast themselves out from the ranks of revolutionary democracy and openly assume their place in the ranks of the counter-revolution.
>
> The Ivanovo-Voznesensk Soviet promises full support by all available means to the new provisional government – the government of revolutionary soldiers, peasants and workers which has been created from the midst of the soviets and is responsible to them.[63]

A few days later, a delegate returned from Petrograd to report the Menshevik and SR condition for joining a coalition – that the government have a base broader than the soviets, including the dumas, elected by universal suffrage, and other organisations which included representatives of the propertied classes. This broader base would also ensure that the Bolsheviks, the majority at the Soviet Congress of 25 October, be a minority partner in the coalition government. The new resolution of the Ivanovo soviet stated:

> Decisively rejecting these treacherous proposals [... the soviet] declares that power must remain in the hands of the soviet and must not be transferred to any ... 'popular soviet', which the Mensheviks and SRs want to pack with supporters of Kerensky.
>
> The Ivanovo-Voznesensk Soviet demands a complete end to negotiations on an agreement with the Mensheviks and Right SRs. At the same time, it proposes that the Left SRs [politically

close to the Bolsheviks] decisively adhere to the workers' and
peasants' revolution and enter the Council of People's Commissars ... Rykov, Nogin and the other [members of the Soviet
government who had resigned from the Bolshevik Central Committee over what they felt to be its intransigence] should not
abandon their posts.[64]

In contrast to Petrograd, there is no evidence that the workers here
were particularly agitated by the issue of a socialist coalition. They
based their judgement on their own experience, and in urban centres
of the region the moderate socialists did not have a politically significant base. What base they did have was, in any case, hostile to the
workers. In the countryside, the SRs did have support among the
peasants (though it became weaker the closer one came to industrial
centres). But the issue of a socialist coalition really involved the Left-
leaning elements in the educated stratum of Russian society, the
socialist intelligentsia, which almost unanimously supported the
moderate socialist parties. There was a real dearth of educated people
among the supporters of soviet power, and this posed real problems for
the revolutionary régime.[65] But the peasants were not a matter of
immediate concern to the workers. They might continue to vote for the
SRs because of their historic identification with the populists, but their
interests lay with the soviets which alone sanctioned their seizure of
the land and would defend it against the counter-revolution.

The only ones who really seemed to waver over this question were
the Bolsheviks in Ivanovo's duma. As they were involved in the day-
to-day city administration, they were more sensitive than most to the
shortage of cultural forces among the partisans of soviet power and to
the importance of securing the cooperation of the educated elements of
society. Their work put them in daily contact with these 'intermediate
strata', and they could not help but be influenced to some degree by
their outlook. On the same day as the Ivanovo Soviet called for an end
to negotiations with the moderate socialists, an editorial in the duma's
paper took the side of the Bolshevik leaders who had resigned from the
Central Committee, accusing it of intransigence in the question of a
socialist coalition.[66] On 2 November, a resolution sponsored jointly by
the Bolshevik, Menshevik and SR fractions of the duma called for a
socialist coalition 'resting upon the soviet of workers', peasants' and
soldiers' deputies of the second convocation, supplemented with
representatives of the socialist parties and public organisations, and
based upon an agreement among the socialist parties'.[67] This was a
significantly more conciliatory position than that of the Ivanovo

Soviet. Yet, it too was doomed once it became clear that the intention of the moderate socialists was a Bolshevik minority in the coalition. This was unacceptable even to the more cautious Bolsheviks of the duma.

Another difference arose between the Bolsheviks in the soviet and those in the duma when the soviet executive decided on 12 November to stop the sale of the 'bourgeois [i.e. non-socialist] press' in the city, pending a new law on the press. Workers' meetings had been passing resolutions since the Kornilov affair demanding the closure of the non-socialist press. During the strike, the textile union had called for a boycott. After the October revolution, this press refused to recognise Soviet power and called, directly and indirectly, for its overthrow. On 15 November, the soviet approved its executive's decision to allow the sale only of socialist papers and it called on the Moscow Soviet to shut down the others. But the next day, the Ivanovo branch of the All-Russian Teachers' Union complained about this to the duma. After a discussion, the duma, which had a Bolshevik majority, called on the soviet to review its decision, as it seemed unjustified. The soviet agreed to re-open the question, but on 22 November it reaffirmed its original decision with only eight opposing votes.[68]

But protests continued, especially among the non-working-class population. On 23 November, a general assembly of white-collar factory employees condemned the soviet's decision. The clerks of the local regiments did the same a few days later, noting that the papers were being sold all the same. On 26 November, a crowd gathered at the railway station to receive the Moscow papers and was dispersed by the Red Guards. The soviet took up the matter for a third time on 29 November. The Bolshevik leader, Samoilov, speaking on behalf of the executive, admitted that the measure was ineffective – the papers continued to be sold. He proposed to lift the ban. This resolution was carried by a vote of fifty-six to thirty-six, with six abstentions. The SR Maximalists, led by Furmanov, registered their opposition.[69]

But the debate did not end here. The city committee of the Bolshevik party decided on 1 December to propose that the central government close the non-socialist press. It also resolved to fight against its distribution locally. On 4 December, the general assembly of the Ivanovo garrison called for the closure of *Russkii Manchester* for its 'slander of the soviets of workers and soldiers and its defence of Kaledin, Kornilov and Rodzianko'.[70] (These were two Tsarist generals and a right-wing industrialist-politician respectively. *Russkii Manchester*, which began publishing in Ivanovo on 5 November, set as its goal 'to facilitate the implantation in our region of new English and

Western European ideas, customs and labour-capital relations'.) The same day, the city-wide Bolshevik party conference voted by nineteen to eleven, with seven abstentions, to demand the closure of the bourgeois papers in the centre and the adoption of energetic measures in Ivanovo to prevent their distribution. It was claimed that the papers used slander as a weapon to 'obscure the consciousness of the popular masses'. On 22 December, the soviet closed *Russkii Manchester*, citing the regiment's decision and the paper's refusal to recognise the Soviet government.[71] Before long, with the first battles of the Civil War in the south, the last of the non-socialist press was closed in the centre, thus finally putting the issue to rest in the Ivanovo-Kineshma region.

The Ivanovo post and telegraph employees, who had struck when the soviet had placed them under surveillance, rejected the duma's proposal of conciliation. Citing the instructions of the Central Committee of Post-Telegraph Employees, they threatened to sabotage the machinery. On 26 October, the General Command of Revolutionary Organisations ordered them to return to work and to repair their machines, threatening 'revolutionary methods'. When this failed, 200 employees were arrested. Shortly afterwards, they agreed to end their strike.[72] But they continued to annoy the soviet. On 4 November, they posted and distributed a false telegram that had been received, announcing a revolt of officers in Ivanovo and calling for the arrest of the Bolsheviks.[73]

This was the limit of resistance to the October revolution in Ivanovo. The situation was similar in the region's other industrial centres. In Shuia, a joint meeting of the soviet, the duma and the zemstvo, together with the factory and soldiers' committees, was convened on 26 October in the hall of the People's House. A huge crowd of workers and soldiers filled the building to overflowing. The news of the insurrection in Petrograd was received with jubilation, and the meeting voted unanimously to give all possible support to the Soviet government, as the only way out of the existing situation. It temporarily gave full power in the town to a revolutionary committee, consisting of one delegate each from the duma, the zemstvo, and the workers', soldiers' and peasants' sections of the soviet.[74]

Frunze, who chaired both the Shuia Soviet and duma, wrote that he

> could not recall a single manifestation of protest or dissatisfaction
> on the part of any group. All opponents of the insurrection in
> Shuia among the intelligentsia and petty bourgeoisie dared not
> utter a word in the atmosphere reigning among the people. Of
> course, the insurrection in Shuia took place without any blood-

shed or gunfire ... We saw scarcely any of the sabotage on the part of the bureaucrats that was so widespread in Petrograd and Moscow. True, there were some hints of it from the post and telegraph employees, but this was cut short, and, in general, the entire local government apparatus continued to function without interruption. We had actually had our October earlier.[75]

The Shuia garrison proceeded to elect a new command. At a meeting of over 300 officers, the latter were offered the option of pledging loyalty to the soviet or of resigning with a guarantee of safe passage. Only a few resigned. At the end of October, a special peasant congress also voted to support the Soviet government.[76]

In the mill village of Vichuga, a Revolutionary Command was created even before the insurrection in Petrograd. Upon receiving a telegram telling of the insurrection, the soviet met with representatives of the textile union, the mill and strike committees and also the local zemstvo. Again the news was received enthusiastically and there was no noticeable opposition.[77]

The crucial factor in this smooth transition was that the Bolsheviks already held majorities in the local governments, elected by universal suffrage, in the industrial centres. The only people who experienced any immediate change in their situation were the employees of the central state in the post and telegraph offices. It was not until many weeks later that the day-to-day local administration was fully transferred to the soviets.

But matters were different in the district capitals of Kineshma and Iurevets, where the local government was not in Bolshevik hands and mill workers formed a relatively small minority of the population. Kineshma was one of the few places in the region with a significant Menshevik organisation, many of whom worked in the cooperative movement that was centred here. The Bolsheviks won a majority in the Kineshma Soviet only in early September, following the abortive Kornilov rising. In the duma, the Bolsheviks held only a minority, though they were stronger in the Kineshma district zemstvo, thanks to the mill villages that surrounded the town.[78] The Bolsheviks in Kineshma were slow to respond to the news of the Petrograd insurrection. The local garrison demonstrated on 27 October under the slogan 'All Power to the Soviets', but the soviet was not convened until the 28th. It voted by forty-nine to nine, with four abstentions, to take power. But an attempt to establish surveillance over the post and telegraph found the building empty. The city administration also went on strike.[79]

On 30 October the new district zemstvo met. (Elections had been held a few weeks before.) It took five days of fractional fighting to reach an agreement on the composition of the executive: three Bolsheviks and three SRs. Then the Mensheviks proposed a resolution condemning 'the attempt by the Bolsheviks, having split off from united revolutionary democracy, to seize supreme power, to the obvious detriment of the revolution'. It proposed the formation of a 'district committee of salvation', consisting of the executive of the zemstvo, representatives of the duma, soviet, socialist parties, garrison, officers, the Post-and-Telegraph union, the white-collar railway employees, and, finally, the district commissar (the local representative of the defunct Provisional Government). The resolution also condemned the Kineshma Soviet for seizing power illegally and against the will of the 'other organs of revolutionary democracy'. The SRs adhered to this resolution, which was passed by a vote of twenty-nine to seventeen. Following the vote, most of the Bolsheviks walked out, declaring that they would not participate in the zemstvo executive. Left without a quorum, the meeting was unable to form a new executive.

On 2 November, a meeting of representatives of neighbourhood street committees also condemned the soviet. They recognised only the Committee of Salvation that had been formed. The Kineshma duma followed suit the next day, voting unanimously in the absence of the Bolshevik deputies for a Menshevik resolution to condemn the Petrograd insurrection and calling on the 'revolutionary democracy' to rally round the dumas and zemstvos. This stand was endorsed the next day by the government employees, who promised to strike if the soviet sought to establish control over their activity. The executive of the peasant soviet also condemned the Petrograd insurrection.[80]

The Bolshevik leaders of the Kineshma Soviet decided to retreat in the face of such resistance. They negotiated an agreement with the other socialist parties to form a 'popular soviet', consisting of two representatives each from workers', soldiers' and peasants' soviets, and the zemstvo, and one each from the duma, All-Union Railway Union (white collar), Post and Telegraph Union, and the Textile Workers' Union. This body was to wield full power, working in close contact with the duma and soviet. On 5 November, this agreement was presented to the soviet in the form of a resolution that argued that full power should really be in the hands of the local self-governments elected by universal suffrage. 'But recognising the great services rendered to the revolution by the soviets of workers', soldiers' and peasants' deputies, the Kineshma revolutionary democracy wishes to strengthen, by means of soviet authority, the position of the young organs of local self-government.'

Many of the soviet delegates disliked this compromise and had harsh words for the leadership. They felt that it was impermissible for the soviet to accept an accord with the Mensheviks, who only a few days earlier had led the zemstvo in condemning the soviet. A delegate from a large textile mill declared that 'the workers will recognise no organs [of power] other than the soviets'. The accord was nevertheless ratified.[81] It did not, however, last very long. The Bolsheviks soon left the 'popular soviet', and a sort of dual power reigned in the city and district, the soviet not interfering with the day-to-day administration of the local government.[82] The main card of the moderate socialists was the support of the public employees. On the other hand, the Bolsheviks had the support of the workers and control of the garrison. In mid November, the vote to the Constituent Assembly produced by the civilian population of the town gave the Kadets 1,275 votes; the Bolsheviks – 542; the Mensheviks – 477; SRs – 475; and the clergy 99. However, in the garrison, the Bolsheviks received 1,231 votes out of 1,699; in the suburb of Popovka – 418 out of 849; and at the nearby Konovalov Mill – 1,376 out of 1,589. In all, the Bolsheviks received 61 per cent of the vote in the town and its environs.[83] By now the peasant soviet had also swung to Soviet Power.[84]

Full Soviet Power was just a question of time; the soviet was waiting until it had enough experienced people to face the threat posed by opposition from the government employees. Already on 26 November, over the protest of the zemstvo, the soviet appointed its own delegate to head the zemstvo commissariat, a body that coordinated the activity of the zemstvo and duma. On 10 December, the Bolsheviks left the zemstvo, claiming that it was not representative of the population and calling for new elections. A series of meetings in the smaller rural districts supported the Bolshevik call. But it was only in February 1918 that the Kineshma Soviet fully assumed the functions of the zemstvo.[85]

The working-class element in Iurevets was even weaker than in Kineshma. In the brief reaction following the July Days here, the moderate socialists had managed to obtain representation in the soviet for various white-collar and intelligentsia organisations. As a result, on 28 October, the Iurevets Soviet, which had earlier refused even to send a delegate to the Soviet Congress in Petrograd, condemned the 'criminal attempt by the Bolsheviks to seize power'. The Iurevets Duma did likewise and set to organising a 'Committee of Struggle against Anarchy'. The district zemstvo, thanks to the large mill village of Rodniki, had a Bolshevik majority.[86]

Meanwhile, the workers picketing the Mindavskii Linen Mill, the only large factory in Iurevets, began to seek arms. The soviet responded by attempting to organise a 'popular militia' to defend itself against the workers. The Bolsheviks began laying plans for an insurrection: the Mindavskii strike committee would serve as the centre and the factory committees would force the soviet to call new elections. Workers went out to their native villages to explain the government's Decrees on Land and Peace and to win the peasants over to Soviet Power. The Constituent Assembly elections in November in the Iurevets district gave the Bolsheviks 55 per cent of the vote. On 10 December, a conference of factory committees in the town demanded soviet elections on the basis of new, genuinely representative norms. If the soviet refused, the factory committees would proceed on their own. The soviet had little choice. Following the elections, on 22 December, the new soviet voted unanimously to assume power in Iurevets. By that time, the situation in the town had seriously deteriorated, and the soviet had to turn to Ivanovo and Kostroma for help in controlling criminal elements.[87]

This was the extent of active opposition to the October revolution in the region. The actual transfer of administrative functions from the dumas and zemstvos to the soviets was not completed, however, until early 1918. Osinkin, a Bolshevik deputy to the Ivanovo Soviet, recalled that the question became an object of heated debate among the Bolsheviks after October, even though they controlled the duma. Those who argued on pragmatic grounds to leave the administration temporarily with the old organs of self-government won out. By the time the soviets finally dispersed the dumas and zemstvos, the oppositional zeal of the employees had considerably waned, and in the meantime, the workers had had time to gain some administrative experience of their own.[88]

The October revolution did not affect the workers' resolve to see their strike through to victory. To them the revolution meant above all the opportunity at last to live as human beings, and for this they needed a minimum wage tied to the cost of living. Their leaders understood this, even though they themselves felt that consolidation of the new régime called for a resumption of production. Accordingly, once the fighting was over in Moscow, the union sent two delegates to the owners to propose an end to the strike, and negotiations on the basis of a 6-rouble minimum. This was a concession from the original demand of 7.50. But the owners would accept no preliminary conditions for negotiations. Moreover, they claimed that the strike had broken the workers' individual contracts; and so they had full freedom in the new hiring that would begin on 10 November. Having been rebuffed, the union delegates went on to Petrograd to obtain government help.[89]

In the meantime, the union executive and central strike committee met with representatives of the regional soviets. Their discussion made it clear that a majority felt it inexpedient to continue a strike that played into the hand of the owners, who now wanted to keep the mills shut as long as possible. On the other hand, they knew that they could not call the strike off without giving the workers any concrete results. The meeting decided to make a new offer to the owners as a basis for ending the strike and opening negotiations: recognition of the principle of a minimum wage based upon a minimum living budget, its size open to negotiation; recognition of the individual contracts as still intact; pay for days lost in the strike; a region-wide collective agreement retroactive to 1 August.[90]

Before the offer was presented, the emissaries returned from Petrograd with a message from the Commissar of Labour asking for an end to the strike while he prepared legislation regulating labour–capital relations, including a minimum wage and limitations on profits. The strike benefited only the owners. He noted that the Moscow district union had called off its strike. The Ivanovo-Kineshma union, however, decided to maintain the strike while awaiting a response to its new offer. It repeated that 'it is entirely impossible to call the workers back to work without giving them any results whatsoever from their strike'. The reports coming in from the mills indicated that the strikers remained very determined and in good spirits.[91]

On 11 November, the two sides met. The owners made a counter-proposal: although the contracts were formally broken, all workers would be rehired; issues relating to white-collar employees would not be discussed with the workers' union (most white-collar employees belonged to a separate union); the agreement would be retroactive to October; any minimum wage had to be tied to productivity norms. The union was prepared to yield only on the date from which the contract would begin. The talks thus broke off. But three days later, thanks to the intervention of the Economic Department of the Moscow Soviet, the talks were resumed and soon yielded a preliminary agreement that was to serve as a basis for further negotiations. The union had accepted the majority of the owners' counter-proposals: no pay for time lost; the agreement retroactive to 15 September; white-collar issues not to be discussed; a minimum wage tied to productivity norms. Nevertheless, the union felt it had won the essential – a minimum wage tied to the cost of living and a region-wide collective agreement.[92]

The union instructed the strike committees that work would resume on 17 November. The mill committees were to verify all claims that technical conditions or lack of fuel did not permit a resumption of production. Such claims were widespread, but in most cases pressure from the mill committees was enough to force management to re-open. In some cases, the mill committees started up production in direct opposition to management. On 17 November, the executive of the Ivanovo Soviet ordered the committees to maintain surveillance of production and the movement of goods, intervening where justified.[93]

Among the workers, the feeling was that they had won a major victory. Support for the Bolsheviks remained very strong.[94] In the Constituent Assembly elections in Ivanovo, the Bolsheviks received 64.3 per cent of the vote, as compared to 54.6 per cent in the duma elections at the end of August. The Bolshevik gains, as well as those of the non-socialist parties, were made at the expense of the SRs, who dropped from 23.4 per cent to 12.7 per cent. The Mensheviks fell from 3.8 per cent to 2.5 per cent.[95] In Vladimir province as a whole, the Bolsheviks' list won 56.5 per cent of the vote; in Kostroma province, which was more rural, 40.0 per cent. Where data are available for the industrial centres, they show that Bolshevik popularity was very high. In Ivanovo itself, the well-to-do central city district gave the Bolsheviks only 35.1 per cent, but the working-class district of Grafskaia Zemlia – 95.2 per cent. The workers and employees of the Konovalov Factory, outside Kineshma, voted 86.6 per cent Bolshevik; 9.65 per cent Menshevik; and 5.0 per cent SR.[96]

But the conflict was far from over. In the negotiations, the owners offered 5.25 roubles as the minimum wage for men and 4.50 for women. The union rejected this as too low and discriminatory against women, the majority of the work force. Talks broke off on 29 November. The owners decided to go ahead unilaterally and implement their wage offer. The union responded by directing the mill committees to introduce on their own a 6-rouble minimum for both men and women. The introduction of new wage scales, as well as hiring, dismissals and transfers, were to be overseen by committees consisting of two-thirds of workers and one-third of management. In the case of stoppage related to the owners' opposition to the wage increase, the mill committees were to continue production on their own, informing the soviet of this and using the Red Guards when necessary.[97]

It had become clear that the owners did not fear a strike in the existing political conjuncture. Different measures were needed. On 30 November, the union executive met with representatives of the Ivanovo Soviet, and it was decided to arrest the most prominent of the owners. On 3 December, a detachment of Red Guards from the mill village of Teikovo arrested four owners in Moscow and delivered them to the Ivanovo jail. The union told the owners to address their protests to the government institutions that had issued the arrest orders. Shortly after the arrest, one of the owners accepted the 6-rouble minimum and was released. In the mills, the committees proceeded on their own to introduce the minimum. Citing the likelihood of sabotage, the regional soviet forbade shipment of goods without the authorisation of the local soviets. Henceforth, absences on the part of the owners and managerial personnel also required the authorisation of the mill committee. If they refused to carry out their normal duties, they were to be arrested and dispatched to Ivanovo.[98]

In mid December, the union proposed to re-open negotiations on the basis of the 6-rouble minimum for men and women. There was no reply. About one week later, yielding to the insistent urging of the Moscow Soviet and the Commissar of Labour, the Ivanovo Soviet released the other three owners.[99] The seizure of political power had not made much difference to this economic struggle. Four months later, the union was still negotiating the collective agreement with the owners. At the end of March 1918, the union delegates' council recognised that their struggle had scarcely been facilitated by the acquisition of political power. It warned the central government against any further delay, demanding legislation establishing a minimum wage and obligatory collective agreements.[100]

But if the central government was slow in acting, this was mainly due to the same problem encountered by the regional soviet: political power had limited utility in forcing the hand of mill owners, when one wanted them to continue managing their mills even though they themselves were not at all keen to do so. Sooner or later, this struggle had to lead the workers to nationalisation. This policy had not been one of the original goals of their movement, despite a vague, though widespread, conviction that the mills were the legacy of the entire people. As early as 27 January 1918, the Shuia Soviet decided to 'defend the principle of the nationalisation of the textile industry, as a measure which will become inevitable in the general course of the development of our revolution'.[101] Although full nationalisation in the region was in practice still a year away, the social content of the revolution, still vague in October, had by then been decided.

In the political sphere, there still remained the issue of the Constituent Assembly. In many of the workers' resolutions, the Council of People's Commissars, elected by the Second Congress of Soviets in October, was originally referred to as the 'Provisional Revolutionary Government'. The final decision on the form of government was to be taken by the Constituent Assembly. This was an inherently contradictory position: the workers took power through the soviets in order to put an end to a coalition of the soviets with the propertied classes; they wanted a soviet government: one responsible solely to the popular classes. But the Constituent Assembly was elected by universal suffrage, by all classes of society. In reality, the workers wanted the Constituent Assembly to legitimise their class dictatorship. They did not foresee that the peasants, despite their hunger for land and peace, would still vote massively for the SRs. (An unknown, but large, proportion of these votes would have gone to the Left SRs, had they had time to form a separate list. But the split in the party came too late.)[102] In its editorial of 5 December, *Rabochii gorod*, the paper of the Ivanovo Soviet and the duma, raised the question of what would happen if the Constituent Assembly did not support soviet power. But this possibility was immediately ruled out.

The position of the workers was relatively clear-cut, if not totally coherent: the Constituent Assembly had a role to play only if it supported Soviet Power. What that role might be, except perhaps to give the soviets legitimacy in the eyes of wavering intermediate social elements, was not clarified. On 7 January 1918, the soviet of workers' and peasants' deputies of the mill village of Kokhma was the scene of a 'lively debate' over the Constituent Assembly. A series of speakers expressed the view that the slogan 'All Power to the Constituent Assembly', that had become the rallying cry of all parties opposed to Soviet power, was a slogan directed against the popular classes. The meeting passed unanimously the following resolution, that reflected the thinking of workers across the region:

> The Constituent Assembly will be able to play a beneficial role in
> the development of the revolution only if it decisively takes the
> side of the toiling people against the landowners and bourgeoisie.
> If it consolidates Soviet Power, confirms the decrees on land,
> peace, workers' control of production, nationalisation of the

banks, etc., and recognises the right of all peoples to self-determination.

Only such a Constituent Assembly will be welcomed by us. Otherwise the Constituent Assembly will be subject to dispersal.[103]

Among the peasants, opinion was not so unanimous. Nevertheless, it had the support of the majority in the region. The second congress of soviets of peasant deputies of Kostroma Province that met from 16–20 December was the scene of a bitter debate over this issue. A majority voted for the following resolution:

> Any attempt by the Constituent Assembly to fight the soviets of peasants', workers' and soldiers' deputies, as organs of revolutionary power ... will be seen as an attack against the gains of the revolution and will meet our most decisive counter-action.[104]

The next three years in the region were dominated by the economic crisis – chronic hunger and the collapse of industry – and by the Civil War and foreign intervention, which aggravated the crisis and prevented its resolution. At the same time, the Bolshevik organisation was swallowed up by the tasks of administration and by recurrent military mobilisations (workers from this region formed the backbone of the celebrated Chapaev Division) leaving few people behind in the mills to continue political work among the remaining rank-and-file workers. In these conditions, the region saw numerous protests against the Bolsheviks and the soviets. But despite the terrible suffering, the bond between the Bolsheviks and the workers of the region remained intact. The Ivanovo-Kineshma region continued to be one of the firmest bases of the revolutionary régime.[105]

NOTES

1 *Ivanovo-voznesenskii raion za 10 let Oktiabrskoi revoliutsii* (Ivanovo-Voznesensk, 1927), p. 36; V.Z. Drobizhev, A.K. Sokolov and V.A. Ustinov, *Rabochii klass sovetskoi Rossii v pervyi god proletarskoi diktatury* (Moscow, 1975), p. 104.

2 *Grozovye gody, vospominaniia starykh bolshevikov* (Ivanovo, 1961), p. 32; Tsentralnyi gosudarstvennyi arkhiv oktiabrskoi revoliutsii (TsGAOR), f.6868, op. 1, d. 311, 1. 112; F.N. Samoilov, *Po sledam minuvshego* (Moscow, 1948), p. 170; *Trudy delegatskikh sobranii Ivanovo-kineshemskogo oblastnogo professionalnogo soiuza rabochikh i soiuza rabotnits tekstilnoi promyshlennosti* (Ivanovo-Voznesensk, 1918), p. 32; *Za vlast sovetov. Khronika revoliutsionnykh sobytii v Kostromskoi gubernii, fevral 1917–mart 1918* (Kostroma, 1967),

pp. 47–8; *1917-i god v Ivanovo-voznesenskom raione* (Ivanovo-Voznesensk, 1917), p. 119; *Rabochii gorod*, 6, 23, 34, December 1917; *Rabochii put*, 5 September 1917.

3 D. Mandel, 'The Ivanovo-Kineshma Workers in War and Revolution', paper presented at the conference on 'Strikes, Social Conflict and World War I' in Cortona, Italy, in May 1989 (Proceedings forthcoming, Feltrinelli Foundation).

4 *Materialy po statistike truda*, part 1, p. 10.

5 See Mandel, 'The Ivanovo-Kineshma Workers', pp. 9–14.

6 Ibid., pp. 2–3.

7 Ibid, pp. 11–13.

8 Ts. Zelikson-Bobrovskaia, *Zapiski riadovogo podpolshchika* (Moscow, 1924), pp. 140–1.

9 TsGAOR, f. 5457, op. 1, d. 26, l. 21.

10 *Nasha zvezda* (24 September 1917); *Grozovye gody* (Ivanovo, 1961), pp. 163–4.

11 *Nasha zvezda* (6 September 1917); *Za vlast sovetov* (Kostroma), pp. 79, 80; *1917-i god v I.-v. raione*, p. 205.

12 *Rabochii kontrol i natsionalizatsiia krupnoi promyshlennosti v Ivanov-voznesenskoi gubernii* (Moscow, 1956), pp. 66–7.

13 *Rabochee dvizhenie v 1917 g.* (Moscow, 1926), p. 156; *Nasha zvezda* (21 September 1917).

14 *Ivanovo-voznesenskie bolsheviki v period podgotovki i provedeniia Velikoi Oktiabrskoi sotsialisticheskoi revoliutsii* (Ivanovo, 1947), p. 91.

15 G.A. Trukan, *Oktiabr v tsentralnoi Rossii* (Moscow, 1967), p. 158.

16 *1917-i god v I.-v. raione*, pp. 80–1; D. Mandel, *The Petrograd Workers and the Soviet Seizure of Power* (London, 1984), pp. 122–3.

17 *Trudy delegatskikh sobranii*, p. 24; *Izvestiia Ivanovo-voznesenskogo soveta r.d.*, no. 4 (1917).

18 Mandel, *The Petrograd Workers*, pp. 292–309.

19 *Nasha zvezda* (6 September 1917); *Za vlast sovetov* (Kostroma), pp. 79, 80; *Za vlast sovetov* (Ivanovo), p. 205.

20 *Grozovye gody*, p. 242.

21 *Dvadtsat let (1907–1917–1927)* (Kineshma, 1927), p. 46.

22 *1917-i god v I.-v. raione*, pp. 170–1.

23 *Rabochii krai*, no. 253 (1923).

24 *Nasha zvezda* (13 September 1917).

25 *Ivanovo-Voznesensk* (5 September 1917).

26 Ibid., no. 143 (1917).

27 *1917-i god v I.-v. raione*, p. 216.

28 *Nasha zvezda* (2 October and 29 September 1917); *Grozovye gody*, p. 188.

29 Ibid. (12 October 1917).

30 *1917-i god v I.-v. raione*, p. 228.

31 *Nasha zvezda* (12 October 1917).

32 *1917-i god v I.-v. raione*, pp. 222–4.

33 Ibid., pp. 246–8.

34 Ibid., pp. 101–2, 154–5; *Ivanovo-voznesenskie bolsheviki*, pp. 78–80; *Grozovye gody*, 154–6, 163, 171, 208; *Za vlast sovetov* (Ivanovo), pp. 108–10; *Ivanovo-Voznesensk* (7 and 8 July 1917); *Trudy delegatskikh sobranii*, pp. 48–9.

35 *Trudy delegatskikh sobranii*, pp. 7–36.

36 Ibid., pp. 37–95; G. Korolev, *Ivanovo-kineshemskie tekstilshchiki v 1917 godu* (Moscow, 1927), pp. 91–3.

37 *Trudy delegatskikh*, pp. 96–106.

38 S. Klimokhin, *Kratkaia istoriia stachki tekstilshchikov Ivanovo-kineshemskoi promyshlennoi oblasti* (Kineshma, 1918), pp. 57–73.

39 TsGAOR, f. 6868, op. 1, d. 311, l. 124.

40 Mandel, *The Petrograd Workers*, pp. 284–6.

41 Korolev, *Ivanovo-kineshemskie tekstilschchiki*, pp. 86–8.

42 Ibid., pp. 44–5.

43 Ibid., pp. 91–3.

44 *1917-i god v I.-v. raione*, pp. 248–9.

45 Ibid., p. 253.

46 *Utro Rossii* (22 October 1917).

47 TsGAOR, f. 6868, op. 1, d. 311, l. 134.

48 *1917-i god v I.-v. raione*, pp. 253–4.

49 Korolev, *Ivanovo-kineshemskie tekstilshchiki*, pp. 48–56; *Trudy delegatskikh*, p. 117; TsGAOR, f. 6868, op. 1, d. 311, l. 124.

50 *1917-i god v I.-v. raione*, p. 254.

51 *Grozovye gody*, p. 192.

52 *Krasnyi tkach*, no. 2 (1923), 10–13.

53 *1917-i god v I.-v. raione*, pp. 255–6; *Za vlast sovetov* (Ivanovo), pp. 185–6; *Rabochii gorod* (8 and 9 November 1917); *Ivanovo-voznesenskie bolsheviki*, p. 248.

54 *1917-i god v I.-v. raione*, pp. 259–60; *Rabochii gorod* (9 November 1917).

55 *Rabochii gorod* (5, 8 and 9 November 1917); *Russkii Manchester* (5 November 1917).

56 *Za vlast sovetov* (Ivanovo), pp. 188–9.

57 Korolev, *Ivanovo-Kineshemskie tekstilshchiki*, p. 60.

58 *Maiak* (November 1917); *Rabochii krai* (5 November 1922); *Grozovye gody*, pp. 228, 246; TsGAOR, f. 6868, op. 1, d.33, l. 134.

59 *Moskovksaia provintsiia v 17-om godu* (Moscow and Leningrad, 1927), p. 154.

60 N. Evreinov, 'Iz vospominanii o podgotovke Oktiabria v Kineshme', *Proletarskaia revoliutsiia*, no. 11 (70) (1927), 190.

61 *Rabochii gorod* (5 November 1917); *1917-i god v I.-v. raione*, pp. 264, 266.

62 *Rabochii gorod* (8 November 1917).

63 Ibid.

64 Ibid. (12 November 1917).

65 Mandel, *The Petrograd Workers*, pp. 324–6 and 'The Intelligentsia and the Working Class in 1917', *Critique* (Glasgow), no. 14 (1981), 67–87.

66 *Rabochii gorod* (8 November 1917).

67 *1917-i god v I.-v. raione*, pp. 266–7.

68 Ibid., pp. 277, 281, 290, 292; *Rabochii gorod* (18 November 1917).

69 *1917-i god v I.-v. raione*, pp. 290, 292; *Rabochii gorod* (2 December 1917).

70 Ibid. (8 December 1917).

71 *1917-i god v I.-v. raione*, pp. 270, 301–2; *Rabochii gorod* (23 December 1917).

72 *1917-i god v I.-v. raione*, pp. 259–60; *Za vlast sovetov* (Ivanovo), p. 189.

73 *1917-i god v I.-v. raione*, p. 269.

74 *Maiak* (29 October 1917).

75 *Rabochii krai* (6 November 1922).

76. Ibid.

77 *Grozovye gody*, pp. 116–17.

78 Evreinov, 'Iz vospominanii', p. 186; *Za vlast sovetov* (Ivanovo), p. 86; *Rabochii gorod* (10 November 1917).

79 *Za vlast sovetov* (Ivanovo), pp. 197–8; *Kineshemskii raion za 10 let Oktiabria* (Kineshma, 1927), p. 12; *Ivanovo-voznesenskie bolsheviki*, p. 123; Evreinov, 'Iz vospominanii', pp. 190–1.

80 *Rabochii gorod* (11 November 1917); *1917-i god v I.-v. raione*, pp. 264–5.

81 Ibid., pp. 268, 271, 292.

82 *Rabochii gorod* (12 November 1917).

83 Evreinov, 'Iz vospominanii', p. 189.

84 Ibid., p. 306.

85 Ibid., pp. 290, 308, 310, 313, 317; *1918-i god v Ivanovo-voznesenskoi gubernii* (Ivanovo-Voznesensk, 1930), p. 50; *Grozovye gody*, p. 210.

86 *Grozovye gody*, pp. 210–12; *1917-i god. v I.-v. raione*, pp. 263, 278.

87 Ibid., pp. 212–15. *Za vlast sovetov* (Ivanovo), pp. 213–15.

88 *Grozovye gody*, pp. 231–2.

89 Korolev, *Ivanovo-kineshemskie tekstilshchiki*, p. 61; TsGAOR, f. 6868, op. 1, d. 311, l. 142.

90 Korolev, *Ivanovo-kineshemskie tekstilshchiki*, p. 61.

91 Ibid., p. 63; Klimokhin, *Kratkaia istoriia*, pp. 38–41.

92 *1917-i god v I.-v. raione*, pp. 275–6; Klimokhin, *Kratkaia istoriia*, pp. 40–1; *Rabochii gorod* (15 November 1917).

93 Klimokhin, *Kratkaia istoriia*, p. 46; *1917-i g. v I–v. raione*, pp. 284–5.

94 *Rabochii gorod* (18 November 1917).

95 *1917-i god v I.-v. raione*, p. 290; *Ivanovo Voznesensk*, nos. 129, 132, 137 (1917).

96 *Rabochii gorod* (23 and 28 November, 6 December 1917); *1917-i god v I.-v. raione*, pp. 290, 299.

97 Korolev, *Ivanovo-kineshemskie tekstilshchiki*, p. 67; *Rabochii gorod* (5 December 1917).

98 Korolev, *Ivanovo-kineshemskie tekstilshchiki*, pp. 67–8; *Rabochii gorod* (5 December 1917); *1917-i god v. I.-v. raione*, p. 300.

99 Korolev, *Ivanovo-kineshemskie tekstilshchiki*, pp. 69–70; *Trudy delegatskikh sobranii*, p. 117.

100 Ibid., pp 126–7.

101 *Rabochii kontrol i natsionalizatsiia krupnoi promyshlennosti v Ivanovo-voznesenskoi gubernii* (Moscow, 1956), p. 14.

102 Mandel, *The Petrograd Workers*, pp. 348–9.

103 *Za vlast sovetov* (Ivanovo), p. 246. See also ibid., pp. 247–9; *1917-i god v I.-v. raione*, pp. 306, 313, 316; *1918-i god v I.-v. raione*, pp. 7, 8, 10, 11, 17, 25; *Rabochii gorod* (17 and 18 January 1918).

104 *Severnaia pravda* (21 December 1917); *Ustanovlenie Sovetskoi vlasti v Kostrome i Kostromskoi gubernii* (Kostroma, 1957), pp. 220–6, 375–6.

105 See, for example, *Za vlast sovetov* (Ivanovo), pp. 400–1, and *1918-i god v I.-v. gubernii, passim*.

9

COMMERCIAL–INDUSTRIAL CIRCLES IN REVOLUTION: THE FAILURE OF 'INDUSTRIAL PROGRESSIVISM'

ZIVA GALILI

W HEN the Tsarist government collapsed in February 1917, many believed that Russia would follow the developmental patterns of Western Europe leading to a parliamentary political system and a capitalist economy. Russian entrepreneurs, too, applauded the end of autocracy and the beginning of Russia's 'bourgeois' era, though their enthusiasm for the revolution was tempered by anxieties about their ability to control their work-force. By the summer of 1917, commercial–industrial attitudes towards the revolution had changed dramatically: pessimism, suspicion and intransigence had come to dominate the entrepreneurs' dealings with the Provisional Government, with their socialist partners in the cabinet and above all with their workers.

These two radically different entrepreneurial responses to the revolution – replacing each other in rapid succession – were of critical importance for the national reconciliation that followed the February revolution, the social and political conflict that erupted in the summer of 1917 and the virtual civil war in the midst of which Lenin's Bolshevik party seized power on 25 October. And yet, Russia's industrialists, merchants and entrepreneurs remain, to date, the least studied of the social and political forces that helped shape the course of the revolution.

Only in the past two decades, as historians began exploring the specific circumstances of workers' radicalisation, has attention focused on individual and organised employers in order to see how far their direct interaction with the workers or the policies they successfully forced on the Provisional Government contributed to the process of social polarisation.[1] A few monographs have attempted to explain commercial–industrial policies, but they have emphasised mostly *structural* determinants (and social patterns of *long duration*) with the result that the apparent shifts in attitude and policy during the eight months of revolution have been largely neglected. Soviet historians have referred to the 'backwardness' of the Russian bourgeoisie and its division by 'narrow' regional interests in explanation of what they see as consistent entrepreneurial opposition to labour reforms and economic rationalisation.[2]

On the Western side, Alfred Rieber's formidable study of how Russian merchants and entrepreneurs responded to reform, industrialisation, and revolution has explained many of the internal contradictions and divisions that would play a role in entrepreneurial conduct during 1917. And although he acknowledged the evidence of employers' concessions to workers in the early months of the revolution, Rieber, too, dismissed them as a temporary departure from long-standing patterns of ineffectual entrepreneurial intransigence: a departure that had been, in any case, virtually forced on the employers by their organisational weakness and political isolation at the beginning of the revolution.[3]

This chapter takes a new look at commercial–industrial conduct in the revolution by directing attention to the *immediate* conditions of revolution and to the way in which the various *representations* of social reality – offered by those who claimed to lead the commercial–industrial circles – shaped collective behaviour. Furthermore, it views these perceptual aspects of social identity as having shifted significantly under the impact of revolution.

More specifically, this chapter will show collective entrepreneurial behaviour to have changed swiftly and extensively at two critical junctures during 1917: first, at the outset of the revolution, when a small and self-appointed leadership was able to project a 'progressive' vision of post-revolutionary Russia on to commercial–industrial circles at large and to predispose them to make the concessions that underlay the relatively peaceful labour relations of March to April 1917; then, in the heated social atmosphere of the summer of 1917, when both the 'progressive' leadership and its vision of social relations were rejected by nearly all commercial–industrial circles, which now resorted to policies of intransigence and intimidation though lacking the unity and coherent vision necessary to make such policies truly effective. Whereas the conciliatory approach of the early months had led to political cooperation across social divides, the stance adopted in the latter period both contributed to the process of social polarisation and undermined the defence of commercial–industrial interests against the effects of such polarisation.

MARCH TO APRIL: THE TRIUMPH OF 'INDUSTRIAL PROGRESSIVISM'

Russia's commercial–industrial sector entered the revolution much fragmented and lacking a nationally recognised leadership. The few local employers' organisations that had appeared to counter labour's efforts during the revolution of 1905–7 did not form a national union until the summer of 1917.[4] The older and more numerous producers' associations, though claiming to regulate and represent all producers in a given branch of production, were usually regional in scope. Even the Association of Trade and Industry, nominally the national representation of all producers' associations, served almost exclusively the interests of large industry, especially those of the giant metal-processing and mechanical plants of Petrograd, the mining and metal-lurgical industry of the south and the Petrograd-based investment banks that financed the operations of both. The preference given by the autocratic state to this segment of industry caused deep resentment among smaller producers and served as a powerful deterrent to com-mercial–industrial unity. During the war, however, this same resent-ment (and commercial–industrial fragmentation in general) helped the rise of a new potential leadership from within the commercial–industrial sector dedicated to a vision of what will be called here 'industrial progressivism'.

The origins of this emerging leadership lay in Moscow, especially among the small faction of merchant-entrepreneurs who had parti-cipated in the founding of the Party of Progressists in 1913. From the outset, the Moscow Progressists advocated the building of social co-alitions to resist the domination of economic and political life by the autocracy and the landed gentry.[5] Then, during the war, as defeat and mismanagement discredited the forces of the old régime, P.P. Riabushinskii and A.I. Konovalov, the outstanding figures in the fac-tion, openly hailed the 'bourgeoisie' as the force destined to lead Russia's 'vital forces' in the pursuit of political freedom and economic expansion.[6]

The war also provided the Moscow Progressists with unprecedented opportunities for influence. Their professed patriotism allowed them to articulate and exploit the animosity towards the privileged Petrograd industry, which now stood accused of German sympathies.[7] Also, because they had advocated greater societal autonomy in the past, they gained ranking positions in the new public organisations, especially in the War Industries Committees (WICs).[8] They then

17. Aleksandr Ivanovich Konovalov, Minister of Trade and Industry in the Provisional Government until his resignation on 18 May 1917.

turned these positions into new bases of support among the owners of small and medium plants in the provinces (to whom the WICs awarded state contracts for the first time) and other diverse elements in the commercial–industrial sector which wanted to end the obnoxious autocratic interference in economic affairs.[9]

It was also during the war that several of the Progressist leaders of the WICs, most notably Konovalov, began to develop and advocate the 'progressive' vision, and by doing so provoked a realignment of forces around the committees and within the Moscow business community. Though never summarised quite so neatly, this vision followed essentially two main lines: that of economic progress, which stressed technological innovation and economic efficiency in addition to free enterprise; and that of social progress, which entailed specific labour reforms but implied more broadly the cooptation of workers into the newly emerged civil society.[10] This economic vision elicited the support of the scientific–technological intelligentsia (both in and out of the WICs), the managers of southern industry active in the committees, and certain entrepreneurs, the most important of whom was A.I. Guchkov, the chairman of the Central WIC.

The social vision became the platform for an even broader, more surprising coalition that included Konovalov and a handful of entrepreneurs (who were said to have 'risen above the dominant sentiment of their environment'); the representatives of the democratic intelligentsia in the WICs; and the Menshevik leaders of the Workers' Groups in the committees.[11] But Konovalov's emergence as the spokesman for this vision of social progress also worked to divide him from his old ally, Riabushinskii and the other Moscow Progressists (now in command of Moscow's most important entrepreneurial organisation, the Exchange Committee) who had come to see the interest of the state as standing above the right of society to autonomy and free discourse.[12]

Such divisions notwithstanding, the decidedly oppositional stance of the WICs and their strategy of forging social coalitions placed them at the centre of the anti-autocratic campaign of late 1916 in which the public organisations, the labour groups and various commercial–industrial factions all took some part.[13] When the autocracy collapsed in February 1917, the leaders of the WICs were able to claim the ministries directly concerned with the economy and war industries: Konovalov took over Trade and Industry, War and Navy went to Guchkov and M.I. Tereshchenko (a sugar-industry millionaire and chairman of the Kiev WIC) became the new minister of finance. From these institutional bases and with the help of new allies (especially the employees of Trade and Industry), the 'progressives' began to advocate the economic and social programmes of the WICs which now included some of the workers' newly stated demands. In general, they used their authority as government leaders to project a vision of a

18. Aleksandr Ivanovich Guchkov, Octobrist leader and Minister of War in the Provisional Government until his resignation on 30 April 1917.

new Russia and its new 'bourgeoisie' – for which they sought to act as guides.

To be sure, there was no unanimity in the articles, addresses and interviews issued by diverse elements of the 'progressive' alliance, but ambiguity also helped because the various commercial–industrial constituencies could thus hear all the different arguments in favour of 'progressivism', at least three of which were discernible during the first two months of the revolution. First, there were the intelligentsia acti-

vists of the Moscow and Central WICs and the employees of the
Ministry of Trade and Industry who attempted to invoke the
industrialists' sense of social responsibility and, at times, to manipulate a potentially guilty conscience. Second, the economically oriented
intelligenty who had made careers for themselves in industrial organisations and had earned their reputation as 'state-minded' public activists (among whom were several southern engineers) insisted on the
primacy of 'national' considerations over 'class interests'.[14] And third,
the 'progressive' industrialists themselves emphasised the advantages
of peaceful labour conditions and minimised the sacrifices required to
secure industrial peace.

Taken together these statements offered the Russian commercial–
industrial class, as it entered a confusingly new era, a view of itself and
the revolution that was optimistic even while it stressed the need for
concessions to labour. On the one hand, the industrialists were to
show a readiness to make every sacrifice for the sake of orderly production and increased national output in wartime.[15] They were presented
with the argument that the 'right' of the bourgeoisie to a position of
leadership in the country's economic and political life required that it
demonstrate 'political maturity' and appear to be 'moved by national
and public sentiments and open to the aspirations of the workers'.[16]
On the other hand, they were also promised great rewards:
enlightened legislation and a departure from 'the old prejudices'
would produce a more orderly, even 'peaceful', labour force;[17] a readiness to shoulder sacrifices for the 'general good' would overcome the
legacy of suspicion among social groups which the old régime had
fostered and enable the commercial–industrial 'class' to take its right-
ful place of 'great significance' in a 'great and new' Russia.[18]

Clearly, the purpose of all this was to induce commercial–industrial
interests to behave in a way that would bear out the progressive vision
of Russia's future. Yet, to assume that the rhetoric of industrial progressivism remained alien to all entrepreneurs or that weakness alone
forced them to make concessions would be to miss the full significance
of this short-lived period of industrial 'peace' and to overlook an
important cause of the abrupt shift that would occur after May. In
fact, I would argue, the message of industrial progressivism appeared
very attractive to many of the entrepreneurs because it successfully
integrated the seemingly contradictory elements of reality and the
expectations of the new, post-revolutionary situation. Or, to put matters differently, it was the particular way in which the revolution had
created and combined great hopes for the future with new, compelling

realities which predisposed the majority of entrepreneurs to accept the vision and the sacrifices urged by Konovalov and his colleagues.

The revolution had created a sense of confidence and pride among the men of business. The long-standing contribution of the 'bourgeoisie' to the nation had finally been recognised, as these men argued, because its leading representatives were now ministers of the state in charge of all 'economic' agencies ('our régime', Riabushinskii called it).[19] But the revolution had also brought about a dramatic change in the balance of industrial forces: workers were now free to organise and strike, whereas employers had lost the protection of the police and the army.[20] And the same mixture of opportunity and threat was evident in the workers' initial response to the revolution: in the instantaneous formation of soviets and other labour organisations, the caution shown by workers and their organisations in pursuing their demands, and the favourable response of labour to employers' concessions.[21] Faced with these new and unfamiliar conditions, employers were more willing than before to lend credence to Konovalov's vision of a 'Europeanised' Russian industry: a free capitalist economy complemented by an organised, moderate working class.[22] Moreover, the 'progressive' vision allowed the industrialists to see frequently unavoidable concessions as voluntary acts for the benefit of the country – acts that conferred a measure of moral authority on the entrepreneurs, supported their political aspirations and benefited their economic operations.

Naturally, opposition to the progressive social programme did not disappear. Against Konovalov's vision of direct social contact based on mutual concessions, Riabushinskii argued that the state still had to act as the supreme 'harmoniser' of social relations, while society was to be limited to functional 'unions' rather than political parties. In his view the commercial–industrial class was to assume the task of protecting the government from the pressure of the 'elemental masses' (of standing 'as a mighty wall') and in return to be allowed to 'organise' the country's economy.[23] In Petrograd, too, there were voices protesting at the demands placed by workers (the 'passive', purely physical force in industry) on the 'brains' of the economy (namely, the entrepreneurs).[24] More often, these Petrograd industrialists criticised social reforms in the name of a presumed 'national' interest. They charged, for example, that a shorter work-day would raise production costs, render Russian products uncompetitive on the international market and undermine the national economy. Less genuine, but doubtless effective in stirring up old class hatreds and suspicions, was the accusation that the eight-hour work-day would deprive the army of necessary equipment.[25]

Yet in March and April, for reasons of varying durability and depth, the voices of commercial–industrial belligerence remained largely isolated and ineffectual. In Petrograd, the collapse of the autocracy undermined the strength and confidence of the metal-processing magnates and their bankers, whereas the advocates of progressivism appeared better suited to handling the new situation. Both the Petrograd Society of Factory and Mill Owners (PSFMO) and the Association of Trade and Industry made leadership changes in March.[26] In the country as a whole, the opponents of social and economic reform were divided by traditional rivalries: the Petrograd magnates gave at best perfunctory support to Riabushinskii's organisational efforts – the First Congress of Trade and Industry convened in Moscow on 19 March and the Trade-Industrial Union that was formed by those who attended the congress. The Muscovite leaders of the new union were also weakened by the parochialism of their largest source of support, the provincial merchantry. Encumbered by their small numbers, economic marginality and distance from urban centres, provincial merchants and producers had no more patience for Riabushinskii's grand vision of the 'bourgeoisie' as the champion of the state than for Konovalov's progressivism. They wanted practical help in facing up to the state regulatory agencies and a political stance that would not alienate the peasantry around them.[27]

Of course, the progressive message was received differently by various groups of industrialists and ranged from enthusiasm to resignation. The PSFMO, formerly known for its intransigence, appeared to have accepted the message more fully than all other industrial organisations – which is less surprising if we recall how dependent that society had always been on state orders and on the state's institutions of repression. This dependence made the society more vulnerable to manipulation by the new heads of state after February, though we would do well to remember that the contradictions in the new situation appeared most clearly in Petrograd and also that a small minority within the society had rallied to the progressives' banner as early as the summer of 1916.[28] Be that as it may, the record of the society's activity in March and April was nothing short of astounding.

Some time in early March, the old leadership of the PSFMO was ousted and a provisional committee elected.[29] Within days it issued a public statement of readiness to pay workers for time spent in 'revolutionary' strikes, and on 9 March, it invited the Petrograd Soviet of Workers' and Soldiers' Deputies to send its representatives to negotiate new working conditions for all the city's workers.[30] The agreement reached between the two organisations on 10 March further provided for the institution of an eight-hour work-day (at full pay) and the establishment of factory committees to be elected by the workers as well as conciliation boards in all the factories in the capital.[31] A few days later, a meeting of 300 owners of the largest factories unanimously approved the action of the provisional committee and agreed to pay time-and-a-half for all work done overtime.[32] As a result, during March and April the average work-day in the factories of Petrograd declined from 10.1 to 8.4 hours, while nominal wages rose 35 per cent.[33] A minimum wage of five roubles daily for men and four for women was fixed on 24 April by agreement between the PSFMO and the Petrograd Soviet.[34]

Most remarkable, these significant concessions had not come as a result of extensive strike activity, though doubtless the potential for such activity had contributed to the industrialists' conciliatory mood. The provisional committee itself took care not only to implement the concessions but also to interpret them in the spirit of progressivism: it warned employers that any arrangement for overtime work had to have the consent of the factory committees, reminded them of the obligation to pay workers for time spent in the activities of the soviets, trade unions and factory committees,[35] and explained the importance of the eight-hour work-day as 'one of the best ways of ensuring the further spiritual growth of the working class'.

> It will allow workers time for self-education and for the development of professional organisations whose goal must be the establishment of correct, orderly relations between labour and capital.[36]

No other industrial organisation in Russia appeared to have accepted the progressive vision as completely as the PSFMO, but elements of this vision were employed by other industrial leaders to guide their constituencies in making the necessary concessions. For example, the southern industrialists acknowledged the importance of 'social peace' for economic recovery and did not lag far behind Petrograd in negotiating with the collective representatives of labour and making actual concessions. In joint conferences with workers' organisations in late March and early April, these industrialists agreed to the eight-hour work-day and a higher overtime pay (as much as 35 per cent) as well as to wage increases averaging 50 per cent. They also offered other improvements in living conditions and in return only insisted on the establishment of a network of conciliation boards to handle all labour conflicts.[37]

Among the merchantry of Moscow and the provinces labour demands elicited greater opposition, yet their implementation progressed with relatively little disruption to production. The results were again unprecedented. During the first three months of the revolution, national wages are estimated to have risen on the average by 50 per cent; the eight-hour work-day was instituted almost everywhere, if not by the employers themselves then by a decree of the soviet;[38] and the organisation of conciliation boards, factory committees and trade unions began everywhere. Moreover, in urging member enterprises to make such concessions, provincial industrial leaders rarely used the argument of entrepreneurial weakness as such. The Omsk Exchange Society, for example, urged its members to remember that their factories were helping the war effort and to accept the terms worked out by the Omsk Soviet for the implementation of the eight-hour work-day.

> The committee believes that the industrialists would rather sacrifice a part of their interests and not be guilty of aggravating the class struggle at this exceptionally important historical moment.[39]

The patriotic argument carried particular weight in the provinces where the war had caused intensified economic activity. However, among the most diverse groups of entrepreneurs there were individuals who now argued that 'only social peace could save both industry and the state', as S.S. Novoselov, chairman of the Society of Leather Manufacturers, had put it. The leather and footwear section of the PSFMO echoed the same sentiment in instructing its representatives on the Central Conciliation Board to reach a compromise 'whenever possible'.[40] It was an injunction derived as much from the hopes raised by the revolution as from the urgent needs it had created or the new limits it had placed on the arbitrary power of employers. The point is that during the early weeks of the revolution most entrepreneurs found little to diminish their optimism: both the political disposition of the revolution and the shape of labour relations had given them reason to be hopeful. When the first issue of the *Herald* (published by the PSFMO) appeared several weeks later on 1 June, the leading article declared that Russia had just entered the capitalist stage, so that it was incumbent on industrialists to adjust to life under these new conditions.

> We do not shut our eyes to the inevitable class struggle; but now, it can, and must, proceed under normal conditions . . . We believe that *the free citizen-industrialist and the free citizen-worker will find a common language in which to communicate [and] will find normal forms of mutual relations.*[41]

The significance of this statement must not be lost: the organ of the formerly most intransigent employers' organisation was now calling on its members to embrace industrial progressivism!

UNDER COALITION GOVERNMENT:
INDUSTRIAL PROGRESSIVISM DEFEATED

Historians generally agree that the formation of the coalition coincided with a significant increase in social discord in general and industrial conflict in particular, though it was only after July that these trends produced the social and political polarisation typical of the revolution in its last weeks. As for the shift in commercial–industrial strategy, soviet historians reject the notion that any attitudinal shift occurred either in early March or in early May. They describe the change instead as essentially 'political' in nature: provoked by the strength the soviet had exhibited during the April crisis; by the socialists' entry into the Provisional Government; and by the resolve of the 'bourgeoisie' to regain its natural place as the predominant economic and political force.[42] Alternatively, the shift has been attributed to the reinforcement of entrepreneurial organisations and to their general recovery from the position of powerlessness into which the revolution had initially thrown them.[43] In fact, I argue, these were but two aspects of a complex shift in the collective expectations and behaviour of the commercial–industrial sector – a shift during the first weeks of the coalition government in May and June which involved a virtual revolt, on the part of entrepreneurs everywhere, against their self-appointed progressive leadership and its vision of social accommodation.

The industrialists' reassertion of their own 'class' goals and interests took place against a background of mounting conflicts with other elements of society, the most apparent of which concerned the labour demands for higher wages and shorter working hours. Not only had

19. Pavel Nikolaevich Miliukov, Kadet leader and Minister of Foreign Affairs in the first Provisional Government until his resignation on 2 May 1917 in the wake of the April crisis.

the economic gains made by the workers had the effect of lowering entrepreneurial profits, but in May it became apparent that the early concessions had not put a stop to further economic demands. Old anxieties resurfaced about the economic viability of individual enterprises (unused to operating at less than the extraordinary profits of the past), about Russia's attractiveness to foreign investors, or its ability to compete on the international market at the war's end. Moreover, the continuing economic conflict raised fears about the presumed intention of the workers to 'expropriate' the profits of private entrepreneurs if not their factories.[44] The industrialists also watched in alarm as the worker-elected factory committees gradually expanded their sphere of activity in matters of factory supplies, factory finances and daily managerial decisions.[45] Taken together, these developments threatened the most fundamental sense of the industrialists themselves as owners and entrepreneurs, and, in conjunction with labour's pattern of collective behaviour in the first weeks of the coalition, made the earlier promises of the progressives appear unfounded if not actually misleading.[46]

The second general area of conflict for the industrialists – that of conflict with the government – was slower to emerge, possibly because it was more difficult to admit. To be sure, men as different as Riabushinskii and A.I. Putilov (perhaps the most powerful banker-industrialist in Petrograd) had never shared Konovalov's trust in the moderation of both labour and the socialists, but other industrialists must have doubted, perhaps as early as March or April, whether Konovalov was in fact one of their own or one of the intelligentsia. Yet, not until May were such disagreements openly aired; that is, not until the establishment of the coalition government with the leaders of the Soviet (3 May) and the resignation of Konovalov from the cabinet two weeks later (18 May). At this point, even those measures to which significant segments of the commercial–industrial class had shown little or no opposition when demanded by 'their' ministers – tax reforms, labour legislation and even regulatory measures – were now roundly opposed as the harbingers of socialism.[47]

But what made the industrialists so pessimistic was not only the change in the make-up of the government and its agencies but also the gradual erosion of its traditional authority on which they, at least the Petrograd industrialists but others as well, had customarily depended. By the third month of the revolution many of the government's functions and activities had been assumed by locally elected authorities, local or regional regulatory agencies and various other 'public' bodies in which the intelligentsia generally predominated.[48] Merchants and entrepreneurs now expressed a sense of virtual persecution as they found themselves subject to all sorts of supervisory agencies that were more often useless than efficacious and felt abandoned by a government supposedly 'theirs'.[49]

And of course, as the background to all these conflicts – with the

workers, the oversight agencies, the government – there was the economic crisis which daily embodied the failure of the revolution to fulfil
its promise and made every demand addressed to the entrepreneurs,
every restriction on their freedom of financial manoeuvre seem more
and more ominous. The economic crisis also interfered with the ability
of the employers to respond to their workers' demands or even to
ensure them continuous employment. The prices of raw materials
were rising; there were frequent shortages; and higher wages,
sometimes paid for idle time, rapidly depleted the liquid assets of the
less profitable enterprises or cut into the profit margin of even the most
favoured industrial giants.[50] Beyond these anxieties and difficulties,
however, the economic crisis made it possible for industrial organisations and their spokesmen in the government to employ the rhetoric of
'national interest' as they forsook their earlier conciliatory posture and
embarked on an offensive against labour to reverse its earlier gains.[51]

It is hardly surprising that these conflicts and difficulties – actual and
perceived – should have awakened entrepreneurial groups to their own
'class' interests and prompted them to pitch their claims against those
advanced by the workers. What is striking, however, is the sense of
relief, almost glee, which can be read in the letters of complaint they
addressed to the government and the press. A letter from the PSFMO
on 9 May provides a particularly good example of this new tone of
reproach and self-righteousness:

> Neither in the name of the industrialists' interests nor self-interest
> but out of a feeling of responsibility for the motherland, the society
> . . . sees itself obliged to turn the attention of the Provisional
> Government to the unusually difficult situation in which the
> industry of the Petrograd district now finds itself . . .
>   After the attainment of the political goals of the revolution . . .
> the society . . . thought an internal conflict would affect the inter-
> ests of defence adversely . . . and took the only correct road – the
> road of conciliation with the organised representation of the work-
> ing class . . . The industrialists made very significant concessions
> at great sacrifice . . . Yet, [now] the demands of the workers and
> employees have gone beyond the limits of the possible and a
> catastrophe for industry advances at a dizzying pace.[52]

What was perceived as 'irresponsible' behaviour on the part of
workers was now taken as a justification to deflect whatever moral
pressure had been directed at the industrialists by the progressives in
March   and   April   and   to   claim   government   protection   for

entrepreneurial interests. The *Financial Review*, for example, wherein Konovalov's ideas had never been welcome, could now prove that the workers were 'ignorant', 'lacking in consciousness', and conducting an 'egotistic class struggle'. In contrast, it praised the commercial class for its past and present contributions to the national economy and demanded that the government pledge itself against any 'socialist measure'.[53]

Of course, even now the entrepreneurial press did not speak with one voice. Among those industrialists who had internalised the progressive vision most fully, the most powerful sentiment was one of bitter disappointment, though blame was cast in different directions. The journal *Financial Life*, for example, complained that the revolution which had begun as an 'all-national revolution' had been turned into a 'class revolution' and had in fact put trade and industry under 'a socialist siege'.[54] Even Konovalov seemed paralysed in mid May by the shocking recognition that Russian society might not, after all, have been ready for democracy and freedom both because the masses appeared to have turned easily to excess and because the superstructures of society, such as the state, had proven so fragile.[55]

Similar complaints came from the intelligentsia, allies of the disintegrating progressive coalition. They now saw their vision of Russia as a European society, complete with modern capitalism and parliamentary democracy, destroyed by general economic 'backwardness', socialist 'sectarianism', the 'maximalism' of workers, and the 'egotism' of the industrialists.[56] The tendency to blame the workers and their leaders was particularly characteristic of the engineers who actually worked in the factories and who had often served as the targets of angry actions by the workers.[57] Disillusionment with the workers' 'shallowness of revolutionary discipline' had been observed as well among the employees of the Ministry of Trade and Industry even before Konovalov's resignation.[58] With his resignation, however, the ministry ceased to serve as the focal point of his coalition, and by June it had come under the influence of those groups that had spoken the loudest for entrepreneurial interests.

In another kind of response, some intelligentsia specialists – mostly the engineers and the economists who had become involved in the work of overseeing industry – blamed both the working class and the industrialists for having demonstrated their 'immaturity': the workers because they preferred immediate and local action over a 'collective', coordinated approach to the economic crisis; the industrialists because they had failed to follow the social and economic programme devel-

oped by the progressive alliance on the eve of the revolution.[59] Not
surprisingly, this analysis led the technical intelligentsia to the conclusion that they alone were capable of saving Russia and the revolution
because they not only stood for progress in general, but most important, stood above class interest and thereby for the nation itself.[60] But
there was nothing in this analysis to lead the industrialists to act as an
enlightened, powerful, and magnanimous 'bourgeoisie'. For, after all,
were not the technical intelligentsia – those who had held up this ideal
to them – now condemning the Russian commercial–industrial class
for having failed to live up to its historic task?[61]

A survey of the way in which the industrialists responded in practice to
labour demands shows an unmistakable trend towards greater intransigence, though there remained significant regional differences. The
Moscow industrial organisations were the loudest in expressing their
disapproval of the Provisional Government, even threatening a
'resolute counter-action' by commercial–industrial interests to block
policies they deemed unfavourable.[62] The Muscovites also began confronting workers' demands with coordinated, aggressive lockouts, the
first of which took place in June at Guzhon and other metal-processing
factories in Moscow province.[63] Later, in the post-July period the
Moscow industrialists, both those led by Riabushinskii in the All-
Russian Commercial–Industrial Union and those headed by Guzhon
in the Moscow Society of Factory and Mill Owners, made confrontation their declared strategy.[64] Riabushinskii then appeared to be
deliberately courting catastrophe in the hope that its outcome – 'the
bony hand of hunger' – would teach the workers and members of
'sundry committees and soviets' the lesson of submission to the 'state
interest' as defined by the commercial–industrial class.[65]

   In Petrograd and the south, the change in entrepreneurial strategies
was just as unmistakable, though more gradual. Acting as if caught by
surprise, the industrialists' first response, in May, was to relapse into
their traditional position of dependence on the state, calling on the
government to help counteract the superior strength of the workers,
though as yet the goal was to stop not reverse labour gains.[66] By late
May and early June, however, the entrepreneurs of Petrograd and the
south were publicly expressing their disappointment with the achievements of the Provisional Government as well as their disapproval of its
overall direction and specific solutions.[67] In meetings called by Putilov
on 25 May and 1–2 June (the latter was labelled in the socialist press
the 'Conference of the Big Bourgeoisie'), the assembled magnates of

industry agreed that the government had failed to understand the essential role capitalism was destined to play in Russia, and for this reason they sought to establish the strongest of entrepreneurial organisations to force the government to change both its policies and also the manner of their implementation.[68]

In their dealings with workers, industrialists in Petrograd and the south began in June to reject labour demands outright and to disallow the decisions of the governmental arbitrators.[69] Moreover, June also saw the transition to more 'offensive' strategies, and here too the first steps were organisational, as one speaker at the 'Conference of the Big Bourgeoisie' in early June explained:

> The workers hold us in their hands, intervene in the management of [our] affairs, and arbitrarily dismiss [our] employees. We ... are now prepared to rebuff the attack on private property ... You must defend yourselves by establishing an organisation that will establish unity.[70]

Indeed, the PSFMO demanded (on 13 June) that all its members sign a 'convention' obligating them to consult with the society before responding to their workers' demands.[71] Lockouts were still relatively rare in June (Moscow was the exception), but warnings about the prospects of unemployment and the hunger that would result from labour's 'excessive' demands helped create the impression that every shutdown was in fact a deliberate lockout.[72]

At the same time, the Petrograd-based organisations began to resist government labour legislation, and though this strategy did not have the immediate inflammatory effect of announced lockouts, it proved highly detrimental to the past and future gains of the workers. The laws on the freedom to strike, the eight-hour work-day, a minimum wage and unemployment insurance were defeated by the entrepreneurial opposition and its supporters in the Ministry of Trade and Industry, and this same alliance joined to change labour projects for workers' insurance significantly.[73] The projects of the Ministry of Labour were deemed objectionable both because of the permanence they imparted to the industrialists' *ad hoc* concessions and because they were the work of socialists.[74] Moreover, the rewriting of labour laws became one of the weapons in the struggle of the industrialists to curb the economic gains made by their employees, while the repeated demands for higher wages were used to demonstrate that the government had no choice but to establish legal limits on such demands.[75]

After July, industrialists in Petrograd began preparing themselves for a showdown with workers by adding industrial-branch sections to their society's city-district subdivisions; tightening the control of the PSFMO over the settlements negotiated by those sections; and taking the initiative in organising an All-Russian Union of Societies of Industrialists.[76] Member enterprises and the new sections became perceptibly more steadfast in resisting the demands of labour during individual and collective bargaining.[77] In the south, meanwhile, the industrialists were calling for troops to be sent to the Donbass mines in order to protect property and production.[78] Moreover, the entrepreneurial attack on labour was now intended not only to stop but actually to reverse the workers' earlier gains. In July the PSFMO instructed its sections to renege on promises made during the July Days, to refuse payment for time spent in demonstrations, and to reject 'the procedure practised hitherto' of submitting workers' demands to arbitration boards.[79] Next, the entrepreneurs attacked the right of the workers to be paid for time spent in the activities of the soviets, trade unions and factory committees;[80] in September the eight-hour day and the workers' right even to demand higher wages to compensate for higher food prices likewise came under assault.[81] One leather manufacturer who had previously taken a progressive view of labour relations now called on industrialists to do everything to break the workers' organisations: mechanise production, hire foreign workers and even shift from domestic production to imports.[82]

There were, of course, organisational–political sides to what has been described here as a 'revolt' of commercial-industrial groups against the progressive leadership and its programme. In the Petrograd-based organisations strength had shifted (in May) back to the old oligarchy of investment bankers and metal-processing magnates. These organisations had then become the springboard for the efforts of Putilov and his circle to unite Russia's disparate commercial–industrial groups under the leadership of the Petrograd magnates – in the Union of United Industry and the All-Russian Union of Societies of Industrialists. However, neither the general organisational effort mounted by the commercial–industrial sector, nor the specific leadership changes listed here, can adequately explain the sweeping transformation in entrepreneurial strategies. That the old oligarchy could reassert its leadership, indeed defeat Konovalov's coalition, was itself testimony to a change of expectations and self-perception among industrialists at large. Moreover, as we have seen, the organisational effort of the summer grew out of weakness rather than strength. In the months leading up to October the disintegration of the state would leave industrialists even less capable of protecting their interests than had been the case in March and April.

The argument advanced here, then, is that the commercial–industrial retrenchment that began during the term of the first coalition should not be seen to have been primarily the consequence of organisational and political resurgence. Rather, it was the result of the many diverse ways in which the realities of the revolution, particularly in the areas of labour relations and economic performance, disappointed industrialists and contradicted the vision of industrial peace, economic hegemony and social respectability held up to them by the progressive leadership. The irony was that even though the various commercial–industrial circles had begun to reassert the legitimacy of their 'class interests', they could not unify their ranks for effective action on their behalf.

Indeed, if anything, the divisions between Petrograd and Moscow, the south and the provinces, appeared more intractable – certainly more damaging – in the summer and autumn than they had been in the spring. One immediate cause had been the return to the scene of Moscow's old rivals, the Petrograd oligarchy, which made organisational unity impossible: each capital now headed its own 'national' union. Moreover, the new rhetoric of self-interest was closely linked to particularistic issues and was therefore less suited than Konovalov's progressive rhetoric to unite the commercial–industrial elements into a 'national bourgeoisie' informed by a broad conception of national politics and the national economy.

It hardly needs stating that the shift in the attitudes and collective behaviour of the industrialists had significant political consequences, the most direct of which was the growing opposition of the commercial–industrial forces to any of the reforms demanded by even the most moderate socialists, despite the support of the latter for the Provisional Government. Naturally, this opposition contributed to the political instability of the post-July months and even to General Kornilov's unsuccessful conspiracy on which many industrialists had placed their hopes. Furthermore, such opposition, as well as the aggressive stance of employers in industrial conflicts, also seemed to prove the workers' suspicion that inflation, unemployment and idle plants were all part of a deliberate 'bourgeois' attack on labour and the revolution. This argument predisposed workers to reject the strategies of social accommodation urged on them by the moderate leaders of the All-Russian Executive Committee of the Soviets and to accept the Bolshevik political solution of Soviet Power as unavoidable.

NOTES

1 I have in mind the following studies: Diane Koenker, *Moscow Workers and the 1917 Revolution* (Princeton, 1981); David Mandel, *The Petrograd Workers and the Fall of the Old Regime* (New York, 1983); and his *The Petrograd Workers and the Soviet Seizure of Power* (New York, 1984); William G. Rosenberg, 'Russian Labor and Bolshevik Power After October', *Slavic Review* 42, no. 2 (1985), 213–38; Steven A. Smith, *Red Petrograd. Revolution in the Factories, 1917–18* (Cambridge, 1983); P.V. Volobuev, *Proletariat i burzhuaziia v 1917 g.* (Moscow, 1964), and my own *The Menshevik Leaders in the Russian Revolution: Social Realities and Political Strategies* (Princeton, 1989).

2 P.V. Volobuev, *Proletariat i burzhuaziia*; and his *Ekonomicheskaia politika Vremennogo Pravitelstva* (Moscow, 1962); V.Ia. Laverychev, *Po tu storonu barikad (iz istorii borby Moskovskoi burzhuazii s revoliutsiei* (Moscow, 1967). Contrary to such claims of consistency, however, these works do record evidence of change in entrepreneurial conduct.

3 Alfred J. Rieber, *Merchants and Entrepreneurs in Imperial Russia* (Chapel Hill, 1982).

4 There were only four of these 'societies of mill and factory owners'.

5 For studies of the Moscow entrepreneurial group and its politics on the eve of the war, see T.C. Owen, *Capitalism and Politics in Russia. A Social History of the Moscow Merchants, 1855–1905* (Cambridge, 1981); J.A. Ruckman, *The Moscow Business Elite: A Social and Cultural Portrait of Two Generations, 1840–1905* (Dekalb, 1984); Rieber, *Merchants and Entrepreneurs*, chs. 4, 5, 7; Laverychev, *Po tu storonu barikad*, ch. 2; and L.H. Haimson, 'The Problem of Social Stability in Urban Russia, 1905–1917', *Slavic Review* 24, no. 1 (1965), 4–8.

6 These formulations appeared in two articles published in Riabushinskii's newspaper *Utro Rossii* (3 and 4 September 1915) which offered the fullest exposition to date of the Progressist vision; see no. 243 (3 September), p. 1 and no. 244 (4 September), p. 4, as quoted in V.S. Diakin, *Russkaia burzhuaziia i tsarizm v gody pervoi mirovoi voiny, 1914–1917* (Leningrad, 1967), pp. 146–7.

7 The press representing middle and small industry was filled with attacks on Petrograd's entrepreneurial giants and especially praised the Moscow industrialists for their independence from the large banks of the capital. See *Promyshlennaia Rossiia* no. 1 (15 April 1915), pp. 1–3; nos. 4/5 (7 May), pp. 1–2; nos. 6/7 (31 May), pp. 1–3, 5–7; nos. 10/11 (28 June), pp. 1–5; nos. 14/15 (26 July), pp. 3–4; *Vserossiiskii vestnik promyshlennosti i torgovli* (hereafter *VVPiT*) no. 5 (May 1915), pp. 6–7; no. 7 (July), pp. 1–6; no. 8 (August), pp. 1–8; *Vestnik kustarnoi promyshlennosti* no. 7/29 (September 1915), pp. 1–13 and 24–41.

8 Konovalov and A.I. Guchkov took over the Central WIC, whereas

Riabushinskii headed the Moscow WIC, which acted as a clearing house for the WICs of the Central Industrial region. Two, often complementary, studies were particularly helpful in mapping out the history of the Progressists in the WICs: L.H. Siegelbaum, *The Politics of Industrial Mobilization in Russia, 1914–17: A Study of the War-Industries Committees* (New York, 1983); and W.L. Duggan, 'The Progressists and Russian Politics, 1914–1917', Ph.D. dissertation, Columbia University, 1984.

9 See reports from Odessa, Kursk and Kharkov in *Izvestiia Tsentralnogo Voenno-Promyshlennogo Komiteta* (hereafter *IzvTsVPK*) 2 (29 August 1915), p. 3; no. 15 (13 October), p. 4; no. 68 (8 March 1916), p. 6; and the report on the conference of regional WICs held in Petrograd on 18–19 April 1916 (ibid., no. 86 (23 April), p. 21).

10 The economic programme of the WICs was articulated in the committees' various publications, most clearly in the journal published by the Moscow WIC, *Proizvoditelnye sily Rossii* (hereafter *PSR*). The social vision summarised here was less openly stated, though elements of it were contained in the resolutions adopted by the Second Congress of WICs (see *Trudy Vtorogo sezda Predstavitelei Voenno-Promyshlennykh Komitetov, 26–29 fevralia 1916 goda*, 2 vols., Petrograd, 1916); a fuller exposition was given in Konovalov's memorandum circulated to local and regional WICs in June 1916 (see 'K istorii "Rabochei gruppy" pri Tsentralnom voenno-promyshlennom komitete', *Krasnyi arkhiv* (hereafter *KA*) 57, 1933, 48–84).

11 F. Platonov on the social character of the WICs, *Izvestiia Moskovskogo Voenno-Promyshlennogo Komiteta* (hereafter *IzvMVPK*) 31/32 (October–November 1916), pp. 53–5. See also Siegelbaum, *The Politics of Industrial Mobilization*, pp. 52–8.

12 *IzvMVPK* no. 13 (January 1916), pp. 46–55; no. 14 (January), 1–2.

13 Duggan, 'The Progressists', pp. 337–9, quoting archival sources; B.B. Grave (ed.), *Burzhuaziia nakanune fevralskoi revoliutsii* (Moscow, 1927), pp. 155–6; and A.G. Shliapnikov, *Kanun semnadtstogo goda*, 2 vols. (Moscow and Petrograd, 1923), vol. II, pp. 128–9.

14 A prime example of this type was A.A. Bublikov, whose statements are cited below, a railway engineer, Progressist Duma deputy, head of the Transportation Section of the Central WIC and a member of the management of several companies.

15 See reports of speeches by Bublikov in *Pervyi Torgovo-Promyshlennyi Sezd* (Moscow, 1917); pp. 143–6; *Burzhuaziia i pomeshchiki v 1917 god. Chastnye soveshchaniia chlenov Gosudarstvennoi Dumy* (Moscow and Leningrad, 1932), pp. 31–3, 46–7.

16 Quotations are from articles in the *Commercial–Industrial Gazette*, which was written and edited by employees of the Ministry of Trade and Industry, and *Financial Life*, a Petrograd weekly addressed to commercial, industrial and financial interests. See *Finansovaia zhizn* (hereafter *FZh*) nos. 9/10 (9 March), pp. 141–5; *Torgovo-promyshlennaia gazeta* (hereafter

TPG) no. 50 (10 March), p. 2; *FZh* nos. 9/10 (9 March), pp. 144–5; no. 11 (16 March), pp. 168–9.

17 *TPG* no. 47 (7 March), p. 2; no. 51 (11 March), p. 2; no. 54 (15 March), p. 2; no. 56 (17 March), p. 2; no. 77 (15 April), p. 2.

18 From Konovalov's press conference, 29 March: *TPG* no. 65 (30 March), p. 4; *Vestnik Vremennogo Pravitelstva* (hereafter *VVP*) no. 21 (31 March), p. 4; and his address (on 15 April) to the Moscow Exchange Society: *Izvestiia Osobogo Soveshchaniia [po toplivu]* (hereafter *IzVOS*) no. 3 (April), pp. 88–93.

19 See the reports of the gala meeting held in Petrograd on 3 March in honour of the three ministers from the WICs in *FZh*, no. 11 (16 March), pp. 165–6; *IzvTsVPK*, no. 208 (13 March), pp. 2–3; *TPG* no. 49 (9 March), pp. 3–4; and *VVP* no. 5 (10 March), pp. 2–3.

20 At a meeting on 16 March of industrial leaders with Konovalov, B.A. Efron of the Petrograd Society of Industrialists explained that the industrialists' concessions were only 'temporary' and were necessary 'for the purpose of establishing order in the labour situation of the capital' (*Revoliutsionnoe dvizhenie posle sverzheniia samoderzhaviia*, Moscow, 1957, p. 438).

21 For a discussion of labour's collective behaviour during the early months of 1917, see my *The Menshevik Leaders in the Russian Revolution*, ch. 3.

22 Konovalov had argued in his memorandum from June 1916 that 'European experience' had shown that the general 'consciousness of civic duties' could also be raised 'by raising the cultural level of workers and turning the formless mass of individual workers into an organised, public-minded, productive class' (memo written as a circular to the local War Industries Committees and reproduced in 'K istorii "rabochei gruppy" pri Tsentralnom Voenno-promyshlennom Komitete', *Krasnyi arkhiv* 57 (1933), 48–84).

23 From Riabushinskii's opening address to the First Congress of Trade and Industry which convened in Moscow at his initiative on 19 March 1917 (*Pervyi Torgovo-promyshlennyi sezd* (Moscow, 1917), pp. 7–19.

24 *Promyshlennost i torgovlia* (hereafter *PiT*) nos. 12/13 (15 April), pp. 241–5.

25 *Finansovoe obozrenie* (hereafter *FO*) no. 9/10 (18 March), pp. 4–6; no. 11/12 (29 March), pp. 5–6; *Izvestiia Soveta sezdov predstavitelei promyshlennosti i torgovli* (hereafter *IzvSSPPiT*) no. 3 (23 April), p. 1; *PiT* no. 14/15 (29 April), pp. 265–9. In truth, most Russian factories were technologically unprepared to work in three shifts. As for the army, there is evidence that as late as June 1917 it still had enough munitions for six more months of fighting. See *Zhurnaly osobogo soveshchaniia* [po oborone] (hereafter *ZhOS*) no. 174 (1 July); 'Zadachi', *PiT* no. 22/23 (24 June).

26 The association's decision to name N.N. Kutler as its new chairman ended a year and a half's stalemate between the Petrograd 'oligarchy' and the southern engineer-managers of whom Kutler was a member.

27 These complaints were aired at the First Congress of Trade and Industry (*Pervyi sezd*, pp. 51–8, 78–119, 136–8).

28 During the summer of 1916, and in spite of the PSFMO's official opposition to the labour programme of the Central WIC, specific initiatives received support from individual owners in Petrograd as well as the society's Commission on Workers' Lives and its Commission on Improving the conditions of Workers in the Textile Industry: *IzvTsVPK* no. 139 (30 August 1916), pp. 3–4; no. 143 (10 September), pp. 3–4; no. 144 (13 September), pp. 2–3; no. 145 (16 September), pp. 3–4.

29 The only direct evidence of this change comes from Shliapnikov (*Semnadtstyi god*, 4 vols., Petrograd, 1923, vol. II, p. 126), but it is corroborated by frequent references to the 'Provisional Committee' in March. On 15 April a general assembly of the society elected a new chairman (A.A. Bachmanov), five other committee members and adopted new regulations: *PiT* no. 14/15 (29 April), p. 293; *FO* no. 15 (May), p. 24.

30 *FZh* no. 9/10 (9 March), pp. 144–5; *Izvestiia*, no. 11 (10 March), p. 3; *Petrogradskii sovet rabochikh i soldatskikh deputatov. Protokoly zasedanii Ispolnitelnogo Komiteta i Biuro I.K.* (Moscow and Leningrad, 1925), p. 31.

31 At the same time the society entrusted a commission with preparing a programme for the 'regulation and improvement of working conditions in Petrograd's factories' (*Izvestiia* no. 11, 10 March, p. 1). For examples of workers' success in obtaining similar concessions from employers outside Petrograd see the reports from Odessa, Nizhnii Novgorod, Kharkov, Nikolaev, Iaroslav, Simferopol, Saratov, Rostov, Perm and Ekaterinburg in *Rabochaia gazeta* (hereafter *RG*) nos. 13, 17, 18, 19 and 21 (21, 26, 28, 29 and 31 March) and V.A. Miller and A.M. Pankratova (eds.), *Rabochee dvizhenie v 1917 godu* (Moscow, 1926), pp. 48–9.

32 *TPG* no. 55 (16 March), p. 3.

33 Volobuev, *Proletariat*, pp. 121, 126–8.

34 Ibid., p. 128.

35 T.I. Shatilova, 'Petrogradskaia krupnaia burzhuaziia mezhdu dvumia revoliutsiiami 1917 g.', *Kraznaia letopis* (hereafter *KL*) 6/21 (1926), p. 55.

36 *Ekonomicheskoe polozhenie Rossii nakanune Velikoi Oktiabrskoi sotsialisticheskoi revoliutsii* (henceforth *EPR*), 3 vols. (Moscow and Leningrad, 1957), vol. I, pp. 511–13.

37 *Konferentsii rabochikh i promyshlennikov iuga Rossii*, vol. 1 (Kharkov, 1917), pp. 61–4. At the 16 March meeting of the heads of industrial organisations with Konavalov, N.F. von Ditmar (of the Association of Southern Mineowners) stressed the importance of social peace: *FO* no. 11/12 (29 March), pp. 7–8.

38 See the following sources on the soviet's unilateral institution of the eight-hour work-day in Moscow: *Rabochee dvizhenie*, pp. 44–7; *EPR*, vol. I, pp. 159–61; Laverychev, *Po tu storonu*, pp. 183, 232; Volobuev, *Proletariat*, pp. 161, 175. Soviets in other cities and towns followed the example of

Moscow, either because the industrialists put up strong opposition to the eight-hour demand or, more often, because there was no industrial organisation with which to negotiate. For examples of strikes leading to entrepreneurial concessions on the work-day issue, see reports from Saratov in *RG* no. 17 (26 March), p. 4; and *Pravda* no. 18 (28 March), p. 4. For examples of the latter, see the accounts of events in Kazan in *Rabochee dvizhenie*, p. 49; Iu.P. Denike, 'Mensheviki v dni revoliutsii (v strane)', unpublished typescript, pp. 12–13, 22; and Interview no. 8, pp. 24–6, both in the archives of the Project on Menshevik History, Columbia University.

History, Columbia University.

39 *Rab. dvizh. posle sverzheniia*, p. 50. That the position expressed by the Omsk Exchange enjoyed wide support in commercial–industrial circles is evident from the election of A.A. Skorokhodov of the Omsk Exchange Committee to the Permanent Council of the All-Russian Union of Trade and Industry during its first congress (Rieber, *Merchants and Entrepreneurs*, p. 386).

40 See Novoselov's opening address to the All-Russian Congress of Leather Manufacturers in Petrograd on 8 May: *Vestnik Vserossiiskogo Obshchestva Kozhevnykh Zavodchikov* (hereafter *VVOKZ*) no. 32, (15 May), pp. 190–200. The Association of Leather Manufacturers' Petrograd-based bi-weekly reported regularly and approvingly on the work of Konovalov's Advisory Committee on labour legislation and on the Central Conciliation Board: *VVOKZ* no. 31 (1 May), p. 192; no. 32 (15 May), pp. 222–3; no. 33/4 (15 June), p. 269; it was during the election (17 March) of its four representatives to the board that the instruction to 'compromise' was issued.

41 As quoted in Shatilova, 'Petrogradskaia burzhuaziia', pp. 50–1; italics in the original.

42 See, for example, B.B. Reikhardt, 'Russkaia burzhuaziia v borbe za sokhranenie ekonomicheskogo', *KL*, 1/34 (1930), pp. 5–47.

43 Volobuev, *Proletariat*, p. 164.

44 See, for example, *FO* no. 15 (May), pp. 3–4; *Torgovlia i promyshlennost* (hereafter *TiP*) no. 18/19 (27 May), pp. 351–4; *VVOKZ* no. 32 (15 May), pp. 202–4; V.T. T-ov, *VVOKZ* no. 33/34 (15 June), pp. 239–42; statement issued on 4 May by the Union of Owners of Mechanised Woodprocessing Plants in Petrograd (*EPR*, vol. 1, pp. 514–17). Also, see the southern industrialists' address to the Provisional Government dated 27 May (ibid., pp. 173–80).

45 See, for example, the complaint on this score by the Association of Metalprocessing Industry to the Minister of Trade and Industry dated 2 June (*EPR*, vol. 1, pp. 184–5).

46 This particular point was not made as often as one might expect, but see for example *VVOKZ* no. 36 (15 July), pp. 333–4. For a discussion of the dynamics of labour relations in May and June, see my book, *The Menshevik Leaders*, ch. 6.

47 See V. Shtein in *PiT* no. 16/17 (13 May), pp. 312–16, which expressed the fear that the Soviet's easy victories would produce a 'typically Russian ideological maximalism' and give rise to the belief that socialism was timely. See G. Mertsalov, *PiT* no. 16/17 (13 May), pp. 305–9, for expressions of fear that socialist pressure on the government would turn the monopoly from a measure of regulating fuel consumption into one of 'state socialism'.

48 See *Biulleten Komiteta iugo-zapadnogo fronta* (published by the Union of Zemstva), Kiev no. 80 (2 July), p. 1, for an assessment of the role of the 'third element', 'supra-class' intelligentsia in the *zemstva* and city governments. According to the article, the revolution had transformed these men from 'hired employees' into 'responsible leaders' of the Public Organisations.

49 See S. Rozov on the new bureaucracy, in *PiT* no. 26/7 (22 July), pp. 50–2, for a complaint against the cost of all the new regulatory agencies the writer characterised as 'intelligentsia' creations. In the article, 'Citizens of the First and Second Order', *PiT* no. 24/5 (8 July), pp. 12–14, the author complains that when the workers strike, the government merely appeals to them, but when Guzhon, 'the largest metal producer in Moscow', rejected the workers' demands, the government allowed the Moscow Factory Conference and the Special Conference on the Defence to sequester his factory.

50 The journals of the Special Conference on Defence show a marked increase during May in the number of defence contractors claiming insolvency because of the rising cost of raw materials and labour: see, for example, *ZhOS* nos. 159, 162–6 (3, 20, 24, 27, 31 May and 3 June), pp. 302, 343–52, 357–8, 372, 380–3, 393–5. It is extremely hard to determine whether these claims were made in good faith. The socialist press argued repeatedly that extraordinary war profits in 1915 and 1916 made it possible for entrepreneurs to absorb financial losses. In fact, the *TPG* had warned on 11 April that the enormous profits just reported by joint-stock companies should not be distributed in dividends because entrepreneurs would be called on to pay higher wages and higher taxes: *TPG* no. 73 (11 April), p. 2. This advice was apparently not followed.

51 See for example Kutler's address to the Economic Council in Z. Lozinskii, *Ekonomicheskaia politika Vremennogo Pravitelstva* (Leningrad, 1929), pp. 187–8. Kutler demanded that instead of a law on the eight-hour work-day there should be measures for imposing longer hours.

52 *EPR*, vol. I, pp. 166–8.

53 *FO*, no. 17/18 (June), pp. 4–6.

54 *FZh* no. 20 (25 May), pp. 370–2; ibid., pp. 373–4.

55 See his letter of 8 May to Prince Lvov complaining against the Ministry of Interior's failure to enforce the laws preventing attacks on property: (*FO* no. 16 (May), p. 21; *VVP* no. 53 (13 May), p. 2; his complaints of workers' 'excessive' demands during a cabinet meeting on 15 May:

Novaia zhizn (hereafter *NZn*) no. 26 (18 May), p. 4; N. Avdeev (ed.), *Revoliutsiia 1917 goda. Khronika sobytii*, vol. II (Moscow, 1923), p. 157; and his speech to the Third Congress of WICs (on 16 May) in which he attacked the socialists, the extremists among them for 'hypnotising' the masses with their slogans and the moderates for failing to keep the labour struggle within 'legitimate channels': *IzvTsVPK* no. 230 (25 May), p. 1; *VVP* no. 57 (18 May), p. 3.

56 E.g. *IzvTsVPK* no. 242 (3 July), p. 2; *Proizvoditelnye sily Rossii* (hereafter *PSR*) no. 13/14 (19 September), pp. 1–4.

57 See reports by fon Ditmar and Priadkin, *Tretiia konferentsiia promyshlennikov iuga Rossii, 20–24 sentiabria 1917 g.* (Kharkov, 1917), pp. 1–6, 9–12.

58 I. Derevenko in *TPG* no. 98 (13 May), p. 2; no. 107 (25 May), pp. 1–2.

59 At the Third Congress of WICs in mid-May, Bublikov criticised the industrialists for being continuously more concerned with high profits than the state of the national economy: *IzvTsVPK* no. 231 (22 May), pp. 1–2.

60 Iv. Brashin in *TPG* no. 102 (18 May), p. 2. See also the letter (30 May) addressed by the Central Committee for the Restoration and Support for a Normal Course of Work in Industrial Enterprises (established in early April by the Union of Engineers) to the Minister of War and the Navy (*EPR*, vol. I, pp. 180–1).

61 See, for example, in the *Vestnik* of the Association of Leather Manufacturers the bitter response to an article in the journal of the Union of *Zemstva* and Cities in which a certain Panov advised the government not to listen to the industrialists' appeals that it 'curb the workers' appetites' but instead stop industrialists from shutting down their factories and force them to operate on less generous profits than they had been used to: *VVOKZ* no 35 (1 July), pp. 299–300.

62 *EPR*, vol. I, pp. 171–2. See also Riabushinskii's speech at the Second Congress of Trade and Industry, ibid., pp. 196–200.

63 Another example from Moscow was the provocative decision (22 May) of the Moscow-based Union of United Industry to stop work from 15 June to 15 September (*EPR*, vol. I, pp. 404–5).

64 See, for example, the Moscow Society's circular of 18 July concerning workers' requests for paid leave (*EPR*, vol. I, pp. 527–8); the reports of shutdowns in the factories of Bromel, Bari and M.I. Grigoriev: *RG* no. 108 (16 July), p. 3; and Tretiakov's refusal to take over the Ministry of Trade and Industry until the Provisional Government had renounced its earlier promises to the soviet: V.Ia. Laverychev, 'Vserossiiskii soiuz torgovli i promyshlennosti', *Istoricheskie zapiski* 70 (1961), 46–7.

65 From Riabushinskii's speech at the Second Congress of Trade and Industry (*EPR*, vol. I, pp. 196–201). This and other pronouncements at the Second Congress of Trade and Industry (3–5 August) prompted the liberal newspaper *Russkie vedemosti* to declare that the assembled mer-

chants and industrialists had exhibited an 'exclusiveness and intolerance' worthy of the Bolsheviks: for they 'did not grieve over the grave condition of the motherland but gloated over the mistakes of the Provisional Government': *Russkie vedemosti* (hereafter *RV*) no. 178 (5 August), p. 1.

66 See, for example, the appeals from the southern industrialists, the Association of Trade and Industry and the Petrograd Society of Industrialists to have state contracts rewritten to compensate employers for the higher wages paid to workers: *TPG* no. 110 (28 May), pp. 3–4; *EPR*, vol. 1, pp. 165–71; 403–4. The Association of Trade and Industry also supported the demand of the southern industrialists that the workers' wage demands be curbed in the name of the 'state interest': *TPG* no. 110 (28 May), pp. 3–4.

67 A letter from the Conference of Southern Industrialists to the Provisional Government (dated 27 May) was bitter on the failure to protect the law and instil respect for proprietorial rights (*EPR*, vol. 1, pp. 173–80).

68 *EPR*, vol. 1, pp. 181–4; *PSR* no. 12 (15 August), p. 18.

69 The behaviour of the Donbass owners in a region-wide conflict which started in early May contained elements that would become typical of Petrograd's major owners only in June: they had refused to consider their workers' 'second-wave' demands, had called on the government to intervene, had then rejected the compromise worked out by M.I. Skobelev (the Menshevik Minister of Labour) and met a general regional strike, but had declared themselves resolutely against a policy of lockouts (*Konferentsii rab. i prom. iuga*, pp. 7–8; *EPR*, vol. 1, pp. 196–7, 403–4).

70 Cited by Reikhardt, 'Russkaia burzhuaziia', p. 26.

71 Ibid., pp. 29–31. A circular sent by the society to its members on 3 June explained the need for a new policy specifically given the 'new wave of economic demands' (*EPR*, vol. 1, p. 523). A similar effort to establish employers' solidarity was made in the Donbass (ibid., pp. 523–4).

72 See the warning issued by the Donbass industrialists (28 June) of impending shutdowns because of workers' wage demands (*EPR*, vol. 1, pp. 407–8).

73 *Vestnik ministerstva truda* no. 1/2 (August).

74 See L.I. Shpergaze's statement on behalf of the Petrograd Society of Industrialists, cited in Volobuev, *Proletariat*, p. 186.

75 On 8 June, Palchinskii brought a proposal to set a ceiling on workers' earnings before the cabinet (*EPR*, vol. 1, p. 546).

76 Shatilova, 'Petrogradskaia burzhuaziia', pp. 48–50; *EPR*, vol. 1, p. 452.

77 In the case of the metal-workers' collective wage negotiations, the society changed its team of negotiators after the July Days and rejected wage raises for unskilled workers, though eventually it was forced to accept a compromise agreement. When the coopers struck in mid July in support of wage levels already accepted by many individual owners, the employers' collective representatives argued that such concessions had

been granted under the pressure of 'machine guns in the streets': *RG* no. 119 (29 July), p. 4.

78 On 19 July, fon Ditmar asked the Special Conference on Defence that the proposed institution of military authority in factories producing for the war effort be extended to include all industry in the Donbas: *ZhOS* no. 179 (19 July), pp. 587–8.

79 See the following circulars: from the society's Metalprocessing Section (4 July); its chairman (7 July); and its council (16 July). See *EPR*, vol. 1, pp. 526–7; Shatilova, 'Petrogradskaia burzhuaziia', p. 54.

80 See circulars of the Petrograd Society (12 September) and the Main Committee of United Industry (8 June). See *EPR*, vol. 1, p. 532; *VVOKZ* no. 39 (1 September), p. 433.

81 *EPR*, vol. 1, pp. 534–5, 539–41; *Moskovskoe soveshchanie obshchestvennykh deiatelei* (Moscow, 1918), pp. 60–7, 72–85, 90–4.

82 *VVOKZ* no. 40/1 (1 October), pp. 448–50.

Part 3

NATIONALITIES

I O

NATIONALISM AND CLASS IN THE RUSSIAN REVOLUTION: A COMPARATIVE DISCUSSION

RONALD GRIGOR SUNY

EVER since Stalin's early pronouncements as Commissar of Nationalities the Soviet justifications for 'gathering' the non-Russian peoples into a new federal state have been based on the priority of the claims of class (proletarian; here implying Russia) over nationality (identified with the bourgeoisie, the peasantry or simply the ethnic; here implying the peoples of the periphery). Separatism, it was said, at best reflected the interests of bourgeois parties, at worst the false consciousness of people misled by Western imperialists. In stark contrast Western analysts, by playing down social and class characteristics and emphasising (or even exclusively focusing on) political and ideological aspects of nationalist movements, have argued, sometimes explicitly, for the validity of the nationalist claim that only separation from Russia and the creation of independent nation-states could have satisfied their real aspirations. From these starkly contrasting perspectives the revolution of 1917 and the subsequent Civil War have been interpreted by some as a national war of Russians against minorities, the centre against the peripheries, and by others as a civil war of class against class, worker against peasant and bourgeois, city against country. A surprising number of the standard treatments, however, have noted the complex interplay of social and ethnic features.[1]

In at least three ways the extreme dichotomy between the exclusive claims of nationality and the priority of class should be questioned. First, as many writers have pointed out, in Eastern Europe and the Russian empire class and nationality were complexly related. In my own work I have emphasised how ethnicity has both reinforced and undermined class. In central Transcaucasia, Georgian nobles and peasants, sharing a common ethnic culture and values based on rural, pre-capitalist traditions, faced an entrepreneurial Armenian urban middle class that dominated their historic capital, Tiflis, and had developed a way of life alien to the villagers. To the east, in and around Baku, the peasantry was almost entirely Azerbaijani, and urban society was stratified roughly along ethnic and religious lines, with Muslim workers at the bottom, Armenian and Russian workers in the more skilled positions, and Christian and European industrialists and capitalists dominating the oil industry.[2] At the same time the vertical ethnic ties that linked different social strata or classes together in a single community worked against the horizontal links between members of the same social class.[3]

A second reason for softening the distance between class and nationality is that the intensity with which commitment to either was felt was related to the nature, depth and ferocity of the social and political conflicts of the time. In the context of the Russian empire, at least, the sense of ethnic oppression or superiority, and aspirations to national recognition were reinforced by social status and the unequal relationship between the particular ethnicity and the dominant Russian nationality. The Tsarist state promoted some peoples at some times (the Baltic Germans, the Armenian merchants until the 1880s) and discriminated against others (Jews; Ukrainians; Poles, particularly after 1863; Armenians, after 1885; Finns at the turn of the century). After 1881 the ruling nationality, the Russians, increasingly conceived of social problems in ethnic terms and saw Jewish conspiracies, Armenian separatists and nationalists in general as sources of disruption and rebellion. Such enmity and discrimination directed against whole peoples, regardless of social status, helped develop support for the conceptions of the nationalists, but at the same time the economic developmental policies of Tsarism attracted certain national bourgeoisies to try to work with the Russifying régime.

The development of ethnic cohesion and national awareness – not to mention political nationalism – occurred at different rates for different ethnicities, and this process was connected to the effects on various peoples of the great socio-economic transformation that took place in Russia in the decades preceding the revolution. Peasant peoples with little representation in towns (Lithuanians, Ukrainians, Belorussians, for example) experienced these changes differently from those ethnicities that had already developed a working class (Georgians, Latvians, Estonians, Jews and, to some extent, Armenians) and therefore participated more directly in the coming of capitalism. As the seigneurial economy gave way to market relations and new forms of the exploitation of labour replaced more tradition-sanctioned and paternalistic ones, it is not surprising that socialist movements found it much easier to mobilise support among the more developed nationalities.

The third reason for questioning the class/nationality dichotomy follows from the second. Both formations are not only socially as well as intellectually determined but are products of real history, not simply dictated by disembodied social forces or eternal essences. Following the meanings given by the work of E.P. Thompson, class can 'happen' or not happen, can be made and unmade, and the same, I would argue, is true for nationality. Similarly the particular conjunctures that create mobilised classes or nationalities, class consciousness or political nationalism, are often fleeting (one remembers Lenin's desperate plea to his comrades when they failed to appreciate the fragility of the workers' and soldiers' militance in October 1917 and take action: 'History will not forgive us'). In 1917 hopes for a constitutional solution to the problem of multi-nationality moderated the demands of the nationalists, and social concerns were far more widely articulated than ethnic concerns. But after the October revolution, the domestic armed opposition to Bolshevism and the intervention of foreign armies abruptly launched a more vociferous nationalism among many non-Russian peoples. In part this was due to the spread of the revolution outside urban centres into the countryside where the non-Russian majorities lived. Lines of conflict were drawn up that emphasised ethnicity (Russian workers against Ukrainian peasants, Armenian bourgeois against Georgian workers and peasants). In part it was the product of the hostility felt by nationalist intellectuals to the ostensibly internationalist, but evidently Russo-centric, Bolsheviks; and in part it was a phenomenon encouraged and financed by the interventionists. In any case the rise of nationalism in the Russian Civil War was no more the natural outcome of an inevitable historical process, the inherent and organic working out of the 'natural' aspirations of the minorities, than was the rise of articulate and conscious class formations during the first year of revolution. Both the development of class consciousness in the cities in 1917 and the subsequent spread of nationalism beyond the intelligentsia were phenomena to be explained both by the long-term social, cultural and intellectual processes that began in the past century and by the more immediate experiences of the revolutionary years.[4]

Given the problem we are analysing, it must already be apparent that Thompson's 'ethnographic' and cultural notion of class fits neatly into a discussion of nationality. Like a Thompsonian class, a nationality can be seen to be the product of 'common experiences', and the articulation of common, shared interests, on the one hand, and opposition to others who do not share them. For Karl W. Deutsch, one of the most influential theorists of nationality, the 'making' of nationality is an historical process of political integration that increases communication among the members of an ethnic group or a 'people'. A people, 'a group of persons linked ... by complementary habits and facilities of communication', had the ability 'to communicate more effectively, and over a wider range of subjects, with members of one large group than with outsiders'.[5] Deutsch links the increase of social communication that is basic to the formation of nationality to other processes of social change – urbanisation, the development of markets, railways and other forms of communication. A progression is made from a 'people' to a 'nationality' ('a people pressing to acquire a measure of effective control over the behaviour of its members ..., striving to equip itself with power') and eventually (though not necessarily) to a 'nation-state'.

Theorists and historians of class, like E.P. Thompson, Eric J. Hobsbawm, Ira Katznelson, William H. Sewell, Jr., Gareth Stedman-Jones and others, as well as those of nationality (Benedict Anderson, Ernst Gellner, Geoff Eley and Eric Hobsbawm again), have also stressed that these social and cultural processes cannot be conceived simply as objective forces existing outside the given class or nationality but rather are mediated and shaped by the social and cultural (even linguistic) experience of individuals and groups within the social group. Class and nationality make themselves as much as they are made; that is to say, the active work of individuals, parties, newspapers and activist intellectuals is key to the creation of social and national consciousness. Class and national traditions are invented and reinvented, discarded and revived; their rhetoric, symbols and rituals are borrowed, refined and passed down by intellectuals and activists. Thus, not only nationalism but the formation of nationality has a history, one that can be empirically elaborated and placed in time. Like other social and cultural relationships, nationality has a reality in the social world and is not merely the liberation of a priori *Volksgeist*, the realisation of a timeless essence.

It is here that the work of the Czech historian Miroslav Hroch is particularly revealing. Hroch argues that the nationalist movements he has studied, largely those of smaller Eastern European peoples, grew through three phases (A, B and C): first, a small number of scholars demonstrated 'a passionate concern ... for the study of the language, the culture, the history of the oppressed nationality'; the second stage witnessed 'the fermentation-process of national consciousness', during which a larger number of patriotic agitators diffused national ideas; and finally the stage of full national revival saw the broad masses swept up into the nationalist movement.[6]

When the formation of class and nationality is understood to be a contingent and historically determined occurrence rather than the essential outcome of natural or historical logic, one must also discard the comfortable notion (for socialists) that a militant, revolutionary, class-conscious proletariat was the natural product of labour history, as well as the conviction (equally dear to nationalists) that nationalism leading to the goal of an independent, sovereign nation-state was the natural and inevitable outcome of the national struggle.

Even the most cursory look at the revolution in the central Russian cities reveals the depth and intensity of the struggle between social classes.[7] Less apparent at first, but equally compelling after immersion in the monographic literature, is the revelation of social conflict of very great intensity in the national borderlands, obscured at times by the ethnic colouration, but in fact made all the more ferocious by cultural as well as class cleavages. Here the social and the ethnic are so closely intertwined that separation of the two can be artificial and misleading. One gigantic social upheaval engulfed the whole of the Russian empire in the third year of the First World War, bringing down the unifying imperial authority and launching a prolonged crisis of authority that continued well into the Civil War years. During the whole period an ever-widening economic disintegration shredded the social fabric of the old order. Everyone everywhere was affected, and physical survival became the first requirement for millions of people. In this great turmoil various regions, some of them ethnically distinct, had their own particular experiences, but rather than dozens of separate national histories they were part of the general experience fatally linked to the whole history of Russia. The sundering of political and economic links opened the way for some parts of the empire, like Finland and Poland, to opt for a viable independence (though not without dissenters and, in the case of Finland, a bloody civil war); other parts were simply set adrift. Because fifty or sixty years later, after decades of Soviet or independent development, many of the incipient nations of 1917 had firmly established national–cultural identities, state structures and even manifestations of political nationalism, retrospective histories describe the revolutionary years as if that future had already existed in 1917. Much of the story of nation-building, and even nationality-formation, belongs as far as many peoples of the Russian empire are concerned more appropriately in the post-revolutionary period than in the years before the Civil War.

The story of national formation and nationalism in the revolutionary years is seen here as part of the intricate mosaic of the Russian Civil War with social and ethnic conflicts inextricably mixed. The Civil War in the disintegrating Russian empire was a civil war everywhere, right up to the pre-1914 borders, and though in the national peripheries it took on aspects of national warfare, the social struggle between workers and peasants, *tsentsovoe obshchestvo* and *demokratiia*, city and countryside remained determinant. This perspective of a single, gigantic revolutionary process engulfing the whole of the now-defunct empire is close to the view of many Bolsheviks and other Russian socialist and non-socialist parties during the revolution and the Civil War. On the other hand, nationalist parties, and most Western historians (E.H. Carr and Richard Pipes most particularly), have viewed the experiences of the borderlands as unique events, in many ways fulfilling a particularly national historical evolution. And their example is followed by most of the monographic studies of individual nationalities.

From the perspective of the Civil War, Soviet power or Bolshevism never simply meant Russia, and the extension of that power was not simply the Russian conquest of other peoples. Bolshevism, for better or worse, was the actual achievement of the revolution of the lower classes as they stood after October 1917, and Russian and Russified Ukrainian workers in Kiev and Kharkov; Russians and Armenians in Baku; and Russians and Latvians in Riga, supported local soviet power (and even Bolshevism) as the preferred alternative to a national independence promoted by a small nationalist élite in the name of a peasant majority. The difficult choice placed before both the Russians and the non-Russian peoples was whether to support the central Soviet government and the revolution as now defined by it, or accept a precarious existence in alliance with undependable allies from abroad with their own self-aggrandising agendas. In making that choice social structure, experience and concerns were often much more determinate than ethnic considerations.

Almost everywhere the nationalist movements were either strengthened or fatally weakened by the nature of their class base. Because ethnic solidarity, activism, Russophilia or Russophobia were very often primed by social discontents, nationalist leaderships had a greater chance of success when they were able to combine social reform with their programme of self-definition, autonomy or independence. Where social, particularly agrarian, reform was delayed or neglected, ethnic political aspirations alone did not prove strong enough to sustain nationalist intellectuals in power. For those ethnic leaders facing a peasant majority indifferent to their claims to power, and threatened by the Bolsheviks, an appeal to the Great Powers of Central and Western Europe became the last resort. And the intervention of foreigners, particularly the Germans in the crucial first months after the October revolution, radically distorted the developmental lines of the first revolutionary year.[8]

While most of the non-Russian peoples of the Tsarist empire were overwhelmingly peasant, they differed radically one from another in the degree of national consciousness. At one extreme

> the Belorussians were predominantly a peasant people hardly touched by the consciousness of a unique national identity. The political cause of Belorussian nationalism commanded the barest following . . . Socialism and assimilation into the Russian nation vied with Belorussian nationalism for the loyalties of the Belorussian people.[9]

The towns and cities of the region were dominated by Russians, Poles and, most importantly, Jews. In 1897 Belorussian-speakers made up only 9 per cent of the inhabitants of Minsk, the city that eventually would be selected as the capital of the Belorussian Soviet Republic. Over 51 per cent were Yiddish-speakers, 25.5 per cent Russian and 11.4 per cent Polish. Given less than 2 per cent of Belorussian speakers living in towns with over 2,000 inhabitants, and the very low literacy rates, the Belorussians had only the smallest of nationalist élites to define and propagate their cause. National awareness came late and did not take hold among the peasants before the revolution. Socialism or assimilation were far more powerful contenders for Belorussian loyalties than nationalism, and the nationalist 'movement', if it can be called that, was almost always 'a pawn in the larger schemes of the German military, Polish nationalists and Russian revolutionists'.[10] Without a mass base, it remained locked into Hroch's phase B until well after the establishment of Soviet Power.[11]

Like the Belorussians, their neighbours, the Lithuanians, had come to nationalism late and had barely moved into phase C. Without an urban presence to speak of, nationalist sentiments did not reach much beyond the intelligentsia and the large Lithuanian diaspora. The creation of a Lithuanian National Council, the Taryba, in September

1917 and the declaration of independence in December were both carried out under German supervision. As in many other regions in the western borderlands, the creation of independent Lithuania, rather than a broad-based and coherent nationalist movement realising long-held aspirations to nationhood, was the artificial result of German politics and the immediate weakness of the central Russian state. Here 'nationality' was the instrument that a Great Power used for its own end of destroying the Russian empire and creating mini-states under its control; as elsewhere and at other times 'class' would be the basis on which the Soviets would reconstruct a multi-national state.

In the Ukraine, scholars agree, 'to an unusual degree, nationality coincided with economic class. Ukrainians were, with the exception of a small intelligentsia, almost entirely peasants; the landowners and officials were Poles or Russians, while the commercial bourgeoisie was largely Jewish.'[12]

> Class and ethnic cleavages were closely related ... Russians manned the oppressive bureaucracy and were heavily represented among the principal landowners. Poles dominated the *pomeshchiki* class in the right-bank provinces of Kiev, Podolia, and Volhynia. Petty trade, commerce, and much of industry on the right bank were controlled by Jews who were therefore the peasantry's most visible creditors. As a consequence, the ethnic and socio-economic grievances of the Ukrainian peasant proved mutually reinforcing and provided the foundation for a political movement which combined nationalism with a populist social programme.[13]

Ukrainian peasants were very active in 1905–7, though the movement in the first revolution had only very superficially nationalistic characteristics. In great degree a protest over land shortages, which were blamed on the large holdings by noble landlords (most of them Polish and Russian), social discontent led to violence, but with minimal ethnic expression. Even the supposedly traditional Ukrainian antisemitism was largely absent, and Jewish revolutionaries were welcomed as supporters of the peasant movement. Peasant grievances were sufficient to generate protests without consistent intervention from outsiders, though, on the right bank, *Spilka* (the Ukrainian Social Democratic Union) and, on the left bank, the Socialist Revolutionaries (SRs) and the Peasants' Union were active.[14]

Historians differ in their evaluation of Ukrainian nationalism in 1917–18. Without question an articulate and active nationalist élite, made up of middle-class professionals, was prepared to confront both the Provisional Government and the Council of People's Commissars with its demand for autonomy and self-rule.[15] The Rada was committed to a democratic solution to the political crisis, to remaining within a federated Russian state and to a radical programme of land reform. Its support in the cities was minimal – in the elections in July to the municipal duma in Kiev, Ukrainian parties won only 20 per cent of the vote while Russian parties garnered 67 per cent (Russian socialists, 37 per cent; 'Russian voters', 15 per cent; Kadets, 9 per cent; Bolsheviks, 6 per cent) – but it was backed by Ukrainian soldiers, particularly interested in the formation of ethnic military units, as evidenced in the resolutions of the First Ukrainian Military Congress in May 1917.[16]

Far more problematic, however, is the estimate of the level of national cohesion among Ukrainians and the degree of support for the national programme among the peasants. For John Reshetar nationalism is a middle-class movement and the peasant 'was enslaved by his locale and regarded the inhabitants of the neighboring villages as a species of foreigner'. The absence of a Ukrainian bourgeoisie of any weight and the

> essentially agrarian character of late nineteenth century Ukrainian society, with its emphasis on the locale, tended to retard the development of that sentiment of group cohesiveness which transcends localism and is termed national consciousness. The peasant, because of his conservatism, was able to retain his language, peculiarities of dress, and local customs despite foreign rule, but initially he resisted the notion that all Ukrainians, whether living in Kharkiv province, in Volynia, or in Carpatho-Ukraine, belonged to the same nation.

Though this peasant parochialism was partially broken down by the spread of currency, the building of railways, and the dissemination of newspapers and periodicals, the protracted process of nationality-formation 'had not been consummated as late as 1917'. Reshetar points out that even in 1917 peasants in Ukraine referred to themselves not as a single collective but with regional terms: *Rusiny* (sons of Rus), Galicians, Bukovinians, Uhro-rusins, Lenki and Hutsuli. Russophilia was still strong in many parts of the country, even among the peasantry, and much of the middle class and working class was Russified.[17]

Richard Pipes agrees with Reshetar that 'the weakest feature of the Ukrainian national movement was its dependence on the politically disorganised, ineffective, and unreliable village', but he emphasises their 'political immaturity, which made them easily swayed by propaganda, and . . . their strong inclinations toward anarchism'. Nevertheless, nationalism was a reality in Ukraine, 'a political expression of genuine interest and loyalties', which had its roots in

> a specific Ukrainian culture, resting on peculiarities of language and folklore; a historic tradition dating from the seventeenth-century Cossack communities; an identity of interests among the members of the large and powerful group of well-to-do peasants of the Dnieper region; and a numerically small but active group of nationally conscious intellectuals, with a century-old heritage of cultural nationalism behind them.

But 'the fate of the Ukraine, as of the remainder of the empire, was decided in the towns, where the population was almost entirely Russian in its culture, and hostile to Ukrainian nationalism'.[18] Contingent factors such as the inexperience of the national leaders and the shortage of administrative personnel are mentioned as part of the toxic mix that destroyed the Ukrainian experiment in independence.

While one might hesitate to accept Reshetar's firm requirement that a middle class must exist for a nationalist movement to succeed or Pipes' assumption that there was a conscious community of interests between intelligentsia and peasantry in 1917, the argument that the fate of the movement would be decided by the peasantry seems compelling. In a most intriguing article Steven L. Guthier argues, in contrast to Reshetar, that the Ukrainian peasantry was nationally conscious in 1917, as demonstrated in their choices in the November elections to the Constituent Assembly when they overwhelmingly supported Ukrainian parties. In the eight Ukrainian provinces (Kiev, Poltava, Podolia, Volhynia, Ekaterinoslav, Chernigov, Kherson and Kharkov) '55 per cent of all votes cast outside the Ukraine's ten largest cities went to lists dominated by the UPSR [Ukrainian Party of Socialist Revolutionaries] and *Selianska Spilka* [All-Ukrainian Peasants' Union]; another 16 percent went to Left PSR/UPSR slates'.[19] The cities, on the other hand, went for Russian and Jewish parties, though heavy turnouts among Ukrainian soldiers gave substantial backing to Ukrainian parties.

Guthier concludes that 'Ukrainian nationalism as a substantial political force was a one-class movement', but one in which identification between peasant aspirations and the programmes of the national parties was quite close.[20] He assumes that peasants voting for the Ukrainian peasant parties were aware of and accepted the national planks in their programmes. 'The peasants were committed to the creation of a Ukraine which was both autonomous and socialist. They wanted land rights to be reserved for those who farmed the land with their own hands.'

A useful distinction, however, might be made between cultural or ethnic awareness and full-blown political nationalism, an active commitment to realising a national agenda. While the election results show that peasants in Ukraine preferred parties and leaders of their own ethnicity, people who could speak to them in their own language and promised to secure their local interests, they do not provide sufficient evidence either that the peasantry conceived of itself as a single nationality or that it could be effectively mobilised to defend ideals of national autonomy or independence. Though more work is needed to determine the mentality of the Ukrainian peasants of 1917, an impression is left that they had some ethnic awareness, preferring their own kind to strangers, but were not yet moved by a passion for the nation and certainly not willing to sacrifice their lives for anything beyond the village.

Defeated nationalists, as well as 'class-conscious' Bolsheviks, considered the peasants of the Ukraine 'backward', 'unconscious', unable to be mobilised except for the most destructive, anarchistic ends. But more generously one might argue that, rather than being backward, Ukrainian peasants had their own localistic agenda in the chaos of the Civil War, one that did not mesh neatly either with that of urban intellectuals, nationalist or Bolshevik, or with that of workers, many of whom despised those living in the village.

Guthier may be closer to the mark when he sees the momentary coincidence of peasant voters and Ukrainian populists as the specific conjuncture when 'national autonomy was seen as the best guarantee that the socio-economic reconstruction of the Ukraine would reflect local, not all-Russian conditions'.[21] Here once again both the contingent and evolving character of nationalism (and class, for that matter) and the closeness of ethnic and social factors become clear. At least in 1917–18, the Ukrainian peasants were most concerned about the agrarian question and their own suffering in the years of war and scarcity.[22] They thought of themselves as peasants, which for them was the same as being 'Ukrainian' (or whatever they might have called themselves locally). Their principal hope was for agrarian reform and the end of the oppression identified with the state and the city. Russians, Jews and Poles were the sources of that oppression, and it is conceivable that for many peasants the promise of autonomy was seen as the means to put an end to the condescension and arbitrary power of those outsiders. But ethnic claims had no priority over social ones in these early years of revolution, and alliances with nationalists (or more frequently, ethnic populists) could easily be replaced by marriages of convenience with more radical forces.[23]

When the nationalist Rada was unable to resist the Bolshevik advance effectively in January 1918, it turned as a last resort to the Germans, who then requisitioned grain and terrorised peasants. When the nationalists failed to back up their own agrarian reform, support for the first generation of revolutionary nationalists among many peasants rapidly evaporated. As a consequence of the German occupation, the nationalist forces in Ukraine splintered into competing groups and the nationalist cause was identified by many as linked to foreign intervention. And to anti-nationalist elements, particularly in towns, the only viable alternative to social chaos, foreign dependence and Ukrainian chauvinism appeared to be the Bolsheviks.[24]

Sadly for the nationalists and happily for 'the Bolsheviks, the peasantry proved to be an unsteady social base for a political movement. When the Directory, which came to power in November 1918 and tried to place itself at the head of the peasant risings against the hetmanate,

> faltered in its implementation of new programs, turning cautious and conservative in order to preserve its very life, the forces of the Jacquerie swept past it to embrace another, more radical political group, which seemed to promise a program that *would* suit peasant tastes. Specifically, even before the year 1918 had run its course, many of the Directory's peasant-Cossack supporters were already going over to the Bolsheviks . . . For a few months in early 1919 there was an illusion that the two forces had joined for a common cause.[25]

But the Bolsheviks effectively disenfranchised the middle and wealthier peasantry and instituted a new round of requisitioning. Formerly sympathetic villagers turned against the Soviets, and the final Bolshevik victory depended on support from the workers, Russian and Russified, of the cities, the Donbass and the Red Army. Here the Bolsheviks were stronger than any of their contenders.

While Belorussia had never been a historic nation and the Ukraine had first been conceived independently of Russia only in the nineteenth century, Georgia and Armenia had existed historically long before the first Russian state had been formed. The sense of a continuous existence was fundamental to the national self-conceptions of the Armenian and Georgian intelligentsias of the late eighteenth and early nineteenth centuries as they revived the study of national history and literature. Their struggles for national emancipation began as liberal and democratic movements of writers, journalists and teachers, but by the last decade of the nineteenth century the first generations of nationalist intellectuals had been shunted aside by younger, more radical, socialists.[26] For these peoples, as for other small nations in Hroch's analysis, the struggle for national emancipation was also a struggle against the non-national or denationalised bourgeoisie.

Though the similarities between the origins and initial stages of Armenian and Georgian nationalism are striking, the different social structures of the two nationalities and their different political imperatives led to quite different nationalist ideologies and political trajectories. Georgians were a largely rural people without a significant urban presence until the late nineteenth century. The Georgian *aznaureba* (nobility) had survived the annexation of the country by the Russians and had, in fact, become part of the Russian *dvorianstvo* (gentry). But the noble élite failed to make a successful adjustment to the post-Emancipation economy, and their ideal of national harmony cutting across classes failed to attract support beyond the ranks of the intelligentsia.

In the 1890s younger Georgian intellectuals adopted a specifically Marxist world view that saw both the bourgeoisie (which in this case was largely Armenian) and the autocracy (which was Russian) as enemies of Georgian social and political freedom. Given the particular social composition of Georgian society, the social and national struggles were successfully merged under a Marxist leadership that claimed not to be nationalist and was willing to link up with the all-Russian Social Democratic movement.

In Georgia, the natural Marxist constituency, the proletariat, had by 1905 been supplemented by broad support (almost unique in the Russian empire) among the peasantry. Thus, by the years of the first revolution, Georgian Marxist intellectuals found themselves at the head of a genuinely supra-class national liberation movement. The Mensheviks easily won the elections to the four State Dumas, controlled soviets and councils in the towns and countryside in 1917, and were the overwhelming choice of Georgians in the elections to the Constituent Assembly. In Georgia, Hroch's phase C had been achieved in the first decade of the twentieth century, but instead of a vertically integrating nationalism, Georgians adopted an avowedly non-nationalist socialist movement as their preferred form of political expression.

Armenians were a largely peasant people divided between three great empires, the Russian, the Persian and the Ottoman-Turkish, which at the same time had a centuries-old diaspora that connected the educated and business people of the homeland with Europe, the Middle East and even India. Their ancient nobility had largely been eliminated by the time of the Mongol occupation and the fall of the last Armenian kingdom in the late fourteenth century. By the early nineteenth century the leading class among Armenians was the merchants and petty industrialists of Tiflis, Baku, Istanbul and Smyrna. Among non-Armenians the most prevalent image of the Armenian was that of the merchant, and both in Turkey and the Caucasus Armenians played a highly visible role in the development of industry and trade. The oil industry in Baku was pioneered by Armenians, and the economic growth of the ancient Georgian capital, Tiflis (Tbilisi), was largely an Armenian enterprise. Here was an historic nation, then, with an educated urban bourgeoisie, but one disconnected socially and by virtue of distance or international borders from the heartland of its own people.

Though the absolute number of Armenians continued to grow in the nineteenth and early twentieth centuries and though they continued to dominate the largest cities of the Caucasus economically and politically, Armenians found themselves in a precarious demographic position. Their relative position in the Armenian plateau of eastern Anatolia worsened. The in-migration of Balkan Muslims, Circassians and the rapid growth of the Kurdish population combined with the out-migration of Armenians, particularly after the massacres of 1894–6, to make the Armenians even more of a minority in a heavily Turkish and Kurdish population.

Impressed by the urgency of a political solution, the nationalist intelligentsia disavowed joint solutions with other parties in the Russian empire. The Armenian revolutionary parties took the battle to Turkey, and by means of the 'propaganda of the deed' and examples of militant sacrifice, attempted to mobilise a rather passive and demoralised peasantry. Though there were a number of spectacular examples of 'resistance' by armed Armenians (Zeitun, Sassun), the revolutionaries never achieved a high degree of mass mobilisation. Their tactics were largely limited by virtue of their relative weakness first in the face of terrorist attacks and, later, against a dangerous policy of alliance with the Young Turks.

The Armenian revolutionary nationalists, who in fact had come out of the middle, and lower-middle, classes, turned their venom (and occasionally even their weapons) against property-owning Armenians who refused to contribute to the national cause. Wary of the revolutionaries, the Armenian bourgeoisie in Turkey clung to the national church which they largely controlled; in Russia they remained liberals hoping for a more reformist evolution of the Tsarist order. Because of the self-destruction of one major party, the Social Democratic Hnchaks, and the relative isolation of the liberals and of the 'internationalist' Social Democrats in the cities, the most nationalist of the socialist parties, the Dashnaktsutiun, emerged by the early twentieth century as the only real contender for Armenian loyalties. In 1903 it gained wide support among city dwellers and even peasants in the Caucasus as the principal defender of the church, the properties of which had been requisitioned by the Tsarist government. In Hrochian terms one might claim that in the years before the First World War the patriots of phase B were attempting, though not yet fully successfully, to enter phase C.

The war, however, and the subsequent genocide of Armenians in eastern Anatolia, created an entirely new situation. Thousands of refugees fled to the Caucasus with retreating Russian armies, and the cities of Baku and Tiflis filled with Turkish Armenians. Armenian volunteer military units fought on the Caucasian front, and when Russian troops 'voted with their feet' late in 1917 and abandoned the Caucasus, Armenians found that they possessed one of the most powerful military forces in the region. For Armenians the principal source of danger came from their ethnic and religious enemies, the Ottoman Turks and the Azerbaijanis, and the very acuity of that danger completed what two decades of revolutionary propaganda had been working to accomplish – the effective mobilisation of the Caucasian Armenian population to vote for and fight for the national future as defined by the Dashnaktsutiun. Overwhelmingly Armenians voted for the Dashnaks in the elections to the Constituent Assembly.

Ethnic conflicts were largely subordinate to social conflicts throughout the first year of revolution in Transcaucasia, but Armenians, traumatised by the mass killings and deportations in Turkey, maintained their separate national position on all major political questions. Still, economic pressures and the question of state power, along with the issue of the war, relegated ethnic matters to second place. Though ethnic tensions appeared in the newly elected municipal duma in Tiflis, as Georgians replaced the formerly hegemonic Armenian middle class, they were contained within a political framework that promised democratic solutions to these perennial problems. But the victory of the Bolsheviks in Petrograd, their relative strength in Baku and weakness in Tiflis, and the removal of Russian troops from the Caucasian front and urban garrisons, created a new political environment, one in which the danger of Turkish invasion threatened some nationalities (the Armenians) and was seen as an opportunity by others (the Azerbaijanis). Choices had to be made between siding with Soviet Russia, the Entente or the Germans, and each national leadership chose a different path. The central political issue became self-defence, and in the context of Russian retreat and Turkish–German advance it quickly took on an ethnic dimension. A brief experiment in Transcaucasian autonomy was followed by an even briefer one in an independent federative republic. By late May 1918 the Georgians opted for the Germans rather than the Bolsheviks; the Azerbaijanis turned expectantly towards the Turks; the multi-national city of Baku opted for Soviet power; and the Armenians were left to their fate.[27]

The only realistic hope for an ethnic Armenian homeland in the post-genocide period was the small enclave around Erevan, which in May 1918 became the centre of a fragile independent republic. Armenian political leaders had not been anxious to attempt independence, but now they were forced to take control of their refugee population. They alone of the Transcaucasian peoples turned to the Entente for support. The ostensibly socialist ideology of the Dashnaktsutiun was largely neglected, and the party became the representative of all classes of Caucasian Armenians as they faced together the common threat from Ottoman and post-Ottoman Turks.

Azerbaijanis, who long had felt victims of the Christian overlords and bourgeoisie in Transcaucasia, welcomed the leverage and support offered by their Turkish brethren. The nationalist leaders, located in Ganja (Elizavetpol), entered Baku with the Ottoman army and took their revenge on the local Armenians (September 1918). But there they were faced by a mixed population of Russian, Armenian and Muslim workers who had undergone a long socialist and trade-unionist education. The nationalists were never fully secure in the city where Bolshevism had deep roots. Among the peasantry on whom they depended, national consciousness was still embryonic.[28]

Certainly the most viable and stable state in Transcaucasia was Georgia. Here the Social Democratic movement was well grounded both in the working class and in the peasantry. German intervention was needed, not to shore up the régime, but to prevent attack from outside. Ironically, the Georgian nation-state was formed and led by Marxists whose expectation had been of a democratic revolution in Russia that would have solved at one sweep the ethnic and social oppression experienced by their people. Instead they found themselves at the head of an independent 'bourgeois' state, the managers of the 'democratic revolution' in one small country, called upon to fulfil the national programme of parties far to the right of them. Unquestionably they had excellent chances for success; the Mensheviks were supported by the great majority of the Georgian people; but the larger geo-political and strategic imperatives of the central Soviet government did not permit them to demonstrate the potential for democratic socialism in a post-revolutionary state. By 1920 a powerful group within the Bolshevik party was pushing for an uprising within Georgia to be followed by an invasion by the Red Army. Lenin was initially opposed to this cynical disregard for the evident influence of the Georgian Social Democrats, but he backed down before the *fait accompli* engineered by Orjonikidze and Stalin.[29]

The only states to remain independent after the Civil War were, of course, in the northwest of Russia, along the Baltic – Poland, Finland, Estonia, Latvia and Lithuania. Here, as well, complex ethnic–class relationships existed. In the Baltic littoral, German nobles dominated rural life in areas of predominantly Estonian and Latvian peasantry. Polish and Jewish city dwellers almost exclusively ran Vilna, which was surrounded by Belorussian and Lithuanian villages.[30] The demographic situations in Tallinn (Reval) and Riga were more complex. The German bourgeoisie and nobles dominated local governing institutions, but the number of Estonians and Latvians in the towns grew rapidly until the local peoples became the largest nationality in their respective capitals.[31] A Latvian and an Estonian working class and a small bourgeoisie had developed by the early twentieth century. In terms of social structure – the presence of an alien ruling élite, and a growing native working class – as well as the difficulty of achieving political influence under Tsarism, the Latvians and Estonians were in a political impasse with evident similarities to that of the Georgians.

Estonian nationalism had developed relatively late. Only in the 1860s did the first generation of Estonian patriots free themselves of their original German patrons who had initiated interest in Estonian folkways. Village school-teachers and university-educated intellectuals joined with peasants in forming choruses and patriotic clubs and reading the national press. Yet the patriotic intelligentsia faced serious difficulties as it tried to penetrate the largely peasant population. Estonians had no political past with which to identify, no written language, no national literature. They were kept out of institutions of education, religion and politics by the ruling Germans. Tallinn was a German town surrounded by relatively passive peasants. Yet these 'disintegrating factors', writes Hroch, were offset by 'the class antagonism between the feudal German landowners and their Estonian subjects' which was

> the fundamental and probably most decisive factor which from a certain date onwards stimulated the spread of national consciousness among broad strata of the oppressed Estonian nationality.

Popular nationalism was further promoted in the last decades of the nineteenth century when Estonians entered the towns, gained higher education, and, together with the Latvians, achieved the highest level of literacy in the Russian empire. 'The sphere of integrating factors', Hroch continues, 'expanded to include the antagonism between the small-scale Estonian commodity-producers and the middle and upper German strata there.'[32] The Tsarist campaign of Russification in the Baltic helped to stimulate national awareness in the broad population, among Estonians, Latvians and Finns.

The parallels between Latvia and Georgia are particularly striking. In both countries the older generation of national patriots (in Latvia 'Young Latvia'; in Georgia the *pirveli dasi* and the *meore dasi*) were supplanted by Marxists (the Latvian 'New Current' and the Georgian *mesame dasi*). The brunt of national hostility was directed not against the Russians, but against the locally dominant nationality (in Latvia, the Germans; in Georgia, the Armenians) and refracted through the class rhetoric of Marxism. From the first days of the revolution Menshevism in Georgia and Bolshevism in Latvia were the strongest local movements, with little competition from the nationalists.

As Andrew Ezergailis has shown in two monographs, Bolshevism had exceptionally strong support among Latvian and other workers and among the famous Latvian riflemen (*strelki*). In the August elections to the municipal council of Riga Bolsheviks won 41 per cent of the vote (60 per cent among ethnic Latvians).[33] A week later Bolsheviks won 63.4 per cent of the vote to the major rural institution, the Vidzeme Land Council, and in November they carried the elections to the Constituent Assembly in those parts of Latvia (Vidzeme) that were not yet occupied by the Germans, winning 71.85 per cent. Among the *strelki*, Bolsheviks won 95 per cent of the votes.[34]

This extraordinary showing stems from a number of factors: the general Latvian alienation from the Germans and the relatively less hostile attitude towards Russians; the high proportion of landless peasants (more than 1,000,000 in 1897) that favoured the Social Democratic cause and opposed the 'grey barons' (Latvian small-holders) almost as much as they did the German nobles; the support of the Social Democratic Party (SD) among a militant working class that had experienced a bloody baptism in 1905, as well as among intellectuals, school teachers and students; the particularly devastating experience of the First World War, which had brought the fighting deep into Latvia, dividing the country, causing great hardship and radicalising the population; and finally the ability of the Bolsheviks to develop and propagate a programme that at one and the same time attempted to deal with social and ethnic grievances.[35] In 1917, it appeared to a great number of Latvians that the solution to their national future was within a Russian federation but one which had moved beyond the bourgeois revolution. The brief experiment in Bolshevik rule after October, the Iskolat, fell before the Germans when they moved into unoccupied Latvia in February 1918. Bolshevism would have been the eventual victor in Latvia but for the German intervention which gave the nationalists an initial chance to create their own republic.

The Estonians were far less radical than the Latvians, but Bolshevik strength grew steadily during 1917. The May 1917 elections to the *Maapaev* (the provincial assembly of Estonia) produced the following party alignment:[36]

Agrarian League	13
Labour Party	11
Estonian SDs (Mensheviks)	9
Estonian SRs	8
Democrats (Estonian)	7
Bolsheviks	5
Radical Democrats	4
German and Swedish minorities	2
Non-party	3

By late July–early August, the Bolsheviks, whose greatest strength was in the larger industrial towns of Tallinn and Narva, polled 31 per cent of the vote in municipal council elections (SRs, 22 per cent; Estonian SD – Russian and Latvian Menshevik Bloc, 12 per cent).[37] Here, as in the elections to the Tallinn Soviet, large numbers of voters were soldiers (16 per cent in Tallinn) and non-Estonians. Bolsheviks did less well in Tartu and the rural areas. Still, in the November elections to the Constituent Assembly, the Bolsheviks outpolled the other parties (40.2 per cent; Labour party, 21 per cent), though socialists as a whole won just over 50 per cent and the non-socialists nearly matched them. Bolsheviks won in Tallinn (47.6 per cent), followed by the Labour party, but the non-socialist Democratic Bloc won in Tartu (53.4 per cent) and southern Estonia.[38]

After the October revolution, Bolshevised soviets ran many of the towns in Estonia, but support for the soviets began to erode rapidly. The Bolsheviks were unenthusiastic about Estonian independence, failed to expropriate the estates of the Baltic barons and tried to suppress opposition parties. When elections were held for the Estonian Constituent Assembly late in January 1918, the Bolsheviks polled only 37.1 per cent while the Labour party rose to 29.8 per cent and the Democratic Bloc held steady at 23.2 per cent. The elections were incomplete, for the Bolsheviks first postponed and later cancelled them, and it appears that sentiment in the area was moving in favour of independence. When the Germans advanced late in February, the nationalists used the opportunity to declare Estonia independent of Russia.

CONCLUSION

The relative strength or weakness of class and nationality in various areas of the empire was crucial in determining the lines of battle and the commitment of actors. In the great sweep of the Russian revolution and Civil War nationalism was still largely a phenomenon centred in the ethnic intelligentsia, among students and the lower middle classes of the towns, with at best a fleeting following among broader strata. Among Belorussians, Lithuanians and Azerbaijanis, rather than a sense of nationality the paramount identification was with people nearby with whom one shared social and religious communality. Among these peoples neither nationalism nor socialism was able to mobilise large numbers into the life-and-death struggle then being waged across the land.

For several other nationalities, among them the Latvians and Georgians, class-based socialist movements were far more potent than political nationalism. Socialism as presented by the dominant intellectual élite answered the grievances of both social and ethnic inferiority and promised a socio-political solution to the dual oppression determined by class and nationality. For still other nationalities, like the Ukrainians and the Estonians, nationality competed with a sense of class for primary loyalty of the workers and peasants. In the absence of detailed social historical studies of the national borderlands, it is still too early to achieve a full sense of the reasons why neither a political class consciousness nor a political nationalism dominated among these peoples. In the case of the Armenians, a most unusual example of a people divided between two empires, without a secure area of concentration, and faced by the imminent danger of extermination, a non-class, vertically integrating nationalism overwhelmed all competitors.

Nationalism, like class consciousness, was a disturbingly ephemeral phenomenon among most non-Russians in these turbulent years, especially once the revolution outgrew the cities. Whatever their cultural and ethnographic preferences, non-Russian peasants did not automatically opt for the national programme of their urban ethnic leaders.[39] The peasant relationship to nationalism as well as other possible reasons for the relative weakness of nationalism in 1917–18, and even further into the Civil War, require further attention by scholars. Tentatively one might suggest that the social distance between villagers and townspeople, between peasants and intellectuals, was great enough to muffle the supra-class message of nationalism. The most successful appeals were populist or even socialist, especially when they were enhanced by ethnic arguments. Furthermore, long-established trade patterns and complex economic relations tied most of the non-Russian peoples of the old empire to the centre (Finns and Poles are perhaps an exception here). The way the empire had developed economically was a powerful force for integration with the rest of Russia rather than for national separation. A bid for independence from Russia was almost always a political decision based on need for support by an outside power, at first Germany, later the Entente powers, and had far less intrinsic appeal to the mass of the population than has been customarily accepted.

The ebb and flow of socialism or nationalism was tied to the ebb and flow of the war and revolution, to the relative fates of the Great Powers and their ability to act within Russia. In the twentieth century intervention has become an unwelcome but ubiquitous guest at the revolutionary table. When Bolsheviks were relatively weak and Germans strong, separatism and the fortunes of the nationalists rose; when the Germans were defeated and the Entente withdrew, the appeals of the Bolsheviks in favour of social revolution, land to the peasants, and even a kind of broader Russian 'nationalism' found supporters. Neither nationalism nor a sense of class were ends in themselves for ordinary people, as they often were for intellectuals. They resonated within the *demokratiia* in so far as they promised to overcome profound social dislocations aggravated still more by war and revolution.

Lenin's estimation that national separatism would be reduced by central Russian tolerance and a willingness to allow national self-determination to the point of independence has appeared, understandably, to be either a utopian fantasy or an example of political dissembling. But if in fact nationalism was far weaker than most nationalists have allowed; if in Russia it was almost invariably connected with real social and political discontents caused by years of discrimination and hardship under Tsarism; and if, indeed, significant groups within the non-Russian peoples responded well to the socialist programmes of social transformation and national self-determination, then perhaps Lenin's views on the near future of the nationalities was less a fantasy than another example of his political style, an uneasy combination of 'hard-nosed' realism and the willingness to take extraordinary risks.

NOTES

1 See, for example, Firuz Kazemzadeh, *The Struggle for Transcaucasia (1917–1921)* (New York, 1951); and Richard Pipes, *The Formation of the Soviet Union: Communism and Nationalism, 1917–1918* (Cambridge, Mass., 1957).

2 'Nationalism and Social Class in the Russian Revolution: The Cases of Baku and Tiflis', in Ronald Grigor Suny (ed.), *Transcaucasia, Nationalism and Social Change: Essays in the History of Armenia, Azerbaijan, and Georgia* (Ann Arbor, 1983), pp. 239–58; 'Tiflis, Crucible of Ethnic Politics, 1860–1905', in Michael F. Hamm (ed.), *The City in Late Imperial Russia* (Bloomington, 1986), pp. 249–81; *The Making of the Georgian Nation* (Bloomington and Stanford, 1988); *The Baku Commune, 1917–1918: Class and Nationality in the Russian Revolution* (Princeton, 1972).

3 'Nationality reinforced class, but at the same time national loyalties cut across class lines. A poor unskilled Muslim worker had little in common with a skilled Armenian worker apart from their memories of the massacres of 1905, whereas he had the bonds of religion and custom tying him to a Moslem peasant and, indeed, to a Moslem capitalist. Moslem workers occupied the bottom of the labour hierarchy while at the same time Moslem industrialists experienced condescension from Armenian, Russian, and foreign capitalists' (Suny, *The Baku Commune*, p. 14).

4 Though the historical and theoretical literature on nationality and class goes in many directions, a significant number of works suggest similar conclusions about the emergence of these formations. Marxist writers in particular, though hardly exclusively, make the point that neither class nor nationality are fixed categories inherent in social relations or certain periods of history. Rather, to quote E.P. Thompson on class, they happen when people, 'as a result of common experiences (inherited and shared), feel and articulate the identity of their interests as between themselves, and as against other[s] . . . whose interests are different from (and usually opposed to) theirs'. As part of that common experience people find themselves in historically created productive relations or enter them voluntarily, and those relations make up the context and much of the content of their social experience that may create a sense of class loyalty. Thompson again: 'Class-consciousness is the way in which these experiences are handled in cultural terms: embodied in traditions, value-systems, ideas, and institutional forms. If the experience appears as determined, class consciousness does not' (E.P. Thompson, *The Making of the English Working Class*, London, 1963, pp. 9–10).

5 Karl W. Deutsch, *Nationalism and Social Communication. An Inquiry into the Foundations of Nationality* (New York and Cambridge, Mass., 1953), pp. 70–1.

6 Miroslav Hroch, *Social Preconditions of National Revival in Europe: A Comparative Analysis of the Social Composition of Patriotic Groups among the Smaller European Nations* (Cambridge, 1985), pp. 22–3. See also his earlier work, *Die Vorkämpfer der nationalen Bewegung bei den kleinen Völkern Europas* (Prague, 1968). As Eley points out in an important essay, Hroch 'pioneers a social-historical approach to the study of nationalist movements and their uneven penetration. In some ways it amounts to a much-needed specification of Deutsch's theory of social communications through the kind of concrete historical investigation that Deutsch himself never really engaged in' (Geoff Eley, 'Nationalism and Social History', *Social History* 6, 1981, no. 1, 101).

7 For a review of Western writing on 1917 in Russia proper that emphasises the importance of deep social polarisation as an explanation for Bolshevik victory, see Ronald Grigor Suny, 'Toward a Social History of the October Revolution', *American Historical Review* 88, no. 1 (1983), 31–52.

8 This point has been made by Geoff Eley: 'By interposing itself between the peoples of the Russian empire and their practical rights of self-determination at a crucial moment of revolutionary political rupture – after the old order had collapsed, but while the new was still struggling to be born (to adapt a saying of Gramsci) – the German military administration suspended the process of democratic experimentation before it had hardly begun. The Germans' essentially destructive impact explains some of the difficulty experienced by the competing political

leaderships in the western borderlands of Russia during 1918–20 in creating a lasting relationship to a large enough coalition of social support. The various political forces – Bolshevik, Left-nationalist, autonomist, separatist, counter-revolutionary – operated more or less in a political vacuum in a fragile and indeterminate relationship to the local population, not just because the Belorussian and Ukrainian societies were so "backward" (the explanation normally given), but because the cumulative effects of war, Imperial collapse, and German occupation had radically dislocated existing social organisation, strengthening old antagonisms between groups and inaugurating new ones' (Geoff Eley, 'Remapping the Nation: War, Revolutionary Upheaval, and State Formation in Eastern Europe, 1914–1923', in Peter J. Potichnyj and Howard Aster (eds.) *Ukrainian–Jewish Relations in Historical Perspective*, Edmonton, 1988, p. 207).

9 Steven L. Guthier, 'The Belorussians: National Identification and Assimilation, 1897–1970', *Soviet Studies* 29, no. 1 (1977), 37, 39.

10 Ibid., pp. 49–50.

11 Nicholas Vakar in his study of Belorussian nationhood writes: 'It has been said that nationhood came to the Belorussians as an almost unsolicited gift of the Russian revolution. It was, in fact, received from the hands of the Austro-German Occupation Army authorities and depended on their good will. The Belorussian National Republic held no general election, and the self-appointed administration lacked the elements necessary for international recognition. It may have been well-meaning, but it had neither the power nor the time to make reforms effective. Furthermore, its subservience to the Central Powers alienated many loyal elements in the population' (Nicholas P. Vakar, *Belorussia, The Making of a Nation: A Case Study*, Cambridge, Mass., 1956, p. 105).

12 John Armstrong, *Ukrainian Nationalism* (New York and London, 1963), p. 10.

13 Steven L. Guthier, 'The Popular Base of Ukrainian Nationalism in 1917', *Slavic Review* 38, no. 1 (1979), 32. In 1897 Ukrainians made up only 35 per cent of the population in the 113 towns in Ukraine; the larger the town the smaller the Ukrainian proportion. In Kiev Ukrainians made up 22 per cent, Russians 54 per cent, Jews 12 per cent, and Poles 7 per cent; in Kharkov Ukrainians were 26 per cent, Russians 53 per cent, Jews 6 per cent and Poles 0.3 per cent (Steven L. Guthier, 'Ukrainian Cities during the Revolution and the Interwar Era', in Ivan L. Rudnytsky (ed.), *Rethinking Ukrainian History*, Edmonton, 1981, p. 157; Patricia Herlihy, 'Ukrainian Cities in the Nineteenth Century', ibid., p. 151).

14 For a recent treatment of the peasant movement in right-bank Ukraine (Kiev, Podolia and Volynia provinces), see Robert Edelman, *Proletarian Peasants: The Revolution of 1905 in Russia's Southwest* (Ithaca, 1987).

15 John Reshetar, the author of the first major scholarly monograph on the

Ukrainian revolution, writes: 'Immediately after the March Revolution, leadership in the Ukrainian national movement was assumed by the democratically inclined petite bourgeoisie, the intelligentsia with nationalist sympathies, and the middle strata of the peasantry which supported the cooperative movement. The peasant masses, the soldiers, and the urban proletariat were not participants at this early period, and it cannot be said that the national movement permeated their ranks to any significant extent in the months that followed since it was competing with more urgent social and economic issues.'

And still later: 'Most of the men who undertook the propagation of the national idea in Ukraine were intellectuals with a middle-class background although many of them were of peasant stock. Hrushevsky was the son of an official in the Russian Ministry of Public Instruction, and Dmitro Doroshenko was the son of a military veterinarian. Colonel Eugene Konovalets and Volodimir Naumenko were the sons of teachers. Nicholas Mikhnovsky, Volodimir Chekhovsky, Valentine Sadovsky, Serhi Efremov, and Colonel Peter Bolbochan were the sons of priests' (John Reshetar, *The Ukrainian Revolution, 1917–1920: A Study in Nationalism*, Princeton, 1952, pp. 48, 320–1).

16 Pipes, *The Formation of the Soviet Union*, p. 63; Reshetar, *The Ukrainian Revolution*, pp. 50–1, 102n–103n.

17 Reshetar, *The Ukrainian Revolution*, pp. 319–23.

18 Pipes, *The Formation of the Soviet Union*, p. 149.

19 Guthier, 'The Popular Base of Ukrainian Nationalism in 1917', *Slavic Review* 38, no. 1 (1979), 40.

20 Ibid., p. 46.

21 Ibid., p. 41.

22 'The Central Rada and the Directory failed to solve the agricultural problem; the hetman government did worse. It was constantly a step behind the revolutionary spirit of the peasants. Its policy was to carry out the land reform legally for approval by a future Constituent Assembly. For this reason it was not able to compete with the Bolsheviks, who were promising the land to the peasants immediately, or even with Makhno, who was giving the land to the peasants as soon as it was captured. For the peasants, the land was a primary question and those forces that would not interfere in the division of land would get their support' (Michael Palij, *The Anarchism of Nestor Makhno, 1918–1920: An Aspect of the Ukrainian Revolution*, Seattle, 1976, pp. 54–5).

23 For another point of view on Ukrainian nationalism and the peasantry, see Andrew P. Lamis, 'Some Observations on the Ukrainian National Movement and the Ukrainian Revolution, 1917–1921', *Harvard Ukrainian Studies* 2, no. 4 (1978), 525–31. Lamis argues that Ukrainian nationalism from Taras Shevchenko on had a dual nature: glorification of the homeland and a demand for social reform. Often these two components

remained separate and in a state of dialectical tension (p. 528). He takes issue with Arthur Adams, who claimed that Ukrainian peasants revolted during the German occupation primarily because of the grain requisitions and fear for their land. Lamis contends that the Jacquerie was nationalist, aimed at one and the same time towards national and social freedom, even though the peasants and the intelligentsia did not act in concert (p. 530). For Adams' argument, see his essay, 'The Great Ukrainian Jacquerie', in Taras Hunczak (ed.), *The Ukraine 1917–1921: A Study in Revolution* (Cambridge, Mass., 1977), pp. 247–70.

24 A German report of March 1918 gives a sense of the fragmentation in Ukraine in early 1918, the uncertainty of nationalist influence, and the relative strength of the Bolsheviks: 'It is not true that the Bolsheviks are supported only by the Russian soldiers who remained in the Ukraine . . . They have a large following in the country. All the industrial workers are with them, as is also a considerable part of the demobilised soldiers. The attitude of the peasants, however, is very difficult to ascertain. The villages that have once been visited by Bolshevik gangs . . . are, as a rule, anti-Bolshevik. In other places Bolshevik propaganda seems to be successful among the peasants. The peasants are concerned chiefly with the dividing up of the land; they will follow the Rada if it allows them to take the estates of the landlords . . . as proclaimed in the Third and Fourth Universals . . . Otherwise they will go with the Bolsheviks. Although the Bolsheviks lost out in many places because of their system of terror, their slogan "Take everything, all is yours" is too attractive and tempting to the masses. The Ukrainian separatist movement, on which the Rada is relying, has no true roots in the country and is supported only by a small group of political dreamers. The people as a whole show complete indifference to national self-determination.' (By the German writer, Collin Ross, this report was first published in *Arkhiv russkoi revoliutsii*, 1, 288–92, and translated and reprinted in James Bunyan, *Intervention, Civil War, and Communism in Russia, April–December 1918: Documents and Materials* (Baltimore, 1936), pp. 4–5.)

25 Adams, in Hunczak, *The Ukraine 1917–1921*, pp. 259–60. See also his *Bolsheviks in the Ukraine: The Second Campaign, 1918–1919* (New Haven, 1963).

26 On the formation of the Armenian national intelligentsia, see the articles by George A. Bournoutian, Ronald G. Suny, Sarkis Shmavonian, Vahe Oshagan and Gerard J. Libaridian in *Armenian Review* 36, no. 3 (1983), 143; Suny, 'Populism, Nationalism, and Marxism: The Origins of Revolutionary Parties Among the Armenians of the Caucasus', *Armenian Review* 32, no. 2 (1979), 126, 134–51; and 'Marxism, Nationalism, and the Armenian Labor Movement in Transcaucasia, 1890–1903', ibid. 33, no. 1 (1980), 129, 30–47. On the Georgians, see Suny, 'The Emergence of

Political Society in Georgia', in R.G. Suny (ed.), *Transcaucasia*, pp. 109–40.

27 The best account of Transcaucasian politics during the revolution and Civil War remains Firuz Kazemzadeh, *The Struggle for Transcaucasia (1917–1921)* (New York, 1951).

28 In a recent study of Azerbaijani national identity, Tadeusz Swietochowski writes: 'While the intelligentsia experiences an evolution that took it in quick succession from Pan-Islamism to Turkish to Azerbaijanism, the masses remained on the level of *'umma* consciousness with its typical indifference to secular power, foreign or native. The idea of an Azerbaijani nation-state did not take root among the majority of the population; the very term *nationalism* was either not understood by them or, worse, it rang with the sound of a term of abuse, a fact the Communists exploited in their propaganda against the Azerbaijani Republic. This might help explain why the overthrow of the republic was amazingly easy. Even those who subsequently rebelled against Soviet rule did not fight for the restoration of the fallen regime' (Tadeusz Swietochowski, *Russian Azerbaijan, 1905–1920: The Shaping of National Identity in a Muslim Community*, Cambridge, 1985, p. 193).

29 On the Menshevik republic, see Suny, *The Making of the Georgian Nation*, pp. 185–208; and chapter 11 in this volume by Stephen Jones.

30 In 1897 Vilna was 40.3 per cent Jewish, 30.9 per cent Polish, and only 7 per cent Lithuanian; Vilna district, excluding the city, was 35 per cent Lithuanian; the whole province was 56 per cent Belorussian and 17.5 per cent Lithuanian (Alfred Erich Senn, *The Emergence of Modern Lithuania*, New York, 1959, p. 42).

31 By 1913 Estonians made up 69.2 per cent of the urban population of Estonia; Russians 11.9 per cent; and Germans 11.2 per cent; in Tallinn Estonians were 72 per cent, though that figure declined during the war because of the influx of Russian and other workers to 58 per cent by 1917 (Toivo U. Raun, *Estonia and the Estonians*, Stanford, 1987, p. 91). In Riga, Latvians had become a plurality by 1881, and by 1913 they made up 38.8 per cent of the city's population; Russians 22·4 per cent; Germans, 16.4 per cent (Anders Henriksson, 'Riga: Growth, Conflict, and the Limitations of Good Government, 1850–1914', in Hamm (ed.), *The City in Late Imperial Russia*, p. 182).

32 Hroch, *Social Preconditions of National Revival*, p. 85.

33 Andrew Ezergailis, *The 1917 Revolution in Latvia* (Boulder, 1974), p. 145; *The Latvian Impact on the Bolshevik Revolution, The First Phase: September 1917 to April 1918* (Boulder, 1983), p. 75.

34 Ezergailis, *The Latvian Impact*, pp. 79, 87, 89.

35 For an attempt to deal with the different choices of the Estonians and the Latvians in 1917, see Stanley W. Page, *The Formation of the Baltic States: A*

Study of the Effects of Great Power Politics upon the Emergence of Lithuania, Latvia, and Estonia (Cambridge, Mass., 1959; reprint: New York, 1970), pp. 83–5.

36 Raun, *Estonia and the Estonians*, p. 100.

37 Ibid., p. 101.

38 Ibid., p. 103.

39 Mobilised in the aftermath of the October revolution, the peasantry was, in Eley's words, 'a class restlessly *in motion* – passing in and out of armies, regular and irregular; migrating for food and work, over short and long distances; experimenting with the full repertoire of violent, direct-action, and peaceful protests; meeting locally to discuss and formulate grievances; combining more ambitiously at the district and regional levels; issuing petitions; instructing deputies; and, of course, voting' (Eley, in Potichnyj and Aster, *Ukrainian–Jewish Relations*, p. 232).

I I

GEORGIAN SOCIAL DEMOCRACY
IN 1917

STEPHEN F. JONES

G EORGIA was one of the most economically backward regions of the empire and yet a socialist movement directed by self-declared Menshevik leaders evolved into one of the largest and most effective political organisations in pre-revolutionary Russia. By 1905, thirteen years after the formation of the first Georgian Marxist group, the Social Democratic movement commanded a mass following in Georgia and it continued to do so for some years after the Red Army invasion of the Georgian Democratic Republic in 1921.[1] At its height the Georgian Social Democratic Labour Party (as it became after 1918) claimed 75,000 members.[2] Paul Axelrod – in Boris Sapir's view the founder of Menshevism – commented in 1920 that 'from the very beginning Menshevism has had its deepest roots in Georgia'.[3]

Before 1917 the Georgian section of the Russian Social Democratic Labour Party (RSDLP) had a major influence on internal party debates and was a mainstay of the Menshevik wing, providing approximately one quarter of the Menshevik delegates to the Fourth and Fifth Congresses of the RSDLP.[4] In common with other revolutionary parties, the Georgian organisation suffered a decline in membership between 1906–17 but won almost all the Georgian seats to the Dumas and produced a continuous stream of legal and illegal papers.[5] At the (Menshevik) Unification Congress of the RSDLP in August 1917, the Transcaucasian membership, which was predominantly Georgian, stood at 43,000, a quarter of all Menshevik RSDLP members.[6] In February 1917, only the Social Democratic party was capable of stepping into the political vacuum in Georgia, and throughout the year it maintained its dominant position in both countryside and town through its control of the Tiflis Soviet of Workers' Deputies and the Regional (*Krai*) Soviet of Workers' and Peasants' Deputies.

247

GEORGIAN SOCIAL DEMOCRACY BEFORE 1917

When the Georgian territories were annexed by Russia in the early decades of the nineteenth century, Georgians were a divided pre-modern people of little over half a million, although they had experienced periods of unity and statehood in the past.[7] Russian rule set in motion the familiar processes of 'modernisation' which by 1917 had transformed the Georgian population into a socially and ethnically integrated Georgian nation.[8] However, in the Georgian cities, especially in eastern regions where the capital of Tiflis (now Tbilisi) was situated, Armenian merchants and Russian administrators dominated. In 1917, despite the Georgian influx from the countryside, Armenians were still the single largest ethnic group in Tiflis at 33.7 per cent. Georgians made up just over a quarter and the Russians and other Slavs 28.1 per cent.[9]

The last decades of the nineteenth century saw the rise of a native working class in Georgia although it remained small (never exceeding 50,000 before 1917) and was employed mainly in small-scale workshops.[10] The largely monoethnic character of the working class (being predominantly Georgian) was a major factor in Social Democratic success in the region. Ethnoclass divisions – between a native working class and an Armenian bourgeoisie – made class war and the liberation struggle against foreign exploiters (the Armenians and Russians) virtually synonymous. Acaci Chkhenceli, a prominent Georgian Social Democrat, admitted that in 1905, although Georgians were united 'behind the flag of international Social Democracy', the protest was in the minds of many against 'national oppression'.[11] Chkhenceli himself felt the task of Georgian Social Democracy was 'to express and defend the local interests of the Georgian people' and that it was 'first and foremost the leader of oppressed nations.'[12]

The Georgian Social Democrats extended their influence into the countryside during the agrarian revolution of 1905. The Georgian peasant movement was the best organised and most tenacious in the Russian empire in 1905.[13] Led by Social Democrats, it transformed the Georgian Social Democratic movement into a mass organisation. Georgian Social Democrats did not restrict their political campaigning to the peasantry. They developed more successfully than their colleagues elsewhere in the empire Axelrod's thesis that the proletariat should go 'into all classes'. Like the Austrian Social Democratic Party, the Georgian organisation made a special (and successful) effort to extend its power into non-proletarian groups, including the lower and middle strata in Transcaucasian towns. Noe Zhordania, the leader of the Georgian Social Democrats, termed this concept 'the hegemony of the working people', which in contrast to Plekhanov's formula, the 'hegemony of the proletariat' allowed the party and the revolutionary movement a broad social basis.[14]

The Social Democratic party in Georgia was a Marxist movement with many political and economic demands attractive to the Georgian peasants and workers, from its collectivism, utopianism and anti-statism to its advocacy of equality and justice. Its internationalism appealed in particular to Georgians who had been the frequent victims of national animosity in the past. At the same time, Marxism's acceptance of the proletariat as the 'leading class of the nation', as expressed in *The Manifesto of the Communist Party*,[15] gave Georgian (and other non-Russian) Marxists an opportunity to combine policies of national and socialist development. In backward regions like Georgia, bourgeois development provided the basis for nationhood as well as socialism. Just as Axelrod could not imagine socialism without political democracy, Zhordania could not conceive of it without national growth and self-rule.

Georgian Menshevism: its theory and practice before 1917

Georgian Social Democrats kept to the central tenet of Menshevism – the Russian revolution would be bourgeois and the socialists' primary task was to promote an independent and politically conscious working class.[16] Their policies coincided closely with the views expressed by Axelrod on the need for political democracy, class education, practical work and the rejection of intelligentsia leadership. By 1917 Georgian Menshevism had evolved into a doctrinally and organisationally cohesive movement. It had a history of tactical successes and a broadly unified leadership which set it apart from the Russian organisation and which gave it the confidence to tackle decisively the dilemmas of revolutionary power. The Georgians had also developed distinctive viewpoints on party organisation, the national issue, the peasantry and on the question of how to exploit power (part of what Abraham Ascher calls the 'moral dimension' of Russian Menshevik politics).[17] These differences, which led to serious conflict and finally a break with their Russian colleagues, could be described broadly as follows.

First, Georgian Social Democrats failed to understand the exclusive approach to party recruitment and opened local party doors wide.[18]

Low socio-economic differentiation in Georgia, particularly between the group of poorer gentry (from which the majority of the Social Democratic leadership came) and the peasantry, and the sense of solidarity which often characterises embattled ethnic groups such as the Georgians, meant that the mutual suspicion which marred working-class–intelligentsia relations in Russia and which underlined the whole debate on party organisation had little place in Georgia.[19] The success of 1905, when the party in Georgia received mass support from all native social strata, as well as the Georgian revolutionary tradition of national unity, led the Georgian Social Democrats to develop a theory of a broadly encompassing 'people's party'.[20] By 1917 this inclusive approach had given the Georgian section of the RSDLP a solid base among a wide spectrum of social groups which Russian Menshevism, to its cost, neglected.

Second, the Georgian Social Democrats who in 1906 had defended the orthodox Russian Marxist formula of regional self-government, by 1917 – influenced by the debates among European socialists – had come to support national-cultural autonomy which implied significant legislative and administrative decentralisation, a Caucasian Sejm and separate national-cultural units. In Zhordania's scheme, each national unit would have its own constitution, and administration would be in the native language.[21] Although by 1917 the Russian Mensheviks had likewise accepted the principle of national-cultural autonomy, it was in reality a concept unwelcome to a Russian party instinctively attached to Marxist notions of centralisation, and the Georgian Social Democrats soon found themselves in opposition to their fellow Mensheviks in Petrograd who supported the confused and inadequate nationality policies of the Provisional Government.[22]

Third, in contrast to the orthodox Marxist view, shared by the Russian Mensheviks, that the peasants were a reactionary force better left to the Socialist Revolutionaries (SRs), the Georgian Social Democrats successfully promoted peasant interests in the countryside. They, like the Bavarian section of the Social Democratic Party of Germany (SPD), regarded the poor and middle peasants as semi-proletarian inasmuch as they did not exploit the labour of others and shared the workers' conditions of poverty and powerlessness. A major reason for the Georgian Social Democrats' success in the countryside was their accommodation to peasant demands for the division of land. There was little basis for a socialised land policy in Georgia where the commune hardly existed and where small landholding peasants had a strong attachment to individual land proprietorship. By 1917 the

Georgian Social Democratic movement, in contrast to Russian Menshevism, had established a clear policy attractive to the native peasantry and based on the latter's self-interest.[23]

Fourth, the Georgian Menshevik leaders, though not as erudite as a Dan or a Potresov, showed a flexibility and daring absent in their Russian confrères. This was reflected not only in the Georgians' singular attitude to the peasantry, party organisation and the Duma (they were the only section of the RSDLP not to boycott the First Duma) but also in their practice of terrorism and expropriations, even after such activities were condemned by the Fourth and Fifth Congresses of the RSDLP.[24] After 1907, the movement in Georgia developed *de facto* as an autonomous national Social Democratic party. It worked out its own tactics without reference to the Menshevik central organs, which were in disarray. The Georgians' frustration with the Russian Mensheviks became more apparent in 1917 when the stakes were higher and tactical differences took on decisive importance. The Georgians proved themselves to be far more adept at wielding power and manipulating the opposition than their comrades in Petrograd.

REVOLUTION

When Russia entered the war, the Georgian Social Democratic organisation adopted an internationalist position of 'neither victory nor defeat', but after the arrival of Zhordania from Switzerland, and largely through his influence, 'defencism' was adopted as official Georgian policy at a conference in October 1915.[25] Zhordania declared that defence of one's country, as opposed to attack on another, was compatible with internationalism. He argued that Germany should be opposed because it threatened the free development of nations. 'Internationalism', he wrote, was 'built on the free existence of nations and on their free development.'[26]

The sudden political vacuum created in Transcaucasia in February 1917 led to a scramble for power by a myriad of organisations. Although all major political parties and soviets rallied behind the Provisional Government, the conflicting national and political interests of the Transcaucasian nationalities were soon reflected in a fractionalisation of authority along ethnic as well as class lines. In Tiflis the largely Armenian commercial class united behind the nationalist Dashnaktsutiun,[27] the Russian peasant soldiers behind the SRs and the Georgian workers behind the Social Democrats. The Georgian Mensheviks, organisationally stronger and politically more experienced than the other parties, dominated Transcaucasian politics throughout 1917 (excluding Baku which was controlled by the SRs and the non-Georgian Mensheviks). They established hegemony in the Tiflis Soviet of Workers' Deputies, the real power in the city, despite a challenge from the Military Regional Centre of the Caucasian Army, and from the Soviet of Soldiers' Deputies which was dominated initially by the SRs and later by the Bolsheviks.

The Georgian Menshevik revolutionary strategy was laid down at the first Regional Congress of Caucasian Soviets of Workers' Deputies on 18 March. The Congress, reflecting Menshevik strategy, adopted a resolution declaring its aim to be a 'democratic republic standing on the basis of a radical solution of the worker and national questions within the limits of the bourgeois structure ... proletarian interests demand the unity of all revolutionary and opposition forces'.[28] Concerned with preserving civil peace and restraining national animosities, the Georgians, backed by the SRs and Dashnaktsutiun, stressed allegiance to the all-Russian revolution, to a united democratic front and to moderation in social issues so as not to alienate the bourgeoisie and encourage reaction.

The Georgian Social Democrats: relations with the centre

Until the October revolution, and for some time afterwards, the Georgian Mensheviks declared that nothing could be decided outside the all-Russian context. Zhordania insisted at the Transcaucasian Congress of Workers' and Peasants' Deputies in May that the proletariat's national demands concerned culture and language, not the setting up of a separate government. However, throughout 1917 the relations of the Georgian Mensheviks with the Provisional Government and its Russian Menshevik supporters deteriorated and their disagreements encompassed issues ranging from coalition to the organisation of local government.

The Georgian Mensheviks opposed socialist participation in the Provisional Government except for a brief period after the 'July Days' when they rallied behind Alexander Kerensky's measures against 'counter-revolution from the left'.[29] Their position conflicted with the view of the Russian Menshevik organisation (excluding Martov's followers and Axelrod who concurred with the Georgians) even though that organisation was led in part by their own Georgian colleagues, Carlo Chkheidze and Irakli Tsereteli.

Following the Kornilov rebellion in August, the Georgian Social

Президіумъ 1-го Всероссійскаго съѣзда Совѣта Рабочихъ и Солдатскихъ Депутатовъ.   12
М. И. Скобелевъ.   Н. С. Чхеидзе   Г. В. Плехановъ.   И. И. Церетелли.

20. Moderate socialist leaders on the platform of the first All-Russian Congress of Soviets, June 1917. Left to right: M.I. Skobelev, N.S. Chkheidze, G.V. Plekhanov, I.G. Tsereteli.

Democrats and the Tiflis Soviet moved to the Left, and a commission was set up to purge all 'counter-revolutionary elements' from government institutions. Zhordania declared that there were now only two types of power, 'the purely revolutionary or the purely counter-revolutionary, there is nothing in between'.[30] There was no longer any place in government for the bourgeoisie who had joined the camp of counter-revolution. Power had to be transferred 'into the hands of the democratic and socialist parties' including the Bolsheviks if need be. This was the position only finally adopted by the Russian Menshevik organisation at its Extraordinary Congress in December 1917 when Martov assumed leadership.[31] Zhordania told a regional congress of Caucasian Social Democrats in September that the Russian Mensheviks, by their reluctance to split from the bourgeoisie had 'isolated themselves from the working class'. He went on:

> The policy of the Petrograd Mensheviks in many ways is like the position of the former liquidationists, . . . [they] think about the construction of a ministry, search for ministers and forget about the general class struggle.[32]

Although there was some dissent, the majority in the Tiflis Soviet supported Zhordania and condemned coalition with the bourgeoisie as 'the grave-digger of revolution'. The call for an all-socialist government represented a major shift for the Georgian Mensheviks who had formerly opposed proletarian involvement at any level in state power. The new policy resembled Lenin's scheme of 1905, a 'revolutionary dictatorship of the proletariat and the peasantry', which, although it envisaged the possibility of socialists seizing power, did not foresee any move directly into socialism. However this strategy did not solve the paradox of a socialist government leading a bourgeois revolution, an idea which Marx and Engels had tried to reconcile with scientific socialism in their 'March Address' and had subsequently rejected as premature and bound to lead to disaster.[33] However, by the autumn of 1917, Lenin and (most of) the Bolsheviks had moved beyond the concept of such self-limiting restrictions on Bolshevik power.

At the Democratic Conference in Moscow in September, the two Georgian Menshevik representatives (Isidor Ramishvili and Noe Zhordania) supported Martov's call for a democratic socialist co-alition. Despite a majority vote in support, no such coalition emerged from the conference. Those in favour of a continuation of bourgeois participation in government led by Tsereteli and Chkheidze still controlled the Menshevik organisation and effectively blocked the adoption of Martov's policies. The confused stalemate at the Conference convinced Zhordania 'that the centre no longer offered any hope and that the strengthening of local power was the only way out'.[34]

Other issues which soured relations with the centre concerned the prevarication of the Provisional Government over land reform, the war and nationality affairs. The Georgians took unilateral action in a number of areas, most notably in the organisation of local power. The complex ethnic divisions in Transcaucasia demanded prompt action. The Provisional Government proved particularly inept at handling the borderlands and antagonised potential support among the nationalities. In Transcaucasia, the government set up a Special Transcaucasian Committee (Ozakom) as the highest organ of local power. Its membership, drawn from ethnically representative city duma deputies, ignored the Social Democratic hegemony in the region and immediately provoked the Tiflis Soviet to demand its abolition. After much debate, Chkhenceli, as a Tiflis Soviet representative, was coopted and put in charge of the Internal Affairs Department. It made little difference. Ozakom, in the words of one contemporary witness, 'did not create any authority for itself, became muddled in piles of paper and drowned in a morass of petitions and requests'.[35] Unclear as to the nature of its powers, and unable to enforce its decrees, it was practically ignored by the local soviets.

The Kornilov revolt produced the first serious break with the centre when on the initiative of the Georgian Social Democrats and SRs, a local 'revolutionary democracy' was set up to rule in lieu of the 'bourgeoisie'. A Caucasian Revolutionary Committee (Revkom) containing representatives of the soviets and socialist parties, but dominated by the Mensheviks and chaired by one of their leaders, E. Gegechkori, declared itself the supreme regional power. Its self-declared purpose was to 'fight against anarchy and counter-revolution'. Gegechkori announced his intention to reorganise the Ozakom which, he claimed, had 'done nothing' over the previous six months. When Kerensky ordered the Revkom's dispersal in early September, he provoked a serious breach in the local united front between the SRs and the Mensheviks. The former, in an apparent change of heart, feared that the policy of the Revkom was the first step to secession and through the Regional Military Soviet of Soldiers' Deputies which they controlled, ordered its dispersal. After acrimonious accusations of 'sabotage' and 'cowardice' from both sides, a compromise was reached with the creation of a Public Safety Committee which included Ozakom and duma representatives. Although a coalition with bourgeois forces, the very thing Georgian Mensheviks had fulminated against, it remained under socialist control.[36]

The Georgian Social Democrats and the United Front

In Transcaucasia, despite serious disagreements on land and labour reform, the parties were united in their attempts to avoid partisan or inter-ethnic strife which might spark off a bloodbath. Between February and October, although the major parties consolidated their ethnic bases, and separate national bureaux or soviets appeared with armed national militias at their disposal, the Menshevik-dominated Tiflis Soviet and the SR-dominated Soviet of Soldiers' Deputies attempted to restrain nationalist activity. The Tiflis Soviet threatened any party that indulged in nationalist agitation with expulsion, and all talk of autonomy was ordered to be removed from public discussion.[37] The Soviet of Soldiers' Deputies took similar action by forbidding any party agitation at the front. Both soviets supported the continuation of the war (although the Mensheviks urged an international socialist conference to bring it to an end), and felt that any politicisation of the army would hinder its defensive capacity. In May, in an attempt to reduce the growing tension between the Russian soldiers and native workers (the former, according to Chkhenceli were sceptical of native loyalty to the war and central government),[38] the workers and soldiers formed a united soviet in Tiflis, electing Zhordania as chairman. This was followed by the formation of an inter-party bureau in the summer. However, with the failure of the June offensive, the split of the Bolsheviks from the Caucasian Social Democratic organisation[39] and the deteriorating position on the Turkish front,[40] the cleavage between the indigenous workers who supported the local parties and the soldiers who supported the SRs and the Bolsheviks reopened. The vote for the Tiflis City Duma in July gave the Bolsheviks and SRs together just a little over a quarter of the vote (the Bolsheviks came bottom of the poll), with the Georgian Social Democrats acquiring twice as many seats as any other party.[41] The trade unions and the Central Trade Union Council were almost all under Menshevik control.[42] On the other hand, elections to the soldiers' section of the Tiflis Soviet in June gave the Bolsheviks fourteen seats, the SRs twelve, and the Mensheviks only eight seats. As soldiers' meetings became more anti-war in tone, Zhordania reported to the Tiflis Soviet Executive Committee in mid June that 'anarchy among the troops of the Tiflis garrison' was leading to a 'dangerous situation'.[43]

On 25 June, there was a Bolshevik-inspired rally of troops from the Tiflis garrison which supported Bolshevik resolutions and shouted down Menshevik orators. Alarmed, the Tiflis Soviet newspaper, *Izvestiia Tifliskogo soveta rabochikh i soldatskikh deputatov*, claimed that the meeting revealed a 'counter-revolutionary force' in the army which 'under the cover of extremist slogans does its evil business'.[44] Zhordania in a tough speech the following day condemned the 'black forces disguised in Bolshevik slogans' and urged a 'fight with arms' and preparation for civil war. At this stage, the Bolsheviks had insufficient control over a wildly susceptible force of soldiers and insufficient courage to challenge Menshevik supremacy. Under all-party pressure they signed a declaration condemning further demonstrations without the sanction of the Tiflis Soviet. Nevertheless, their influence among the troops continued to grow and at an Ozakom meeting in the middle of October, General Przhevalskii, Commander-in-Chief of the Caucasian Army, reported that the troops in the rear were becoming a serious threat and had to be dispersed.

The split between soldiers and workers was partly a result of the monoethnic nature of the Social Democratic movement in Georgia which in February 1917, despite several prominent non-Georgian members, resembled a national party. It was also caused by the differing attitudes to the war. The Georgian Social Democrats concentrated propaganda on their natural constituency – the Georgian workers – in their native tongue. It was not until May that they began to publish a Russian-language paper, *Borba* (*The Struggle*), edited by W. Woytinsky, which was of smaller circulation and poorer quality than the Georgian equivalent *Ertoba* (*Unity*). Similarly, the Bolsheviks (and SRs) failed to publish much in Georgian. The Bolsheviks' propaganda struggle against the Mensheviks, according to one participant, was 'conducted largely in the Russian language, in *Kavkazskii rabochii*'.[45] Only in June did the Bolsheviks bring out a Georgian-language paper. On the question of war, the soldiers by the late summer of 1917 wanted to go home, but the Georgian workers, fearful of their old Turkish enemy, wanted military protection. No doubt these conflicting interests were underlined by old ethnic prejudices and the Russian soldiers' suspicions of the *tuzemtsy* (natives). The local Bolsheviks were in the unenviable position of having to justify the Bolshevik policy of defeatism which, by encouraging the soldiers to return home, undermined their own power base and alienated the Georgian working class.

Until the departure of the army in the winter of 1917–18, the workers and soldiers dominated Tiflis politics and other social forces such as the Armenian bourgeoisie and Georgian peasantry remained peripheral to the central power struggle. Although national issues played a major role in Transcaucasian politics in 1917, they did so within the context of social divisions. The soviets in Transcaucasia were seen by the lower classes of each national group as in some way representative of their interests, and in the early days of the revolution in particular, class solidarity across ethnic lines was evident in the soviets, factories and on the streets. Most of the parties, too, were not simply nationalist organisations; they also advocated socialist policies. The relationship between class and nationality was a complex one; at times they reinforced each other, at times they were in conflict, and it was not until after October and the withdrawal of Russian military protection that in the crisis atmosphere of national survival, nationalism completely dominated class concerns.[46] However, it is significant that in the various elections to the regional soviets in 1917, the only areas in Transcaucasia which voted predominantly for the Bolsheviks were those of Russian population.[47]

The Georgian Social Democrats: moderate socialism

The social and economic programme of Georgian Menshevism in 1917 differed little from the one set out in July 1919 in the document of the Russian Mensheviks, *What Is To Be Done?*, and from the New Economic Policy (NEP) finally adopted by the Bolsheviks in 1921. However in 1917 three factors hindered its implementation. First, every decision had to be made after balancing extraordinarily complex political and ethnic interests. The usual result was an unsatisfactory compromise which no one had much incentive to implement. Second, nobody was clear on the juridical and legislative rights of the various local institutions, and there was a reluctance to force the issue before the Constituent Assembly. Third, there was no suitable executive office or administration to see the reforms through. Nevertheless a blueprint of reform was set out by Georgian Mensheviks, most of which was subsequently implemented by the government of the Georgian Democratic Republic. It was a revolutionary strategy of controlled socialist direction, but quite at odds with either Lenin's 'commune' or 'labour' state.[48]

Although the land question was not resolved until Georgian independence, the Transcaucasian Congress of May 1917, in line with Georgian Menshevik policy since 1905, rejected the SR socialisation programme, arguing that the present stage of economic development dictated support for the small landholder. The SRs were criticised for failing to take local conditions into account. The state would nationalise land of national significance and only confiscated property would be handed over to the organs of local self-government. There was no call for the immediate confiscation of land, and rents to landowners were to be paid into banks until the Constituent Assembly decided on the final land reform. Until then arbitration committees would settle disputes.[49] Despite additional resolutions, no further steps were taken to lay down the norms of confiscation or to set up peasant committees, and the Menshevik plans for conciliatory procedures remained on paper. The practical solution to providing the cities and army with foodstuffs which the peasantry was reluctant to supply in exchange for increasingly worthless money, was to requisition and establish monopolies. This began in November.

The Mensheviks took a moderate line on the worker question. Concerned above all else with continuing production at a time of chronic shortages, the Georgian Social Democrats, as well as demanding an eight-hour day, full social security and wage increases, proposed measures to reduce class conflict in factories, such as arbitration courts comprising equal numbers of employers and employees. They also personally intervened to end strikes and on occasion, such as in the June water strike, recommended the arrest of ringleaders.[50] They opposed soviet control of industry which they argued would lead to lockouts, and the power to hire and fire and ownership rights remained with the employers although the sacking of workers required the approval of the arbitration committees.[51]

The food and production crisis, which worsened after October when the northern grain supply almost ceased, soon taught the Mensheviks the contradictions of socialist power in a backward country. It was a problem they shared with the Bolsheviks. Although the latter were trying to impose a socialist system directly, and the Georgian Mensheviks were promoting a bourgeois revolution (playing according to the Marxist rules), both found that backwardness accentuated by the economic chaos of war and revolution, forced them into taking action against the very class they represented. In both cases it led to increasing authoritarianism, although the Mensheviks did not resort to terror. Both frequently had to consider the choice between protecting working-class or peasant interests on the one hand (during a strike for example), and maintaining production and supply, the lifeblood of the new state, on the other.

As one Transcaucasian economist put it, the state had to defend the workers while making sure their rights did 'not obstruct and hold back the development of productive forces'.[52] Leading a bourgeois revolution and defending proletarian or peasant interests was a rather contradictory position, as Zhordania was only too well aware. 'There is no doubt', he wrote, 'that all government operating within the limits of bourgeois society will inevitably serve the interests of the bourgeoisie.'[53] It was a situation Engels had warned against in his *Peasant War in Germany*. A party leader who takes power 'when the movement is not yet ripe for the domination of a class which he represents' is compelled 'to represent not his party or class, but the class for whose domination the movement is then ripe', he wrote.[54]

The Georgian Social Democrats and the October revolution

The October revolution, which Georgian Mensheviks refused to oppose by arms but considered doomed to failure, removed Russian responsibility for the revolution in Transcaucasia as well as its protective army. Isolated from the centre and faced with a rapacious Turkish enemy, the question of local power took on new urgency. The Georgian Mensheviks, in common with the other major Transcaucasian parties, still clung to the hope of remaining within a Russian democratic state, but were conscious of the need to establish a firm locus of regional power in order to 'lead Caucasia out of this catastrophic situation'.[55]

The urgency was reinforced by a growing Bolshevik challenge to SR control of the army. Thirty-six units of the Tiflis garrison, led by the Bolsheviks, formed a 'Delegates' Commission' to agitate for new elections to the Military Regional Soviet at the end of October. A joint meeting of the Tiflis Soviet and worker organisations, after listening to a report by Zhordania condemning 'supporters of the [Bolshevik] uprising in the garrison', resolved that 'any armed manifestation on the streets of Tiflis is a manifestation of the disorganised against the organised'.[56] After initially refusing to disperse the Delegates Commission and resigning from the Tiflis Soviet Executive Committee, the Bolsheviks, conscious of the unstable nature of their peasant soldier base and the irony of a rising against soviet power, withdrew from the commission on 11 November when new elections were set. That same day, on Menshevik initiative, 'representatives of all revolutionary democratic organisations of national, local or social significance' met to discuss the creation of a new organ of supreme power in the region. Four days later the Transcaucasian Commissariat was formed. Its twelve portfolios were carefully balanced among the parties and ethnic groups (the Mensheviks took the most important posts),[57] and included 'bourgeois' representatives from the Kadet and Musavat parties. It announced an ambitious programme of reform, but in the five months of its existence achieved none of its self-imposed tasks. The soviets retained their authority, and the Commissariat, immobilised by conflicting internal ethnic and political interests, confirmed Zhordania's warnings about the danger and confusion which surrounds inclusive coalitions. Resignations and walk-outs by the national parties and the refusal to compromise on issues such as land reform (the Muslim Musavat were against any radical measures) produced an administration which in the words of Chkhenceli was 'terribly like the government of Kerensky'.[58]

The most serious challenge to the Commissariat in its first few weeks of power was the influx into Tiflis of Bolshevik-oriented army units. The Mensheviks, as the senior partners in the coalition, accepted the challenge head on and showed a boldness that their Russian counterparts lacked in similar crises. (The latter, according to

Zhordania, 'slept and slept and the next morning found themselves in Bolshevik shackles'.[59]) The returning Russian soldiers were forcibly disarmed, sometimes at bloody cost,[60] martial law was declared, and a warrant for the arrest of the Bolshevik leader, Stepan Shaumian, was issued. But, most important, the Tiflis arsenal was seized by a Menshevik worker militia in order to release arms for distribution by the Tiflis Executive Committee.[61] At the same time the Bolshevik papers were temporarily closed and a number of Bolshevik activists arrested. Valico Jugheli, leader of the newly formed workers' militia, the Red Guard, declared that the seizure of the arsenal 'largely determined the revolution . . . in Caucasia'.

Lenin, on hearing the news, agreed and declared the Georgian Mensheviks to be 'masters of their own affairs'.[62] The Bolsheviks were also outmanoeuvred when they obtained a majority at the Second Congress of the Caucasian Army in December. The Menshevik and SR members, a minority of the Executive Committee, simply walked out over a contentious issue,[63] seized the soviet's inventory and declared themselves the properly constituted soviet. The Bolsheviks failed to rally the soldiers against this move and took their half of the soviet to Bolshevik Baku. With the soldiers' abandonment of the front, the local Bolsheviks, who had been hesitant to use the army against the Transcaucasian Commissariat, lost the opportunity to do so. In the following months, the soldiers' section of the Tiflis Soviet and the Military Regional Soviet dissolved without a murmur and all soviet power passed to the Mensheviks. On 19 December, the Second Congress of the Regional Soviet of Workers' and Peasants' Deputies confirmed the Mensheviks' supremacy, giving them 155 of the 248 delegates.[64] The Menshevik-led Red Guard was declared the official armed defence force of the revolution and replaced the army as the most powerful military force in Tiflis.

The Mensheviks polled a similarly impressive victory in the elections to the Constituent Assembly, receiving over half a million votes excluding all other Georgian parties.[65] However, of the eleven Menshevik delegates, only Irakli Tsereteli decided to attend the Assembly in Petrograd. The Georgian Mensheviks by this time had lost faith in the centre's ability to re-establish strong central government. E. Gegechkori reported to the Tiflis Soviet on 13 January that henceforth 'Caucasia has to rely on its own strength' and the Regional Centre of Soviets confirmed that with the fall of the Constituent Assembly 'the last thread which could have united Russia and the all-Russian democracy' has been severed.[66]

The move towards independence

In 1917, each national group developed its own ethnic organisation. By October, both the Armenians and the Azerbaijani Muslims possessed national councils which had extensive control over national political life and, ominously for future Transcaucasian unity, put forward territorial demands. The Georgians were the last to establish a national council. The Social Democratic organisation claimed to represent the Georgian people as a whole (a 'people's party') and was in a position to resist coalition within a national council. The Social Democrats participated in a Georgian inter-party bureau in April, but later withdrew from a Georgian inter-party soviet in August. In September, as a response to an increase in desertion from the front, they finally agreed to the formation of national military units, following the example of the Azerbaijanis and Armenians.

After the October revolution, the Georgian Mensheviks shifted their ground completely, and assumed the leadership of the first Georgian National Congress. Zhordania was elected chairman of this distinctly non-proletarian assembly.[67] He called for a Transcaucasian Sejm, a local constitution and 'complete self-government, with the power to make our own laws, to direct our own national administration, courts, schools, in a word, the nationalisation of all our institutions'.[68] He envisaged the National Congress as a 'guarantee of our national existence' and the 'base on which can be built the free cultural development of our people'.[69] Zhordania's speech represented a shift from his pre-October stand. He was now advocating a national coalition, not some kind of revolutionary democracy. Second, although he had conceded the right of Caucasian nationalities to establish self-governing bodies along territorial lines for the administration of national cultural affairs at the first Transcaucasian Congress of Workers' and Peasants' Deputies in May 1917, he was now proposing, in the absence of a strong unified centre, much broader legislative competence for the region. However, there was no mention of independence and he reiterated his loyalty to the Russian revolution.

In February 1918, as a result of a joint Menshevik–Musavat bloc in the Transcaucasian Commissariat, part of Zhordania's plan – the creation of a Transcaucasian Sejm – was achieved despite SR–Dashnaktsutiun (and some Menshevik) opposition to what was seen as a separatist step. Based on the results of the Constituent Assembly elections in Transcaucasia, it gave the Mensheviks 33 of the Sejm's 112 seats. The Musavat gained 30 and the Dashnaktsutiun 27.[70] The

Sejm, which went on to declare a Democratic Federative Republic of Transcaucasia in April, lasted 105 days and failed to establish effective land or labour reforms, and did not solve the problem of regional power and administration. National councils and parties rather than the Sejm continued to attract the Transcaucasians' allegiance, and in the atmosphere of insecurity produced by revolution and war, the Sejm failed, despite initial declarations of unity from all parties, to overcome conflicting national interests.[71] This was evident in the peace negotiations with Turkey from January 1918 onwards, when, in the absence of the Russian army, the nationalities were forced to think in terms of self-preservation. The pressure of Turkish territorial claims finally broke the fragile Transcaucasian alliance.

The Georgian Marxists took the leading role in each step towards Transcaucasian autonomy and independence despite some internal party resistance[72] and opposition from the Dashnaktsutiun and Russian SRs. The Armenians, despite their hankering for autonomy, wanted it under the Russian umbrella, ever fearful of neighbouring Turkey which in 1915–16 had massacred up to a million Turkish Armenians, perhaps even more. The Georgian Menshevik leaders, on the other hand, having learnt from the indecisiveness of their Russian counterparts, argued that the pressing problems of peace, land and national relations could not be decided before the question of regional power was resolved. In an address to the Sejm on 15 February, Zhordania, on behalf of the Social Democratic fraction, informed the representatives that his party could no longer wait for the juridical form of Transcaucasian power to be 'achieved within a Russian context'.[73] But it was the Turkish claim on Transcaucasian territory resulting from the Brest–Litovsk treaty (Kars, Ardahan and Batumi) which finally pushed the Social Democrats towards Transcaucasian independence. For Zhordania, the question was quite simple: 'Either here in Caucasia there will be Turkish rule, or the region will become independent.'[74] On 6 April, with Turkey already occupying parts of western Georgia, the Social Democratic Caucasian Regional Committee voted in favour of independence (the Georgian National Council did so three days later).

Zhordania, the 'orthodox Marxist' was unable to follow his own logic and abstained. Similarly, during the Sejm debate on independence, the Menshevik leaders remained demonstrably silent, leaving the floor to their deputies. Irakli Tsereteli later expressed what was probably a shared feeling among Georgian leaders dedicated for so long to the Russian revolution and internationalism, when he said that 'independence was a renunciation and defeat for the proletariat, and I could not add my voice to that'.[75] However, a few days after the declaration of Transcaucasian independence, he declared that the Bolsheviks had left them with the alternative 'either to destroy with our own hands the physical and political existence of our peoples . . . or to separate from Russia'. This became the Georgian Mensheviks' standard defence for their support of Transcaucasian independence.[76]

Throughout the long peace negotiations with Turkey, the Georgian Mensheviks staunchly defended Transcaucasian territorial integrity, particularly the threatened Georgian areas such as Batumi. However, as Transcaucasian unity broke down over Turkish territorial demands, the Georgians decided to save themselves by striking a bargain with Germany which was concerned at the activity of its Turkish ally in the region.[77] Tsereteli, in a frank expression of *Realpolitik*, told the Sejm that the Georgian Social Democratic Party had 'to employ all its efforts for its country within the limits of what they call bourgeois-internationalist guarantees, to get the best results possible'.[78] He went on to justify the decision in terms that Zhordania, Chkhenceli and other Georgian Social-Democratic activists had been repeating for years. 'National self-preservation was not opposed to democracy', he declared. On the contrary,

> it is the best base for the realisation of our final ideal, socialism. A nation, a people, a state cannot enter socialism if they cannot defend when necessary the national interests of their democracy.[79]

Although socialist cooperation with imperialism was acceptable to Lenin, this was not so for the ideologically more scrupulous Russian Mensheviks. At a party conference in Moscow in May 1918, the Russian Mensheviks pointedly rejected 'soliciting, in whatever form, the assistance of foreign powers in the task of overcoming Russia's internal political crisis'.[80] In their defence, Tsereteli and Zhordania replied to the Central Committee of the Menshevik RSDLP, that they were motivated not by 'the demand for national self-determination' but by the 'defence from Bolshevism on the one hand . . . and from the invading Turkish army on the other'.[81] Further argument on this issue became irrelevant when the Georgian organisation, following logically on Georgia's declaration of independence (on 26 May), formed its own independent Social Democratic Party in November 1918. Separation from the centre was complete and the Georgian Social Democrats began to develop their three-year experiment in Menshevik government.

CONCLUSION

The Georgian Social Democratic organisation, like the Bund and the Latvian party, was one of the most successful Marxist movements in the Russian empire. What all three had in common was identification with a single ethnic group and the association of political or economic oppression with a different nationality. Where national and class discrimination combined, then nationalism and socialism seemed natural allies. In the debates then current in the European socialist movement on the relationship between class, nationality and revolution, the Georgian like the Austro–Hungarian Social Democrats supported national-cultural development as the proper revolutionary strategy in a multi-ethnic state. At this stage of Georgia's development, they argued, proletarian interests were at one with national and social interests. The liberation struggle was proletarian and national at the same time. This concept proved to be popular and was reflected in the mass following of the Georgian Social Democratic organisation. In short, Georgian Social Democracy became one of the first examples of a Marxist national-liberation movement demonstrating the intimate relationship between socialism, nationalism and the agrarian struggle, which became the common pattern among Third World revolutionary movements following the Second World War.

This 'nationalisation' of Georgian Menshevism was the key to its success in 1917. In contrast to the Russian Menshevik organisation, which dominated the Petrograd Soviet but failed to sink deep organisational roots in the masses, Georgian Menshevism had a wide organisational and social base from which to operate. It also had a united leadership which commanded national loyalty and which demonstrated both greater pragmatism and political will than its Russian counterpart, particularly in its dealings with the army. Class loyalties remained important in 1917, and much of the organisation's appeal was its defence of the oppressed groups in society; but ethnicity was the foundation, in the Transcaucasian context, of class allegiance, underlining rather than undermining working class loyalty to the Georgian Social Democratic movement.

NOTES

The transliteration from Georgian is based on the system adopted by the library of the School of Oriental and African Studies, London.

  1 At the Ninth Congress of the Russian Communist Party in 1923, even Stalin admitted that there were 10,000 Menshevik Party members in

Georgia at a time when the official membership of the Communist Party of Georgia was 10,964 (*Dvenadtsatyi sezd RKP(b) 17–25 aprelia 1923 goda. Stenograficheskii otchet*, Moscow, 1968, p. 69).

2 A. Inghels, 'Une république socialiste', in *L'Internationale Socialiste et la Georgie* (Paris, 1921), p. 134.

3 Cited in Abraham A. Ascher, *Paul Axelrod and the Development of Menshevism* (Cambridge, Mass., 1972), p. 366.

4 There were seventeen voting delegates from Georgian committees at the Fourth Congress. Stalin was the only Bolshevik. Approximately 62 of the total 112 voting delegates were Menshevik (*Chetvertyi obeditelnyi sezd RDSRP, aprel (aprel–mai) 1906 goda: Protokoly*, Moscow, 1959, pp. x–xi). At the Fifth Congress, the Georgian committees provided 25 voting delegates (including G.V. Plekhanov who represented Tiflis) out of a total of approximately 85–90 Mensheviks. See *Piatii (Londonskii) sezd RSDRP, aprel–mai 1907 goda: Protokoly* (Moscow, 1963), pp. 651–2. Noe Zhordania, the acknowledged leader of Georgian Social Democracy, was elected to the RSDLP Central Committee at the Stockholm Congress in 1906 and Noe Ramishvili, another Georgian leader, at the Fifth Congress in 1907.

5 Irakli Tsereteli, Noe Zhordania, Carlo Chkheidze and Acaci Chkhenceli played outstanding roles in the Social Democratic fractions at the various Dumas. Tsereteli and Chkheidze went on to play a major part in the Petrograd Soviet and Menshevik organisation in 1917. For a list of Menshevik newspapers published in Georgia between 1905 and 1917, see S.F. Jones, 'Georgian Social Democracy: In Opposition and Power, 1892–1921', unpublished Ph.D. thesis, University of London, pp. 573–4. Also G.I. Bakradze, *Karthuli periodica 1819–1945. Bibliographia* (Tbilisi, 1947).

6 The terms, Transcaucasia (*Zakavkaze*) and Caucasia (*Kavkaz*), were often used interchangeably by political activists and writers of this period. Strictly speaking, Transcaucasia refers to the more limited area between the Greater Caucasian range and the southern frontiers with Iran and Turkey (the area presently occupied by the Soviet republics of Azerbaijan, Armenia and Georgia). Caucasia includes territory further north such as the Kuban, Terek, Daghestan and Stavropol regions. When quoting from original texts, I have simply translated what was written, making a note about geographical accuracy if necessary. On the Unification Congress, see Leo Lande, 'Some Statistics of the Unification Congress, August 1917', in L.H. Haimson (ed.), *The Mensheviks: From the Revolution of 1917 to the Second World War*, trans. Gertrude Vakar (Chicago and London, 1974), p. 391.

7 For literature on this period of Georgian history in English, see D.M. Lang, *A Modern History of Georgia* (London, 1962); D.M. Lang, *The Last Years of the Georgian Monarchy 1658–1832* (New York, 1957); W.E.D. Allen, *A History of the Georgian People: From the Beginning Down to the Russian Conquest in the Nineteenth Century* (London, 1932).

8 R.G. Suny has written extensively about the formation of national con-

sciousness in Georgia in the nineteenth century. See for example his 'Russian Rule and Caucasian Society in the First Half of the Nineteenth Century. The Georgian Nobility and the Armenian Bourgeoisie', *Nationalities Papers* 7, no. 1 (spring 1979), 53–78; 'The Emergence of Political Society in Georgia', in R.G. Suny (ed.), *Transcaucasia: Nationalism and Social Change* (Ann Arbor, Michigan, 1983), pp. 109–40.

9 *Sabdchotha Sakarthvelos 10 tseli: statisticuri crebuli* (Tphilisi [*sic*], 1931), pp. 24–5.

10 According to S. Khundadze, in 1900 Tiflis contained approximately 2,000 craftshops with one to two workers each, 439 'factories' of 7–8 employees and no more than 7 enterprises with over 300 workers each. The largest employer was the railways, with almost 4,000 workers at the Tiflis Railway Depot (S. Khundadze, *Sotzializmis istoriisathvis Sakarthveloshi: tsigni pirveli*, Tbilisi, 1927, p. 52).

11 A. Chkhenceli, 'Erovnuli citkhva chvenshi', *Khomli (Constellation)* no. 9 (23 July 1908), p. 1.

12 A. Chkhenceli, in *Shurduli (Catapult)* no. 3 (4 September 1908), p. 2.

13 Between 1903 and 1905, a large-scale west Georgian peasant movement known as the 'Gurian Republic' established a system of self-government, and with the help of the Social Democrats, excluded Tsarist authorities from the region for two years. Its fame spread wide. Leo Tolstoy declared that the Gurians were doing what he had been thinking and preaching for twenty years, namely 'setting up their own life without the need of authority' (cited in I.M. Avazashvili, *Bolshevistskie organizatsii Zakavkazia v period pervoi russkoi revoliutsii. 1905–7*, Tbilisi, 1968, pp. 97–8). The Italian historian and journalist, Luigi Villari, also travelled to Georgia to record events in Guria (L. Villari, *Fire and Sword in the Caucasus*, London, 1906). The best account is in the memoirs of Social Democrat Grigol Uratadze, *Vospominaniia gruzinskogo sotsial-demokrata* (Stanford, 1968). See also my 'Marxism and Peasant Revolt in the Russian Empire; the Case of the Gurian Republic', *The Slavonic and East European Review* 67 (1989), 403–34.

14 R. Kaladze, an Old Bolshevik, wrote: 'The national struggle and the hegemony of the working people's democracy are the two principles which Zhordania introduced to Georgian Social Democracy and from which Georgian Menshevism later developed.' R. Kaladze, 'Tribuna: criticuli shenishvnebi Ph. Makharadzis da S. Thalacvadzis saistori natserebis shesakheb', *Revolutziis matiane (Chronicle of the Revolution)* no. 3/13 (1925), p. 228. In some sense, Zhordania's formula resembled Mao's idea of the New Democratic Movement, which was a broad national alliance directed against foreign rule.

15 See K. Marx and F. Engels, *Manifesto of the Communist Party*, in Lewis S. Feuer (ed.), *Marx and Engels: Basic Writings on Politics and Philosophy* (New York, 1971), p. 67.

16 For attempts at definition of Menshevism, see Abraham Ascher (ed.), *The*

Mensheviks in the Russian Revolution (Ithaca, 1976), pp. 41–2; Leonard Schapiro's 'The Mensheviks', in Ellen Dahrendorf (ed.), *Russian Studies: Leonard Schapiro* (London, 1986), pp. 259–61; and Israel Getzler, *Martov: A Political Biography of a Russian Social Democrat* (Cambridge, 1967), ch. 10.

17 Abraham Ascher, *Paul Axelrod*, p. 383.

18 In the west Georgian region of Ozurgethi, for example, a Menshevik newspaper noted that 'peasants from different economic strata, traders, gentry, shop assistants, hired labourers and intelligentsia members are all in the party', *Grigali (Hurricane)* no. 1 (9 December 1906). On the debate over party composition in Georgia, see Uratadze, *Vospominaniia*, pp. 168–73.

19 Numerous observers of Georgian rural society have noted this phenomenon. The French socialist Odette Keun, who travelled extensively in Georgia during the independence period of 1918–21, declared that the vast majority of the country gentry 'only had limited estates which they cultivated themselves without having recourse to paid labour. Hence in their way of life and simplicity of their minds, they were very much akin to the peasants.' W. Woytinsky, a resident in Georgia during the same period, also talks of the 'solidarity of Georgian Social Democracy'. In his view, the intelligentsia were not considered 'apart' from the people and the former's links with the village kept the two classes close together (Odette Keun, *In the Land of the Golden Fleece: Through Independent Menshevist Georgia*, trans. from the French by Helen Jessima (London, 1924), p. 209; W. Woytinsky, *La Démocratie Georgienne* (Paris, 1921), pp. 37–8).

20 In a society dominated by a history of regional disunity and foreign domination, it is not surprising that national unity became the keystone of nearly every Georgian revolutionary programme from the early intelligentsia circles of the 1860s to the Georgian anarchists and populists of the 1880–90s. Georgian Social Democrats, as Chkhenceli reminded his readers in 1908, 'come largely from the Georgian national school; this fact has a great influence'. Chkhenceli, *Khomli* no. 9 (23 July 1908), p. 1.

21 Zhordania wrote extensively on the future Transcaucasian administrative structure. See, for example, his *Natsionaluri sakitkhi chvenshi* (Kutaisi, 1913), published under the pseudonym 'Naridze'; *Natsionaluri kitkhva Amier-Kavkasiashi* (1916?), published in *N.N. Zhordania: misi natserebis krebuli erovnuli sakitkhebis shesakheb* (Tiflis, 1922), pp. 244–69 and *Pederalistebi da chven* (Tiflis, 1917). In these monographs (all in Georgian), his concern was to devise a plan whereby the three major Transcaucasian nations could share power in a single Transcaucasian administrative unit. His solution was a combination of the territorial and cultural principle, with the central government reserving for itself major legislative, executive, diplomatic and military powers, leaving to the national cultural units competence over national-cultural and local questions. See

also his 'Erovnuli sakitkhi amier-kavkasiis sotzial-democratiul organizatziebis me-VI qrilobaze', in *N.N. Zhordania: misi natserebis krebuli erovnuli sakitkhebis shesakheb* (Tiflis, 1922), pp. 271–6.

22 The Russian Menshevik nationality policy was expressed in a resolution presented by F. Dan and V.M. Chernov to the Provisional Council of the Republic in October 1917. It declared, with an ambiguity more akin to Bolshevik statements, that 'all nationalities have the right to determine their own fate. But that does not mean giving them independence. We feel that the right must be directed toward the preservation of tight bonds with Russia.' Cited in Marc Ferro, 'La politique des nationalités du Gouvernement Provisoire', *Cahiers du Monde Russe et Soviétique* no. 2 (April–June 1961), p. 164.

23 As far back as 1903, Zhordania was emphasising the importance of the peasant struggle to the proletarian cause when he declared at the RSDLP Second Congress: 'We must put ourselves in the forefront of the peasant struggle and lead it under the banner of the proletariat and not abandon it to the fates', *Vtoroi sezd RSDRP. Iiul-avgust 1903 goda. Protokoly* (Moscow, 1959), p. 216. The different Russian and Georgian attitudes towards the peasantry often led to misunderstandings. In the Second Duma for example, when Tsereteli advocated closer cooperation with the peasant parties, this was seen by many Russian Mensheviks as capitulation to the Left-bloc tactic of the Bolsheviks, whereas Tsereteli saw it simply as a means for putting further pressure on the Kadets (B.I. Nicolaevsky, 'Pamiati I.G. Tsereteli. Stranitsy biografii. Statia sedmaia', *Sotsialisticheskii vestnik* nos. 2–3, 1960, 50). Boris Nicolaevsky later wrote that 'the attempt to free Russian Menshevism from its elements of peasant phobia was one of the main services of Georgian Social Democracy for the All-Russian movement'. Ibid., p. 51. However, it is worth noting two points. First, at the RSDLP Fourth Congress, which had a Menshevik majority, the resolution on the agrarian question accepted that if conditions necessitated it the distribution of land to the peasantry on the basis of 'small-scale husbandry' was acceptable (Ascher [ed.], *The Mensheviks*, pp. 64–5). Second, after Georgian Mensheviks attained state power and faced a restless peasantry provoked by a deteriorating economic situation, attitudes changed. Zhordania declared in 1918 that the 'single serious danger to the Republic and revolution comes from inside – the peasantry' (N. Zhordaniia, *Za dva goda: Doklady i rechi (mart 1917–mart 1919 g.)*, Tiflis, 1919, p. 116).

24 Georgian Menshevik detachments cooperated willingly with Bolsheviks in bank robberies and assassinations, and in 1906, had their own 'expropriation group'. Kote Tzintzadze, the first commissar of the Georgian Cheka and later a stubborn oppositionist, writes in his memoirs that the Mensheviks were still operating an expropriation group in 1908. Tzintzadze, 'Chemi mogonebani', *Revolutziis matiane* no. 4 (1923), 57.

25 According to Zhordania's memoirs, on his arrival in Georgia at the end of 1914, there was a 'Germanophile' position in the local organisation (*Chemi tsarsuli*, Paris, 1958, pp. 98–9). Forbidden to publish his defencist views in the official Social Democratic organ, he set up a rival newspaper with Grigol Urutadze in Kutaisi. The local organisation removed this paper from Zhordania's control but by the summer of 1915, Zhordania was winning the arguments. 'Kakheli' (pseud.) in a collection of articles on the war edited by Plekhanov in 1915, declared that two-thirds of Georgian workers backed Zhordania (*Voina. Sbornik statei*, Paris, 1915, p. 95). Half of the delegates to the conference in October were from Guria (Zhordania's home region) which may partly explain Zhordania's success in changing official policy. Although the conference decided not to oppose the war actively and to support the War Industries Committees, it refused to sanction Zhordania's most extreme proposal to call on the Duma fraction to vote for war credits. For an account of the debate in the Georgian organisation, see Uratadze, *Vospominaniia*, pp. 267–75.

26 Naridze (pseud.), 'Omi da zavi', *Akhali azri (New Thought)* no. 106 (30 December 1914), 3.

27 The Hai Heghapokhakan Dashnaktsutiun (Armenian Revolutionary Foundation), established in 1890, was the leading party in both the Turkish and Transcaucasian Armenian communities. Dedicated to the defence of Armenians in Turkey, it also professed socialism, and was a member of the Second International.

28 S. Beridze (ed.), *Borba za sovetskuiu vlast v Gruzii: Dokumenty i materialy* (Tbilisi, 1958), p. 14.

29 During the war, Zhordania had defended the participation of socialists in bourgeois government, arguing that the special conditions of national defence demanded it. Naridze (pseud.), 'Omi da zavi', *Akhali azri*, no. 106 (30 December 1914), 3.

30 *Za dva goda*, p. 35.

31 Getzler, *Martov*, p. 162; and S.E. Sef, *Revoliutsiia 1917 goda v Zakavkazi: Dokumenty i materialy* (Tiflis, 1927), p. 212.

32 *Za dva goda*, p. 40.

33 For discussion of Marx's view of the 'permanent revolution' and his subsequent rejection of the idea, see the introduction to David Fernbach (ed.), *Karl Marx: The Revolutions of 1848. Political Writings*, vol. 1 (Harmondsworth, 1973), pp. 9–61. On the Russian Marxist debate concerning the dilemmas of revolution in backward Russia see Israel Getzler, 'Marxist Revolutionaries and the Dilemma of Power', in A. Rabinowitch, Janet Rabinowitch and Ladis K.D. Kristof, *Revolution and Politics in Russia: Essays in Memory of B.I. Nicolaevsky* (Bloomington, 1972), pp. 88–112.

34 *Chemi tsarsuli*, p. 116.

35 B. Baikov, 'Vospominaniia o revoliutsii v Zakavkaze (1917–1920 gg.)', in I.V. Gessen (ed.), *Arkhiv russkoi revoliutsii*, vol. 9 (Berlin, 1923), p. 91.

36 For composition of the new organ, see Sef, *Revoliutsiia*, pp. 227–8. There were four representatives from the Ozakom and military organs and two from the duma. All the rest were soviet, trade-union or party representatives.

37 *Protokoly Zakavkazskikh revoliutsionnykh sovetskikh organizatsii*, vol. 1, (Tiflis, 1920), p. 26.

38 Ibid., p. 136.

39 The Bolsheviks did not split with the Georgian Mensheviks until after the Bolshevik Seventh All-Russian Conference in April. They formally left in June despite considerable resistance from local Bolshevik members.

40 Although the Russian army had done extremely well on the Caucasian front capturing Trebizond in 1916, after the February revolution, as supplies (including medicines) dried up and disease spread, soldiers began to leave for home. For an account of the military situation on the Caucasian front during the First World War, see W.E.D. Allen and Paul Muratoff, *Caucasian Battlefields. A History of the Wars on the Turco-Caucasian Border 1828–1921* (Cambridge, 1963).

41 The Mensheviks received 50 seats, the Dashnaks 24, the SRs 20, the Kadets and the Bolsheviks 7 each, Sef, *Revoliutsiia*, p. 203.

42 The Georgian Bolshevik, M. Orakhelashvili, wrote that after February 1917 trade unions 'everywhere seemed to be in the hands of the Mensheviks', M. Orakhelashvili, *Zakavkazskie bolshevistskie organizatsii v 1917 g.* (Tiflis, 1927), p. 41.

43 *Protokoly Zavkavkazskikh*, p. 85.

44 Cited in 'Otsdakhuthi ivnisis mitingi Nadzaladevshi, *Revolutziis matiane* 1 (1927), 84.

45 R. Kaladze, 'Mushata karthuli' zhurnal-gazetis istoria', *Revolutziis matiane* 5 (1923), 46.

46 R.G. Suny comes to the same conclusion in his 'Nationalism and Social Class in the Russian Revolution: The Cases of Baku and Tiflis', in Suny (ed.), *Transcaucasia*, pp. 239–58.

47 See Sef, *Revoliutsiia*, pp. 51–2.

48 For an interesting account of these two models of socialism adopted by Lenin after 1917, see N. Harding, 'Socialism, Society, and the Organic Labour State', in N. Harding (ed.), *The State in Socialist Society* (Oxford, 1984).

49 The resolution is in *Borba za sovetskuiu vlast v Gruzii*, pp. 27–30.

50 'Zhurnali osobogo Zakavkazskogo komiteta', *Georgian Archive*, box 1, no. 49. (The Archives of the Delegation to the Conference of Peace and the Government in Exile are deposited at the Houghton Library, Harvard.)

51 For Georgian Menshevik proposals on labour reform, see Sef, *Revoliutsiia*, pp. 123, 162; *Protokoly Zavkavkazskikh*, p. 107.

52 Report by the Minister of Labour at the First Congress of Georgian Trade Unions (April 1919), in *Georgian Archive*, box 3, book 24, pp. 4–5.

53 N. Zhordania, *Za dva goda*, p. 111.

54 *Marx and Engels: Basic Writings*, p. 475.

55 N. Zhordaniia, *Za dva goda*, p. 51.

56 Sef, *Revoliutsiia*, p. 328.

57 The Mensheviks took the Chairmanship and Commissariat of Labour (a joint post held by E. Gegechkori) and the Commissariat of the Interior. The SRs took the Commissariat of Land and the Dashnaktsutiun the Commissariat of Finance. For the full distribution of posts, see 'To the People of Transcaucasia', Kantselariia Zakavkazskogo Seima, *Georgian Archive*, box 1, book 1/1157.

58 Ibid., box 1, book 1/1589.

59 Cited in K. Ivanidze, *Slavnye stranitsy borby i pobed: Istoriia deiatelnosti Kavkazskogo Kraiego Komiteta RKP(b) 1917–20* (Tbilisi, 1975), p. 137.

60 The most serious clash occurred at Shamkhor in January 1918 between Russian troops returning from the front and Azerbaijanis who were in desperate need of arms. Up to 1,000 soldiers died in the ensuing battle (Baikov, 'Vospominaniia', p. 113; *Borba za sovetskuiu vlast v Gruzii*, pp. 194–6).

61 It was an extremely risky venture and Zhordania recalls receiving a terrible shock when he reviewed the 300 or so badly armed workers who were to carry out the mission. Although in Zhordania's view they 'resembled a band of robbers' (*Chemi tsarsuli*, p. 118) they took the garrison by surprise and without firing a shot.

62 Orakhelashvili, *Kavkazskie bolshevistskie organizatsii*, p. 51.

63 The issue was over the Bolshevik refusal to recognise the authority of the Regional Centre of Workers' and Peasants' Deputies.

64 S. Chkhartishvili, *Sabdchoebi Sakarthveloshi oktombris revolutziis momzadebisa da gatarebis periodshi: 1917 tslis marti–1920 tseli* (Tbilisi, 1977), p. 158.

65 For a breakdown of the Menshevik vote to the Constituent Assembly, see Leo Lande in L.H. Haimson (ed.), *The Mensheviks*, pp. 389–91.

66 F. Kazamzadeh, *The Struggle for Transcaucasia: 1917–21* (Oxford and New York, 1951), p. 85.

67 Among the 324 delegates were, besides the 82 from the parties and soviets, 26 from trade, commercial and banking institutions, 6 from the gentry, 7 Georgian Muslims, 7 Georgian Catholics and 9 from the teacher's union. It was clearly a national phenomenon but many Mensheviks felt it was quite unfit to decide any major political questions. G. Urutadze, *Obrazovanie i konsolidatsiia Gruzinskoi Demokraticheskoi Respubliki* (Munich, 1956), pp. 36–7.

68 Ibid., p. 92.

69 Cited in F. Makharadze, *Sovety i borba za sovetskuiu vlast v Gruzii 1917–1921* (Tiflis, 1927), p. 131.

70 For these figures see R.G. Hovannisian, *Armenia. On the Road to Independence 1918* (Berkeley and Los Angeles, 1967), p. 126. There is some

dispute about the party numbers. See for example *Borba za sovetskuiu vlast v Gruzii*, p. 214, and F. Kazamzadeh, *The Struggle for Transcaucasia*, p. 87, which present slightly different figures.

71 The conservative Georgian National Democrats wrote in January 1918 with great prescience that 'in Transcaucasia, centrifugal forces dominate centripetal ones . . . The rights of the Transcaucasian Sejm will be challenged by the National Soviets . . . the life of the Sejm as a government will be very short lived.' Cited in E. Drabkina, *Gruzinskaia kontrrevoliutsiia* (Leningrad, 1928), p. 64.

72 For example, Chkhenceli firmly opposed the first step in the organisation of local power (the Caucasian Revkom) believing it to be an abandonment of the Provisional Government. In the spring of 1918, there was considerable resistance to the declaration of Transcaucasian independence from Carlo Chkheidze, Inna Zhordania (Noe's Russian wife) and another Russian member M.N. Smirnov (S. Ia. Kheifits, 'Zakavkaze v pervuiu polovlnu 1918 g. i Zakavkazskii seim', *Byloe* no. 21, 1923, 307). See also the report on the Eighth Congress of the Caucasian Social Democratic organisations in *Svobodnaia Mysl* no. 71 (3 December 1918) in Georgian Archive, box 20, book 17.

73 Zhordaniia, *Za dva goda*, p. 65.

74 Ibid., p. 74.

75 Cited in Kheifits, 'Zavkavkaze', p. 307.

76 I.G. Tsereteli, *Séparation de la Transcaucasie et de la Russie et Indépendence de la Georgie. Discours prononcés à la Diète Transcaucasienne par Irakly Tseretelli* (Paris, 1919), p. 21.

77 At the Batumi peace talks between Transcaucasia and Turkey, secret negotiations were held with the German representative, Major-General von Lossow. Germany, fearful that Turkish intervention in Transcaucasia could block Germany's strategy of creating a corridor to the Orient and prevent access to raw materials (oil, manganese), was quite ready to strike a deal with Georgia.

78 *Séparation*, p. 51.

79 Ibid., p. 53.

80 George Denicke, 'From the Dissolution of the Constituent Assembly to the Outbreak of the Civil War', in L.H. Haimson (ed.), *The Mensheviks*, p. 148.

81 'Platforma po natsionalnomu voprosu', *Sotsialisticheskii vestnik*, nos. 7/8 (1929), 14.

places, founded and built factories and plants, and many of our brothers have served in the army and served their homeland in faith and truth. Thousands have given their lives in fulfilling their honourable duty to their fatherland. That is our history.[3]

It was the peculiar circumstances of the Russian-German community that led the Union to limit its programme to economic and cultural autonomy at a time when other national groups were developing more far-reaching political platforms. The dispersal of the community throughout the Russian empire militated against the development of any homogeneous political platform and strategy, and similarly made unrealistic any idea of territorial autonomy within the framework of a federal republic; the territorial idea was only viable for the Volga Germans, and for those of the community in the Black Sea and Siberian regions.

The Union adopted the organisational structure of the large political parties. It appointed a Provisional Central Committee to be based in Petrograd, district committees in provincial capitals of areas with substantial German settlement, and local committees in provincial towns. Confronted with the need to fight elections to the *zemstva* and town dumas as well as to the Constituent Assembly, the various committees were forced to formulate a variety of political programmes.

Thus, the Provisional Central Committee, consisting of disillusioned Russian-German and Baltic-German Octobrists under the leadership of the dynamic professor of jurisprudence, Baron Alexander Meyendorff, adopted an independent liberal stance. The Moscow regional committee, under Lindemann, pursued specifically national goals. Its programme contained the significant phrase: 'The union is based upon a strictly national foundation without following any party political goals.' Its electoral strategy consisted in forming national German lists and barred the formation of electoral alliances with other groups. The national stance of the Moscow committee was regarded with disapproval by the south Russian regional committee which had its headquarters in Odessa. Moscow's attitudes were also overtly criticised by the Saratov regional committee.

The Odessa committee, representing the most economically and socially powerful group of Russian Germans, while close to the Kadets – notably on the agrarian question – nevertheless remained open to all democratic and left-wing parties. The congress of the south Russian committee, which was convened in mid April, adopted the platform of a democratic republic based on universal, free, equal and secret suffrage; on the nationality question, it upheld the right to national self-determination, expecting that right to be realised within the existing framework of a united, free and democratic Russian state and not by secession.

The Saratov regional committee, consisting of Kadets, Social Democrats and Socialist Revolutionaries, adopted an independent position halfway between the liberals and the socialists. In line with the Kadets, the Saratov congress, convening at the end of April, upheld the right to own a limited amount of private land, but, with the Social Democrats, espoused a programme of national self-determination. It also advocated the formation of a republican party of Volga-German colonists.

In Siberia, both the regional committee based in Omsk, and the Siberian regional congress, convening in Slavgorod in May, advocated national self-determination and territorial autonomy, including the right of secession. But in Bessarabia (Tarutino) and Transcaucasia (Tiflis and Veliko Kniazhesk), the regional congresses of the German community – aligned with the Kadets in their general platform – did not uphold the right to self-determination.

The Mennonite conventions in Halbstadt (June 1917) and Georgevka (July 1917), as well as the first general Mennonite congress in Orlov (August 1917), adopted positions similar to those of the Saratov committee. But on the agrarian question, while some veteran representatives of large landed property owners favoured moderate Kadet positions, the young, radical intelligentsia urged the general expropriation of landed property and its just redistribution (socialisation) among the needy population. A compromise formula was found, but all it did was temporarily to paper over the deepening ideological gaps.

In general, all regional groups of the All-Russian Union of Russian Germans and Mennonites claimed the right to private land ownership and/or private use at least for some limited area and time. On the national question, all groups demanded economic and cultural autonomy, the right to use their own language and to have their own schools and educational institutions. Some groups, such as the Siberian and Volga Germans, claimed the right to national self-determination and territorial autonomy, while others, such as the south Russian Germans, kept an open mind on the issue. The large majority of the community favoured the establishment of a parliamentary republic on democratic foundations based on the so-called 'four-tailed formula'. Some groups, such as the Siberian and Volga Germans and a section of south Russian Germans, advocated a federal democratic republic. On the all-important question of peace, the community in general remained prudently silent.

It was with these basic commitments that the Russian Germans entered the election campaign to the Constituent Assembly. German participation was expected to be relatively high. Indeed the community's newspapers had made their readers aware of 'the immense importance' that these elections were bound to have for them. As the *Wochenblatt* put it:[4]

> They must give us a new form of government, must guarantee us all the liberties which the great political transformation called revolution has brought us, such as personal freedom, freedom of belief, freedom of the written and spoken word, of assembly, of sojourn and of ownership. Moreover, the Constituent Assembly must come to a final decision on the extremely important agrarian question: whether the right to private ownership of land should continue to exist, to what extent and so on. There is nobody, whether Russian, German or Jew, for whom these issues are not of the greatest importance. Consequently, it rests entirely in our hands whether we have our representatives in this Constituent Assembly, that is, men who will both fight for the above-mentioned liberties in general and also ensure that these freedoms are accorded to us to the fullest extent. We must seek to bring *our* men into the Constituent Assembly.

There was, however, little agreement on how to bring German representatives into the Constituent Assembly, and it was not until September 1917 that there emerged a growing consensus that it would be better to have separate German lists. In that, the Russian Germans did not differ from most other national groups. On 3 September, the south Russian Germans resolved that

> the Germans must participate in the elections as an independent German [national] group; the electoral lists of Germans will be made known in the election districts under the name *Spisok russkikh nemtsev*; in every district, a commission for electoral propaganda is to be elected forthwith; landless and poor peasants must be taken into account in the compilation of lists of candidates.[5]

However, the question of election agreements with other all-Russian parties in regions where exclusively German lists did not promise success remained open and subject to debate. The Moscow regional group vehemently rejected electoral alliances with other national groups. The Volga-German congress in Schillings split evenly over the question whether the recommendations of the Moscow committee should be debated at all – while a large socialist wing insisted on the right to enter into electoral alliances with suitable all-Russian parties, the Centre tended to prefer exclusively Volga-German lists.

Singular difficulties bedevil any attempt to analyse the electoral behaviour of Russian Germans in the elections to the Constituent Assembly in mid November 1917. Results for the Saratov, Kherson and Tauride provinces are very incomplete, while none are available for some districts such as Kamyshin in the Saratov province (with a particularly large German population), and the Caspian, Terek and Kuban regions. Moreover, no elections could be held in Bessarabia and the northern Caucasus. In other areas, for instance the city of Saratov, political turmoil in the form of street fights made normal election procedures impossible, while the forced expropriation of local newspapers, including German-language dailies, prevented the regular publication of election results. Even where elections were held more or less normally, there were a number of cases of moral pressure and physical intimidation.

While the resulting picture remains fragmentary and somewhat problematic, some patterns of German–Russian electoral behaviour can be identified.[6] Thus, out of the 1.2 million votes in the Volga district of Samara, where 8.1 per cent of the population were Germans, 47,500 votes were cast for the German national list and 42,156 for the German socialist list. In Saratov province, with 6.9 per cent of the population being Germans, around one million votes were counted. There is no information available about national electoral returns here, but it seems reasonable to assume that the German community in Saratov would have followed the Samara pattern and achieved similar results. In the south Russian province of Ekaterinoslav (3.8 per cent being Germans), out of 1.2 million votes cast, 25,977 went to a German national list.

Results in the other two south Russian provinces, Tauride – with a German population of 5.4 per cent – and Kherson – with 4.5 per cent Germans – afford no information regarding German lists. But the total number of votes cast in the Tauride province (524,750) contained, along with 61,509 votes for Ukrainian and 60,958 votes for Moslem parties, a group of 45,519 'not particularly specified' votes – among these, one can assume, there must have been a fair number of German votes. Likewise, in Kherson province, out of a total of 694,391 votes, 72,500 were cast for the Ukrainian parties and 43,608 for unspecified other national lists – the latter number might also have contained a large number of German votes.

Altogether between 121,000 and 130,000 votes were cast for German national lists, while from 42,000 to 44,000 went to German socialist lists. Thus, a total of between 163,000 and 175,000 German votes (that is, less than 10 per cent of the total Russian-German population) have been identified, and this is probably only a modest part of the total poll since for the first time women too were entitled to vote.

It must be assumed that much of the vote went not to the German national lists but to the front-line soldiers' lists and to the all-Russian parties. While the number of those who backed the German lists appears low, 37 of the 715 deputies sent to the Constituent Assembly can be identified by name and family connections as ethnic Germans.[7] If this is accurate, then the Russian Germans, who constituted only 1.4 per cent of the total population of the Russian empire, were represented by over 5 per cent of the Constituent Assembly, a situation comparable to that in the State Dumas of the Tsarist period.

Delegates of ethnic-German background were not affiliated to any German list, national or socialist, nor did they represent the interests of Germans in any visible manner; indeed no specifically German mandate can be identified among any of the 715 delegates. Moreover, none of the candidates of the All-Russian Union of Germans and Mennonites such as Baron Meyendorff, Ludwig Lutz, Benjamin Unruh and Pastor I.I. Winkler made their way into the Assembly; yet most of the larger national groups, such as Georgians, Armenians, Poles, Jews, Bashkirs, Kirgiz and Cossacks and even such small minorities as Buriats, Chuvash or Cherimissians did manage to have their own representatives. It is difficult to pinpoint the reasons for this failure on the part of the Germans. As the success of the Jews proved, mere territorial dispersal will not provide an answer. Perhaps the main reason may have been the wide party-political and ideological spectrum that characterised the German community.

However, numerous ethnic-German candidates graced the lists of other ethnic minorities: thus, among the sixteen ethnic-German deputies in the Socialist Revolutionary group, four represented the Ukrainian SRs, among them Nikolai Ilich Schrag, from Chernigov province, whose father, Ilia Ludvigovich von Schrag, had represented the Left Kadets of Chernigov in the First State Duma. One Baltic German from Estonia, Rudolf Johann Backmann, represented the Estonian Trudoviki; another four of the German SRs were deputies representing front-line units: one SR of German origin was the illustrious revolutionary, Vera Figner.

Among the Bolsheviks, the ethnic Germans were even more strongly

represented, with 14 deputies out of the party's 175. While the Bolsheviks made up only 24 per cent of the total Assembly, ethnic-
German Bolsheviks apparently constituted 39 per cent of all ethnically
German deputies. Of the German Bolsheviks, 2 had been elected by
front-line soldiers (the western and Romanian fronts) and the remaining 12 in the province of Minsk (3), in Estonia (2), Petrograd (2), and
one each in Chernigov, Viatka, Tambov, Tver and Priamurskii Krai.

Four ethnic-German delegates belonged to the non-Bolshevik Social
Democratic fractions (Mensheviks and Internationalist Social
Democrats). They had been elected in the Province of Livonia
(twenty-two) and one each in Tula and Petrograd. Among the Kadets
there were two leading German liberal intellectuals, Lev Iacob Kroll,
from Perm province and Professor Nikolai Nikolaevich Kutler, from
Petrograd. A considerable part of the Russian-German vote in both
capitals seems to have gone to the Kadets who were highly regarded
by the German bourgeois intelligentsia which had joined the party's
ranks in great numbers.

Russian-German votes may also have been given to religious lists.
And in the countryside of various provinces, especially those in the
south, Russian-German landowners may also have voted for the Russian Landowners Party which received the fairly solid result of 215,542
votes.

The fragmentary results available make it still more difficult to
assess the voting patterns of Russian-German soldiers. So that they
would not have to fight against their own kinsfolk, the overwhelming
majority had been removed from the western to the Caucasian front in
the spring of 1915. But the election results from the Caucasian front
contained no national lists. One may only assume that Russian-German voters were far more numerous among the 360,000 SR voters
than among the 60,000 Bolsheviks.

Similarly, there is no evidence of votes along national lines among
the sailors in the Baltic fleet, and while sailors in the Black Sea fleet
did support national lists there is no mention of a German list. The
same applies to the armies along the northern front and the western
and south-western Romanian fronts.

To sum up, in the elections to the Constituent Assembly some 130,000
of the 175,000 identifiable Russian-German votes went to the German
national list and consequently voted for the right to own a limited area
of private land, for economic and cultural autonomy, for a democratic
republic and for the possibility of a federal solution for certain border

regions; in short, they backed a basically Kadet programme. Some 30 per cent of the Russian-German votes in the Volga region went to the German socialist list which advocated a just redistribution of land among the needy and working populations. As far as the Russian-German deputies of the Constituent Assembly are concerned, a proportionately strong representation among the Bolsheviks is evident, perhaps because the Bolsheviks appeared as the peace party *par excellence*.

Lenin's forcible dispersal of the Constituent Assembly must have alienated many Russian Germans who had pinned their hopes on a democratic Russia. Likewise, the Bolsheviks' agrarian programme turned many German landowners and prosperous peasants into bitter enemies of the Soviet state. But the same programme must equally have been greeted with satisfaction by the community's agrarian proletariat and poor peasantry. In attacking German schools and church institutions, the Council of People's Commissars alienated the religious and traditional German urban population. But that attack on traditional institutions and ways of life, which characterised the entire period of the Civil War, was essentially a matter of the class struggle. That being so, many Germans in leading positions in the army, the civil service and industry seem to have accepted the régime, trusting that it was capable of restoring law and order. It took the advent of Stalinism to dash all hope in the Russian-German community of a restoration of that free and democratic society, the *Volksherrschaft*, which they had so eagerly hailed early in 1917.

NOTES

1 See Axel von Gernet, 'Die Deutschen in Russland', *Deutsche Monatsschrift für Russland* no. 1 (Reval, 1912), pp. 1–7; no. 2, pp. 97–103. Later studies include: Ingeborg Fleischhauer and Benjamin Pinkus, *The Soviet Germans Past and Present* (London, 1986); Ingeborg Fleischhauer, *Die Deutschen im Zarenreich: Zwei Jahrhundert deutsch-russischer Kulturgemeinschaft* (Stuttgart, 1986); Benjamin Pinkus and Ingeborg Fleischhauer, *Die Deutschen in der Sowjetunion. Geschichte einer nationalen Minderheit im 20. Jahrhundert* (Baden-Baden, 1987).

2 'Obrashchenie ko vsem nemtsam', *Ezhenedelnik: Organ Vserossiiskogo Soiuza russkikh nemtsev* no. 1 (16–22 April 1917), p. 3.

3 'Kak nam sleduet organizovatsia', *Ezhenedelnik* no 4 (May 1917), pp. 3, 7–13.

4 'Die verfassunggebende Versammlung (Uchreditelnoe Sobranie)', *Wochenblatt* no. 18 (19 August 1917), pp. 2–3.

5 *Wochenblatt*, no. 20 (September 1917), p. 2.
6 My findings are based on *Vserossiiskoe Uchreditelnoe Sobranie*, Podgotovil k pechati S. Malchevskii (Moscow and Leningrad, 1930); V.I. Lenin, 'Vybory v uchreditelnoe sobranie i diktatura proletariata', *Sochineniia*, 3rd edn., vol. xxiv (Moscow, 1932), pp. 631–49; Oliver Henry Radkey, *The Elections to the Russian Constituent Assembly of 1917* (Cambridge, Mass., 1950).
7 The names of the deputies of German origin have been spelt in the German manner; where there is some doubt as to their German background, a question-mark is added:

1. APEIER, Hans Andreas, western front, RSDRP(b)
2. BOSCH, Eugen Gottlieb, Chernigov, RSDRP(b)
3. BRUSCHWIT, Hans Michael, Samara, SR and Soviet of Peasant Deputies
4. BACKHANN, Rudolf Johannes, Estonia RSDRP(b)
5. DETLAV, Anton Osip (?), southwestern front, SR and Soviet of Peasant Deputies
6. EIDEMANN, Robert Peter, Ufa, SR and Soviet of Peasant Deputies
7. FIGNER, Vera Nikolaevna, Astrakhan, SR and Soviet of Peasant Deputies
8. FREIMANN, Basilius Nikolaus (?), Minsk, RSDRP(b)
9. GERSTEIN, Leo Nikolaus, Perm, SR and Soviet of Peasant Deputies
10. KAUL, Alexander Joseph, Tula, Revolutionary SD(b)
11. KORSCH, Kuzma Alexius (?), Ekaterinoslav, Soviet of Peasant Deputies and Ukrainian SD and SR
12. KROLL, Leo Jakob, Perm, CD (Constitutional Democrats)
13. KUTLER, Nikolaus Nikolaus, Petrograd City, CD
14. LANDER, Karl Johannes, Minsk, RSDRP(b)
15. LÖWENBERG, Eduard Alexander, southwestern front, SR and Soviet of Peasant Deputies
16. LINDBERG, Michael Jakob (?), Tomsk, SR
17. MORGENSTJERNA, Viktor Theodor, western front, SR and Soviet of Peasant Deputies
18. NEUBUI(H), Arnold Jakob, Amur region, RSDRP(b)
19. PEGELMANN, Hans Gustav, Estonia, RSDRP(b) and Executive Committee of Landless and Poor Peasants
20. PETERSON, Karl Andreas, Livonia, Latvian SD
21. PORSCH, Nikolaus Woldemar, Kiev, Ukrainian SR
22. POSERN, Boris Paul, Petersburg (*sic*), RSDRP(b)
23. RICHTER, Woldemar Nikolaus, Kherson, Soviet of Peasant Deputies, SR, Ukrainian SR
24. ROSEN, Friedrich Adam, Livonia, Latvian SD
25. SACK, Samuel Sergius (?), Tauride, SR and Soviet of Peasant Deputies
26. SCHLEGEL, Nikodim Valerian (?), Minsk, RSDRP(b)

27. SCHLICHTER, Alexander Georg, Tambov, RSDRP(b)
28. SCHMIDT, Basilius Woldemar, Tver, RSDRP(b)
29. SCHOT[T]MANN, Alexander Basilius, Petrograd, RSDRP(b)
30. SCHRAG, Nikolaus Ilia, Chernigov, Ukrainian SR
31. SCHREIDER, Georg Ilia, Petrograd City, SR
32. SCHWEIZ, Theodor Peter, Kiev, Ukrainian SR
33. SOLERS, Boris Johannes (?), Romanian Front, RSDRP(b)
34. SPUNDE, Alexander Peter, Viatka, RSDRP(b)
35. UNSCHLICHT, Joseph Stanislav, Petrograd City, Central Committee SD
36. UTHOF(F), Woldemar Leo, northern front, SR and Soviet of Peasant Deputies
37. WILMS, Georg Reinh., Estonia, Estonian Workers' Party, Trudovaia Partiia

Part 4

LENINISM AND THE MAKING OF OCTOBER

13

LENIN, SOCIALISM AND THE STATE IN 1917

NEIL HARDING

For differing reasons both Soviet and Western historians and political commentators have found it convenient to assume that the Bolsheviks came to power in October 1917 ready armed with a well-articulated theory of legitimacy which had the dictatorship of the proletariat at its core. As Soviet historians have been concerned to demonstrate the seamless web that ties the initial revolutionary starting-point to present practice, so, for very different motives, do Western historians seek comfort in easily discoverable continuities that appear didactically convincing: the seeds of the later monolith were planted in the revolutionary beginning.

For Soviet historians the dictatorship of the proletariat was the necessary form that proletarian state power had to assume from the very outset. It was the state form appropriate to the organisation of resistance to the régime's internal and external enemies. In more general historical terms it was the necessary transitional stage to the abolition of classes which would consequently secure the preconditions for the emergence of the 'state of the whole people' appropriate to the phase of 'developed socialism'. Mistakes, misjudgements and abuses there might have been during the dictatorship of the proletariat, but its necessary place in the evolution towards full communism has not been open to doubt (even by Gorbachev). For Western historians the dictatorship of the proletariat was the predictable outcome of policies and dispositions long previously advertised by the Bolshevik party.

The party had, after all, arrogated to itself the duty of articulating the interests of the proletariat which, already in 1902, was found by Lenin to be incapable of self-articulation. After the revolution it was, therefore, unsurprising that the party should continue this process of substitution and claim the right of exercising a dictatorship on behalf of the working class. Equally unremarkably it formed that dictatorship in its own organisational image, transposing to it the hierarchical pattern of accountability of all the lower organs to the higher organs. The organisational pattern that rejoiced under the name of democratic centralism was simply applied to the state machine. Thereafter, we are told the familiar tale of how irresponsible yet tightly disciplined power of this sort, wedded to extravagant plans for social-economic and social-psychological transformation, ineluctably developed into totalitarianism. Both accounts give us over-determined outcomes; inexorable histories to shore up ideological antipathies.

This whole analysis is complemented, particularly in Western scholarship, by the almost unanimous conclusions of prominent commentators that Lenin, particularly in 1917, demonstrated that superbly timed adaptability to popular moods which was the mark of his success as a political strategist and tactician. In his quest for power he let no ideological hindrance stand in his way. Forget Marxism and adopt the agrarian programme of the Socialist Revolutionaries if that will keep the peasants sweet. Forget the constraints of the 'objective' levels of social and economic development that make the 'bourgeois revolution' the only one practicable and skip straight to the socialist revolution. Adopt Trotsky's programme of permanent revolution, if only that will keep the industrial workers happy. Never mind the Marxist insistence upon a single, unified state, play to the anarchic native populism of the Russian tradition expressed in the soviet movement, if only it secures the predominance of the Bolsheviks. Play to the mutinous discontent of a disillusioned soldiery by calling for an end to the imperialist war, an end to the prerogatives of officers, if only this propaganda dissolves the power of the Bolsheviks' opponents.

Here Lenin is presented as the adroit opportunist. His purpose is essentially negative – to exacerbate the chaos and dissolution of a war-ravaged Russia, to expose the ineptitude of a weak, unstable and inexperienced Provisional Government and to bring about its collapse by making Russia ungovernable. He does this by stimulating and encouraging the most disparate and extravagant aspirations of the Russian people – land to the peasants, factories to the workers, peace to the soldiers and bread for everyone. He capitalises on the psychological mood of the times, its angry desperation and the uncontrollable explosion of ancestral grievances. And in the resultant chaos of the foundering of all the old social ties, conventions, forbearances, law, administration and order, the organisational integrity and rigid discipline of the Bolshevik party will stand out greatly magnified. It would emerge as the sole remaining agency able to bring order out of chaos and to re-establish a centralised state made in its own image.

Things appeared this way even to some of Lenin's erstwhile supporters who listened in stupefaction to his first pronouncements on returning to Russia in 1917. His April theses left the party reeling. Goldenberg, an old Bolshevik, was moved to declare that Lenin had stepped forth to assume a throne that had been vacant in Europe for forty years – the throne of Bakunin. Not a single prominent Bolshevik leader was prepared to endorse Lenin's theses and they were published with the pointed reservation that they expressed only the 'personal' opinion of comrade Lenin. An editorial note cautioned the reader that Lenin's general scheme 'appears to us unacceptable, since it starts from the assumption that the bourgeois revolution is *finished* and counts on the immediate transformation of this revolution into a socialist revolution'.[1] We can, perhaps, understand and excuse the confusion of those contemporary witnesses who had no opportunity to reconstruct the extraordinarily rapid and radical development of Lenin's thought over the previous year or so. For them the complex chain of reasoning behind Lenin's astonishingly bold conclusions was not yet apparent. We need hardly be as sympathetic to modern commentators who continue to tell the same undemanding tale.

If we make the effort of actually examining the evidence of Lenin's own writings and actions in 1917 and attempt to make them intelligible, then a stranger and more complex story by far begins to emerge. We discover that the man was propelled, in almost all he did and said, by an intensely theorised project. Lenin's absolute surety of purpose (without which, as Trotsky remarked in his *History of the Revolution*, the October revolution quite simply would not have happened) was given by an unshakable *theoretical* conviction. He was, in 1917, the very type and paradigm of an ideologue. The revolution he made, the vision its complex hierarchy of objectives generated and the strategies he adopted to implement them, are unintelligible when divorced from the chain of reasoning (or theorised obsessions) from which they sprang.

Returning to Russia in April 1917 Lenin did not arrive with a mind like a new film in a camera. He was not there to take snapshots of a multi-faceted reality in order to put together a composite montage. There was no such modesty or hesitation. He did not wait, he had not come on a fact-finding mission to learn the intricacies of the current situation. He had come to teach, to impose his view upon reality, to make that reality conform to a theory that was fully formed and quite resolute.

Sukhanov, in his memoirs, seizes exactly on Lenin's implacable surety. At the Finland Station he is greeted by Chkheidze with cautionary words about the necessity of preserving the unity of the democratic forces, 'but Lenin plainly knew how to behave. He stood there as though nothing taking place had the slightest connection with him.'[2] Then, totally ignoring the advice given, he exploded his theses – down with the imperialist war, respond to Liebknecht's call and start the international revolution and the civil war for socialism: 'Lenin's voice, heard straight from the train, was a "voice from outside".' Lenin's theses quite simply did not fit 'the "context" of the Russian revolution as understood by everyone, whether they were witnesses or participants'.[3]

That the Bolsheviks were scandalised by his April theses, the public uncomprehending and the government outraged, did not matter a whit. Never in his life had he estimated the value of ideas and programmes by the sheer weight of numbers that supported them. In the maelstrom of movements, ideas, personalities, shifting allegiances and alliances that the succeeding months were to witness, he stood implacable. He would not revolve around events, they would have to spin around *him*. We are examining an extreme case of an ideological disposition constructing reality.

The metamorphosis of Lenin's thought began with the outbreak of the First World War and the socialist reaction to it. What was the nature of the war? Why had Marxists and socialists of good standing abruptly reneged on their internationalist duties and thrown in their hand with their own national states for the duration of hostilities? What had become of the transcendent obligation to the international solidarity of labour? Out of these questions there grew a comprehensive transformative analysis and out of that grew not only the imperative for an international socialist revolution but also the outline of its substantive content and the forms it should assume specifically in Russia. The April theses announced the *conclusions* of this process of development. They did not disclose its grounding.

At the same time as he propounded his April theses Lenin began writing a 'Draft Programme for the Proletarian Party', published in September 1917, under the title 'The Tasks of the Proletariat in Our Revolution'.[4] It was the most authoritative available statement of Bolshevik policy in the run-up to the Bolshevik conquest of power. Among other strident assertions Lenin contended that, 'Democracy is a form of *state*, whereas we Marxists are opposed to *every kind of state*.'[5] This was, by any standards, an extraordinary statement and we need to unpack it.

In matters of theory Bukharin was undoubtedly Lenin's mentor during this period and he had, by 1916, moved on from his socio-economic analysis of monopoly capitalism (or imperialism) to consider its implications for the state. He operated on the basic Marxist notion that state and society were locked in a zero-sum game. The growth of the one could only be effected at the cost of the other. The diversity of competing interests of differing sorts of capital (landed, manufacturing, merchant, banking, etc.) during the period of competitive capitalism was reflected at the superstructural level, in a variety of competing political parties and potential governing élites. This was the heyday of capitalism (and liberalism) as an emancipatory and relatively permissive economic, social and political culture. As the nineteenth century progressed competition gave way to monopoly. And banking or finance capital absorbed or thoroughly marginalised other forms of capital. The ideological, party and state forms of bourgeois domination grew similarly monolithic and increasingly oppressive.

The culmination of this process was state monopoly capitalism (or simply state capitalism). This was the *last* feasible historical form of the state that increasingly acted as *the principal means* of guaranteeing the reproducibility of capitalism as a mode of production. The state now became as rapacious, violent and exclusive as the monopoly capitalism whose last desperate bastion it was. It survived only on militarism, war and blood. Its last fragile ties were the bonds of patriotism that the war itself would finally sever. For Bukharin the state was the engine of internal tyranny and external catastrophe. Together with the parasitic capitalism it served, it had long declared its redundancy and had to be smashed.[6]

By September 1916 Lenin had come to the conclusion that national states were a thing of the past for western Europe.[7] Against Bukharin, though, he argued that for those countries where the national movement had not yet exhausted itself, the state still had a role to play. In any case socialists could not agree to Bukharin's conclusion that the state had to be 'blown up' or 'abolished'. Even in the most developed countries what distinguished socialists from anarchists was their recognition that existing state institutions would have to be used in the transition to socialism. As late as early December 1916 Lenin was still maintaining this orthodox opinion and rounding on Bukharin for his wild formulations.[8] By the end of that month, however, Lenin was signalling the beginning of a truly dramatic shift in his position. For the first time, in late December, he acknowledged Bukharin's account of the metamorphosis of monopoly capitalism into *state capitalism*[9] – a process which the war itself had consummated.[10]

Capitalism and its political formation were now at their terminus.

They were indissolubly fused together and the logic of Bukharin's argument was now inescapable – monopoly capitalism becoming *state* monopoly capitalism could not be vanquished unless and until the state form in which it was enmeshed was simultaneously overthrown. But if this were the case then a positive alternative to the coercive administrative structures of the political state had to be discovered. New participatory modes of deciding upon and executing public policy imperatively had to be outlined to inform a genuine socialist practice. The old patterns of domination and subordination inherent in capitalism, raised to their ultimate expression in monopoly capitalism and replicated in its legal structures and state forms, could only be transcended by a positive alternative. And that alternative, to be acceptable, had to have a warrant in Marxism.

It was in this intellectual context that Lenin began his feverish researches into the works of Marx and Engels that were, eventually, to be published as *The State and Revolution*. By March of 1917 he had arrived at the *idée fixe* that was to guide him for the rest of the year. As the Commune had, for Marx, represented the inspired antidote to the suffocating bureaucratic militarism of Louis Bonaparte's imperial régime, so its contemporary manifestation – the Soviet/Commune form – was the antidote to the threatening totalitarianism of state capitalism. Both were the spontaneous creations of ordinary working men roused to creativity by the necessities of their situation in moments of acute crisis. The Russian workers in their soviets had *in practice* revived the institutions and practices of 1871. Lenin saw his task as fortifying and strengthening their resolve by rescuing from the oblivion into which they had fallen Marx's fulsome and extensive writing on the Paris Commune. It was his role to provide a cohesive theoretical justification for soviet power, to end the dangerous ambiguities of dual power by firing his supporters with the confidence to smash the old state structures and to rely exclusively on the Soviet/Commune form as the only one appropriate to save Russia from ruin, thus securing the conditions for an advance towards socialism. By the time he wrote his 'Letter From Afar' (in March) Lenin had already come to these extraordinarily radical conclusions. In the first three months of 1917 his thought had moved with astonishing rapidity and he had arrived at the slogans and the strategy that were (apart from amplification) to serve him and the Bolshevik Party for the rest of the year.

It was in the third of his 'Letters from Afar' written from Zurich on 11 March 1917,[11] that Lenin first conflated the soviets with the Com-

mune and outlined the programme that so stunned his Bolshevik
colleagues in Russia that they refused to publish it in *Pravda*. It was the
idea of the Commune that distinguished Lenin's conception of the
prospects of the Russian revolution throughout 1917. 'Only the Commune can save us. So let us all perish, let us die but let us set up the
Commune.'[12] It was a conception that was unique to him.

The programme that Lenin spelt out during this period was the
most radical programme ever to be put to a mass electorate and the
most radical ever to enjoy the ostensible support of millions of people.
And yet this same programme had about it an aura of ambivalence as
to its actual *socialist* content. For all his commitment to the cause of a
global socialist revolution and his conviction that the honour and duty
of launching it fell to Russia, there still remained an element of ambiguity in Lenin's position with regard to the goals of the revolution in
Russia. He was, as we have seen, absolutely adamant that dual power
could not last long. He was convinced that there was no way forward
out of war and economic ruination without smashing the orthodox
nation state. He was, against all detractors, an unambiguous proponent of the Commune in its contemporary soviet form, *but* on the
crucial question of whether the revolution in Russia could frankly
espouse *socialist* goals there remained an element of doubt. The substantive goals of the movement were, like those of the Commune it
lauded, socialist only in potential but not in substance.

Lenin is, of course, generally presented as the supreme voluntarist of
the Marxist tradition. He allegedly substituted party for class as the
agency of historical progress in the modern world and, crucially in
1917, ignored the 'objective' constraints that Marxist methodology
enjoined and that should have restricted the Russian revolution to
bourgeois-democratic objectives. I have argued elsewhere that by late
1916 Lenin had, in his endorsement of the theory of international
finance capital, set this argument in a quite new global context.[13] The
crucial factor for him now became the analysis of the *global* contradictions of capitalism and the *global* maturation of the conditions for the
implementation of socialism. Russia was, in short, perceived as the
weakest link in an imperialist chain.[14] There the *ancien régime* was
thoroughly discredited, the attachment of the people to the old state
form was most tenuous, alternative radically democratic institutions
had been established, the press was free and, above all, the insurgent
masses were armed. For all these reasons it fell to Russia to begin the
process of worldwide socialist transformation. In this way Lenin, it is
argued, either rendered redundant and outmoded the question of Rus-

sia's own objective maturity for socialism, or adroitly used the theory of international finance capitalism and the global appraisal of the balance of socialist revolutionary forces to sidestep the question altogether. It now seems to me that there are important reservations to be made about either conclusion.

It is too easy to assume that because (i) Lenin was adamant that international finance capitalism had become retrogressive and oppressive, because (ii) he therefore endorsed a programme of imminent world socialist revolution and because (iii) he believed that this process could and should begin in Russia, *therefore* (iv) the revolution in Russia must unambiguously, and from the outset, be frankly socialist in its objectives. The fourth term in the progression did not necessarily follow from the first three. It is not at all clear that Lenin, in 1917, was unreservedly a proponent for the here and now of socialism pure and simple. There is evidence that the objective level of economic and social development specifically in Russia weighed with him and constrained his options. There is, furthermore, evidence that what he had in mind was nearer to the most radical possible variant of the democratic revolution than to an expressly socialist revolution (at least as conceived in the Marxist tradition). The catalyst of the world revolution was not to be, and could not be, expressly socialist in the *content* of its policies. It could qualify as 'socialist' only in the far more limited sense of the *form and practices* of its institutions. It was, in short, immanently socialist in its content but that potential could only be realised if the *form* of its administration proved sufficiently inspirational to galvanise the developed West into frankly socialist revolutions.

If this was the case then a number of things would follow. In the first place, Russia could not possibly project itself as the model for expressly socialist revolution in the more developed world. Second, the October revolution and the triumph of the Bolsheviks could in no way be represented as the final or deciding event in the transition to socialism in Russia. The significance of October, at least in the eyes of its single most prominent actor, must therefore be re-appraised. It was less a decisive watershed (promoting and guaranteeing with the power of the state the dominance of socialism) than an historical enabling act that released the potential for a future advance to properly socialist goals. Without the revolution, without the Bolshevik-inspired assumption of power by the soviets, the prospects for an advance to socialism would, in Lenin's view, have been minimal. But the assumption of power itself in no way implied the hasty introduction of socialist policies nor, certainly, did it guarantee their future predominance. It has suited both Soviet and Western schools of interpretation to gloss over Lenin's relativistic, ambiguous and, at times, tortured, accounts of the objectives of the revolution in Russia.

In the third (and most radical) of the 'Letters from Afar' Lenin – having impressed upon the Bolsheviks the need to break completely with the existing state and the Provisional Government and to substitute for it a proletarian militia, a proletarian 'state' – nonetheless insists, in what seems a puzzling qualifier, that

> Those measures do not yet constitute socialism. They concern the distribution of consumption, not the reorganisation of production. They would not yet constitute the 'dictatorship of the proletariat' only the revolutionary-democratic dictatorship of the proletariat and the poor peasantry.[15]

His famous 'Farewell Letter to Swiss Workers', written in late March and the last thing he wrote before the April theses, several times over repeats the point that as far as Russia is concerned 'Socialism *cannot* triumph there *directly* and *immediately*' but that circumstances might well 'give tremendous sweep to the bourgeois-democratic revolution in Russia and *may* make our revolution the *prologue* to the world socialist revolution, a *step* towards it'.[16] The pursuit of radical democracy and the nationalisation of the land 'would not, in itself, be socialism'.[17] It is often remarked that the moderation of this letter stands in stark contrast to the radical utopianism of his April theses. It would appear almost that the scales had fallen from his eyes in the sealed train. And yet, if we examine the substance of his proposals in the theses, we see that here too he was *not* commending the immediate introduction of socialism.[18] He went no further than recommending 'the amendment of our out-of-date minimum programme'.[19] This was his consistent stance right up to the Bolshevik seizure of power. His programme was that of the most radical possible extension of the democratic revolution and he criticised, as he had done in 1905, those Mensheviks like Skobelev who proposed fundamental alterations of property-owning relationships.[20] 'We cannot be for "introducing" socialism – this would be the height of absurdity.'[21] 'I not only do not "build" on the "immediate transformation" of our revolution into a *socialist* one, but I actually warn against it, when in thesis no. 8, I state "It is *not* our *immediate* task to 'introduce' socialism."' [22]

The fruitless talk of 'introducing socialism' and 'permanent revolution' and similar 'nonsense' was in Lenin's view 'ridiculously stupid, for what makes socialism objectively impossible is the *small-scale* economy which we by no means presume to expropriate, or even regulate or control'.[23] The vast mass of small-scale peasant and artisan productive units formed a huge and insurmountable obstacle to the immediate introduction of socialism in Russia. But it was equally clear that only the triumph of the soviets could secure to the peasants the gains they had made since February 1917. There could be no question of attempting

> to 'introduce' socialism in Russia by decree, without considering the existing technical level, the great number of small undertakings, or the habits and wishes of the majority of the population.
>
> That is a lie from beginning to end. Nobody has ever proposed anything of the kind.[24]

Throughout 1917 Lenin insisted that the fundamental question at issue in the revolution was not the question of socialism but the issue of state power. 'Which class holds power decides everything.'[25]

It was not simply on historical/theoretical grounds that Lenin called for the overthrow of the conventional form of the state (the Provisional Government) and its replacement by the Soviet/Commune variety. Increasingly, as October approached, his tone becomes more practical and immediate. He insists more and more that catastrophe for the whole people is approaching at a constantly accelerating pace. Economic ruination is already apparent, the supply of basic provisions has broken down, profiteers are holding the nation to ransom, the bosses are forsaking their factories, production slumps and unemployment assume a mass scale, the government is about to sell out Kronstadt and Petrograd to the Germans. It can neither feed its people nor defend them from aggression. Its bankruptcy is increasingly demonstrated with every passing day. *Only* the soviets, only the Commune can, by galvanising the initiative of tens of millions of people, hope to fend off the impending catastrophe.[26] Only by vesting them with full powers to regulate investment and production can devastation be avoided. 'Control, supervision and accounting are the prime requisites for combating catastrophe and famine.'[27]

Specifically he recommended five measures:

(1) Amalgamation of all banks into a single bank, and state control over its operations, or nationalisation of the banks.
(2) Nationalisation of the syndicates, i.e. the largest monopolistic capitalist associations (sugar, oil, coal, iron and steel, and other syndicates).

21. Lenin in disguise, summer 1917.

(3) Abolition of commercial secrecy.
(4) Compulsory syndication ... of industrialists, merchants and
     employers generally.
(5) Compulsory organisation of the population into consumers'
     societies.[28]

All these measures, he emphasised, in no way involved expropriation.
Confiscation, Lenin asserted, led nowhere; it was not on the agenda.[29]
The continued ownership of capital resources in private hands would
be assured. Nationalisation of the banks 'would not deprive any
"owner" of a single kopek'.[30] All these measures have, to varying
degrees, been adopted by explicitly anti-socialist state capitalist
régimes; 'it is not a question of introducing socialism now, directly,
overnight, but of *exposing plunder of the state*'.[31]

Lenin does, however, concede that these measures, when combined
with a genuinely revolutionary-democratic power of the soviet type,
will produce a historically unique and hybrid form of rule. If 'carried
out in a revolutionary-democratic way', that is, if these measures
instead of bolstering monopoly profit are applied to serve the interests

of the labouring classes, *then*, inevitably, they would represent steps towards socialism. They would not, frankly, constitute socialism (for private property-owning relations would remain intact and the great mass of petty producers would remain outside the realm of government control) but they would mark a break with capitalism. They would, in a sense, go beyond it and, Lenin argues, they have to go beyond it in order to meet the practical crises that state capitalism in its terminal decline has bequeathed. And these measures themselves – the nationalisation of the banks, the national mobilisation of capital and labour resources,[32] control over production and consumption – have all been experimented with by state capitalism and form part of its portfolio of survival strategies: 'the new means of control have been created *not* by us, but by capitalism in its military-imperialist stage'.[33]

The only difference – but this in Lenin's view is a crucial and qualitative difference – is that such measures should be implemented by and in the interests of, a genuinely revolutionary, genuinely democratic régime of the Commune type. When that happens there is a qualitative transformation. These measures are no longer the final desperate resorts of a bankrupt political form but the harbingers of a new one. They are now purposefully employed to construct the foundations for socialism. The issue then is not the content of the measures proposed. The issue is what goals do they subserve? The issue is who controls whom – is finance capital to control the revolutionary democracy; or revolutionary democracy, finance capitalism? 'Not regulation of and control over the workers by the capitalist class, but *vice versa*.'[34] One way leads to catastrophe and emasculation, the other towards socialism and empowerment. 'There is', he asserts, 'no middle course.'[35] 'For socialism is merely the next step forward from state-capitalist monopoly. Or, in other words, socialism is merely state-capitalist monopoly *which is made to serve the interests of the whole people* and has to that extent *ceased* to be capitalist monopoly.'[36]

The argument could no longer, he urged, revolve around theoretical niceties such as when the bourgeois stage of the revolution had exhausted itself, or what was appropriate to capitalism and what to socialism. 'Nowhere in the world is there pure capitalism developing into pure socialism', he told the First All-Russian Congress of Soviets, 'but there is something in between, something new and unprecedented.'[37]

We should, at this point, be clear that Lenin's programme for the organisation of public life – the deliberation, execution and policing of public policy – was not, in and of itself, inherently socialist. It represented, in his mind, the most radical possible extension of democracy and it had to do not with the transformation of property-owning relationships within society but with the ancestral relations of domination and subordination at the apex of which stood the perfected machinery of the state. It signalled an end to the 'disgusting prejudice'[38] that only the wealthy and educated could play a part in the management of public affairs. Its object was the empowerment of the masses of ordinary people – the ending of their alienation from control over public affairs. He was however, in retrospect, extra-ordinarily cautious and circumspect about projects to transform ownership relations within Russia, to introduce an unambiguously socialist content into the revolution. All the economic measures which he proposed, he considered to be firmly within the 'minimum pro-gramme' of the Social Democratic ideology.

These planks in the minimal programme did not go beyond the framework of private property relations. They were the demands of the working people for the radical realisation of democracy. Convention-ally they had included demands for legal, political and civic rights; economic demands for limiting the working day, guaranteeing minimum pay and health, pension and educational provision. They had also (as in the Social Democratic programme for 1905) included demands for the abolition of the standing army and for the nationalisa-tion of land. This was, precisely, the programme of the cumbersomely entitled 'Revolutionary-democratic dictatorship of the poor peasants and the proletariat' that Lenin repeatedly invokes in 1917.[39] It was not a 'dictatorship of the proletariat' nor a workers' government, and its proximate goals were not socialist. In his programmatic 'Tasks of the Proletariat in our Revolution', written in May 1917, Lenin made clear that the package of measures he proposed were indeed minimum-programme demands rather than properly socialist ones:

> Such measures as the nationalisation of the land, of all the banks and capitalist syndicates, or, at least, the *immediate* establishment of the *control* of the Soviets of Workers' Deputies, etc. over them – measures which do not in any way constitute the 'introduction' of socialism – must be absolutely insisted on.[40]

Many of these measures, Lenin reminded his colleagues, had in fact been adopted by the wartime state-capitalist trusts without in any way altering the reality of the dominance of finance capital. Banks could be nationalised without assets being confiscated; the nationalisation of land had been canvassed by Marx himself as a measure likely to

accelerate rather than to retard the development of capital concentration in agriculture. The wartime state-capitalist trusts had, indeed,
gone further and actually introduced compulsory labour direction and
state-supervised allocation of consumption through rationing. All
these measures, far from undermining capitalism were, Lenin argued,
system-sustaining and essential to its economic and political
reproducibility. To cite this package of measures as 'socialist' was, in
his view, to display profound ignorance of the manner in which contemporary state capitalism conducted its business and maintained its
control.

There is implicit in Lenin's writings in 1917 a distinction that is ill-
elaborated but which, nonetheless, he was acute enough to recognise.
In his *The State and Revolution* he had somewhat uncritically accepted
Engels' cavalier and off-the-cuff identification of the dictatorship of the
proletariat with the Commune.[41] Here, clearly, Lenin is at pains to
distinguish the two. The dictatorship of the proletariat, as well he
knew from his recent researches into Marx and Engels on the state,
was emphatically a form of state. It was, moreover, in all Marx's
references to it, a very highly centralised state formation. Its programme was outlined exclusively in terms of economic objectives and
not at all in terms of its administrative arrangements. Those economic
objectives were, in turn, unambiguously socialist in the sense that they
proclaimed the swiftest possible transference of all resources into the
hands of the state. The Commune, by contrast, was not properly
speaking a state at all (as Lenin repeatedly reminds his colleagues in
1917); it was always portrayed as highly decentralised, with initiative
always proceeding from the bottom upwards rather than vice versa.
Its programme was wholly concerned with transforming administrative arrangements and the patterns of social and political domination
within society and had nothing whatever to say about the transformation of property rights.

The Commune is not necessarily incompatible with the maintenance of private property and the only sense in which it could qualify
as 'socialist' would be in the qualified sense in which socialism is
equated with humanism, as it was in Marx's early writings. The
Commune is the administrative model befitting unalienated man. The
dictatorship of the proletariat, by contrast, is the model befitting unex-
ploited man. Its promise is not freedom, autonomy and dignity
through participation but sufficiency, security and reward according
to productive endeavour. Its principle is the labour principle of dis-
tributive justice. 'The right of the producers is proportional to the

labour they supply; the equality consists in the fact that measurement is made with an *equal standard*, labour.'[42]

Nowhere, to my knowledge, does Lenin, in 1917, commend the programme of the dictatorship of the proletariat in this economic and statist sense as appropriate to Russia. There may well be a number of reasons for this and amongst them was, undoubtedly, Lenin's own awareness of the relative backwardness of the development of Russian industry, and therewith of its working class. In choosing to concentrate almost exclusively on the Soviet/Commune model Lenin showed, in retrospect, considerable astuteness. In the first place its libertarian theme of popular empowerment accorded well with the revolutionary spirit of the times – the allegiance of millions of activists to 'their' soviet institutions and their mounting contempt for the vacillations and inertia of the 'official' government. It flattered (and fomented) the widening temperamental and institutional gap between official, wealthy and educated Russia and the militant strivings of popular Russia. It was also the only plausible basis upon which to appeal to the international working class. It was to light (at least in Lenin's eyes) the beacon of hope that things *could* be differently arranged, that the exploited and downtrodden *could* become masters in their own house and put an end to bossing – thus as Lenin confidently expected, igniting the great bonfire of the international revolution.

It simply would not have been credible, as an example to the rest of the world, for the Bolsheviks to have pretended, in a ruined and war-ravaged Russia, to light the path to the realm of plenty. Others, later, would no doubt blaze that trail but the promise of the Russian revolution, as conceived by Lenin, was more modest by far. It was no more than to consummate the democratic revolution in the most radical conceivable way and, thereby, to ensure, in the future, the most propitious circumstances for the transition to socialism step by step with the international spread of the authentic socialist revolution in the West. The revolution, as conceived by Lenin in 1917, was more modest in its objectives, more hybrid in composition, more equivocal in its profession of socialist goals than commentators of Left and of Right have led us to believe.

NOTES

1 E.H. Carr, *The Bolshevik Revolution* (Harmondsworth, 1966), vol. 1, p. 91.
2 N.N. Sukhanov, *The Russian Revolution 1917* (London, 1955), p. 273.
3 N.N. Sukhanov, *Zapiski o revoliutsii*, kniga tretia (Berlin, 1922), p. 15.

4 V.I. Lenin, *Collected Works* in 45 vols. (hereafter Lenin *CW*) (Moscow 1960–70) vol. XXIV, pp. 57–88.
5 Ibid., p. 85.
6 For a fuller account of the influence of Bukharin upon Lenin's theory of the state see my 'Authority, Power and the State', in H. Rigby, A. Brown and P. Reddaway (eds.), *Authority, Power and Policy in the Soviet Union: Essays Dedicated to Leonard Schapiro* (London, 1980), pp. 32–56.
7 Lenin, *CW* vol. XXIII, p. 38.
8 Ibid., p. 165.
9 Ibid., p. 212.
10 Ibid., p. 267.
11 Ibid., pp. 320–39.
12 Lenin, *CW*, vol. XXV, p. 313.
13 See my *Lenin's Political Thought* (London, 1981), vol. II, especially ch. 3.
14 Much is made of the notion of 'the weakest link in the imperialist chain' in accounts of Lenin's theory of revolution, yet Lenin himself barely mentions it in the run-up to the October revolution. He certainly did not at this time provide any substantial elaboration of this idea. To my knowledge the first reference he makes to it is in the brief statement in his Preface to *The State and Revolution* written in August 1917: 'but this revolution as a whole can only be understood as a link in a chain of socialist proletarian revolutions being caused by the imperialist war' (Lenin, *CW*, vol. XXV, p. 388).
15 Lenin, *CW*, vol. XXIII, pp. 229–30.
16 Ibid., p. 371, repeated in virtually the same formulation on p. 372.
17 Ibid., p. 372.
18 Lenin, *CW*, vol. XXIV, p. 24.
19 Ibid.
20 Lenin, *CW*, vol. XXV, p. 425.
21 Ibid., p. 242.
22 Ibid., p. 52. Lest it be thought that these are isolated or uncharacteristic references the reader might care to check a sample of the following: Lenin, *CW*, vol. XXIV, pp. 48, 53, 74, 180–1, 194–5, 290–1, 307, 323, 329–30, 373, 429; *CW*, vol. XXV, pp. 44–5, 63, 68, 69, 303, 328, 344.
23 Ibid., p 45.
24 Ibid., p. 303.
25 Ibid., p. 370.
26 See 'The Impending Catastrophe and How to Combat It', ibid., vol. XXV, pp. 327–69.
27 Ibid., p. 328.
28 Ibid., p. 333.
29 Ibid., p. 334, repeated p. 348.
30 Ibid., pp. 107–8.
31 Ibid., p. 344.

32 'Universal labour conscription, introduced, regulated and directed by the Soviets of Workers' Soldiers' and Peasants' Deputies will *still not* be socialism, but it will no longer be capitalism' (ibid., p. 364).

33 Ibid., vol. xxvi, p. 108.

34 Ibid, vol. xxv, p. 45.

35 Ibid., p. 362.

36 Ibid.

37 Ibid., p. 19.

38 Ibid., vol. xxvi, p. 409.

39 See, for example, ibid., vol. xxiv, p. 45.

40 Ibid., p. 74.

41 F. Engels, Introduction to K. Marx, *The Civil War in France* in Marx/ Engels *Selected Works*, 2 vols. (Moscow, 1962), vol. i, p. 485. Marx himself had never identified the Commune with the dictatorship of the proletariat.

42 K. Marx, in Marx/Engels *Selected Works*, vol. ii, pp. 23–4.

14

THE BOLSHEVIKS ON POLITICAL CAMPAIGN IN 1917: A CASE STUDY OF THE WAR QUESTION

ROBERT SERVICE

THE most stimulating recent development in the historiography of the Russian revolution has been the emergence of studies of institutions, social groups and the non-metropolitan regions. Less attention has as yet been paid to economics; perhaps this will be the next topic for intensive investigation. In any case it is being widely recognised that, until just over a decade ago, virtually all the major accounts of 1917 were preoccupied with the ideas and activity of individual leaders such as Nicholas II, Aleksandr Kerensky, Lavr Kornilov and Vladimir Lenin. Institutional, social, regional and economic history was largely ignored. The newer historiography, while rightly and successfully reversing the neglect, must nevertheless evade a new danger which would hardly have been imaginable two decades ago: the danger of relegating the central political leaders to the lowermost rung on the ladder of explanation of the revolution. The Bolsheviks came to power partly because they expressed the aspirations of ordinary urban working people who had already disrupted the Provisional Government through their own mass organisations and who voted for the Bolsheviks in the elections of representatives in such organisations. This expression was in many ways a genuine reflection of the party's analysis of the domestic and foreign situations; but it also resulted from a thrust to adapt policies for the specific objective of grasping power. The adaptation was undertaken not least because of the energies and calculations of the party's central leadership. As Lenin was the most influential of all Bolsheviks, his impact on Bolshevik strategy will remain crucial to an understanding of 1917.

Lenin's policies covered many domestic problems. He spoke and wrote often about the economic crisis, about political polarisation, about nationality tensions and about the possibilities for action by large social groups. He campaigned for his strategy not only in the party but also at mass rallies of workers. Not having impressed everyone in the party by his demeanour as a leader in 1905–6, he proved himself a master of the mass politics of 1917.

He fought also for his opinions on foreign policy throughout the year. Lenin's perspective on international relations in 1917 has been endlessly described. Throughout the First World War he had maintained that capitalism had attained its final stage of development, imperialism, and that the era of socialism was at hand; and that Europe stood on the threshold of a continent-wide socialist revolution. After Russia's February revolution, Lenin repeated these contentions. He did not claim that European socialist revolution would definitely happen all at once. Further wars and counter-revolutions might occur. The transition to socialism, according to Lenin, might be a lengthy epoch. But he also believed that, whichever country turned out to be the first to obtain a socialist government, socialism was unlikely to be containable within that country's frontiers by the foreign forces of counter-revolution. The existence of any socialist state would transform the consciousness of workers, peasants and soldiers not only at home but across Europe. The 'masses' would be activated to move from war-weariness to participation in uprisings against their governments. Bourgeois rule would be overturned. The continent would be liberated from military devastation, political oppression and economic exploitation. Such were Lenin's thoughts both in the early years of the First World War and in the months after the February revolution.

Fellow Bolsheviks agreed with Lenin that the era of socialism was nigh in Europe. There was no unanimity as to precisely how near it was; but about its nearness there was no doubt among them. All the party's leaders took it for granted that the more advanced industrial societies, especially Germany, were ready for socialism.[1] Furthermore, the notion that the European socialist epoch was approaching was not confined to Bolsheviks in Russia. It was a widely held idea among Mensheviks and Socialist Revolutionaries, particularly those who belonged to the left wing of their respective parties.

Bolsheviks in 1917, however, differed from the Mensheviks and the Socialist Revolutionaries in arguing that even semi-industrialised Russia was poised to initiate a 'transition to socialism'. There were disputes in the Bolshevik Party itself on this. But those leading Bolsheviks who challenged Russia's readiness for socialism left the party either before or shortly after the Seventh Party Conference in April 1917;[2] or else they remained and attempted, like L.B. Kamenev, to compel Lenin to moderate his more radical ideas and to agree to compromise.

Most Bolsheviks assumed that the major industrial countries would accomplish their own socialist revolutions. But they had to consider the possibility that Russia, because of the Provisional Government's extraordinary difficulties and the extraordinary opportunities available to the Bolsheviks for propaganda and organisation, might have her socialist revolution much earlier than Germany. In such an eventuality the Bolsheviks might have to take active measures to accelerate the German revolutionary process. Accordingly the Bolsheviks had to decide what to do if a German socialist revolution either did not precede or did not quickly follow a Russian socialist revolution. For no one was so naïve as to assume that the Bolsheviks would be left alone by the world's great capitalist states once socialism had come to power in Russia.

This was not the only hypothetical question which the Bolshevik party needed to address before its accession to government. Its various projects for economic reconstruction were linked to the anticipation that the First World War would be swiftly ended and a democratic peace brought about. But what if such a peace did not emerge? The Bolsheviks also argued that the Russian forces of counter-revolution would be weak since the interests of the vast majority of the population lay with the policies of Bolshevism. But what if large numbers of peasants and even workers proved to think otherwise? The Bolshevik party based its programme on the premise that the working class could establish and maintain a revolutionary central and local government without prior training. But what if the administrative tasks turned out to demand technical expertise and lengthy specialist training?

The question about the Bolshevik party's plans for promoting international revolution in the event of a 'failure' of foreign socialists to take power in their own countries was equally important. All accounts rightly assert that Lenin and his colleagues suggested that, if socialist revolution in any European country did not quickly lead to a general 'democratic peace', it was the duty of socialists to engage in a 'revolutionary war'; and that the intra-Bolshevik debate from January to March 1918 was provoked principally by Lenin's contention that a revolutionary war was no longer a practical option for the Bolsheviks. A number of problems remain to be answered. It has to be ascertained when and why Lenin started to withdraw his support for revolutionary war, and what indeed he meant by 'revolutionary war'. This leads to a further problem: to what extent did he alter his mind independently of Bolshevik central colleagues about the prospects of revolutionary war? The Bolshevik party was not a one-man brigade; and, although Lenin was easily the most influential Bolshevik, his word was not law for his associates. Disagreements about policy persisted throughout 1917. We need to inquire what was thought by other Bolsheviks about the contingency policy for revolutionary war. And, finally, it is important to know how party pronouncements on international policy were relayed to the general public.

Indisputably, Lenin in March and April 1917 still openly advocated revolutionary war as a contingency policy; and he recalled that his advocacy had been consistent since 1915, when he had proposed that such a war would be undertaken if revolution occurred first in Russia and if the proposal for a 'democratic peace' were to be rejected by 'German, English, French and other capitalists'.[3] This attitude stemmed from Lenin's general strategy to transform the European 'imperialist war' between rival capitalist coalitions into a 'civil war' between the European working classes and the European bourgeoisies. From Switzerland he repeated this argument in March 1917.[4] In his 'Farewell Letter to Swiss Workers', he repeated what would happen if a democratic peace failed to be agreed: 'We would have to wage a revolutionary war against the German bourgeoisie and not only the German bourgeoisie. *We would wage it.*'[5] And in a pamphlet written in Petrograd on 10 April he reasserted that the European imperialist war should be turned into a European civil war.[6] On 22 April at the Bolshevik City Party Conference in Petrograd, he defended his 1915 standpoint by urging that, in the event of a democratic peace not occurring after a socialist revolution in Russia, 'we ourselves would wage a *revolutionary war*, calling the workers of all countries to a union with us'.[7] It is statements from the first three weeks after Lenin's return to Russia that are most frequently quoted in favour of the idea that his international policy remained unchanged during 1917 until the very end of the year.

The exact nature of a revolutionary war, as anticipated by Lenin up to April 1917, remains unclear. He did not state whether it would be fought offensively or defensively; he therefore did not commit himself to the idea of spreading socialist revolution westward by a military thrust into Germany. Nor, on the other hand, did he specify that he would prefer to fight on defensively in the hope that merely the precedent of a Russian socialist revolution would stir up the German workers to a campaign of political emulation. Neither option was approved or rejected. 'Revolutionary war' was consequently more a slogan than a fully elaborated policy; and it became all the more mysterious in its practical implications, from the time of the April theses onwards, when Lenin simultaneously proposed that Russian and German soldiers should fraternise.[8]

In any case, Lenin's thinking was far from being fixed and consistent. Even in Switzerland his thoughts had shifted quickly after hearing about the February revolution and the rapidity of mental movement increased in Petrograd. It would have been astounding if this had not been so. Lenin the veteran revolutionary was able to observe a real revolution with his own eyes and draw practical conclusions about its political, social and economic processes. He was not an armchair observer but the leader of a mass party and was obliged to hearken to some extent to what his colleagues thought about the same processes. The issue of revolutionary war was a case in point. Discussions between Lenin and Kamenev occurred between the end of the Petrograd City Party Conference on 22 April and the start of the All-Russian Party Conference on 24 April. This produced an agreement by Lenin to moderate his earlier insurrectionary sloganeering, as Kamenev delightedly noted.[9] There must also have been negotiations about the official party policy on the First World War. Time had run out at the City Party Conference in Petrograd, and Lenin's motion which had included a contingency scheme for revolutionary war was not voted on.[10] When Lenin put forward the Central Committee's motion on the same subject to the All-Russian Party Conference on 26 April, important changes had been made to the wording. In particular, the clause on revolutionary war had entirely disappeared.[11]

In introducing the re-formulated motion, Lenin emphasised that no exact predictions on the timing of the German socialist revolution could be given. He also stated: 'It is said to us: If the revolutionary class in Russia takes power into its hands and there is no insurrection in other countries, what will the revolutionary party do then?' Days earlier, Lenin's reply would have been unequivocal. But now he strangely omitted to give an answer. Instead he answered a different question, namely, what would the 'revolutionary class' of Russia do to facilitate revolutions abroad before that class came to power in Russia?[12] No one at the conference commented on this omission, and Lenin was relieved of the necessity to explain himself before the vote of approval was passed on his motion.[13] No details have been revealed about the behind-the-scenes debate in the central party leadership. Consequently it is impossible to gauge the exact pressure from Central Committee members in shifting him away from open support for revolutionary war; but there can be little doubt that Kamenev and the

Bolshevik Right had at least some influence on Lenin's thinking and actions.

But what of the remaining months up to October 1917? The main thing to note, in relation to revolutionary war, is the scarcity of Lenin's public comments. 'Revolutionary war' was not a slogan which flowed often from Lenin's lips or from the tip of his pen. In mid May he wrote a pamphlet entitled *War and Revolution*. Denying any intention of signing a separate peace with Germany and Austria–Hungary, he addressed the policy to be adopted if a German socialist revolution did not swiftly occur. In such a contingency, declared Lenin, the Bolsheviks would be in favour of war (*za voinu*).[14] And yet this short phrase should not be construed as signifying that the entire Bolshevik party and all its supporters knew that, in following Lenin, they were committing themselves to a war against the German army if a German socialist revolution failed to take place. Such an interpretation would be guilty of that excessive 'textualism' afflicting studies of Lenin in all countries and is reminiscent of the methods of European sixteenth-century religious controversies. For Lenin's remark was not published until 1929. No party member outside the few leaders in the Central Committee, and possibly not even they, would have been acquainted with his words.[15]

Another comment occurred in an article that was published at the time, in *Pravda* on 13 May. Lenin argued that, if a democratic peace was not forthcoming after the Bolsheviks seized power, firm measures would be required: 'Then we ought to prepare [*podgotovit*] and carry through a revolutionary war.'[16] But is Lenin's statement completely unambiguous? He could, for example, be interpreted as having implied a need to 'prepare' the war before waging it.[17] At any rate, Lenin refrained from specifically declaring that a revolutionary war would immediately follow the failure of the German socialists to take power in Berlin. His words were more carefully chosen and more opaque than has widely been proposed. Nor, again, did he define 'revolutionary war'.

The last major public occasions between the April Party Conference and the October Revolution when Lenin even mentioned revolutionary war openly as an immediate contingency objective came in the first half of June. He gave two lengthy speeches to the First All-Russian Congress of Workers' and Soldiers' Soviets. In the first, on 4 June, he noted that, 'if circumstances . . . placed us in the situation of a revolutionary war', the Bolsheviks would not refuse the challenge.[18] In the second, on 9 June, he stated that 'in certain circumstances we cannot get by without a revolutionary war'.[19] He repeated this line of argument in his article in *Pravda*, 'The Foreign Policy of the Russian Revolution' on 14 June.[20] Neither in his two speeches nor in his article could he fairly be said to have evinced a zeal for an offensive; and, in contrast with his prognosis in 1915, the statements in June 1917 were characterised by a more or less reluctant acknowledgement that war might be forced upon the Bolsheviks whether they liked it or not: the tone of menacing determination had already vanished. Furthermore, it can scarcely have been a coincidence that Lenin was making his two speeches at a time when anti-Bolshevik newspapers and politicians were voicing suspicions that the Bolshevik party was planning a separate peace with the Germans. Lenin absolutely denied this, and renounced in advance not only such a peace but even separate negotiations.[21] His talk of the acceptability of a revolutionary war must have helped to bolster such arguments.

Thus the number of these open discussions by Lenin was small indeed; and, from mid June up to and beyond the October revolution, he more or less avoided the topic in public. This cannot have been a statistical fluke. Lenin was a formidably fluent and articulate writer; and, whereas his freedom to speak his mind could be inhibited at a party conference or congress by his role as Central Committee rapporteur, he was not someone to avoid expressing it on other occasions. It seems likely that other Bolshevik leaders put pressure on him in late April to desist from advocating revolutionary war as a contingency policy; but, since he continued to have arguments with the Central Committee about other policies, his reticence about revolutionary war probably indicates that he accepted the logic of the case put to him by his colleagues.[22]

The explanation for his reticence can only be guessed at. He divulged his motivations on this matter neither in 1917 nor thereafter; he continued, as with the rationale which led him to effect a radical transformation of the Bolshevik programme with his April theses, to keep quiet on his reasoning. We are therefore left with hypotheses. One possible reason was that he had already concluded that a revolutionary war was simply impracticable; and that, on those few occasions when he advocated such a war, he did so only for reasons of political tactics: namely to protect the Bolsheviks against the charge of favouring the signing of a separate peace with Germany and Austria–Hungary. War-weariness, which had already been noticeable before the fall of the Romanovs, was growing in the summer of 1917. Both the

Russian army and the civilian population were affected, and a flood of desertions occurred on the Eastern front. Yet the army's decomposition had hardly begun in the spring of 1917 whereas Lenin's reticence was already perceptible from late April. It may well be that the condition of the armed forces became a factor in his calculations by midsummer; but it can scarcely have made him desist from talking about revolutionary war in earlier weeks.

Another possibility was that he feared less the imbalance between Russian and German armed might than the prospect of losing the German government's financial assistance. That some money was passed from Berlin into the coffers of the Bolsheviks is probable. But 'German gold' cannot be turned into a basic explanation for the Bolshevik political success in 1917. The scale of the alleged subsidy is unascertainable: there is no way of knowing how much money reached Petrograd through the hands of the various intermediaries and how much was pocketed by the intermediaries themselves. The charge has been made that Berlin's financial support was crucial to the establishment of Bolshevik newspapers in March and April. But it would be difficult to demonstrate that the Bolsheviks, once they had set up their network of newspapers and had made gains in the soviets, still felt financially dependent on Berlin to the extent that Lenin was ready to alter his statements on international relations.

A stronger likelihood was that Lenin from late April recognised that the advocacy of a revolutionary war was a political liability for the party while it struggled for votes in the soviets, and that a 'peace' slogan was more effective. Throughout the First World War, while issuing his chilling plea for a European civil war between the continental bourgeoisie and the continental working class, he had also spoken of the need for a 'democratic peace' which would enshrine the principle of national self-determination. This was a popular proposal; the Mensheviks and Socialist Revolutionaries, too, campaigned for it. But these moderate socialists confined themselves to putting pressure on the Russian Provisional Government and to helping with the arrangements for the abortive international socialist conference in Stockholm; and their activities were transparently ineffectual. In addition, a Socialist-Revolutionary minister, Aleksandr Kerensky, helped to instigate the re-opening of the military offensive on the Eastern front late in June. His behaviour gave rise to further suspicions that the coalition of liberals and moderate socialists, so far from aiming to end the war quickly, were doing their utmost to prolong it in the hope of a conclusive victory for Russia. In such circumstances it made pragmatic sense for Lenin to desist from associating himself publicly with proposals which could involve the Russian army and its society in yet further military exertions.

Indeed it is a sign of his earlier inflexibility that he came so late to this conclusion. Other Russian Marxists on the left had seen the usefulness of a peace slogan since the beginning of the First World War. The Menshevik leader Iu.O. Martov was so convinced about the war's awful consequences for world civilisation that, for most practical purposes, he became virtually a pacifist in international policy.[23] Another non-Bolshevik, L.D. Trotsky, took a more ambivalent approach. It was his opinion that Russian Marxists should, without believing in pacifist propaganda, exploit the pro-peace movement for their own ends; and he was not without support among Bolsheviks: N.I. Bukharin was keen that Lenin should not pass up the opportunities for making full use of anti-war sentiments throughout Europe.[24] Presumably such arguments, put to him by many of his natural political allies immediately after his return to Petrograd, helped to win Lenin round; and no doubt he also benefited from his opportunity to talk directly and regularly with Russian workers and Russian soldiers for the first time in the First World War.[25] And yet Lenin was a highly complex individual. There is yet another possibility (which by its nature is unlikely to be proved or disproved by fresh documents). This is that he was edging towards an abandonment of the contingency objective of revolutionary war without yet having entirely given up hope that the situation in the armed forces might change. He may have supposed that a socialist revolution led by the Bolsheviks would put a stop to the demoralisation evident in the armed forces, and that a Bolshevik-led Russian army could fight with renewed vigour. Thus Lenin, who always liked to keep his options open, may simply have been undecided about his international policy.

So far we have looked at the public Lenin. But what of the Lenin who argued his case among other high-ranking Bolsheviks behind the scenes? Not all the Central Committee minutes which are known to exist have been published, so that we cannot discover whether they would tell us much about Lenin's comportment on matters like revolutionary war. On the other hand it is at least known that on a few occasions even after mid June 1917, when he ceased to advocate revolutionary war in public, he advocated it to fellow members of the Central Committee.[26]

This would seem to demonstrate that Lenin's lack of public commitment to revolutionary war was merely a political device to allay popular feelings that the Bolsheviks might not intend to end the war. Perhaps he was still fully committed to revolutionary war. Perhaps. But the sources do not close off another interpretation. First, Lenin seldom privately discussed revolutionary war; second, when he did so it was only in parenthetical remarks: he never made a large issue of the matter from late April onwards. Some evidence, at least, implies that he remained in favour of his old contingency policy. But quite possibly it counted for less in his calculations than before. It is extremely difficult to probe the labyrinthine passages of his mind at the best of times; and it is not inconceivable that he himself was not well acquainted with its geography. What is irrefutable, however, is that the public Lenin in contrast with Lenin the intra-party debater had no constant and strong commitment to revolutionary war for several months before the October Revolution; and that, when he did advocate such a war, it was in qualified terms. And Lenin's lack of frankness about his intentions, whatever they were, must have been deliberate. Open as he was about some questions, he kept his thoughts to himself on other matters, or shared them only with members of the Central Committee.

Perhaps there was also an ingredient of casualness at work. Revolutionary war, when all is said and done, was only a contingency policy; indeed it was so unspecific in content that it was more a slogan than a policy. Lenin professed to believe that by far the likeliest consequence of a Russian socialist revolution was the undertaking of a socialist revolution in Germany by the German working class. Throughout the First World War until the Russian February revolution he had concentrated his attention upon Germany. In 1917 he repeatedly affirmed that a German socialist revolution could not long be delayed. The thrust of his statements on international policy was directed at convincing his readers and hearers of this. Consequently he gave the impression that the military contingency plan was for a highly improbable contingency. He often argued that the chances were ninety-nine out of a hundred that the German workers would rise up and overthrow Wilhelm II and establish a fraternal socialist régime.[27] And, of course, Lenin was like every other politician in Russia in 1917 in being caught up in a giddying swirl of events. He did not have the historian's advantage of calm, retrospective analysis. His time before July 1917 was taken up also with active politics: he addressed mass workers' meetings, he edited *Pravda*, he worked in the Central Committee's offices. After July, although the day-to-day routine tasks decreased in number, Lenin's work load was far from being a light one.

Be that as it may, Lenin was not the only leading Bolshevik to draw back from frequent public advocacy of a revolutionary war; on the contrary, it was the general trend. This is hardly surprising since several of them, notably Trotsky (who formally joined the Bolsheviks in the summer of 1917) and Bukharin, had continually argued that the party should exploit opportunities offered by the pro-peace movement in all European countries.[28] Furthermore, the debates among Bolsheviks in April at the Petrograd City Party Conference and the All-Russian Party Conference demonstrated an implicit reluctance to parade revolutionary war as party policy.[29]

A survey of *Pravda* demonstrates that calls for revolutionary war were not entirely absent. But they were rare; and, as in Lenin's case too, they tended to be phrased in qualified terms. Thus the anonymous piece on 7 June that declared that 'the oppressed classes of both Russia and other countries will not fear a revolutionary war *against capitalists*' fell well short of an unequivocal summons to arms in the event of a 'failure' of the German workers to make their own socialist revolution.[30] Apart from Lenin, the main Bolshevik commentator on international relations in the spring and summer of 1917 was G.E. Zinoviev. On 8 April *Pravda* printed an article of his on the possibilities of socialist revolution at home and abroad; it contained no mention of contingency military plans.[31] On 12 April a report on one of Zinoviev's speeches appeared. Zinoviev had two main themes: his denial that Bolsheviks wanted a separate peace and his call for Russian and German soldiers to fraternise as a means of hastening the composition of a general peace in Europe.[32] On 25 April he at last broached the matter of revolutionary war, stating that such a war could only be supported if the soviets already held power.[33] Such statements by Zinoviev, however, were extremely few after mid June. On 9 September he noted that if the German government refused Bolshevik peace overtures, the Bolsheviks would have to continue with the war.[34] But this was an exceptional statement by Zinoviev in these months. Like Lenin, he preferred to dwell on the inadequacies of the Provisional Government's foreign policy and on the need to encourage fraternisation and install a soviet government.[35]

Nor must it be overlooked that *Pravda*, as a daily newspaper, did not carry complete verbatim accounts of everything said by Zinoviev and Lenin at the various meetings attended by them in April. This was true even of the Petrograd Bolshevik City Conference (where Lenin mentioned revolutionary war as a contingency plan) and the All-Russian Bolshevik Conference in that month (where he was more circumspect). It was the will for a democratic peace that was stressed in *Pravda*.[36] Consequently only those Bolsheviks who had been party members at least since February 1917 and who had also followed official party debates with considerable thoroughness would be aware that revolutionary war had ever been Lenin's policy. The vast majority of Bolsheviks joined the party from the summer of 1917 onwards. It is reasonable to suppose that most rank-and-filers would not have appreciated all the nuances of discussions among the central party leaders.

This is all the more plausible when we consider the advice given by the Central Committee to local activists campaigning for election to the soviets in the summer. The resolutions adopted by the All-Russian Bolshevik Conference were obviously too lengthy and recondite to be useful for such campaigns. And yet mere slogans like 'peace', 'bread' and 'land' were not self-explanatory either. The Central Committee therefore formulated a pithy, punchy summary of party policies which could be taken up by the activists, and *Pravda* printed it in full on 7 May.[37] It is not known how many activists used the summary. But the contents are highly instructive, not least in showing how the Bolshevik Central Committee wanted its policies presented to the general public. The summary will also, of course, have been important reading material for the new rank-and-file Bolsheviks who had only a dim awareness of the nature of the party's policies. On international policy, it opened with the claim that the First World War was the result of collusion between kings and capitalists throughout Europe to fight to annex new territories. It stated that only governments of workers, soldiers and peasants could produce 'a just peace'.[38] There was no other mention of ways of ending the war; and there was no reference whatever to the possibility of a revolutionary war.[39]

Unfortunately the various extant records of Central Committee discussions in May and June 1917 remain mostly unpublished, so that the debates on both policies and the presentation of policies remain inaccessible. Yet the implication of the *Pravda* summary is clear enough: the Central Committee wanted to steer clear in public from advocacy of revolutionary war.

This does not mean that such a war was no longer in the minds of Bolshevik leaders. The Sixth Party Congress proceedings, which occurred in July 1917, show that quite the contrary was true. The Congress took place during the absence of Lenin and Zinoviev in Finland, where they hid from Kerensky's police. Most current major political and economic matters were discussed, including international policy; and Lenin did not have the degree of influence over these proceedings which he had wielded at the party conference in April.[40] Central Committee members could therefore speak without feeling inhibited by the presence of the party's most authoritative leader and theoretician. The Congress was held in a hasty and clandestine fashion; there was a constant fear lest the Ministry of Internal Affairs might discover its whereabouts and arrest the delegates. In such turbulent circumstances, understandably, the Central Committee gave much latitude to its representatives in the composing of their reports. And perforce these were closed proceedings. The Central Committee could not risk publishing them on security grounds. The indirect result was that Bolshevik leader could speak fairly freely with Bolshevik leader. All these aspects of the Congress make the proceedings an excellent, if underused, source on the Bolshevik party.[41]

The contingency policy for international relations cropped up exclusively with Bukharin's Central Committee report 'on the current moment'. Bukharin is conventionally portrayed as an unbridled leftist between 1917 and 1919 – even in the detailed accounts which are sympathetic to him.[42] Yet Bukharin in fact took care to declare to the Congress that an offensive revolutionary war might already be beyond the capability of the Russian armed forces. Since he was not speaking on the public record, there is no reason to suppose that he was being disingenuous. Bukharin recommended that, if a German socialist revolution failed to occur, the Bolsheviks should fight only a defensive revolutionary war. There was no talk from him or from other leftists of throwing the Russian army westwards.[43]

Neither Lenin nor any other Bolshevik leader had expressed a commitment to an offensive revolutionary war; there had been a universal reluctance to describe what a revolutionary war would involve. Bukharin had therefore been the first to put the task of definition on the Bolshevik party agenda. Both Bukharin's report and Stalin's report 'on the political moment' provoked sustained debate at several points (although, admittedly, the contingency plan on revolutionary war was accompanied by direct, open controversy). A Congress commission was formed to expedite business. The commission's deliberations remain unknown. But Bukharin, in introducing the motion as amended by the commission, significantly no longer stipulated even a defensive revolutionary war as being a Bolshevik contingency plan. Instead the official resolution spoke only of 'the task of rendering every kind of support, including armed support, for the militant proletariat of other countries'.[44] Bukharin was being forced to compromise; his

22. Delegation to the Soviet–German peace negotiations at Brest-Litovsk (seated, left to right: L.B. Kamenev (1st) and A.A. Joffe (2nd); standing: (1st) E.M. Sklianskii (3rd) L.D. Trotsky).

behaviour in 1918 showed that he had not changed his personal opinion (even though it is noteworthy that, in the Brest-Litovsk discussions, he continued to call for a war of defence rather than attack). Yet it is clear that the Sixth Congress, with its 157 voting delegates from virtually every Bolshevik party organisation in the country, did not want too closely to specify a contingency policy in the light of the difficulties that might impede its implementation.

Bukharin and the future Left Communists presumably made concessions since they, too, hoped that the outbreak of a German socialist revolution would make the need for a contingency plan unnecessary. Such a revolution did not occur and a near-destructive debate on revolutionary war as an alternative to an 'obscene' separate peace was to rack the body of the Bolshevik party in the first months of 1918. But the Congress minutes show that non-leftist Bolshevik leaders already felt edgy about even a defensive war with the Germans; and that even the leftists, months before the October revolution, saw that an offensive war was decreasingly feasible. It is also noteworthy that Bukharin's reasoning was premised not on tactical considerations of politics (such as the need to present the Bolsheviks as the peace party in Russia) but on a pragmatic recognition that Russia lacked the military capacity to launch an offensive.

Too often the Left Communists have been portrayed as persons with unswerving commitment to their ideas without the slightest inclination to adjust them to currently developing circumstances. To be sure, the Left Communists were more inflexible than Lenin. But the picture should not be drawn in black-and-white terms. By the same token, Lenin's flexibility must not be exaggerated. As an observer of the European labour movement in the First World War, he displayed persistent defects of perception. Among Bolsheviks in 1914–16, Lenin had always been the most optimistic about the chances available to the German Social Democratic Party (SPD) to lead a socialist revolution in Germany. Despite the doubts of many associates, including others in the so-called Zimmerwald Left,[45] he contended that the failure of revolution to break out in Germany at the beginning of the First World War was predominantly attributable to the acts of betrayal by the German Social-Democratic leadership. Yet nationalism in general and support for the German war effort in particular were not alien to the German Social-Democratic rank and file; and the whole blame could not reasonably be heaped on Kautsky and his associates. Several Bolsheviks perceived this, and the perception was not confined to any one section of the Bolshevik faction. Many leftists shared it before and during 1917. It was highlighted in the writings of Bukharin; and it appeared in the work of the leading left Zimmerwaldist and future Bolshevik, L.D. Trotsky.[46] Their knowledge about the obstacles in the path of a German socialist revolution must have assisted them, after the Russian February revolution, in seeing the obstacles in the path of a revolutionary war (even though they continued to believe in the need for it as a contingency policy).

Lenin himself became somewhat more sober about the German prospect in mid 1917. He never ceased to proclaim that revolution was imminent across the continent as a whole. But he also now began to emphasise, as he had not done before February 1917, that revolution in Germany with its powerful militarist government would be more difficult than in Russia.[47] He tended to abandon his earlier stress on the possibilities for revolt if only the SPD's central leaders were to show the necessary nerve and determination. Following Trotsky and (to a lesser extent) Bukharin, he came to accentuate the social and economic factors likely to come into play in the creation of a revolutionary crisis in Germany.[48]

Even so, nearly all Bolsheviks continued to overestimate the likelihood of German socialist revolution; it was an article of faith among them. Lenin, as usual, put the matter as vividly as he could in order to rally his party behind him. He asserted that the economy in Germany, especially the food-supplies sector, presented the Berlin authorities with greater problems than in Russia.[49] This was not a view shared by the Central Committee economic spokesman at the Sixth Party Congress, V.P. Miliutin.[50] But Lenin was resolved to see the European political situation in as favourable a glow as he possibly could. In Russia, the information on German political events was inevitably sketchy. A fully satisfactory contemporary assessment was impossible; and undoubtedly the supplies of foodstuffs to German towns and to the German army, while not as paltry as Lenin contended, were dropping to dangerously low levels. The last months of 1916 and the first ones of 1917 had been known popularly as the 'turnip winter'. Popular discontent grew throughout 1917. And yet the Mensheviks in their comments were nearer to the truth when they affirmed that German working-class war weariness should not be treated as proof of overwhelming mass support for violent socialist revolution.[51] Lenin's appraisal of the German situation, despite its adjustments in 1917, remained inadequate.

In his favour it can be said that after the February revolution he perceived that it no longer made sense to speak of the defeat of Russia, which now had a democratic régime, as a lesser evil than the defeat of militarist Germany. In 1917 Lenin ceased to take a 'defeatist' line in international policy. There is no reason to suppose that this change of stance was only tactical. It has sometimes been suggested that he was simply hoping to avoid being portrayed as a German spy. No evidence has been produced in corroboration. On the other hand, Lenin did not zealously seek the maintenance of order in the Russian army. Obviously he could see the high command as a potential domestic-political threat. The Kornilov coup attempt, despite being abortive, demonstrated the realism of Lenin's thinking. He contented himself by avoiding active, direct encouragement of the break-up of the Russian army under the Provisional Government even though the involvement of soldiers in the kind of politics recommended by the Bolsheviks was partly instrumental in bringing this about. Throughout the summer he portrayed the Provisional Government as a dangerously militarist cabinet.

But he altered his propaganda in September after the German army's advance along the Baltic littoral. His accusation was that the country's defences were no longer safe in the hands of Kerensky. Lenin even claimed that the Provisional Government was deliberately abandoning land to the Germans in order to make the task of maintaining its own control of Petrograd easier. He went so far as to allege that Kerensky wanted Petrograd to fall to the Germans.[52] This extreme charge was hotly disputed; and it fits badly with everything else that is known about Kerensky's vision of his patriotic duty. Yet Lenin's words illustrate that he was at least trying to present himself as someone who would not dream of colluding with the national enemy of the moment. He also denied that his agrarian policy, which included a promise of the transfer of land to the peasantry, would disrupt the army in the trenches. He expressed the hope that peasant soldiers would stay at their posts and not desert to their villages in search of a share in the land that was about to be divided amongst the peasantry.[53] In summary, the last few weeks before the October revolution witnessed Lenin, who had already donned the frock-coat of the peacemaker, putting on the cape of the true patriot who alone would save his country from dismemberment and dishonour.

What conclusions are we to draw from this survey of Bolshevik party policy and discussions between the February and the October revolutions? First, Lenin in public came to drop the policy of an immediate revolutionary war. This does not mean that he had abandoned it in the longer term; his eagerness to use the military victories in the Soviet–Polish war of 1920 as a means of facilitating the outbreak of socialist revolutions in the rest of Europe indicates an enduring feature in his strategical thought.

We cannot be totally sure that he had really dropped it even in the shorter term; but it seems reasonable to suppose that he was already experiencing doubts (as were even leftists like Bukharin, albeit to a more limited extent). In addition, Lenin was shifting away from a public commitment to revolutionary war without openly acknowledging the fact. Lenin was in many ways an exceptionally frank politician; but he was also capable of fudging issues in pursuit of intra-party and general political objectives. He and other leading Bolsheviks were marching to power by presenting the pieces of their programme to the general population, and indeed to the mass of their own party, which were most likely to garner and retain support. A further conclusion is that the leftists recognised the impracticability of an offensive revolutionary war, and that this recognition was made even before the October revolution. This presumably made it all the easier for Lenin to dent their self-confidence in the Brest-Litovsk controversy of 1918. Even so, Lenin was far from being the sole Bolshevik to affect his party's policies and intentions; his shift away from open advocacy of revolutionary war as a contingency policy followed rather than directed the opinion of the Bolshevik party leadership. Moreover, the debate on the war question was only intermittently engaged. Like much that happened among Bolsheviks in 1917, many issues were left in a poorly and irresponsibly elaborated condition. This was both an asset to them in approaching a seizure of power and a disadvantage once they had seized it.

A further conclusion is that Lenin's statements always have to be considered in relation to the circumstances of their expression and to the audience or readership he was addressing. There were different levels to his thinking; and an accurate summary requires that we do not seek to impose consistency where it did not exist. Discussion of Lenin's 'thought' necessarily involves investigating his ideas for their intrinsic logic, originality and development. But he was not a thinker first and an active politician only second; nor was the reverse true. He was both at once. The balance between the two sides of his career has to be assessed for each particular conjuncture: it was not at all a fixed balance.

This brings us to the issue of the connection between Bolshevik policies and popular aspirations in 1917. Until the 1960s most Western historians, though by no means all of them, assumed that the Bolsheviks came to power by means of both superior political organisation and comprehensive political manipulation. Thus the 'masses' were hoodwinked into voting for the Bolsheviks. In the 1970s several studies appeared which indicated that mass political action was not exclusively or even mainly Bolshevik-directed; and that the Bolsheviks in many ways reflected popular aspirations. But to draw a rigid dichotomy between 'manipulation' and 'reflection' is mistaken. For the Bolsheviks both manipulated and reflected popular opinion. Even this contention is too crude. There were Bolsheviks and Bolsheviks. The pro-peace campaigning undertaken by low-level activists was surely not a manipulative ploy on their part. Rather it coincided with their own opinions; and they had many reasons to suppose that they had the genuine encouragement of the Central Committee. And even those central party leaders who, more or less privately, supported revolutionary war as a contingency objective were not complete political frauds. Their basic expectation was that a German socialist revolution would save them from ever having to engage in such a war.

In addition, Bolshevik leaders at the centre and in the localities faced problems in communicating their policies. Most of their potential recruits and supporters had only a patchy knowledge about the implications of current political and economic questions. This was especially true as regards international relations. The Romanov absolute monarchy had deliberately hindered the development of independent, informed mass opinion in Russia. Simplification of party policies for general consumption was sensible in such an environment. Not only the Bolsheviks but also all the other contemporary parties tacitly recognised this. Indeed, nearly all parties in all countries simplify their policies in order to stand a realistic chance of increasing their support.

This does not signify that there was no sleight of hand in the Bolshevik Central Committee's presentation of its policies. But the conclusion does not follow that such conjuring was the main reason why they achieved power in 1917. It was indeed a reason; but mass revulsion against the Provisional Government and the fact that, on so many matters, the short-term aspects of Bolshevik policies unforcedly coincided to a large extent with popular aspirations counted for much more. The Bolsheviks were constantly and justifiably harangued by the Mensheviks and the Socialist Revolutionaries that their attitude would cause horrendous problems; but the Bolsheviks ignored them. It was a tragic situation. The opponents of Bolshevism correctly perceived the dangers of Bolshevik policies; the Bolsheviks correctly perceived that the Provisional Government's policies and the Menshevik alliance with the Kadets presaged ruin at home and abroad. Much blame should therefore be attached to Lenin; but understanding should also be his due. There truly was no easy solution to the country's domestic and foreign problems. Historians who eulogise Lenin attribute to him greater responsibility than is justified whereas those who denigrate him exaggerate his blameworthiness.

The way out of this problem is to look at the Bolshevik party as a whole and to abandon the dreary algebra of 'Lenin, the party and the masses'. Attention must be paid also to other Central Committee members and to the lower levels of the Bolshevik party hierarchy as well as to the party's rank-and-filers; and all this has to be undertaken in the framework of the aspirations and understandings of those workers and other social groups who supported the Bolsheviks in 1917. A vast agenda for research on Russian revolutionary politics remains to be accomplished.

NOTES

I should like to express my thanks to Israel Getzler who made many valuable suggestions for the improvement of the several successive drafts on a similar theme. His patience has been as inexhaustible as his generosity in sharing his notes on Lenin's thinking about revolutionary war in 1917.

1 See the contributions to the Seventh Party Conference: *Sedmaia (aprelskaia) vserossiiskaia konferentsiia RSDRP (bolshevikov). Aprel 1917 goda* (Moscow, 1958), pp. 67–78 and 243.

2 R. Service, *The Bolshevik Party in Revolution: A Study in Organisational Change* (London, 1979), p. 54.

3 *Sedmaia konferentsiia*, p. 57.

4 Lenin, *Polnoe sobranie sochinenii (PSS)* (Moscow, 1958–65), vol. XXXI, pp. 13 and 67.

5 Ibid., p. 91.

6 Ibid., pp. 161 and 174.

7 *Sedmaia konferentsiia*, p. 57.

8 *PSS*, vol. XXXI, p. 114.

9 *Sedmaia konferentsiia*, pp. 79 and 85.

10 Ibid., p. 58.

11 Ibid., pp. 173–4 and 241.

12 Ibid., pp. 173–4.

13 Ibid., p. 177.

14 *PSS*, vol. XXXII, p. 100.

15 Ibid., p. 102.

16 Ibid., p. 72.

17 The Russian perfective infinitive (*podgotovit*) could be taken to imply that preparations would have to be completed in advance rather than be made at the same time that the war was being waged.

18 *PSS*, vol. XXXII, p. 274.

19 Ibid., p. 288.

20 *Pravda*, no. 81 (14 June 1917).

21 Ibid. and *PSS*, vol. XXXII, p. 287.

22 See above, note 9.

23 See I. Getzler, *Martov: A Political Biography* (London, 1967), ch. 7.

24 See 'Rezoliutsiia bozhiiskoi gruppy', reprinted in *Proletarskaia revoliutsiia* no. 5 (40) (1925), 171.

25 This is not to imply, of course, that Bukharin and Trotsky were among the first to influence Lenin in Petrograd. On the contrary, they did not secure their return to Russia for some weeks after Lenin's trip in the sealed train.

26 Thus he mentioned the possibility of revolutionary war in cor-

respondence with the Central Committee; see his letter of 30 August 1917: *PSS*, vol. xxxiv, p. 121.

27 Ibid., p. 148.

28 See above, note 24.

29 See above, note 9.

30 'Est li put k spravedlivomu miru?', *Pravda* no. 74 (7 June 1917).

31 Ibid., no. 27 (8 April 1917).

32 Ibid., no. 30 (12 April 1917).

33 Ibid., no. 40 (25 April 1917).

34 *Rabochii*, no. 2 (5 September 1917): 'V chem vykhod?'.

35 See 'Bratatsia li dalshe', *Pravda* no. 49 (5 May 1917).

36 See, for example, ibid., no. 40 (25 April 1917) and 42 (27 April 1917).

37 Ibid., no. 51 (7 May 1917).

38 Ibid.

39 Ibid.

40 But see, on the front of domestic Russian politics, the analyses of A.M. Sovokin, 'Rezoliutsiia VI-ogo sezda partii "O politicheskom polozhenii"', in *Istochnikovedenie istorii Velikogo Oktiabria* (Moscow, 1977), pp. 9–25; and A. Rabinowitch, *The Bolsheviks Come to Power: The Revolution of 1917 in Petrograd* (London, 1976), pp. 83–90.

41 *Protokoly Tsentralnogo Komiteta RSDRP(b). Avgust 1917–fevral 1918* (Moscow, 1958), p. 179.

42 See S. Cohen, *Bukharin and the Russian Revolution: A Political Biography, 1888–1938* (London, 1974), ch. 3.

43 *Shestoi sezd RSDRP (bolshevikov). Avgust 1917 goda. Protokoly* (Moscow, 1958), pp. 104–5.

44 *Shestoi sezd*, pp. 196–8.

45 Even G.E. Zinoviev, Lenin's closest colleague from the period of the First World War until the February revolution, was unwilling to blame only the apex of the SPD. His *O prichinakh krakha germanskoi sotsial-demokratii* (Petersburg, 1917) assertively implied that almost the entire party was pervaded by nationalism: see especially part iii, *Rabochaia aristokratiia*, pp. 24–5. This work was written before 1917 but was not printed until after the February revolution: see ibid., p. 30. Unlike Trotsky and Bukharin, Zinoviev took pains to emphasise his notion that such nationalism was confined to a minority of the German working class: see ibid., p. 15.

46 Nota Bene (N.I. Bukharin), 'The Imperialist Pirate State', from *Jugend-Internationale* (no. 6, 1 December 1916) in O. H. Gankin and H. H. Fisher (eds.), *The Bolsheviks and the World Wars* (Oxford, 1940), p. 239; and L.D. Trotsky, 'Natsiia i khoziaistvo', *Nashe slovo* no. 135 (9 July 1915), reprinted in *Sochineniia*, vol. ix (Moscow and Leningrad, 1927), p. 214, and his 'God voiny', *Nashe slovo* no. 156 (4 August 1915) in ibid., p. 220; and 'K novomu godu', *Nashe slovo* no. 1 (1 January 1916) in ibid., p. 226.

47 *PSS*, vol. xxxiv, pp. 385–6 and 395.

48 L.D. Trotsky, 'God voiny', *Nashe slovo* no. 156 (4 August 1915), reprinted in *Sochineniia*, vol. ix, pp. 220–1; and N.I. Bukharin, 'The Imperialist Pirate State'. It ought to be noted that Trotsky's argument was more clearly articulated than Bukharin's in this respect. Zinoviev, too, took a closer interest in the social dynamics of the German labour movement than did Lenin: see note 26.

49 *PSS*, vol. xxxii, pp. 54 and 96.

50 *Shestoi sezd*, p. 151.

51 See the editorial in *Rabochaia gazeta*, no. 73 (6 June 1917), p. 1 and in particular N. Andreev's article on p. 2; and the editorial in ibid., no. 109 (18 July 1917), p. 2.

52 See, for example, *PSS*, vol. xxxiv, p. 389.

53 Ibid., vol. xxxii, p. 177.

15

LENIN'S TIME BUDGET:
THE SMOLNY PERIOD

JOHN KEEP

THE Bolsheviks' retention of power during the first few months after the October revolution was in large measure due to Lenin's unique combination of pertinacity and flexibility: on this point both his admirers and detractors agree. Yet his actions have hitherto not been subjected to detailed critical scrutiny, as needs to be done if we are to comprehend the inner workings of the 'proletarian dictatorship' in its key initial phase. Fortunately there is a source that makes a quantitative approach possible: the fifth volume of the exhaustive *Biographical Chronicle* (*BK*), published in 1974.[1]

This vast compendium of information – in all some 39,000 items, only half of them previously in print – has a clear hagiographical intent; nevertheless it has been compiled with exemplary thoroughness. Where they have left written trace, *BK* records each of Vladimir Ilich's conversations with visitors to Smolny (by party activists, military and economic specialists, journalists and so on), the messages he sent, and his participation in decision-making by the Council of People's Commissars (CPC or *Sovnarkom*) and other governmental agencies. It has some obvious lacunae, notably in its meagre references to Old Bolsheviks disgraced under Stalin – as well as to Stalin himself, although to a lesser degree.[2] Yet for no other twentieth-century leader do we have such a complete catalogue of his daily doings.[3]

From this source we have compiled a data base of over 1,500 actions which Lenin is known to have taken between 25 October 1917 and 10 March 1918; supplementary information is drawn from over one hundred memoirs as well as other items of historical literature.

This evidence shows that, although Vladimir Ilich displayed phenomenal energy and resilience, he responded to events as much as he shaped them, and that his contacts with other decision-makers were haphazard and episodic. His days started early and ended late;

23. Red Guards at Bolshevik headquarters in the Smolny Institute (October 1917).

frequently he was at work until the early hours of the morning and on at least one occasion did not sleep at all.[4] His life consisted of a continual whirl of meetings as one crisis gave way to another. Everything had to be improvised, partly because he lacked a proper staff. Nor was he good at delegating responsibility. Much time was wasted on trivial housekeeping problems: coping with humble petitioners, arranging for visitors to be given passes, ordering railway tickets or ration cards for Smolny employees and so on.[5] The social chaos and the strikes among communications workers complicated matters.

Lenin obtained much of his information about developments in provincial Russia from conversations with activists, but except for those from the northwest (Petrograd province, Baltic, Finland) they were unevenly distributed. Of eighteen such persons whom he received in his Smolny office (after appropriate screening procedures) before the end of November, half came from Moscow or the Central Industrial region; only then did the first individuals arrive from the Urals (3) and the Middle Volga region (1), and men from the northern Caucasus and Kazakhstan (1 each) did not follow until early in January. Lenin met only one activist from the Ukraine (S.S. Bakinskii),[6] which may help to explain his rash decision to launch hostilities against the Rada government. In this region policy was in fact later made by V.A. Antonov-Ovseenko, the commander of the Red forces there, who in Lenin's view often behaved irresponsibly.[7]

As Nina Tumarkin writes in her recent study of the Lenin cult, Vladimir Ilich 'was a remarkably literary leader [whose] pen had unusual powers of persuasion'.[8] Even in these weeks of intense practical activity his published output runs to over 400 pages. He wrote fewer letters than usual, but his incoming mailbag averaged 300 letters a week.[9] Few of his humdrum correspondents received a personal reply – as did the soviet chairman of inconspicuous Ostrogozhsk (Voronezh province) – although officials might be told to investigate such complaints or requests.

Apart from the mail, four other means of communication lay to hand. Smolny had its own telephone exchange, with a range limited to Petrograd and environs. On 27 October a special switchboard was set up for the leader, with direct lines to his fellow commissars as well as to the Smolny and municipal exchanges. This installation enabled him 'to settle party and state matters operationally by telephone while keeping his conversations secret'[10] – facilities superior to those that Kerensky had enjoyed in the Winter Palace.

Yet Lenin grumbled at the service and preferred to use the telegraph or military direct-wire apparatus. The latter was connected to GHQ (and other fronts), Moscow and Kharkov – but significantly not Kiev, for which purpose he had to resort to the civilian system, or other cities in the interior.[11] The known recipients of his telegrams were geographically scattered: five in Moscow or environs, three in the Ukraine, and one each in Kishinev, Smolensk province (Belaia), Irkutsk, Manchuria and Finland. Radio was used to despatch an official message for the first time on 30 October.[12] In January Smolny acquired its own transmitter, which was useful in diplomacy, notably to contact Berlin once the Germans denounced the armistice and sent troops across the demarcation line.[13]

We may now turn to Lenin's role in the organs of government, beginning with the CPC, where it was indisputably overwhelming. As T.H. Rigby writes,

> Lenin pervaded the whole Sovnarkom system, his activity constantly entering it at all the nodal points, his methods stamped on its very structures and procedures and his attitudes and expectations 'internalised' to a greater or lesser extent in the working personalities of most of the individuals active in the system.[14]

24. The Council of People's Commissars in session, 1918, with Lenin in the chair.

He paid 'infinite attention to detail and behav[ed] towards his colleagues rather like a firm but good-humoured if occasionally irascible schoolmaster'[15]– as when he ordered fines to be levied on members who arrived late for CPC sessions. Not only did he chair nearly all the sessions – seventy-three out of seventy-seven, according to Iroshnikov's calculations[16] – but he also fixed the agenda by adding items of his own and deleting or postponing those he considered of lesser importance. The establishment of the 'Little CPC' (*Malyi Sovnarkom*) in January for routine business[17] helped to reduce the excessive number of agenda items, but even so the Council's sessions often dragged on far into the night. On 5–6 January, when dissolution of the Constituent Assembly was under discussion, it did not even begin its labours until 1 a.m.[18] On this occasion Lenin intervened five times, and on 30 December seven times. (This was less than the record of sixteen times, reached on 21 November 1918!)[19] At some sessions, however, he remained silent.[20]

Lenin encouraged debate but was quick to correct members he thought were straying from the proper 'line'. When faced with matters likely to arouse opposition, he might call an informal conference (*soveshchanie*) of trusted members,[21] and so present the others with a *fait accompli*. A still more effective device was to get the issue referred to the

Party Central Committee, whose members were bound by disciplinary constraints. This became a necessity once the Left SRs entered the CPC late in November, so turning it into a coalition cabinet – on the surface, at least, for one should not anachronistically regard this body as a conventional state institution with legally defined powers. In essence Russia was ruled by a junta which took such action as seemed expedient in order to maintain and extend its authority, and cloaked this in pseudo-legal forms; it blended procedural formality with operational informality in a way that allowed ample scope for arbitrary action.

The CPC issued a stream of decrees and orders, most of which were signed, and many written, by its chairman. According to one Soviet scholar, by 18 January he had written thirty-two laws;[22] another offers a figure of forty-one decrees written and another nineteen amended during the first *year* of Soviet power.[23] But these figures understate the extent of his influence over the Council's legislative activity. One may confidently state that no order was issued by the CPC that did not have his consent.

Actual legislative procedure varied considerably. On important issues Lenin would sometimes first compose 'theses' for discussion and then re-work them as a decree, adding clauses to the draft text as the debate evolved; sometimes he would write 'Confirmed – Lenin' on his own draft, once he was satisfied that it had his comrades' assent; sometimes another Council member would submit a draft, usually based on ideas which he had previously discussed orally with the leader, and he would then approve it.[24] A vivid, if somewhat overdrawn, picture of Lenin at work in the CPC is given by a railwayman, V.N. Fonchenko, who was admitted to a session at 3 o'clock one December morning.

> Vladimir Ilich was in constant movement. He listened to the speakers, put questions, formulated decisions and dictated them to a secretary. At the same time he wrote notes to the PCs and the *rapporteurs*, and called someone up on the phone . . .[25]

The minutes of the CPC, publication of which began in October 1987,[26] have yet to be critically analysed. *BK* allows us to reconstruct the subjects under discussion, if not the positions taken by participants in the debate. We are also told – at some cost to contextual logic – which items Lenin expressed an opinion on or otherwise dealt with personally, and which went through without any active intervention on his part. To examine these topically would make little sense, since the leader interested himself in virtually everything; like many chiefs, he meddled in matters for which subordinates were responsible, while simultaneously insisting that they abide by the rules and reprimanding them in public if they were poorly informed about their department's affairs or slow to execute CPC decisions.

Most prominent Bolsheviks did not expect their party to remain in power for long, so that a great deal of their legislative activity was designed for its demonstrative effect. In the worst possible scenario they saw themselves as leaving behind a monument to maximalist aspirations that would inspire later generations. More optimistically, Lenin told a sceptical A.V. Shotman before taking power that the laws which a Bolshevik government would put out would serve mainly 'to let the entire people see that it is *their* power; once the people see this they'll support us and everything ·else will sort itself out'.[27] Or as Trotsky put it later, the CPC's decrees 'had a propagandist rather than administrative significance'.[28] 'Bourgeois' critics who valued legality objected to this, as did the Mensheviks.[29] So too did some reflective Bolsheviks, such as A.G. Shliapnikov, who in 1922 reminisced that 'the high output of decrees soon bogged down [*zagromozdilo*] the CPC's work'.[30] In self-defence Lenin maintained that 'these decrees, even if they could not be immediately and fully implemented, played a major role in propaganda'.[31]

A close study of *BK* reveals that decrees were only one of at least ten types of 'authority acts' which Lenin issued during the Smolny period. Each had its proper appellation. They are listed in table 1, roughly in declining order of gravity. Other important points relevant to the CPC about which *BK* offers useful information are (i) the growth and composition of its 'apparatus' or administrative staff, which was so to speak an extension of Lenin's own personal secretariat; (ii) its policy in regard to personnel and (iii) budgetary matters.

(i) *The CPC staff*. An Old Bolshevik and personal friend, V.D. Bonch-Bruevich became the CPC's 'office manager' (*upravliaiushchyi delami*) on 29/30 October, even before the Council met for the first time in regular session, and it was he who the next day got N.P. Gorbunov appointed as its secretary.[32] Gorbunov had been a Bolshevik for only three months and had been trained as a chemist.[33] It was he who recruited the first secretary-typist, Anna Kizas. She was soon joined by several other ladies, whom she identifies in her memoirs. (For an attempt at a reconstruction of the staff, see table 2.) In December Mariia Skrypnik was appointed 'second secretary', the deputy of Gorbunov.[34] Sergeeva describes her own job as chief clerk (*deloproizvoditel*);

Table 1. *'Authority acts' issued by Lenin during the Smolny period*

Type of act	Example	References and notes
dekret (decree)	Confiscation of certain factories	238.1, 27.1. The Bolsheviks shunned the Tsarist term *ukaz* (ukase), presumably because of its arbitrary connotations.
rasporiazhenie (instruction, ordinance)	Measures to safeguard security of dispatches abroad on foreign policy matters	254.4, 14.2. A decree with limited scope of application.
postanovlenie (order)	Appointment of board (*kollegium*) member, PC of Internal Affairs	243.4, 30.1. A *change* of jobs, however, might call for an *ukazanie*: 220.3, not later than 19.1.
ukazanie (order)	Subordinate agencies to assist materially Communist workers leaving to establish collective farms	247.1, not earlier than 30.1.
predpisanie (order)	Military agencies to ensure supply of volunteers	260.4, 17.2. Rather less forceful than *ukazanie*, in the sense: 'do what you can within the limits we know constrain you'.
otnoshenie (memorandum)	Moscow soviet praesidium to cooperate with emissaries sent to combat pogroms	258.3, 16.2. More of an appeal than an order.
poruchenie (commission)	Stalin to answer queries from a district soviet, which Lenin then signed	248.5, 31.1.
izveshchenie (announcement)	Grant of funds for Latvian pro-Bolshevik newspaper	241.1, 29.1.
zapiska (note)	PC of Finance to allow depositor to draw savings from State Bank	231.2, 24.1. Such notes might be more peremptory. The secretaries called them 'Ilichevki'.
zapros (inquiry)	Antonov to nominate commander for forces in Odessa	246.3, not earlier than 30.1.

she was a Bonch appointee.[35] All the women depict Lenin as a demanding yet considerate boss, who taught them 'how to keep minutes, find information quickly and send off letters . . . He demanded that we work neatly and swiftly and that we know our job well.'[36] Korotkova speaks of his 'severe but just exactingness'.[37] By mid December the staff had grown to such a point that Lenin had to ask

Gorbunov to compile a list of their names and telephone numbers.[38] This was followed by a 'survey' – presumably an inquiry into their social and political backgrounds – conducted on 22–24 January.[39] In March the total staff numbered sixty-five, or three times as many as in mid November (twenty-one) and twice as many as on New Year's Day (thirty-two).[40]

The CPC spawned a number of administrative offshoots. One was the Press (or Information) Bureau, under T.L. Akselrod, whose functions included transmission of items for publication in Bolshevik-controlled organs and supervision of the non-Bolshevik media.[41] Another was the Financial Department, set up on 20 November; its activities will be discussed shortly. Although formally independent of the 'Secretariat', as the CPC staff was sometimes termed, both these bodies also came under Bonch-Bruevich's direction. Rather different in character were the *ad hoc* commissions of CPC members established to work out policy on contentious issues. The first of these appeared on 5 December, to discuss district land committees (a matter on which the coalition partners were at loggerheads) and relations with the Ukrainian Rada. The latter commission was accorded powers equivalent to those of the CPC as a whole, presumably to avoid having to debate the Ukrainian adventure too openly.[42] Soon afterwards M.L. Lvova was appointed to head an 'Economic Section (*chast*)';[43] its relations with the Financial Department are unclear.

At the end of January the CPC began the practice both of appointing agents ('trouble-shooters') to impose its will in the provinces,[44] and also of establishing 'special commissions' of the CPC, inter-departmental agencies staffed by officials from the PCs concerned. Blessed with such awesome titles as 'Chokprod' or 'Chokrap', which underlined their limitless emergency powers, their main function was to restore order on the railways and to speed supplies. Trotsky headed the former agency, a fact that goes unrecorded in *BK*.

(ii) *Personnel policy.* A. Lomov (G.I. Oppokov), People's Commissar (PC) of Justice for the first few days until he resigned in protest at the drift to dictatorship, later reminisced:

> [Lenin] energetically sought out candidates to be People's Commissars and to hold [other] responsible posts; after that the [Party] CC would formalise [*oformlial*] the appointment; there were no disagreements of any kind.[45]

The main problem was the lack of willing and qualified candidates; another was the need to reshuffle the 'ministerial portfolios'

Table 2. CPC Staff

Name	Function	References
1 Bonch-Bruevich, V.D.	Office manager	Bonch-Bruevich, *Na boevykh postakh*, p. 131
2 Gorbunov, N.P.	Secretary	Ibid; Orakhelashvili, *Lenin*, p. 104
3 Kizas, Anna P.	Secretary-typist	Orakhelashvili, *Lenin*, p. 104
4 Koksharova, E.K.	Secretary-typist[a]	Chervinskaia, *Zhizn*, pp. 416–17
5 Skrypnik, Mariia N.	Secretary-typist[a]	Skrypnik, *passim*; 132.5
6 Sergeeva, Iu. P.	Secretary-typist	Chervinskaia, *Zhizn*, pp. 426–8
7 Ozerevskaia, L.Ia.	Secretary-typist	Ibid.
8 Belenkaia, B.Ia.	Secretary-typist	Ibid.
9 Shakhunova, P.A.	Secretary-typist	Ibid.
10 Gorlova, N.N.	Secretary-typist	Ibid; Klopov, *Lenin v Smolnom*, p. 76
11 Fediushin, G.R.	Secretary-typist	Ibid.
12 Dukhvinskii-Osipov, I.	Junior secretary	Ilin-Zhenevskii, pp. 153–9
13 Korotkov(a?), B.L.	Press distribution worker (secretary)[b]	*Lenin – vozhd Oktiabria* (1956), pp. 278ff.
14 Dmitriev, P.D.	Courier (*vestovoi*)	52.1; Kosobokov, 'U apparata – Lenin', 27; Ilin-Zhenevskii, *Bolsheviki u vlasti* (Leningrad, 1929), p. 171
15 Ivanov, Ia.	Personal secretary[c]	65.1
16 Sidorenko, S.M.	Personal secretary	218.3; *PSS*, vol. L, pp. 48–9; Genkina, *Protokoly*, p. 137
17 Vorobev, N.V.	Personal secretary	141.4
18 Ozerevskii, G.A.[d]	?	200.5

19 Kinkadze, (first name unknown)	'In CPC service'	
20 Shutko, K.I.	?	
21 Astapkovich, G.I.	Telephonist	218.1 Shliapnikov, 'K oktiabru', 26 Chervinskaia, Zhizn, p. 417; Kosobokov, 'U apparata – Lenin', 22
22 Andreev, M.F.	Telephonist	Ibid., 20
23 Kupriianov, N.K.	Telephonist	Ibid.
24 Kalinin, I.Ia.	Telegraphist	Ibid.
25 Diatlov, A.P.	Telegraphist	Ibid.
26 Riatin, N.A.	Telegraphist	Ibid.
27 Gausman, I.K. (female)	Telegraphist	Ibid., 23
28 Sobolev, I.	Telegraphist	Ibid., 28
29 Luther, Heinrich	Telegraphist	Ibid.
30 Vorontsov, G.B.	Guard	Ibid., 24
31 Polovinkin, P.A.	Guard	Ibid.
32 Zheltyshev, S.P.	Guard (temporary?)	Lenin – vozhd Oktiabria, p. 300
33 Li Hu-tsin (et al.)	Guards (temporary?)	Bezveselnyi and Grinberg, O Lenine (Moscow, 1962), pp. 243–5
34 Gil, S.K.	Chauffeur	Lenin – vozhd Oktiabria, p. 346

[a] In December appointed 'second secretary'.

[b] Initials may be B.P. His/her memoirs, completed in 1939, were not published until after Stalin's death: Lenin – vozhd Oktiabria, pp. 278–91.

[c] Ivanov was evidently a replacement for Sidorenko, another sailor, who when drunk boasted of his position close to the Leader and was dismissed; later he was pardoned and given a job in the Cheka.

[d] Presumably the husband of 7.

frequently, as a consequence of the November resignations and the Left SRs' entry into the government, or to appoint deputies for PCs who went off on important missions. The story of S.S. Pestkovskii's appointment as commissar of the State Bank is well known: a degree from the London School of Economics was the decisive factor![46] G.I. Petrovskii, the second PC of Internal Affairs (after A.I. Rykov's resignation), tells how Lenin chanced upon him in his outer office, clapped him on the shoulder and said: 'You've arrived just in time. We'll appoint you PC of Internal Affairs right away. Rykov has just run away from that job.' Petrovskii said that he would rather be a mere deputy commissar. Lenin jocularly responded: 'Get two armed workers to escort him to the ministry and then let him try to refuse'; so he fell silent and accepted his task[47] – which years later led to a spell in the gulag.

Lunacharsky voiced fears that the initial selection had been made too casually, but his chief reassured him: 'For the moment let's [wait and] see; we need responsible people for all positions; if they turn out to be unsuitable, we can change them.'[48] He was over-optimistic, for the number of appointments to be filled grew apace and many had to be left vacant; the rate of turnover was unacceptably high. Only the personnel shortage explains Lenin's embarrassed request to his own brother-in-law, the engineer M.T. Elizarov, to take on the post of PC of Transport; Elizarov found his duties irksome, fell foul of the political zealots, and soon resigned.[49] Krupskaia, of course, served in the People's Commissariat of Education, and a cousin of Bonch-Bruevich's found himself on its board (*kollegium*).[50] There was a clear risk of nepotism here.

Ideally, the People's Commissariats were to consist of a PC as chief and an advisory board.[51] (It was an arrangement that, by the way, had been introduced to Russia by Peter I and had lasted on paper until 1801.) What happened in practice now was that Deputy People's Commissars emerged. Only three complete boards received formal sanction by the head of government during this period. Lenin's confirmations, as registered in *BK*, are set out in table 3. Many other senior officials exercised power without having received the signed certificate of appointment that was sometimes made out by the leader, even for quite junior appointees, such as the commissar of the local branch of the State Bank in Saratov.[52] One might have expected Lenin to leave such details to the man he had appointed commissar in the bank's head office.[53] On the other hand, as table 3 shows, Stalin and Trotsky were each given a free hand in building their staffs.

Table 3. *People's Commissars and board members whose appointments were officially confirmed by Lenin as Chairman of the CPC*

	1917		1918		
Commissariat	October/November	December	January	February–March	Totals
Agriculture	[MILIUTIN, V.P]*,*** / SHLIKHTER, A.G. (td) 13.11 / KOLEGAEV, A.L. 25.11				3
Education	LUNACHARSKY, A.V. 18.11[a] / Leshchenko, D.I. 21.11[b]	Zaks, G.D. 11.12 / Krupskaia, N.K. / Lebedev-Polianskii, P.I. / Pozner, V.M. / Menzhinskaia, L.R. / Rogalskii, I.B. } 30.12	Bonch-Bruevich, V.M. 6.1 / Alekseev, N.N. 6.1	KRUPSKAIA, N.K. (d) 9.3	10
Finance	[SKVORTSOV (STEPANOV), I.I.] / MENZHINSKII, V.R. 30.10 / Bogolepov, D.P. 14.11			Krestinskii, N.N. 2.3	3
Foreign Affairs	[TROTSKY, L.D.]		CHICHERIN, G.V.[c] 29.1		1
Internal Affairs	[RYKOV, A.I.] / PETROVSKII, G.I. 17.11 / Muranov, M.K.[d] / Lazimir, P.E. / Latsis, M.I. } 18.11 / Unshlikht, I.S.[e] / Uritskii, M.S.	Iakovleva, V.N. 11.12 / Smirnov, A.P. 11.12	Pravdin, I.G. 24.1		9
Justice	[LOMOV, A. (Oppokov G.I.)] / STUCHKA, P.I. (td) 16.11 / Krasikov, P.A. 29.11 / Kozlovskii, M.Yu. 29.11	Stuchka, P.I.[f] 9/10.12	SHREIDER, A.A. (d) 30.1		5

Table 3. (*continued*)

Commissariat	1917		1918		Totals
	October/November	December	January	February–March	
Labour	[SHLIAPNIKOV, A.G.]		BRONSKII, M.G. (d) 30.1		1
Military and Naval Affairs	[ANTONOV-OVSEENKO, V.A.][g] [KRYLENKO, N.I.] [DYBENKO, P.E.][h] MEKHONOSHIN, A. (d) 20.11 KEDROV, M.S. (d) 23.11 LEGRAN, B.V. (d) 23.11 SKLIANSKII, E.M. (d) 23.11				4
Nationalities	[STALIN, I.V.]				
Naval Affairs	DYBENKO, P.E. 21.11		RASKOLNIKOV, F.F. (d) 29.1 VAKHRAMEEV, I.I. (d) 29.1	Saks, S.E. 15.2	4
Post and Telegraph	[GLEBOV (AVILOV), N.P.] Kronik, L.B. 25.11 Shotman, A.V. 29.11[i] Zalezhskii, V.N. 29.11		Rabchinskii I.V. 7.1		4
Social Welfare	[KOLLONTAI, A.M.]		EGOROV, I.G. 29.1		1
State Control	ESSEN, E.E. (td) 20.11				1
Supply	[TEODOROVICH, I.A.][j] SHLIKHTER, A.G. (td) Iakubov, A.S. Kalinin, M.I. 19.11 Manuilskii, D.Z. TSIURUPA, A.D. (d) 29.11	SHLIKHTER, A.G. 21.12	Malyshev, S.V. 20.1 MANUILSKII, D.Z. (d) 29.1	12-man board[k] 28.2	6+ 12

Trade and Industry	[NOGIN, V.P.][l]
Transport	ELIZAROV, M.T. (d)
	NEVSKII, V.I. (d) 8.11
	Shelomovich, A.P. 4.12
	NEVSKII, V.I. 10.12[m]
	Bubnov, A.S. 10.12
	Neimant, I.I. 10.12

5

[Health][n]

$$58 + 12 = 70$$

* Capitals for People's Commissars and deputies; upper and lower case for board members.
** Names in square brackets are of People's Commissars appointed on 26 October and endorsed by acclamation at the Second Congress of Soviets, and who therefore did not require personal accreditation by the CPC chairman.

(t) = temporary
(d) = deputy

a 'By the Second Congress of Soviets' (*BK* 69.1), i.e. the CEC?
b 'Senior secretary' (75.6)
c Previously served as temporary (vice) PC; in fact Trotsky retained charge until March.
d 'Dismissed for personal reasons' (8.12).
e Moved to Cheka in December.
f The PC of Justice was I.Z. Steinberg from 9/10 December, when agreement was finally reached on admission of the Left SRs to the CPC. As deputy Stuchka's job was to act as Bolshevik 'watchdog'. At this time P.P. Proshian took over the PC of Post and Telegraph from Glebov-Avilov; V.E. Trutovskii and V.A. Karelin were appointed to new posts as PCs for Local Government and 'Property of the Republic' (i.e. State Domains) respectively. Their appointments do not appear to have received written confirmation from Lenin, unless the fact has been suppressed in *BK*.
g Antonov-Ovseenko was reduced to deputy status on 11.11.
h Dybenko became an independent PC for Naval Affairs a month later: see below.
i Shotman's appointment was confirmed a second time (in error?) on 8.1.
j Teodorovich did not really act as PC and was replaced by Shlikhter 'owing to illness'.
k For full list see 284.2. A ranking order was established: Manuilskii (1), Iakubov (7), Shlikhter (8), Rozovskii (9), Rykov (10), Vladimirov (11): the only time this was done.
l Nogin was among the PCs who resigned on 4.11; he was succeeded by Shliapnikov on 19.11.
m Nevskii was elected (full!) PC of Transport by the Railwaymen's congress in lieu of Elizarov, but Lenin wanted him to remain only a deputy and the PC to be a worker, Rogov A.G. (234.2, 25-.1.) However, the latter's appointment does not seem to have gone through.
n Source: Iroshnikov, p. 161, who states that Dr A.N. Vinokurov became PC on 31 January.

(iii) *Budgeting*. It took time for the new régime to win control of the state's financial institutions. Early orders to open an account in the CPC's favour were simply ignored by the officials responsible, and not until 17 November did the resourceful Gorbunov, aided by G.L. Piatakov and N. Osinskii (V.V. Obolenskii), first State Bank commissar, manage to obtain 5 million roubles – in two sacks, which they heaved to Lenin's office; the loot was kept under close guard and stowed away in a cupboard.[54] A blend of threats and appeals to junior bank employees produced results, and on 14 December access was gained to the Petrograd private banks as well.[55]

With money rapidly losing all value, and the printing-presses adding to the inflationary pressures, there could be no question of proper budgeting. The Financial Department responded in *ad hoc* fashion to pressures from various quarters, by workers who complained that they had not been paid, by military authorities old and new, by PCs who needed funds to meet current commitments, and by soviets and other mass organisations to which the régime looked for support. A leading member of the Supreme Economic Council stated frankly in his memoirs:

> We had to take it upon ourselves to decide a whole range of questions right there in our office; in an extreme case we had to telephone and then decide within five minutes whether or not to give 3 or 5 million roubles to some factory or other which was in deep trouble.

This required, as he puts it, 'keen revolutionary judgement [*glazomer*]'.[56]

But where did the money actually go? Here *BK* is of considerable value, even though it only records *appropriations* of funds and there is no way of knowing how far these decisions were implemented. At least one may concede that the CPC did not spend much money on its members' own material needs, in this contrasting favourably with many other dictatorships. Lenin's puritanical modesty in this regard was extended by fiat to his entourage, who had to make do with workmen's wages (a maximum of 500 roubles a month, later raised to 800 roubles), and the Smolny canteen provided little else than tea and chunks of rye bread. I.P. Aleksandrov, a worker at the Anchor factory, was looking forward to a hearty meal there but all he got was bread, soup and tea; on hearing that this was also the leader's fare, 'the meal we had eaten seemed more tasty'.[57] The ascetic life-style of the new rulers commended itself strongly to the hungry and egalitarian-minded masses and was an excellent means of winning support.

The CPC did not render any account of the expenditure of the initial 5 million roubles; but half-a-million roubles went to pay the wages of postal workers[58] and the rest may have met similar charges. The CPC awarded itself another 2 million roubles on 6 March,[59] but some money must have still been left in the 'CPC fund' at that time, since two days later Lenin authorised payment from it of an identical sum to his chief agent in the Caucasus, S.G. Shaumian.[60]

It is difficult to perceive the logic behind some of the financial appropriations. There is evidence that by late February the CPC was becoming more prudent, since we hear of requests being turned down.[61] Even prior to this not every appropriation discussed in that body was automatically embodied in a signed order, which suggests that it was not acted on.[62] On 4 December it was resolved that routine financial questions should be decided by the People's Commissariat concerned together with those of Finance and State Control, and then referred to the CPC 'for the appropriate signatures'. This implied that the latter's approval could normally be taken for granted. It was, as we know, for this purpose that the Little CPC was set up. It was chaired by Lenin with Gorbunov as secretary.[63] Although *BK* does not register separately Lenin's (regular) attendance at its sessions, it records his ulterior signature of its decisions, so that we may assume that the data on those financial appropriations that he approved are reasonably complete.

When examined topically, they fall into three major categories which can be further broken down as shown in table 4. Adding in a relatively trivial sum of 41,550 roubles for cultural purposes[64] – but omitting as a historical conundrum the loan of nearly 700,000 roubles to the men of a certain customs station in suburban Petrograd! – we arrive at a grand total of over a quarter of a milliard roubles which Vladimir Ilich personally authorised to be spent, or roughly 2 million roubles a day.

So haphazard were these appropriations that we can scarcely speak of orderly financial management. Many public agencies continued to draw funds for a while from their customary sources, which the Bolsheviks did not yet control. Thus government subsidies to the arms industry continued until January 1918, in which month they amounted to 247 million roubles.[65] Only twice did Lenin make appropriations to satisfy the needs of soviets outside the two major cities:[66] they were expected to be financially self-sufficient. In both Petrograd and Moscow the old local-government agencies were allotted funds, even though they were being rapidly phased out (table 4, C2, C3). This

Table 4. *Expenditures authorised by the Chairman of the Council of People's Commissars*

Date		Recipient and purpose	Amount (roubles)	Reference
A. Military				
A 1	13.11	Main Artillery administration: soldiers' pay	670,000	55.5
A 2	18.12	Petrograd Soviet: soldiers in trenches	1,000,000	141.1
A 3	18/19.12	Miroshnichenko, A.: Cossacks fighting in southeast	49,500	142.1
A 4	22.12	Moscow military district: troops in southeast	1,000,000	151.2
A 5	23.12	Podvoiskii: volunteer detachments	10,000,000	153.6
A 6	23.12	PCNA: sailors in Don, Urals	50,000	154.4
A 7	10.1	Krylenko: Rumanian front	6,000,000	195.1
A 8	16.1	Establishment of Red Army	20,000,000	209.1
A 9	16.1	Establishment of Red Army: Red Army ' field staff' (GHQ)	1,000,000	207.1
A10	16.1	[PCMA]: invalid soldiers	3,000,000	210.3
A11	25.1	PCMA: Russian prisoners of war	3,100,000	233.1
A12	25.1	Petrograd 'Socialist detachment'	200,000	233.3, 236.5
A13	2.3	Special Cossack detachments (advance)	15,200,000	291.1
		Sub-total	61,269,500	

B. Economic and social

	Date		Amount (roubles)	Pages
B1	22.1	PC Agriculture: forest workers' pay	24,390,577	227.3
B2	19.11	PC Agriculture: forest workers' pay	7,852,985	73.1
B3	5.12	PC Post and Telegraph: workers' pay	500,000	112.1
B4	not earlier than 13.12	PC Post and Telegraph: workers' cooperatives	1,000,000	130.5
B5	5.12	PC Transport: railwaymen's pay	18,600[a]	110.4
B6	19.12	State Printing Press: workers' wages	448,000	144.6
B7	21.12	State Papers Printing Office: special grant	1,400,000[b]	262.4
B8	21.2	SEC: organisational expenses	100,000	270.1
B9	3.3	SEC: agricultural census	5,950,000	296.3
B10	27.1	SEC: advance	2,000,000	236.6
B11	14.2	Tsentrotkan [textile industry board]	100,000,000[c]	254.1
B12	14.2	PC Supply: emissary (Iakubov A.I.) to south	200,000	254.1
B13	16.2	Northern ports	10,000,000[d]	258.5
B14	25.2	Northern ports: safeguarding 'Russian property'	100,000	280.6
B15	28.2	Evacuation of Petrograd	200,000	285.1
B16	9.3	Evacuation of Petrograd	300,000	307.1
B17	22.2, 10.3	Evacuation of Petrograd	10,000,000	272.1, 307.3
		Miscellaneous	691,000	
		Sub-total	165,151,162	

[a] Preceded by a loan of 3,000 roubles: 96.1, 29.11.
[b] An incentive to the men who printed banknotes.
[c] Designed to encourage direct products exchange with the peasantry for food.
[d] Chiefly to protect military stores as the Allied landings began.

(Continued on the next page)

Table 4. (*continued*)

Date		Recipient and purpose	Amount (roubles)	Reference
C. Political and administrative				
C 1	22.11	Moscow Soviet	5,000,000	73.4
C 2	24.11	Moscow council of district dumas	20,000,000	80.6
C 3	6.12	Petrograd 'public administration'	20,000,000[a]	116.4
C 4	11.12	Petrograd Soviet Investigating Commission	10,000	125.5
C 5	23.11	CEC: despatch of agitators	30,000	79.1
C 6	25.11	CEC: agitational literature	50,000	84.2
C 7	17.12	CEC	500,000	138.5
C 8	28.2	State Papers Printing Office: postage stamps	2,100,000	285.1
C 9	5.12	PC of Internal Affairs: fares, subsistence for Constituent Assembly deputies	500,000	112.2
C 10	18.12	PC of Nationalities: Caucasus	500,000[b]	141.5
C 11	19.12	PC of Nationalities: Polish Affairs	43,000	145.3
C 12	26.1	PC of Nationalities: 1 month's advance	360,000	234.0
C 13	29.1	PC of Nationalities: subsidy for Polish newspaper	50,000	241.1
C 14	28.11	Subsidy for rural newspaper	250,000[c]	92.1
C 15	3.12	Red Guards central *kommandatura*	2,162,000	106.1
C 16	13.12	Extraordinary railwaymen's congress	30,000	131.1
C 17	15.1	Extraordinary railwaymen's congress	40,000	206.3
C 18	14/15.12	Vorovskii V.V. (Stockholm): 'struggle for peace'	2,000,000	133.4
C 19	15.2	Assistance to political émigrés from UK	1,500,000	255.5
		Sub-total	55,125,000	
		Totals: A:	61,269,500	
		B:	165,151,162	
		C:	55,125,000	
			281,545,662	

[a] By a 'guaranteed letter' covering a draft on the State Bank – the only instance of this procedure.

[b] Not included here: the 2 million roubles from CPC funds mentioned above and 10 million roubles for the Terek region (301.5, 8.3).

[a] Not included here: 200,000 roubles for the official government gazette (159.2, 4.12).

suggests that Lenin was anxious to ensure continuity of administration (for these bodies were under Bolshevik control), and that he took the autonomy of the local soviets seriously. The former consideration also explains the generous allocation for printing postage stamps (C8) or safeguarding supplies in northern ports (B12). Welfare considerations were not wholly absent (A2, A11), but played a very modest role, at least until the evacuation of civilians from Petrograd (B16).

In section B the vast allotment to Tsentrotkan (B10) skews the figures: one suspects that very little of this was taken up, at least in the short term, for organised products exchange did not get under way until the late spring of 1918 and even then was notoriously ill managed.[67] The relatively large appropriation for the agricultural census (B8) instituted by the Provisional Government may reflect Lenin's personal interest in agrarian statistics as well as the hope that these data would be used in a second (more closely supervised) land redistribution. The Bolsheviks made no bones about using state funds to promote party-political propaganda, so setting a trend that has lasted to this day. Of the PCs, Stalin seems to have been effective in obtaining his chief's authority for the expenditure of funds (C11–13), especially by comparison with Petrovskii in the People's Commissariat of Internal Affairs or Lunacharsky in the People's Commissariat of Education – not to speak of Trotsky, whose 'nil return' suggests that he took seriously his celebrated dictum that the People's Commissariat of Foreign Affairs could 'shut up shop' once it had published the secret treaties and that international revolution would do the rest.[68] In this connection the 2 million roubles allocated to Vorovskii in Stockholm (C18), flouting accepted diplomatic norms, would hardly suffice to set Europe alight.

During the first year of Bolshevik rule the party was slow to assume its 'vanguard role'. The Central Committee (CC) of the All-Russian Communist Party (Bolsheviks), the RKP(b) – as it would style itself from March 1918 – met on seventeen known occasions during the Smolny period, far less frequently than the CPC.[69] Lenin was present at all but two of these meetings (30 October, 22 February). He permitted a full and frank exchange of opinions, but as always was unwilling to submit to his opponents if they secured a majority on any important policy question. As A. Avtorkhanov points out, he overcame them by 'skilful manipulation' of party opinion and reliance on cadre elements.[70] Particularly useful in this regard was the 'Petersburg' committee, to which he turned in the early days to outbid those 'soft' comrades who sought a political compromise with the moderate socialists that would allow them a say in the government.[71] He attended three of its sessions in this connection.[72] In the second major internal party crisis he employed a modification of this tactic by agreeing to hold an Extraordinary Party Congress (6–8 March) which endorsed his peace policy at the price of a schism. So isolated was Lenin at this juncture that he had to make an unparalleled concession: to allow the Left Communists (who advocated 'revolutionary war') to remain in the CC and to express their views without fear of being disciplined.[73]

No such tolerance was shown towards the Left SRs, whose departure from the government was due as much to conflicts over internal policy issues (agriculture, justice) as to their disapproval of the Brest-Litovsk peace treaty. They had performed the service expected of them by giving the dictatorship an appearance of peasant support, but had made themselves objectionable by their continual criticism; they could be jettisoned without regret.[74]

At this time the term 'soviet democracy' still had some meaning, and the congresses of workers' and soldiers' soviets were genuine public forums. However, delegates to the Second Congress (25–26 October) dispersed as soon as they had sanctioned the formation of an all-Bolshevik government and before they could raise any awkward questions about its future relationship to the soviet movement. The CPC duly rendered an account of its actions to the Third Congress (10–18 January), where the 1,800 or so delegates were in an euphoric mood at the prospect of imminent peace; the real struggle went on behind the scenes at an associated gathering concerned with the land socialisation law.[75] Lenin was greeted with an ovation when he first appeared before the throng (11 January), and he chatted informally to delegates, as he had done in October, even visiting them in their quarters.[76] At the Fourth Congress, held from 12 to 16 March to endorse ratification of the Brest-Litovsk treaty, the tension was too acute for such private conclaves; he met several diplomats but only one known (lady) delegate.[77]

He also had a much more difficult time at the two *peasant* soviet congresses in November, where there was an awkward wrangle over his right to attend and his defence of the repressive decree outlawing the Kadets.[78] At these gatherings Lenin did not have Ia.M. Sverdlov to rely on to take the chair and pull the strings, as he did at the January and March meetings. Sverdlov, a man of considerable organisational talents, took over chairmanship of the Central Executive Committee (CEC) from the errant L.B. Kamenev on 8 November, at Lenin's express request. According to Bonch-Bruevich, Lenin gave Sverdlov some practical advice on how to manipulate the body: he was to form the Bolshevik deputies into a 'fraction' bound by party discipline, and then

> scatter the men of our fraction around the assembly, call lots of intermissions so that they can discuss all questions quietly with the non-party people and – this is the main thing – see that they literally watch over each man, how his mood [develops] . . . We need to know what each comrade is thinking.[79]

Sverdlov coped with his task so well that Lenin needed to attend fewer than half the sessions held during the second convocation (ten out of twenty-four or twenty-five).[80] In the ·third convocation he turned up only twice, on 23 and 24 February (during the Brest-Litovsk crisis). Another reason for this neglect was the CEC's physical relocation from Smolny to the Tauride Palace.[81]

At a lower level in the emerging hierarchy of soviets stood those of the municipalities, among which that of Petrograd itself, naturally, held pride of place. Lenin attended three of its sessions. The first was on 25 October, while the seizure of power was still incomplete; the second occurred five days later, to explain Bolshevik agrarian policy. On the third visit (4 December) he addressed a meeting of the soviet's workers' section, where he made a statement that present-day reformers might be tempted to display on their banners: 'There is not and cannot be a concrete plan for the organisation of economic life.'[82] Here too he took measures to ensure that the Bolsheviks controlled the soviet's praesidium at a moment when it seemed that the assembly might pass a Left SR motion.[83]

The Petrograd Soviet was the nominal master of the famous Military Revolutionary Committee (MRC) which engineered the October coup. Lenin attended its meetings four times in the two weeks that followed,[84] but then phased out this troublesome body, a potential rival to the Sovnarkom. Control over local soviets was left to others, notably the 'commissars' sent out by a whole range of agencies in Petrograd and at the front. It was the same story with regard to Lenin's relations with pre-Bolshevik executive institutions. On 25 November he discussed with Petrovskii, the PC of Internal Affairs, measures to eliminate the Ruling Senate and the Holy Synod,[85] but otherwise limited himself to signing decrees that formalised action taken by his lieutenants.

When we turn to the former legislative bodies, the scoreboard reads: the State Duma 1, the zemstvos 2, the municipal dumas 5 – but the Constituent Assembly 54! Lenin seems to have realised the gravity of the step he was determined to take in dissolving the body which, for all its faults, embodied the aspirations of democrats in all social classes (workers included). There is no need to rehearse here the arguments he used to justify the move, which more than any other plunged Russia into the horrors of civil war, nor the tactical measures which the Bolsheviks adopted to isolate, discredit and intimidate the deputies.[86]

One point that emerges from *BK* is the trouble Lenin took to camouflage his intentions by treating the elections with apparent seriousness. His name was first on the ballot in five electoral districts, of which he chose that of the Baltic Fleet; regularising his status involved him in five recorded actions.[87] Was it the residual lawyer in him that made him observe such formalities? He sent messages clarifying the complicated electoral procedure,[88] and arranged for impoverished deputies to obtain subsidised accommodation and rail travel[89] – while simultaneously making preparations to send them packing! Objections to dissolution were expressed by a delegation from Luga, by the Black Sea Fleet's 'regional commission', and by leading activists like Ludmilla Stal at Kronstadt.[90] They were ignored. When in the hall, Lenin grew 'deathly pale' at the uproar and ordered some sailors who were pointing rifles at Chernov to be restrained.[91] A bloodbath would not have served Bolshevik purposes, which could be much better accomplished by pseudo-legal measures. Afterwards he never expressed any contrition or doubt as to the correctness of dissolution, which cost the lives of several persons who attempted to demonstrate in the Assembly's favour.[92] He ordered an inquiry, but the results were hushed up.[93]

Simultaneously another inquiry got under way into the murder, by 'anarchist' (maximalist) sailors, of two prominent Kadet politicians who had been jailed and, on account of their poor health, removed to hospital.[94] Lenin took this incident more seriously, bombarding the investigators with requests for information (nine actions from 7 to 31 January!) – but in the end the case fizzled out since the perpetrators could not be found.[95]

In general the Bolshevik chief gave little attention to the elimination from public life of the liberal and socialist parties. This was a matter best left to subordinates. He was more concerned with limiting these parties' access to the media: it was no coincidence that he had spent most of his life in journalism. On 28 October he signed a decree

endorsing the closure by the MRC of about twenty publications.[96] The
adverse reaction – it led to the resignation of several of his aides –
forced him to retreat and to apply less abrasive tactics for a while. But
on 21 November he moved to replace a paper serving peasant readers
with a government-subsidised one; in mid December he ordered one
newspaper's staff to be dismissed and another's printing-press to be
requisitioned; and at the end of January *Ekho* was suppressed outright
for reporting (truthfully!) that, in response to Trotsky's 'neither war
nor peace' order, Krylenko had ordered the army to demobilise; this
was treated as revelation of a military secret.[97] On 14 March Lenin
told the Fourth Congress of Soviets that unfortunately some hostile
papers were still appearing, but 'we shall close them all'.[98] Meanwhile,
without his express order, other newspapers had been harassed by the
MRC and the Petrograd Soviet's 'Press Commissariat', under A.E.
Minkin and N.N. Kuzmln, whose aim was to apply 'merciless and
consequential pressure on the [non-Bolshevik] press by fines, closures
and arrests'.[99] The editors resisted by changing titles, borrowing
presses, and other ruses they had learned under the Tsars – but to no
avail.

Destroying the old order took up less of the leader's time than building
the new one. This necessitated creating a state security apparatus that
could cow the people into submission, by terroristic means where these
were called for. The forty-five actions he took in this domain which
have been recorded in *BK* (the list is deficient in some particulars, as
we shall see) began inconspicuously with instructions of 27 October to
the sentries outside his office, followed by a directive to check on the
building's security arrangements, which were entrusted as we know
mainly to sailors and Lettish riflemen.[100] Another early concern was to
bring to heel the activists in the MRC and elsewhere who were engaging in indiscriminate violence against 'class enemies', and to concentrate such functions in Dzerzhinskii's Cheka.[101]

As early as 6 November Lenin asked Gorbunov to look into the
composition of the so-called Investigation Commission of the
Petrograd Soviet, headed by P.A. Krasikov.[102] Krasikov was an old
comrade of Lenin's whose machinations had played an important role
in the 1903 schism of the party.[103] He is characterised by Steinberg, the
Left SR and PC of Justice, as a 'Balalaikin' with wildly flowing hair
and a brutal way of expressing himself.[104] Still more unsavoury was his
comrade M.Iu. Kozlovskii (Kozlowski), whom he describes as *ein
verbissener und giftiger Winkeladvokat*. Kozlovskii's role in channelling

German funds to the Bolsheviks in 1917 aroused the concern even of some members of the party's Central Committee, which in September set up a commission to look into the allegations against him.[105]

As leading lights on the Investigating Commission, the two men made a name for themselves in Petrograd by getting posses of Red Guards to carry out arbitrary searches, arrests and confiscations of property – some of which they kept for themselves or traded. Steinberg set out to turn the agency into a regular procuracy organ that would prepare cases for hearing before a revolutionary tribunal. Some of the materials he sent it had to do with a notorious miscarriage of justice in 1915 in which a Jew named Freinat (whose brother turned to Steinberg for aid) had been put to death.[106] The commissioners had more topical matters to deal with, and may have harboured anti-semitic prejudices that helped to poison their relations with Steinberg. He paid an unsolicited visit to their headquarters. Sacks of flour and sugar were being loaded on to a truck, apparently destined for the black market. He demanded to see the files containing the evidence against A.I. Shingarev – the Provisional Government minister who would shortly thereafter be murdered – and the Right SR leader N.D. Avksentev, who were confined in the Peter and Paul fortress. The files were empty. 'We don't need evidence', said Kozlovskii, 'their counter-revolutionary deeds are common knowledge.' Steinberg left 'with shame and anger in [his] heart'.

A few days later, told that the commissioners were taking bribes for the release of prisoners, he went straight to Lenin[107] and secured his approval for an investigation of the investigators. Lenin had their papers placed under seal, but was clearly unhappy about this 'counter-commission'.[108] No sooner had it been set up (11 January) than Kozlovskii went to Lenin to put his case.[109] Three days later Lenin warned Steinberg in the CPC not to listen to gossip and suggested submitting all the materials to a 'revision commission' of the CPC staff – or in other words, to bury the matter.[110] N.V. Krylenko, an ex law student who would soon swap his military job for that of chief of the 'special courts' section of the Justice commissariat, seems to have brought his influence to bear in Kozlovskii's favour, and by 17/18 January Lenin again reprimanded Steinberg in public. Shreider, Steinberg's deputy, a Left SR and Jewish like his chief, resigned his post in protest.[111]

For some reason the pendulum then swung the other way, for on 21 January the CPC resolved to add two more members, one from each party, to the commission and urged it to speed its inquiries.[112] Ten days later Steinberg secured a CPC decision delimiting the functions of the Cheka and the Petrograd Soviet's Investigating Commission; the People's Commissariat of Justice was to have the right to nominate candidates for membership in the latter.[113] But this was of little use to Steinberg unless he could produce hard evidence of Kozlovskii's wrongdoing, but this would have taken longer than the two weeks he had been accorded for the purpose. Thus when on 26 February the CPC met to settle the matter the chips were stacked against him. Lenin absented himself from this part of the proceedings – perhaps deliberately – leaving Trotsky in the chair. 'Now the floodwaters poured upon our heads.' He gave the floor to Krasikov and Kozlovskii, who 'with tearful voices . . . presented themselves as sacrificial lambs for Bolshevism'. Trotsky indignantly asked why Steinberg had instituted proceedings without evidence, to which he replied with bravado that if he had had evidence he would simply have arrested the wrongdoers on the spot. By eleven votes to five the CPC endorsed Trotsky's motion exonerating the accused and condemning the counter-investigation as 'part of the general campaign of lies and slander unleashed by the bourgeoisie against the Soviet government'.[114] Kozlovskii and his colleagues were to be reinstated.

Yet this was not quite the end of the matter. Zinoviev, boss of the Petrograd Soviet, did not trust Kozlovskii – or Trotsky, for that matter – and refused to readmit them. With his encouragement the investigators soon came up with a long list of abuses, including physical maltreatment of prisoners, by agents of Kozlovskii's organisation and Chekists. When this came before the CPC, 'Lenin and all the others were sombre and silent.'[115] However, no Bolshevik leader would openly consider, still less repudiate, the antisemitic overtones of the affair. Nor did they wish to curb the Cheka's powers, least of all when the régime's security was gravely imperilled. Nevertheless, this first (largely Jewish) effort to impose some quasi-judicial check on the terror apparatus deserves to be recorded. Although these fellow-travellers did not stand for the rule of law, they appreciated the dangers latent in the Leninist position.[116]

A closely related matter was the arbitrary detention of political opponents. Lenin's view of such matters is well brought out by one memoirist, the sailor S.N. Baranov, who overheard Lenin conversing with the commandant of the Peter and Paul fortress (presumably G.I. Blagonravov). Referring to the prisoners held there, Lenin allegedly said:

What are they complaining about? They are ordinary prison

25. Lev Davidovich Trotsky.

regulations which I remember well; they helped to frame them, so tell them that I have sent their statement on where it should go but we cannot alter the general prison régime.[117]

Study of the CPC minutes may tell us how often he took this line and how often he acted to ease the prisoners' lot. From *BK* we know that he intervened four times in the CPC on such matters: relocating prisoners to more favourable conditions; improving food supplies; and permitting communications with relatives;[118] approving four men's release.[119]

But he refused to permit the release of several mine-owners held in Kharkov or the officer Rutkovskii,[120] and one of his first acts on arriving in Moscow was to write to M.F. Andreeva *refusing* to overrule subordinate agencies so that prisoners might receive visitors.[121] He displayed an ambivalence on this point which, as we have shown elsewhere,[122] would continue throughout the Civil War.

Walter Laqueur has recently remarked that 'not much new can be said on Lenin and Leninism; few stones have been left unturned in this particular field of study'.[123] Raising up this particular boulder reveals no great surprises. Lenin was hyperactive, hard-working, politically astute, unafraid of responsibility, and accessible to supporters, if not to the general public. He did not rule as a personal dictator but through a junta or coterie of men and women who accepted his authority and cooperated eagerly, if not always efficiently, in putting his will into practice. If they disagreed, they could leave Smolny without suffering anything more unpleasant than verbal criticism, and if they chose to return, on Lenin's conditions, they would be made welcome. But the institutional basis of the new order was weak; there were no checks to the exercise of arbitrary power by the leader or those who modelled their conduct on his. Lenin's intransigent spirit was clearly expressed in the resolute tone of CPC instructions. (They did not need the artificial products of the Lenin cult that would develop later.) Lenin's emphasis on the demonstrative nature of these orders applied equally to his activity as a whole: his conversations with plebeian visitors, for example, had an obvious pedagogic intent, as did his speeches and writings.

Nevertheless precisely this didactic approach to government blinded Vladimir Ilich to the dangers latent in the institutional framework he was creating as well as in the political culture that sustained it. Put succinctly, the contemptuous attitude he displayed towards basic human rights and freedoms (or national rights, for that matter) encouraged the Bolshevik cadres to act ruthlessly and violently against real or presumed adversaries, whether this was necessary or not. They were led to assume that any natural obstacles they encountered must be the result of counter-revolutionary scheming, and so to seek out scapegoats whom they could punish. Such punitive actions could then be rationalised as 'objectively necessary' or as means of preventing others from being tempted to side with the victims – in short, as 'prophylactic terror'. Within months of leaving Smolny Bolshevik zealots would be shooting innocent hostages out of hand.

Granted, this descent to barbarism was in part an inevitable concomitant of civil war conditions; yet civil war was a predictable consequence of the seizure of power, a risk which the Bolsheviks knowingly
ran. While it would be unfair to blame their leader for all the excesses
perpetrated by his desperate and fanatical followers, it is also true that
Lenin openly incited such actions. To Blagonravov and Bonch-
Bruevich he wrote on 8 December: 'The arrests to be carried out as
comrade Peters [of the Cheka] directs are of exceptionally great
importance and must be pushed through with maximum energy.[124] A
month or so later he publicly urged a mass audience to *shoot* presumed
enemies. The Petrograd workers, he declared, were themselves to
blame if they were hungry:

> Until we apply terror – shooting on the spot – against speculators,
> nothing will come of it. If the [search] detachments consist of men
> chosen at random, who aren't in collusion with each other, they
> won't pillage. Anyway, looters must also be dealt with firmly, by
> shooting on the spot.[125]

This was probably the first occasion in the twentieth century when the
head of a European government issued such a blood-curdling licence
to kill.

Both the institutional structure of the Soviet régime and its essentially repressive character were clearly formulated during the Smolny
period. Each would develop a life of its own and lead to pernicious
results that Lenin did not anticipate and, though he had second
thoughts before he died, was powerless to check. Had Stalin not mum-
mified his body, one might have said of Lenin, as Mark Antony said of
Julius Caesar,

> The evil that men do lives after them,
> The good is oft interred with their bones.

NOTES

1 *Vladimir Ilich Lenin: biograficheskaia khronika*, ed. G.N. Golikov (Moscow,
  1970–82), 12 vols. The copious memoir literature, which underwent
  extensive 'rewriting' in the Stalinist era and later, is the subject of a
  separate forthcoming study. For analysis of another source, see my
  'Lenin's Correspondence as a Historical Source', in B. Eissenstat (ed.),
  Lenin and Leninism: State, Law and Society (Lexington, 1971), pp. 245–68, to
  be reprinted in *Power and the People: Essays on Russian History* (Irvine,
  1989).

2 In his memoirs Trotsky states: 'I was throughout in the closest uninter-
rupted collaboration with Lenin' and that they would consult each other
several times a day. There is no mention of these meetings in *BK*, and
Trotsky's role at Brest-Litovsk is distorted: 171.4, 1.1; 172.1, 1/2.1; 175.5,
3.1. (References to *BK* will be given with page and item no. (from top of
page), followed by the date.) An informal conference with Stalin, Trotsky
and Lunacharsky is referred to with personal names replaced by job
titles: 94.2, 29.11. Source references exclude relevant works critical of the
Bolsheviks, such as the memoirs of I.N. Steinberg, the Left SR People's
Commissar (PC) of Justice, which were published in the West.

3 *BK* has had Western emulators: G. and H. Weber, *Lenin: Life and Works*,
ed. and trans. M. McCauley (Basingstoke, 1983); for the Smolny period
see pp. 140–7. A comparable compilation of Adolf Hitler's actions after
the *Machtübernahme* (M. Hauner, *Hitler: A Chronology of his Life and Times*,
New York, 1983) records only 60 items for the first 124 days, the
equivalent of Lenin's Smolny period.

4 262.4, 264.1, 18.2.

5 128.4, 12.12; 151.4, 22.12; 198.6, 12; 214.3, 18.1; 218.1, 19.1, etc.

6 90.3, not later than 27.11; 99.1, late 11.

7 217.2, 19.1; 224.2, 21.1; 244.2, 30.1; 259.3, 27.2; cf. V.I. Lenin, *Polnoe
sobranie sochinenii* (hereafter *PSS*), vol. L, pp. 17–18, 34–5, 40.

8 N. Tumarkin, *Lenin Lives! The Lenin Cult in Soviet Russia* (Cambridge,
Mass. and London, 1983), p. 42.

9 M.P. Iroshnikov, *Sozdanie sovetskogo tsentralnogo gosudarstvennogo apparata:
SNK i narodnye komissariaty, oktiabr 1917–ianvar 1918* (Moscow and Leningrad, 1966), p. 80 (December 1917).

10 S.N. Kosobokov, 'U apparata – Lenin', *Voprosy istorii KPSS* no. 10
(1985), 27.

11 20.5, 31.10; 268.1, 20.2 (Moscow); 134.4, 15.12; 198.4, 12.1 (Kharkov);
147.8, 20.12; 176.4, 4.1 (Ukraine).

12 19.6.

13 264.1, 19.2; 279.4, 24/5.2; R.K. Debo, *Revolution and Survival: The Foreign
Policy of Soviet Russia, 1917–1918* (Toronto, 1979), pp. 129, 144.

14 T.H. Rigby, *Lenin's Government: Sovnarkom, 1917–1922* (London, 1979), p.
108.

15 Ibid., p. 34.

16 Iroshnikov, *Sozdanie*, p. 100; for the year 1917–18 E.B. Genkina, *Protokoly
Sovnarkoma RSFSR kak istoricheskii istochnik dlia izucheniia gosudarstvennoi deiatelnosti V.I. Lenina* (Moscow, 1982), p. 15; cf. also E.V. Klopov, *Lenin v
Smolnom: gosudarstvennaia deiatelnost V.I. Lenina v pervye mesiatsy Sovetskoi
vlasti, oktiabr 1917–mart 1918* (Moscow, 1965), pp. 59–60.

17 Rigby, *Lenin's Government*, p. 36; he points out that this body, popularly
known as the 'vermicelli commission', was a re-creation of a Tsarist
institution. It met only eight times between 9 January and 2 March:
Genkina, *Protokoly*, p. 161n.

18 181.4.

19 Genkina, *Protokoly*, p. 43.

20 E.g., 116.9, 7.12.

21 128.8, 12/13.12, on nationalisation of private banks; 270.3, 21.2, on defence of Petrograd.

22 Iroshnikov, *Sozdanie*, p. 120.

23 Genkina, *Protokoly*, p. 124. The total number of CPC decrees is hard to establish. Genkina puts the number of *clauses* in CPC decrees (including those issued jointly with the Central Executive Committee (CEC)) at 479: table 4, p. 121. In addition many orders were issued by other central bodies; these altogether had a total of 1,033 clauses. (This does not take into account *departmental* orders.) By 1924 Lenin had personally written or amended 680 decrees and signed over 3,000, or three-quarters of the total: ibid., p. 122. I.I. Mints calculates that over 250 'acts-decrees', instructions and ordinances were issued by 10 January 1918, and offers a breakdown by topic (*Istoriia velikogo oktiabria*, vol. III (1973), p. 739).

24 Based largely on Genkina, who does not, however, make such a differentiation. For the second practice: Gorbunov, in M.D. Orakhelashvili (ed.), *Lenin v pervye mesiatsy Sovetskoi vlasti: sbornik statei i vospominanii* (Moscow, 1933), p. 107; for the third practice, see e.g. 154.4, 23.12.

25 N.S. and N.S. Chervinskaia (comps.), ed. V.I. Startsev, *Zhizn v borbe: po vospominaniiam sovremennikov o V.I. Lenine (peterburgsko-petrogradskii period)* (Leningrad, 1975), p. 444.

26 *Voprosy istorii KPSS*, no. 10 (1987), 29–34 (continued in subsequent issues).

27 A.[V.] Shotman, 'Lenin nakanune Oktiabria', in L.B. Kamenev (ed.), *O Lenine: sbornik vospominanii* (Leningrad, 1925), vol. I, p. 118.

28 L.D. Trotsky, *Moia zhizn*, vol. II (Berlin, 1930), p. 65.

29 'These decrees, usually drafted and always signed by Lenin . . ., gave a spurious impression of energy and determination but did little to create order in the existing chaos': V. Broido, *Lenin and the Mensheviks: The Persecution of Socialists under Bolshevism* (Boulder, 1987), p. 20.

30 A.G. Shliapnikov, 'K oktiabriu', *Proletarskaia revoliutsiia* 9 (1922), 35.

31 'Doklad o rabote v derevne' (23 March 1919), *PSS*, vol. XXXVIII, p. 198.

32 Bonch-Bruevich, *Na boevykh postakh fevralskoi i oktiabrskoi revoliutsii*, 2nd edn (Moscow, 1931), p. 131; Orakhelashvili (ed.), *Lenin*, p. 104.

33 *Modern Encyclopaedia of Russia and the Soviet Union* (hereafter *MERSH*), vol. XIII, p. 41. He died in a Stalinist prison in 1944.

34 132.5, 14.12.

35 *Lenin – vozhd Oktiabria: vospominaniia petrogradskikh rabochikh* (Leningrad, 1956), p. 271.

36 Koksharova, in Chervinskaia, *Zhizn*, pp. 426–8.

37 *Lenin – vozhd Oktiabria*, p. 289.

38 129.2, not later than 13.12.

39 222.1, 20.1.

40 Iroshnikov, *Sozdanie*, pp. 69, 76, 91. Klopov (*Lenin v Smolnom*, p. 77) puts the figure at 48 for the end of 1917, including typists, accountants and canteen workers – but excluding guards and communications workers? The figure for the last-named group is put at 45 (12 telephonists, 20 telegraphists and 13 radio operators), as early as late October (Kosobokov, 'U apparata – Lenin', p. 23).

41 106.2, 3.12. Not to be confused with the Petrograd Soviet's Press *Commissariat*, under A.E. Minkin and N.N. Kuzmin, which closed down opposition papers and supervised the Press Tribunal (see below); Iroshnikov, *Sozdanie*, p. 85; *Novyi luch*, 30 January, 19, 20, 22 February.

42 111.3, 5.12.

43 116.5, 7.12.

44 247.5, 31.1: P.A. Koboev to Orenburg; 292.4, 3.3; N.G. Poletaev and his son to southern Russia.

45 A. Lomov, 'V dni buri i natiska', *Proletarskaia revoliutsiia* 69 (1927), 172.

46 S.[S.] Pestkovskii, 'Ob oktiabrskikh dniakh v Pitere', *Proletarskaia revoliutsiia* 9 (1922), 100.

47 G.I. Petrovskii, *Velikoe nachalo: vospominaniia starogo bolshevika* (Moscow, 1957), p. 20.

48 A.V. Lunacharsky, 'Smolnyi v velikuiu noch' [1925], reprinted in Orakhelashvili (ed.), *Lenin*, p. 51.

49 40.4, not later than 8.11; 40.6, 8.11.

50 183.3, 6.1.

51 Rigby, *Lenin's Government*, pp. 3–5.

52 196.1, not earlier than 10.1.

53 56.2, 13.11.

54 Gorbunov, 'Kak sozdavalsia', p. 109.

55 I.F. Gindin, *Kak bolsheviki zakhvatili Gosudarstvennyi Bank* (Moscow, 1961); Bonch-Bruevich, *Na boevykh postakh*, pp. 197–207; Rigby, *Lenin's Government*, pp. 45–6; J.L.H. Keep (ed.), *The Debate on Soviet Power: Minutes of the All-Russian Central Executive of Soviets: October 1917–January 1918* (Oxford, 1979), pp. 318ff., 376–8.

56 Gorbunov, 'Kak sozdavalsia', p. 116.

57 *Lenin–vozhd Oktiabria*, p. 299.

58 73.1, 19.11.

59 298.5.

60 301.5, 8.3.

61 282.1, 26.2; 285.1, 28.2.

62 E.g., $11\frac{1}{2}$ million roubles to the People's Commissariat of Education for an increase in teachers' pay (161.5, 30.12), 12 million roubles to the People's Commissariat of Agriculture for firewood (135.6, 15.12), 125,000 roubles for naval college teachers (74.2, 20.11), 450,000 roubles

for flood relief in the Ukraine (84.2, 25.11). On 19 December Lenin held up 'publication' of (i.e. action on?) a 200-million-rouble appropriation to cover loans concluded by the old local government agencies.

63 142.2, 18/19.12; 154.4, 23.12.

64 269.5, 21.2; 307.3, 10.3.

65 S.A. Somov, 'Poslednaia stranitsa istorii Osobogo soveshchaniia po oborone, oktiabr 1917–fevral 1918 gg.', *Istoricheskie zapiski* 90 (1972), 92–3; P. Scheibert, *Lenin an der Macht* (Weinheim, 1984), p. 193. Lenin all but abolished the naval shipbuilding programme, reducing the appropriation to a derisory sum: 232.1, 24.1.

66 They were Vologda (an instruction transmitted through Stalin, not an appropriation: 241.2, 29.1) and Soltsy in Pskov province (25,000 roubles; 258.5, 16.2) – the latter for 'urgent needs of the population', presumably protection against the German threat.

67 By the summer, appropriations had reached 1 milliard roubles, but the amount of cloth available did not exceed 400 million arshins, which 'had to be distributed prudently': M.I. Davydov, 'Gosudarstvennyi obmen mezhdu gorodom i derevnei v 1918–1921 gg.', *Istoricheskie zapiski* 108 (1982), 37–8.

68 Pestkovskii, 'Ob oktiabrskikh dniakh', p. 49. Conceivably Trotsky's appropriations may have been suppressed in *BK*.

69 *The Bolsheviks and the October Revolution*, a translation by A. Bone of the minutes of the CC, first published in 1928 and republished in 1958 (*Protokoly TsK*). No minutes were kept of sessions between 1 and 8 November, nor of those on 14 November or 21 January, but Lenin's presence at the latter is attested by *BK* (59.3, 225.3).

70 A. Avtorkhanov, *Proiskhozhdenie partokratii*, vol. 1: *TsK i Lenin* (Frankfurt, 1973), p. 430.

71 Keep (ed.), *The Debate on Soviet Power*, pp. 275–81, 288–90, 308f.

72 21.1, 31.10; 25.5, 1.11; 32.2, 4.11 (extended); plus another on 28.10 (11.3) concerned with the city's defences.

73 Avtorkhanov, *Proiskhozhdenie*, p. 499; R.V. Daniels, *Conscience of the Revolution: Communist Opposition in Soviet Russia* (Cambridge, Mass., 1960), pp. 76–7.

74 On the troubled relationship between the two parties, see the classic study by O.H. Radkey, *The Sickle under the Hammer: The Russian Socialist Revolutionaries in the Early Months of Soviet Rule* (New York, 1963); more recently, J.L.H. Keep, *The Russian Revolution: a Study in Mass Mobilization* (London, 1976), pp. 314–16, 320–1, 444–8.

75 Keep, *Russian Revolution*, pp. 333–8, 444–8; 194.2, 215.1.

76 8.1, 9.1, 27.10; 196.5, 11.1; 197.3, 11/12.1; 215.1, 18.1.

77 S.I. Gopner from Ekaterinoslav; 321.5, 16.3.

78 53.1, 12.11 (extraordinary congress); 104.3, 2/3.12 (regular congress).

The peasant soviets merged with those of workers and soldiers at the Third Congress.

79 Bonch-Bruevich, *Na boevykh postakh*, p. 169; cf. C. Duval, 'I.M. Sverdlov, Founder of the Bolshevik Party Machine', in R.C. Elwood (ed.), *Reconsiderations on the Russian Revolution* (Columbus, 1976), pp. 223–4.

80 27.10; 4/5.11; 8.11; 10.11; 14.11; 21/22.11; 23.11; 1.12; 14.12; 6/7.1. In *The Debate on Soviet Power* I published in translation the minutes of the twenty-four sessions; the existence of a twenty-fifth (9 January), reported solely in the non-Bolshevik newspaper *Novaia zhizn* of 11 January and concerned with preparations for the Third Congress of Soviets, has been pointed out recently by N.N. Smirnov in *Vspomogatelnye istoricheskie distsipliny* 17 (1985), 261–9, but he makes no mention of the English edition. Will the Soviet authorities perhaps now publish the full verbatim record, to replace the makeshift and defective edition of 1918?! Such a step has been foreshadowed: *Voprosy istorii*, no. 10 (1987), p. 36.

81 223.2, 20/21.1; 256.1, 15.2; 262.4, 18/19.2; Lenin went to the Palace a third time on 18/19 February (263.1), but characteristically only to consult privately with Sverdlov on how the CEC should deal with the crisis caused by the German offensive.

82 1.3, 25.10; 19.5, 30.10; 108.5, 4.12; *PSS*, vol. xxxv, p. 147.

83 131.2, not later than 13.12.

84 4.2, 26.10; 12.2, 28.10; 28.3, 3.11; 42.2, 8/9.11.

85 86.2.

86 J. Bunyan and H.H. Fisher, *The Bolshevik Revolution: Documents and Materials* (Stanford, 1934), pp. 338–99; Scheibert, *Lenin*, pp. 16–22; Bonch-Bruevich, 'Sozyv Uchreditelnogo sobraniia', *Na boevykh postakh*, pp. 227–53 (the 1965 edition is expurgated!); W.-A. Kropat, 'Lenin und die Konstituierende Versammlung in Russland', *Jahrbücher für Geschichte Osteuropas* 5 (1957), 488–98; B. Williams, 'The All-Russian Constituent Assembly, January 5/18 1918', *Parliaments, Estates and Representation* 5, no. 2 (1985), 119–29.

87 53.2, 12.11; 78.2, 3, 22.11; 90.2, 27/28.11; 91.5, 28.11; 98.4, 5, 30.11; cf. M.[G.] Fleer, 'Izbranie V.I. Lenina v Uchreditelnoe Sobranie', *Krasnaia letopis*, 16 (1926), 21–2.

88 35.5, 5.11; 53.3, 12.11; 55.2, 13.11; 98.3, 30.11.

89 112.2, 5.12.

90 97.4, 30.11; 178.1, 4.1; 184, 6.1; *Novaia zhizn* (7 January 1918).

91 Bonch-Bruevich, *Na boevykh postakh*, pp. 248–9.

92 179.1, 5.1.

93 Scheibert, *Lenin*, p. 19; Keep, *Debate*, pp. 417–19, 432.

94 Bunyan and Fisher, *Bolshevik Revolution*, pp. 386–7; L.B. Schapiro, *Origin of the Communist Autocracy: Political Opposition in the Soviet State, First Phase, 1917–1922* (London, 1955), p. 298; I.N. Steinberg, *Als ich Volkskommissar*

war: Episoden aus der russischen Oktoberrevolution (Munich, 1929), pp. 139–63; I.N. Steinberg, *In the Workshop of the Revolution* (London, 1955), pp. 74–83 (where the culprits are named). The commission's report is said to have been published in *Katorga i ssylka* no. 2 (1934), but post-1931 issues of this journal are a bibliographical rarity.

95 186–90 *passim*, 250.4; cf. *PSS*, vol. L, p. 26.

96 11.5, 28.10; on this see A.I. Sergeev, 'Borba Kommunisticheskoi partii protiv kontr-revoliutsionnoi pressy v pervye mesiatsy Sovetskoi vlasti', in E.F. Erykalov *et al.* (eds.), *Mezhdunarodnoe znachenie istoricheskogo opyta bolshevistskoi partii v Oktiabrskoi revoliutsii* (Leningrad, 1977); cf. Schapiro, *Origin*, p. 173; Scheibert, *Lenin*, pp. 328–31.

97 75.5, 21.11; 130.2, 3, 13.12; 249.2, 31.1.

98 *PSS*, vol. XXXVI, p. 100; Sergeev, 'Borba', p. 182.

99 Sergeev, 'Borba', p. 180.

100 E.F. Koksharova, in Chervinskaia, *Zhizn*, pp. 416–17; 26.2, 1/2.1; cf. 137.1, mid 12.

101 15.3, 29.10; 115.2, 6.12; for the formation of the Cheka see G. Leggett, *The Cheka: Lenin's Political Police* (Oxford, 1981), pp. 1–27.

102 35.2, 6.11. Its other members were P.I. Stuchka, B.D. Mandelbaum and L.N. Alekseevskii: I.I. Mints, *Istoriia velikoi oktiabrskoi revoliutsii*, vol. III, p. 752.

103 I. Getzler, *Martov: A Political Biography of a Russian Social Democrat* (Melbourne, 1967), pp. 73–80. For his authorised autobiography see *Deiateli SSSR i Oktiabrskoi revoliutsii: avtobiografii* (Leningrad, 1925(?), reprinted Ann Arbor, 1964), vol. I, pp. 218–26.

104 Steinberg, *Volkskommissar*, pp. 123–4.

105 Lenin intervened energetically on his and Fuerstenberg (Hanecki)'s behalf. On the question of German funds see M. Futrell, *Northern Underground* (London, 1963), esp. pp. 174–5, 197, and on Kozlovskii, pp. 177–8, 220; Z.A.B. Zeman, *Germany and the Revolution in Russia* (London, 1957).

106 Steinberg, *Volkskommissar*, p. 125. On the 'Miasoedov affair' see P.J. Rollins in *MERSH*, vol. XXII, pp. 34–6; cf. also G. Katkov, *Russia 1917: the February Revolution* (London, 1967), pp. 119–32. Miasoedov had Jewish connections. One of those responsible for the accused's fate was none other than General Bonch-Bruevich, whom the Bolsheviks were recruiting to their service, but it is not clear whether this affected the outcome.

107 Steinberg, *Volkskommissar*, p. 128. This encounter is not listed in *BK*, which records only that Lenin had the CPC debate the matter (177.6, 4.1). He saw Steinberg on 7 January to discuss the Shingarev and Kokoshkin murders (186.3).

108 200.5, 13.1.

109 197.1, 4, 11.1; Steinberg, *Volkskommissar*, p. 131.

110 204.2, 14/15.1; *PSS*, vol. LIV, p. 693; G.A. Belov (ed.), *Iz istorii VChK, 1917–1922: sbornik dokumentov* (Moscow, 1958), p. 90.

111 213.6, 17/18.1. Shreider's appointment dated only from 7 January.

112 226.1; *PSS*, vol. LIV, pp. 388, 694; Belov, *Iz istorii*, p. 91.

113 249.2; *PSS*, vol. LIV, p. 391.

114 Steinberg, *Volkskommissar*, pp. 135–6, reproduced in part in *PSS*, vol. LIV, p. 693, where Trotsky's role is of course suppressed.

115 Steinberg, *Volkskommissar*, pp. 136–7.

116 The conflict between the PC of Justice and the Cheka is considered by Leggett, *Cheka*, pp. 45–9, 52; but he does not use *BK*.

117 Chervinskaia, *Zhizn*, p. 441. Conditions in the Kresty prison at this time were reported to be good. F.V. Vinberg, *V plenu u obezian* (Kiev, 1918).

118 173.5, 2.1; 174.1, 2.1; 228, 23.1; cf. *PSS*, vol. LIV, p. 388.

119 A.I. Konovalov and S.N. Tretiakov (239, 29.1); M.F. Tereshchenko and N.M. Kishkin (267.2, 20.2).

120 253.1, 14.2; cf. 235.6, 26/27.1. Rutkovskii was released by the Left SR Chekist, P.A. Aleksandrovich. Steinberg, *Workshop*, pp. 68ff.

121 *PSS*, vol. L, p. 49; 311.2, 11.3.

122 Keep, 'Lenin's Correspondence', p. 261.

123 W. Laqueur, *The Fate of the Revolution: Interpretations of Soviet History from 1917 to the Present*, revised edn (London, 1987), p. 222.

124 *PSS*, vol. L, p. 18.

125 *PSS*, vol. XXXV, p. 311 (14 January).

Part 5

**1917 IN RETROSPECT:
HISTORIOGRAPHY AND THEORY**

16

IAKOVLEV'S QUESTION, OR THE HISTORIOGRAPHY OF THE PROBLEM OF SPONTANEITY AND LEADERSHIP IN THE RUSSIAN REVOLUTION OF FEBRUARY 1917

D.A. LONGLEY

In his last book, Leonard Schapiro briefly compares George Katkov's and Tsuyoshi Hasegawa's work on the February revolution:

> Very different in treatment, these two books provide as complete a picture of the revolutionary days of February and March 1917 as we are likely to get. Katkov's is the more dramatic and imaginative, with much hitherto unknown material; Hasegawa's is a more factual and detailed analysis of events. His access to Soviet archives, however, does not seem to have contributed much new information.[1]

At first sight, he is too generous to Katkov, whose darker obsessions have rightly given offence to many scholars, and too harsh on Hasegawa, whose 600-page book is the result of more than a decade's careful scholarship and access to Soviet archives unrivalled among Western scholars, as well as access to those of the Hoover Institution and of the London School of Economics.[2]

This chapter will argue that Schapiro's judgement is essentially just, that although Hasegawa's book is more subtle than its Soviet equivalents (he does, after all, examine the activities of parties other than the Bolsheviks), and produces a wealth of new detail to give us 'as complete a picture . . . as we are likely to get' of the events it portrays, it is nonetheless the wrong, or at least a misleading, picture; that the reason for this is that Hasegawa questions the detail but not the composition, focus and general outlines of the currently accepted picture of the February revolution, a picture which evolved, not as the result of dispassionate scholarship, but from the struggle for power in the USSR in the 1920s; that Katkov's approach, which attempted to shift the focus of our attention and tackle some of the questions left unanswered by the current consensus, is, despite the unacceptable prejudices of the man himself and the unsatisfactory nature of his answers, ultimately the one which will lead to a greater understanding of the events of February 1917; and that the first stage in this process is to examine the way in which the current picture was formed and in particular what was excluded from it for political reasons.

The first Soviet historians of the revolution on the whole showed no interest in the question of leadership in February 1917. Those who did, usually referred to it obliquely, and took it for granted that the revolution was spontaneous.[3] This should not surprise us, since they were merely thereby following the earliest accounts of the February revolution, the contemporary Okhrana reports, which all agreed that the revolution was spontaneous, leaderless, primarily caused by the shortage of food in the cities and was something they had been predicting since at least the middle of 1916.[4] What makes these police reports particularly convincing is that, as Richard Cobb has pointed out in his studies of the French revolution, policemen love villains. Police spies were paid to find them, and sometimes invented them to enhance their own importance, and would be unlikely to attribute unrest to spontaneous causes if a villain, any villain, could be found.[5]

This consensus was threatened, however, not by any work of scholarship, but by the political offensive against the Mensheviks in the middle of 1918. Their expulsion from the Central Executive Committee of the All-Russian Congress of Soviets, and the closure of *Novaia zhizn*, Gorky's inconvenient newspaper for which N.N. Sukhanov had worked, left the latter with a grudge and with time on his hands, which he used to write his memoirs. In the first volume, published in Russia in 1919, he argued that the revolution had only been spontaneous because the leaders on the spot had been 'utterly second rate . . . routine hacks . . . from whom, in most cases one could expect nothing'; that the Bolsheviks in particular had shown 'their inability to think over and then formulate a political problem'; that Shliapnikov, the senior Bolshevik in Petrograd at the time, had been incapable of 'grasping the essence of the state of affairs that had arisen or generalising on it', and that 'if he had any political ideas, they derived from the clichés of ancient party resolutions'.[6]

Sukhanov could not have hit upon an issue more likely to disrupt the Bolshevik party from within, for 1919 saw the re-emergence of the long-standing tension between the party's intelligentsia leadership and its proletarian 'periphery', many of whom resented the ease with which *intelligenty*, who had deserted the party during the war and been absent during the February revolution, had returned in softer times to positions of leadership over the heads of the worker militants who had kept the party going, however tenuously, when times were hard. This antagonism was to focus on the relationship between the trade unions and the party, and would emerge in 1920 as the Workers' Opposition, the leader of which was Aleksandr Shliapnikov.

What distinguished Shliapnikov from many other dissident Bolsheviks was his refusal to be intimidated, even by Lenin. In March 1921, the Tenth Party Congress banned the Workers' Opposition, but Shliapnikov continued to criticise the party leadership publicly. On 9 August 1921, at a plenary meeting of the Bolshevik Central Committee and the Central Control Committee, Lenin failed to obtain the two-thirds majority needed to expel him from the party. In February 1922, Shliapnikov signed the 'Declaration of the Twenty-Two', the case of the Workers' Opposition against the Bolshevik party leadership, submitted to the Executive Committee of the Communist International (which rejected it). Shliapnikov was back on the attack on 6 March 1922, when he clashed with Lenin at the Fifth Congress of the All-Russian Metal Workers' Union, when Lenin managed to get him removed from the congress praesidium, despite considerable support for Shliapnikov within the union. Undeterred, at the Eleventh Party Congress later in the month, Shliapnikov accused Lenin of using 'criticism by weapons instead of the weapon of criticism' against the opposition. Again, Lenin tried to get him expelled and, although he failed to win a majority for this proposal, he did obtain a vote threatening Shliapnikov with expulsion if he continued his factional activity.[7]

It was at this point that Sukhanov's complete memoirs, seven volumes in all, were published in Berlin, and Shliapnikov's reply, eventually to consist of two volumes on party work during the war and four on the revolution of 1917, began to appear in Russia. Sukhanov represented everything that Shliapnikov opposed: an intellectual, not even a Bolshevik, who had opposed the Bolsheviks at critical times like the October revolution, but who had nonetheless found his niche in the state apparatus of Soviet Russia. Sukhanov's verdict on the Bolshevik party was that it 'was the work of [Lenin's] . . . hands, and his alone' and that 'except Lenin, there was nothing and no one in the party . . . Lenin the Thunderer sat in the clouds and then – there was absolutely nothing right down to the ground'.[8]

Shliapnikov's whole political platform was based on the opposing thesis that the worker Bolsheviks inside Russia were the backbone of the party and that, although none of them knew that 23 February 1917 was the beginning of the revolution, they were expecting revolution at any moment, and so were able to take the leadership, despite being cut off from Lenin and abandoned by the intellectuals.[9] Shliapnikov's work, therefore, was a manifesto for the Workers' Opposition, his way of continuing the struggle when all other paths had been cut off, and the fact that it was published by *Istpart*, the official Bolshevik party commission for the study of the revolution, showed that Shliapnikov still enjoyed support.

The Eleventh Congress was the last that Lenin attended. In May 1922, he suffered his first stroke, and what had begun as a dispute between workers and intellectuals in the party was overtaken by the struggle for the succession, between Trotsky and the ' Old Bolsheviks' (Kamenev, Zinoviev and Stalin). Trotsky's case for his own candidacy was based on his brilliance as a leader and his closeness to Lenin in the period since he joined the Bolshevik party in August 1917. His case against the 'Old Bolsheviks' was that, notwithstanding their long training in the party, they had failed to give proper leadership at critical moments. In this respect, it is significant that his early statements, like *The Lessons of October*, ignored the February revolution as such, presumably because he too considered it to have been a spontaneous event in which the party had played no part.[10] The 'Old Bolshevik' troika, on the other hand, had every reason to force the discussion back to the period before August 1917, when Trotsky had not been in the party and when Lenin's writings had been full of disparaging comments about him. However, they could find no support for their case in either Sukhanov's or Shliapnikov's books.

Sukhanov, as a non-Bolshevik 'capable of standing by a revolutionary conception only up to the time when it was necessary to carry it into action',[11] was not particularly dangerous and could safely be left to Shliapnikov to destroy.[12] But Shliapnikov was dangerous, for any case that the troika might make that the party had led the working class during the war and the February revolution would also strengthen Shliapnikov's case against the entire intellectual élite, Stalinist or Trotskyist, since the party at that time had been led by its working-class cadres. Since Shliapnikov, a former People's Commissar and Central Committee member, refused to be silenced, was still publishing articles in the party press to this effect,[13] and could still command respect among the worker members of the party whose support the troika needed, he had to be discredited.

Zinoviev began the attack, in his *History of the Communist Party*, which appeared in 1923 and went through four editions in its first year, dismissing Shliapnikov's case in a characteristically high-handed way:

the February revolution found part of our Central Committee abroad and part in prison or in exile. It was as though the party did not exist, it was dispersed and broken ... It did not play a decisive role in the February revolution and could not, for the working class at that time leaned towards defencism.[14]

However, while this effectively removed any credit from Shliapnikov, it did so at the expense of denigrating the working class (in Bolshevik terms), by calling it 'defencist', and risked offending the very rank-and-file worker militants, whom the troika wished to win. It also threatened to undermine the whole 'Old Bolshevik' case, based on the continuity of the party tradition, which alone could secure the 'correct' leadership for the working class. Zinoviev desperately tried to retrieve ground by what James White has called the 'theory of ghostly leadership by the Bolsheviks',[15] an argument that verged on the metaphysical:

> But regardless of all this, the work that [the party] had carried out over twenty-five years still bore fruit. Our party was the truly revolutionary party and thus did not only work when it existed as a hierarchical and closely united organisation, but also at times when, at first sight, it seemed not to exist, when it had gone completely underground. Such is the dialectic of the revolutionary process and precisely such was our party too. How many times in the long years of Tsarism did it seem that it was entirely destroyed, comprised only a few individuals and yet, as a result of its work, those elements necessary for the creation of a great all-Russian party of the working class had accumulated in the consciousness of the working masses, and our party was reborn, like the phoenix from the ashes.[16]

Stalin's attack, if indeed it was he, for it is difficult to be certain that he lay behind it despite certain characteristic features, was more subtle. In 1922–3, a spate of memoirs appeared, written ostensibly by 'ordinary workers', the general message of which was that, although the intellectual leaders of the party, and in particular Shliapnikov, had proved bankrupt during the war and the February revolution, the party tradition had been maintained by its worker cadres. According to these 'worker' memoirists, the February revolution may have begun spontaneously, but the political alertness of the worker Bolsheviks enabled them to take over the leadership and ensure its victory.[17] This was a far more promising line of attack than Zinoviev's, for it discredited Shliapnikov and maintained the continuity of the party without resorting to the theory of ghostly leadership or denigrating the working class. In fact, the story that they tell accords with Shliapnikov's, with the one exception that they attack him personally for failing to give leadership.

The suspicion that this rash of memoirs was in fact a campaign mounted by Stalin arises when one looks more closely at the 'worker' memoirists. James White has shown us that the memoirist most referred to by historians, Vasilii Nikolaevich Kaiurov, far from being an 'ordinary worker' in 1923, had by then become a party functionary with a number of purges to his credit and, although he died in the inauspicious year of 1936, he did so from old age.[18] Another, Taras Kondratev, was a member of the Petrograd Cheka and at some stage became a candidate member of the Central Committee;[19] a third, Nikolai Sveshnikov, lived until 1969,[20] a sign that his memoirs at least did not displease Stalin. A further curious aspect of this attack was that Shliapnikov was not an intellectual but a worker, whom Lenin had taunted at the Tenth Party Congress for always harping on his genuinely proletarian nature.[21]

But this is not all. James White has shown that Kaiurov, Sveshnikov and most of the leaders of the Bolshevik party in Petrograd in the February revolution were members of a *zemliachestvo* of former Sormovo workers;[22] the implication of his argument, as I understand it, is that they attacked Shliapnikov as an outsider. But Shliapnikov, a native of Murom in Vladimir *guberniia*, had worked at the Sormovo factory as a boy of fifteen, and was in contact with the Sormovo Social Democrats in 1902–4, precisely the time that White sees as critical in the forming of the links that gave rise to the *zemliachestvo*.[23] Thus Shliapnikov was most probably a member of the *zemliachestvo* in St Petersburg and the fact that, in 1916–17, he regularly spent the night at the flat of Dmitrii Pavlov, who had been prominent among the Sormovo Social Democrats in 1901, and that this flat was the headquarters of the Russian Bureau of the Central Committee from December 1916 until the February revolution, appears to confirm this proposition.[24] In other words, the attack on Shliapnikov by the 'worker' memoirists most probably did not arise out of tensions existing in 1917, but was the result of new loyalties formed after the October revolution. The suspicion must be that this new loyalty was to Stalin.[25]

However, the more subtle method of attack, the cutting of Shliapnikov's proletarian roots from under him, still did not bring him down and, in 1927, *Istpart* published the third volume of his book on 1917. The Stalinist camp now abandoned the attempt to portray the Bolshevik party as leading the February revolution, even in a ghostly

way, but reverted to the view that it had been entirely spontaneous. A
new campaign of vilification against Shliapnikov began, this time conducted by overtly Stalinist hacks.[26] One of these, Ia.A. Iakovlev, the
scourge of Belorussia, who was shortly to become People's Commissar
for Agriculture in charge of the forced collectivisation, rose above mere
vilification. He argued that Shliapnikov's case for Bolshevik leadership
of the revolution rested on the hitherto unchallenged assumptions that
the revolution had begun on 23 February; that it sprang from the
Vyborg district of the city; and that, after the arrest of the Petersburg
Committee on 25–6 February, the Russian Bureau of the Central
Committee and the Vyborg district committee had assumed the
leadership of the revolution.

Iakovlev did not deny that one possible view of the revolution was
that it had begun on 23 February in the Vyborg district, but he
showed that other dates were also possible, and that one's view of the
revolution as a whole depended on which one was chosen. In
particular,

> one might consider the strike of a single shop in the Putilov Works
> to be the start of the revolution . . . On 18 February, one shop in
> the Putilov Works went on strike. The workers elected a delega-
> tion which went to the director. The revolution made its way into
> the whole of Petrograd through one small shop in the Putilov
> Works. The next day there were disturbances over food shortages
> at the Putilov Works, when women workers demanded bread
> outside food warehouses. The workers were threatened with a
> lockout and this threat was met with meetings in all shops, in all
> departments of the Works. On 22 February, the lockout was
> declared . . . All twenty thousand or so of them were now thrown
> into the city like a great explosive charge. When a revolution has
> matured to the extent that it is looking for an opportunity to
> unfold, a small strike in one shop of the Putilov Works can be the
> starting-point of major events. The movement to support the
> Putilov workers spread through the entire city against the back-
> ground of the thousands of women who clustered round the food
> warehouses.[27]

This view that the revolution began in the Putilov Works, and that the
events in the rest of the city, including those on the Vyborg side, had
merely occurred in response to the Putilov strike, would not be attractive to anyone arguing the Bolshevik case, since it shifted the centre of
attention to a factory where the Bolsheviks were weak.

Since the whole purpose of Iakovlev's work was to denigrate

26. Funeral procession held on 23 March 1917, for those who fell
in the February revolution; the banner reads: 'Sleep you fighters
for freedom! Sleep with a free soul! You gave happiness to the
people! May you be remembered forever! Eternal peace!'

Shliapnikov, he not surprisingly took up the 'worker' memoirists'
attack on Shliapnikov's leadership:

> The fact that Shliapnikov wrote a leaflet which was printed
> nowhere and of whose existence the workers only learned when
> the rough draft appeared in Shliapnikov's book, *1917*, cannot be
> called leadership. Indeed, one could say that the very content of
> this leaflet shows to what extent events had outgrown the
> organisational and political abilities of the Bolshevik centres on
> the spot. The leaflet, written on the morning of 27 February, has
> no slogan calling for the organisation of soviets, and yet the soviet
> had already met the day before.[28]

However, Iakovlev pushed the argument further than the 'worker'
memoirists, asserting that this showed that there was no continuity of
Bolshevik leadership after the arrest of the Petersburg Committee on
25–6 February, and that any claim to Bolshevik leadership had to end
there.

With the true instinct of a political killer, Iakovlev then asked the
single most damaging question about Shliapnikov's account of the
February revolution: if the Bolshevik leadership did direct the course

of events, how did it happen that the revolution did not lead to the establishment of the revolutionary–democratic dictatorship of the proletariat and peasantry, or to the Bolsheviks being at the head of the Petrograd Soviet?[29] What made this question so damaging, was that Shliapnikov, who had anticipated the problem, thought that he had dealt with it, at least insofar as Bolshevik weakness in the soviet was concerned. His treatment is worth citing *in extenso*:

[On 27 February], I argued that we should not be in a hurry to set up the soviet, but should wait for the representatives from the working-class districts, but N.D. Sokolov [N.B. a lawyer D.A.L], persuaded people to proceed with the opening with no more than twenty to thirty workers' representatives present. It was impossible to expect more of them on that day. We agreed to wait for a couple of hours and, meantime, to prepare the room for the opening of the soviet session.

I tried to use the time left before the opening of the soviet to warn our comrades of the impending soviet meeting, but the telephones were not working properly and I had great difficulty in getting through anywhere to warn the comrades and call them to the Tauride.

However, we could not expect any greater influx of our factory representatives, since most of the comrades were engaged in the struggle on the streets. In many parts of the city, it was still necessary to wage war against police ambushes. Officers loyal to the Tsar had locked themselves into some of the barracks and were defending themselves with machine guns. The most active comrades were in the ranks of those who were finishing off the remnants of Tsarism.

When they were released from prison, and from the police and Okhrana cells, our party comrades, including the members of the Petersburg Committee, immediately took up party work. At the very time that the defencist elements and radical *petit-bourgeois* intelligentsia were hurrying to the Duma, in the hope of playing an 'historic role', and stood side by side with their bourgeois friends from the Progressive Bloc, our comrades were in the streets continuing to direct the mass struggle of the workers and soldiers, working among them, explaining the significance and meaning of what was happening.

The room in which it was proposed to open the soviet of workers' deputies gradually filled with delegates and with the intelligentsia community. There was a particularly large number of intellectuals, seeking mandates as representatives to the soviet. In order to prevent the room from becoming overcrowded, it became necessary to post a sentry at the door and to give orders that only representatives of factories or of organisations should be let in. Many of our former members, who had once played some kind of role in our Russian Social Democratic Party, but who had disappeared into obscurity in the last few years, turned up at the Tauride Palace. All those people who until that day had avoided the struggle of the workers and soldiers, clung to them now that they were victorious, vying with each other to offer their services as 'leaders'. The members of the 'Workers' Group of the Central War Industries Committee', just released from prison, used their network to mobilise the representatives at the Tauride Palace. N.S. Chkheidze's Social Democratic Duma faction also collected all the leading lights of Menshevism. K.A. Gvozdev, once he was out of the *Kresty*, managed to phone a telegram to 'his boys' in some of the factories, telling them of the soviet meeting.[30]

What is ostensibly a description of the first soviet meeting is a microcosm of Soviet Russia as seen by the Workers' Opposition. Yet, for all its colour and vehemence, for all that it does contain elements of truth, Iakovlev was right to see that it would not do as an explanation of Bolshevik weakness in the soviet. It might, at a pinch, explain why they were outnumbered on the soviet's Executive Committee, as this was primarily made up of leading party activists, nominated by the parties themselves rather than elected by the soviet delegates. Ironically, Shliapnikov was primarily to blame for this fact, since it was he who had proposed this method of constituting the Executive Committee.[31] It would only be true of the soviet itself if the factories which had been unable to get delegates there on the first night were denied the opportunity to do so until later in the year. Yet over the next few days they did hold elections, in which the Bolshevik workers who, according to Shliapnikov, actually led the revolution were almost all passed over in favour of Mensheviks, Socialist Revolutionaries, and non-party people.

If we accept that the February revolution was the work of the Petrograd working class, then the argument that the Bolsheviks were busy on the streets while others jumped on the bandwagon must apply to the soviet electorate, the factory workers, too. For Shliapnikov's accusations to be true, one would have to believe a number of things that are, frankly, unbelievable. They are:

That at a time of general strike and rioting in the streets, those workers who supported the Workers' Group of the Central War-Industries Committee, the Menshevik deputies in the Duma, and

K.A. Gvozdev, ignored all that was going on and turned up to work as normal, where they could be conveniently contacted by Gvozdev and company in time to attend the soviet meeting.

That once the revolution was won on the streets, and the active workers and party members could turn their attention to the soviet elections, *either* they were denied the right to send those people who had led them during the revolution to the soviet; *or* they ignored the people who had led them in the revolution and instead elected as their representatives people who had opposed it, or remained passive during its course; *or* that the revolution was so unpopular among the working class as a whole that the activists who wished to elect those who had led the movement, were outnumbered in the factories by those who wished to elect those who had opposed it or had remained passive.

Thus one of the key points in Shliapnikov's argument rests on premises that he himself would not have been able to endorse. To accept that Menshevik workers turned up to work as normal during the February Days would be to accept the Stalinist caricature of them as stooges of the bourgeoisie. To accept that the workers wished to send Bolsheviks to the soviet, but were denied the opportunity to do so is to forget that soviet deputies were subject to immediate recall. To accept that the workers ignored those who had led them in the revolution is to accept that either they did not know who they were, in which case it is difficult to know how this leadership had been effected; or that they had changed their minds about the whole affair, in which case it is difficult to understand why there was no counter-revolution. This is also the case if we accept that the revolution was only supported by a minority of the working class, which subsequently lost the political ascendancy. All these hypotheses are possible, but unlikely.

In any case, the time for questions was rapidly drawing to a close. In March 1931, Sukhanov was one of the defendants in the 'Menshevik' show trial. In the same year, Shliapnikov, unbelievably, managed to have the fourth volume of his book published by *Istpart*, but two years later was arrested in his turn. His books were denounced, with the barefacedness that characterised the 1930s, as a 'Menshevik–Trotskyite' falsification of the history of 1917.[32] Inside the Soviet Union, now that Shliapnikov's work had been disposed of by 'administrative methods', history books adopted his view of the February revolution as prepared and led by the Bolshevik party, with the difference that the leader of the Russian Bureau of the Central Committee was now said to have been 'comrade Molotov'.[33] Iakovlev's question was answered in terms similar to Shliapnikov's:

> While the Bolsheviks were directly leading the struggle of the masses in the streets, the compromising parties, the Mensheviks and Socialist Revolutionaries, were seizing the seats in the soviets, and building up a majority there. This was partly facilitated by the fact that the majority of the leaders of the Bolshevik party were in prison or in exile (Lenin was abroad and Stalin and Sverdlov in banishment in Siberia) while the Mensheviks and Socialist Revolutionaries were promenading the streets of Petrograd. The result was that the Petrograd Soviet and its Executive Committee were headed by representatives of the compromising parties.[34]

Meanwhile Trotsky, once again a political exile, had adopted his old enemy Zinoviev's theory of the 'ghostly leadership'.[35] His answer to Iakovlev's question was more sophisticated than that of Shliapnikov/Stalin: the 'leadership proved sufficient to guarantee the victory of the insurrection, but it was not adequate to transfer immediately into the hands of the proletarian vanguard the leadership of the revolution'.[36] But, although it is more sophisticated, it will not do, for Trotsky's analysis betrays the weaknesses of the view of the party held by the émigré intellectuals that Shliapnikov had attacked. When he writes that the revolution was led by 'conscious and tempered workers educated for the most part by the party of Lenin',[37] he is referring to people like Kaiurov, whose memoirs figure so prominently in his analysis, and Chugurin, whose activities on the streets he mentions. But neither Kaiurov nor Chugurin were merely 'conscious and tempered workers'. Kaiurov had been a member of 'the party of Lenin' since 1900, and Chugurin had not merely been a member of the party since 1902, he was also a member of its Vyborg committee and of the executive commission of the party's Petersburg committee.[38] Shliapnikov is right here: these men *were* the 'party of Lenin' in Russia at the time. By calling them merely 'conscious and tempered workers educated for the most part by the party of Lenin', Trotsky betrayed his belief that the only 'real' members of the party were its intellectual élite. In any case, Iakovlev's question remains unanswered, as we still need to know why these party leaders were not elected to the soviet.

Since the death of Stalin, Soviet historians have, within limits, been able to address themselves once more to the problem raised by Iakovlev's question. Potentially the most radical answer was suggested by E.N. Burdzhalov's contribution to the debate that raged on the pages of *Voprosy istorii* in 1956. Burdzhalov examined not the February revolution itself, but its immediate aftermath up to Lenin's return to Russia. He shows that, even after the street fighting was over, the Bolshevik leadership in Russia was uncertain about what should replace the existing régime and seriously divided in its attitude towards the new soviets, and that, whereas some low-level cadres saw them as the Provisional Revolutionary Government, others, including the Russian Bureau of the Central Committee, were at best only lukewarm in their support for institutions that they saw as rivals to the party.[39]

Thus, by implication, he provided a new answer to Iakovlev's question: the Bolsheviks were not represented in the soviets because they were not particularly interested in them. This in turn prompts a further question: since a revolution, as opposed to a riot, involves the substitution of one kind of state power for another, what kind of leadership could the Bolsheviks be presumed to have been giving, if they had no idea of what should replace Tsarism? What is more, it leaves open the question of who, if anyone, did lead the February revolutionaries to the creation of the soviet? Burdzhalov himself was unable to pursue these ideas, as he was fast hounded out of Moscow University and the editorial board of *Voprosy istorii*.

Other scholars did, however. In 1964, *Istoriia SSSR* contained an exchange between G.I. Zlokazov and S.A. Artemev, on the question of why there were so few Bolsheviks elected to the soviet immediately after the February revolution. Zlokazov took a traditional view, based on the argument, first put forward by K.I. Shelavin in 1927, that the electoral system, which gave one deputy per thousand workers to the large factories but one deputy to small factories regardless of size, ensured that representatives from the small factories, in which the Bolsheviks had very little influence, predominated in the soviet.[40] In reply, Artemev showed that Shelavin's analysis was based too uncritically on memoir material, and was mistaken in its assumptions about the way that the soviet electoral system worked. Working from the records of the soviet's credentials commission, Artemev found that small factories of less than one hundred workers normally merged to elect deputies, and had between them about 200 deputies in the soviet, compared to some 250 for medium-sized factories (100–500 workers) and roughly 300 for the large factories (over 1,000 workers). Thus delegates from the bigger factories were actually the largest single group in the soviet.

The problem was that even they did not elect Bolsheviks in any large numbers, and Artemev argued that this was the result of the change in the social composition of the Petrograd working class, including that section of it in the large factories, during the course of the war, when the rapid expansion of industry had led to a great influx of non-proletarians, thereby lowering the average level of political consciousness.[41] Artemev's analysis was taken one step further by Iu.S. Tokarev in his posthumous book, where he argues that the low level of political awareness displayed by the Petrograd proletariat in February 1917 led to all three main proletarian parties, Bolsheviks, Mensheviks and SRs, being under-represented, and that the bulk of the delegates belonged to no party at all.[42]

Interesting though the findings of Artemev and Tokarev are, and although they do add to our understanding of the February revolution, they do not provide a convincing answer to Iakovlev's question. It is certainly true that the Petrograd working class expanded rapidly during the war, absorbing a large number of peasants straight from the country, and that those industries whose products were essential to the war effort, and whose workers were therefore exempt from military service, attracted draft-dodgers (although it is not clear how many of these there were). But it is also true not only that it was this 'diluted' proletariat that turned out for the street demonstrations of the February Days, but that, as Burdzhalov argued in his works published in the 1960s, the spearhead of the revolution was not the organised and politically conscious engineering workers, generally favoured by Soviet historians, but the women textile workers, normally regarded by them as 'backward'.[43]

This politically inexperienced proletariat might not have voted for recognised political parties, might not even have been able to distinguish between them, and there is a good deal of memoir evidence to support this view,[44] but it does not follow from this that they did not vote for those who had led them in the revolution. Indeed, their very lack of any established political allegiance makes it more likely that they would have voted for the people who had led them on the streets, as the only political leaders they would recognise. Thus, one possible conclusion from all this could be that the February revolution was led by non-party people, natural charismatic leaders, who simply rose to the occasion and were then elected to the soviet.

Another aspect of Shelavin's argument was taken up by O.N. Znamenskii, at one of the seminars held as part of the Academy of Sciences' celebrations of the fortieth anniversary of the revolution, in a survey of the Soviet historiography of the question. It is a remarkable article, not least because it is one of the few (perhaps the only one?) which explicitly confronts Iakovlev's question, mentioning Iakovlev by name. Shelavin had argued that the February revolution should not be seen, as Shliapnikov and the 'worker' memoirists of the mid-1920s had seen it, as a spontaneous movement that was gradually brought under control by the Bolsheviks, but as a movement which began spontaneously, over which the Bolsheviks gained temporary control on 25 and 26 February, only to lose it again once the garrison mutinied and all kinds of non-proletarian elements entered the fray.[45]

This approach, for all its more convincing appearance, still fails to answer Iakovlev's question. For it to do so, we should expect the proletarian core of the movement, presumed to have been led by the Bolsheviks on 25 and 26 February, to have returned Bolshevik deputies to the soviets. But, as G.I. Zlokazov has shown, this did not generally happen, even in the engineering factories on the Vyborg side, but 'in those factories where there were strong and close-knit Bolshevik organisations, which paid sufficient heed to the elections to the soviets, Bolsheviks were unanimously elected'.[46] He also demonstrates that where these conditions prevailed, the Bolsheviks could force a successful re-election, even unseating very prominent opponents, and cites the Novyi Lessner factory, to which Taras Kondratev, one of the 'worker' memoirists cited above, returned on 1 March after active participation in the revolution, to find that the factory had elected mostly Mensheviks to the soviet. He forced a re-election, which unseated all the Mensheviks, including Mark Broido, and returned eight Bolsheviks and one Socialist Revolutionary.[47] These findings appear consistent with those of the voting patterns overall, for where the Bolsheviks were strong and united we should expect them to have been prominent in the revolution, and thus to have become known to the soviet electorate. Those who were insufficiently interested in soviet elections, however, may have been active in the streets, but it is difficult to see how they could be described as leading the revolution, since such leadership involved the creation of soviet power as one of the two substitutes for the old régime.

Although Soviet historiography had produced some extremely interesting analyses of certain aspects of the February revolution, its answers to Iakovlev's question thus remain unsatisfactory. This is because, for political reasons, the framework within which Soviet historians are constrained is still essentially that laid down by Shliapnikov in the early twenties, and adopted by Stalinist historiography in the 1930s. The clearest example of this is the case of E.N.

Burdzhalov who was persecuted when his work in the 1950s explicitly broke out of this framework. In the 1960s, however, his books were published, even though he was in disgrace, but the price paid for this concession was that the sometimes exciting detailed research is followed by tired conclusions, which even run contrary to the research itself. Thus the first volume concludes that the workers and peasants of Russia overthrew Tsarism under the leadership of the Bolsheviks,[48] although there is precious little in the book itself that supports this. The second concludes that:

> The strikes and demonstrations of the workers and women of Petrograd broke out spontaneously on 23 February 1917, but as they became a mass movement the Bolsheviks strove to transform them into the decisive battle with Tsarism. They called on the workers and on the women to win the soldiers over to the revolution, so that their united forces could bring about the overthrow of Tsarism. The Bolsheviks called for the establishment of the revolutionary–democratic dictatorship of the proletariat and peasantry, for the formation of a Provisional Revolutionary Government from the soviets,[49]

which is something he had disproved in 1956, and in support of which no new evidence had been produced. It is this inability to realise the promise of their own research that has made so much Soviet writing so disappointing.

Unfortunately Western historiography is in the same sorry state. Hasegawa's book is encyclopaedic in that it contains practically everything that we know about the February revolution. Hasegawa seems to have been possessed by the same zeal as the editors of the first *Cambridge Modern History*, to write the ultimate history, and like the *CMH* it can be seen as the best summation of the 'state of the art' at its time. But it also shares the weakness of its time in its uncritical approach to the memoir literature which leads its author to adopt a view very similar to that of Kaiurov (which he mistakenly attributes to Trotsky). Having rejected spontaneity, he writes:

> But on the other hand, it is difficult to subscribe to the theory of Bolshevik leadership. The Bolshevik party as a whole failed to react to the workers' strike movement quickly and imaginatively. The Russian Bureau led by Shliapnikov was constantly behind the developing events and grossly underestimated the revolutionary potentialities of the movement ... Nonetheless, in such an explosive situation as the February revolution the existence of

3,000 committed revolutionaries cannot be easily dismissed. The most important Bolshevik organisation, the one that exerted a significant influence on the workers, was the Vyborg district committee. Headed by militant Chugurin and led by such experienced party activists as Kaiurov and Sveshnikov, the Vyborg district committee had placed its 500 to 600 members in strategically important factories . . . Considering the important role played by the metal factories in the Vyborg district, these Vyborg Bolsheviks must have contributed to the rapid acceleration of the strike movement. In this sense, Trotsky was partially correct in stating that the February revolution was led by the lower rank Bolshevik activists.[50]

It is the ghostly theory again, with an appeal to the readers' solidarity as a substitute for evidence, and it leaves Iakovlev's question unanswered.

Iakovlev's question, it would appear, cannot be answered within the framework put forward by Shliapnikov. Yet it remains a valid question that demands an answer. What needs to be done, therefore, is to re-examine Shliapnikov's framework. Shliapnikov was arguing a political case, and his *History* was part of that case. This does not mean that he lacked objectivity or honesty, but merely that, on the whole, he selected those facts that supported his political case: that the February revolution was not spontaneous, but was led by the Bolshevik leadership in Petrograd at the time, which alone was up to the task, and which upheld the revolutionary traditions of the Bolshevik party without recourse to any outside help. His case rests on a few simple premises:

(1) that the February revolution began on International Women's Day, 23 February (8 March) 1917, with strikes and demonstrations by women workers who had been influenced by meetings organised by the Bolsheviks;
(2) that the Vyborg district of Petrograd was the centre of the revolutionary movement;
(3) that the Bolsheviks, rather than anyone else, led the demonstrations, imposing their slogans on the crowds, and preventing violence towards the soldiers, with a view to winning them over;
(4) that the arrest of most members of the Petersburg committee of the Bolshevik party, in the early morning of 26 February, did not interrupt Bolshevik leadership of the movement, as Shliapnikov was able to arrange for the Vyborg district committee to take over;

(5)   that the Bolshevik leadership was clear in its idea of what should be substituted for the old régime;

(6)   and that they were only under-represented on the soviet because they were outmanoeuvred by politicians who took advantage of the party activists being occupied leading workers on the streets.

Although the fifth premise has been destroyed by Burdzhalov's work of the 1950s,[51] and the sixth has been undermined by much recent Soviet research, albeit by implication only, it is surprising how little the first four have been challenged. Only the third has attracted any attention from Western historians, most notably and penetratingly from James White and Michael Melançon, but their work is only a beginning.[52] The other three premises have scarcely been criticised at all. No historian has taken up Iakovlev's challenge to Shliapnikov's dating of the revolution, or his argument that this dating was linked to the view that the Bolsheviks led the revolution. Indeed, Hasegawa goes out of his way to endorse Shliapnikov's dates, without examining Iakovlev's critique.[53]

Even more surprising is the fact that Shliapnikov's account of the revolution entirely in terms of the Vyborg district, which he substitutes for Petrograd as a whole, has never been challenged. Here too, Hasegawa clings to the Vyborg-centric view and rejects the argument that the Putilov works played an important part in the movement as 'erroneous', on what can only be described as weak grounds.[54] In the circumstances, it is hardly surprising that Shliapnikov's assertion that, after the arrest of the Petersburg committee on the morning of 26 February, the Vyborg district committee assumed the leadership of the party and the movement as a whole, has not been challenged either.

Whereas Soviet historians have been severely restricted, their Western counterparts have been uninterested in the historiography of the question, and often appear to work on a rule of thumb that if someone was persecuted by Stalin, and had his views distorted, then these must be right. This has led to an exaggerated respect for Sukhanov, Trotsky and Shliapnikov, with little effort to distinguish between their views. But the debate initiated by Sukhanov's book was not an academic one about historical truth, but part of a struggle for political power, whose victims, from all sides, paid the penalty: Sukhanov, Shliapnikov and Iakovlev died in the Gulag. Trotsky was murdered; Kamenev and Zinoviev were executed. We should beware of allowing our sympathy for a man's fate, or our distaste for some of his actions, to determine our attitude to his evidence. All the protagonists used history for political ends, but not all, even on Stalin's side, did so dishonestly. Thus we cannot reject Kaiurov's and Iakovlev's views *in toto* simply because they were unpleasant characters in the 1920s and 1930s. Nor can we accept Shliapnikov's approach uncritically, simply out of admiration for his courageous defence of his views throughout his lifetime. If we are to answer Iakovlev's question, Shliapnikov's mould will have to be broken.

NOTES

1 Leonard Schapiro, *1917: The Russian Revolutions and the Origins of Present-Day Communism* (Harmondsworth, 1984), p. 226.

2 Tsuyoshi Hasegawa, *The February Revolution: Petrograd 1917* (Seattle and London, 1981), contains five pages of archival references (pp. 603–8).

3 O.N. Znamenskii, 'Sovetskie istoriki o sootnoshenii stikhiinosti i organizovannosti v fevralskoi revoliutsii', in *Sverzhenie samoderzhaviia* (Moscow, 1970), p. 284, citing the work of D.Z. Manuilskii and M.N. Pokrovskii.

4 E.g., a report of October 1916 reads: 'The problem of supplying the army with military supplies can be considered solved and proceeding as it should be. On the other hand, the ever growing disorder in the rear, or in other words in the entire country, which is chronic and cumulative, has now attained such an extraordinarily rapid rate of growth that it now specifically threatens our achievements at the front and menaces shortly to throw the country into catastrophically destructive chaos and spontaneous anarchy.' 'Politicheskoe polozhenie Rossii nakanune fevralskoi revoliutsii v zhandarmskoi osveshchenii', *Krasnyi arkhiv* 17/4 (1926), p. 5.

5 Richard Cobb, *The Police and the People: French Popular Protest, 1789–1820* (Oxford, 1970), pp. 5ff.

6 N.N. Sukhanov, *Zapiski o revoliutsii*, vol. 1 (Petrograd, 1919), pp. 7, 36, 39, 72. Joel Carmichael states that there was only one edition of Sukhanov's memoirs, that published in Berlin in 1922–3 (*The Russian Revolution 1917. A Personal Record by N.N. Sukhanov*, edited, abridged and translated by Joel Carmichael, London, 1955, p. xiv). In fact, the first volume had been previously published in Petrograd. Apart from minor stylistic variations, the only difference between the editions that I have been able to detect is in the size of the pages, which makes the pagination different.

7 Vladimir Ilich Lenin, *Sochineniia*, third edition, vol. XXVII (Moscow, 1935), pp. 533 (note 111), 538 (notes 121–2). Larry Holmes ('Soviet Rewriting of 1917: The Case of A.G. Shliapnikov', *Slavic Review* 38 (1979, 224–42)), traces these disputes with the party leadership, but sees the writing of history as something Shliapnikov turned to, once politics were denied him, and 'although he did occasionally use history to support his

politics, a respect for scholarship led him ... to arrive at relatively impartial conclusions' (p. 242). My point is that the writing of history was Shliapnikov's way of continuing the political struggle and that although a respect for scholarship may have made it objective, it did not make it impartial, since his politics affected his selection of the facts.

8 Sukhanov, *The Russian Revolution*, pp. 290–1.

9 A. Shliapnikov, *Kanun semnadtsatogo goda*, 2 vols. (Moscow, 1922); A. Shliapnikov, *Semnadtsatyi god*, 4 vols. (Moscow, 1923–31). See also his more forthright, 'Nasha partiia v "fevralskie" dni', *Pravda* (12 March 1922), p. 2.

10 L.D. Trotsky, *Uroki oktiabria* (Moscow, 1924), especially parts 1 and 2, where he mentions the February revolution, but only as 'having overthrown Tsarism'.

11 Trotsky, *The History of the Russian Revolution*, vol. 1, p. 165.

12 E.g., A. Shliapnikov, 'O knigakh N. Sukhanova', *Pechat i revoliutsiia* 4 (1923), 46–52.

13 E.g., A. Shliapnikov, 'Nashi raznoglasiia', *Pravda* (18 January 1924), pp. 4–5.

14 G. Zinoviev, *Istoriia Rossiiskoi kommunistischeskoi partii (bolshevikov)*, fourth edn (Leningrad, 1924), pp. 184–5.

15 James White, 'The Sormovo-Nikolaev *zemliachestvo* in the February Revolution', *Soviet Studies* 21, no. 4 (1979), 491. In this very perceptive article (p. 490) he calls Zinoviev's view 'the official line'. My argument is that there was no official line in 1923, but a series of different positions taken by the different participants in the power struggle.

16 Zinoviev, *Istoriia*, pp. 184–5.

17 E.g., 'Podpolnaia rabota v gody imperialistischeskoi voiny v Petrograde', *Krasnaia letopis* no. 2/3 (1922), 118. V. Kaiurov, 'Shest dnei fevralskoi revoliutsii', *Proletarskaia revoliutsiia* no. 3 (1923), 169. N. Sveshnikov, 'Otryvki iz vospominanii', *Petrogradskaia pravda* (14 March 1923), reprinted in *Krushenie tsarizma* (Leningrad, 1986), pp. 31–6.

18 James White, 'The Sormovo-Nikolaev *zemliachestvo*', p. 476. On p. 490, White describes Kaiurov's memoirs as following Zinoviev's interpretation of the February revolution and lending it 'substance and authority'. I disagree. Kaiurov did not see the revolution as completely spontaneous, or the working class as defencist. He is clear that people like himself provided leadership, but he attacks Shliapnikov for failing to do so.

19 *Krushenie tsarizma*, p. 405. Unfortunately this source does not date this election, so I am not sure whether he entered the Central Committee before or after Stalin's accession to power.

20 Ibid., p. 397.

21 Vladimir Ilich Lenin, *Polnoe sobranie sochinenii*, vol. XLIII (Moscow, 1974), p. 40.

22 White, 'The Sormovo-Nikolaev *zemliachestvo*', pp. 477ff.

23 Georges Haupt and Jena-Jacques Marie, *Makers of the Russian Revolution* (London, 1974), pp. 213–14; White, 'The Sormovo-Nikolaev *zemliachestvo*', p. 478.

24 Shliapnikov, *Kanun*, vol. I, p. 192; Shliapnikov, *Semnadtsatyi god*, vol. I, p. 54.

25 Sveshnikov published an 'improved' version of his memoirs in 1967 (N.F. Sveshnikov, 'Vyborgskii raionnyi komitet RSDRP(b) v 1917 g.', in *V ogne revoliutsionnykh boev, [raiony Petrograda v dvukh revoliutsiiakh 1917 g.]*, Moscow, 1967, pp. 81–90), in which the attack on Shliapnikov is embellished to the point that he has the latter saying on 25 February, like a latter-day Marie-Antoinette, 'What revolution? Give the workers a loaf of bread and the movement would be gone' (p. 84). The danger of not appreciating the background to these memoirs is illustrated by the fact that Hasegawa cites this source uncritically, adding 'needless to say, the Vyborg district committee was outraged by this statement'! (*The February Revolution*, p. 258.)

26 White ('The Sormovo-Nikolaev *zemliachestvo*', p. 503), lists articles by D.Ia. Kin (*Istorik marksist*, vol. III, 1927); A. Lomakin (*Bolshevik* nos. 11–12, 1927), and Ia.A. Iakovlev (*Izvestiia*, 10 March 1927), to which should be added Ia.A. Iakovlev, 'Fevralskie dni', *Proletarskaia revoliutsiia* 61–2, nos. 2–3 (1927). Iakovlev's extremely interesting article is sadly neglected by modern Soviet and Western historians. Only Znamenskii, ('Sovetskie istoriki', pp. 286–8), I.P. Leiberov (*Na shturm samoderzhaviia*, Moscow, 1979, pp. 6–7) and White ('The Sormovo-Nikolaev *zemliachestvo*', pp. 491ff.) refer to him.

27 Iakovlev, 'Fevralskie dni', p. 81.

28 Ibid., pp. 97–8.

29 Ibid. The formulation 'the revolutionary–democratic dictatorship of the proletariat and peasantry' was, of course, Lenin's.

30 Shliapnikov, *Semnadtsatyi god*, vol. I, pp. 117–18.

31 Ibid., p. 121.

32 Holmes, 'Soviet rewriting', p. 241.

33 *History of the Communist Party of the Soviet Union (Bolsheviks). Short Course* (Moscow, 1939), pp. 175–6.

34 Ibid., p. 177.

35 Trotsky, *History*, vol. I, pp. 136ff. James White argues that Trotsky and Stalin adopted the theory of ghostly leadership simultaneously in the 1920s because 'For Trotsky, as for Stalin, the political stance of the Sormovo and Nikolaev workers in the February revolution was a most unwelcome foil to his own political position at the time' (White, 'The Sormovo-Nikolaev *zemliachestvo*', p. 492). I have been unable to trace any writings by Trotsky that deal with the question before his *History*, written in exile, which, indeed, is the source cited by White. It is possible that one of the reasons for the onslaught on Shliapnikov's line in 1927 by

Iakovlev and company was that Trotsky had by then adopted the 'ghostly leadership' theory because he realised its potential as an argument against the 'Old Bolsheviks'.

36 Ibid., p. 152.

37 Ibid.

38 *Sverzhenie samoderzhaviia*, pp. 381, 399.

39 E.N. Burdzhalov, 'O taktike bolshevikov v marte-aprele 1917 goda', *Voprosy istorii* no. 4 (1956), 38–56. He replied to his critics in a later article, making his points even more firmly: E.N. Burdzhalov, 'Eshche o taktike bolshevikov v marte-aprele 1917 goda', *Voprosy istorii* no. 8 (1956), 109–14.

40 G.E. Zlokazov, 'Sozdanie Petrogradskogo soveta', *Istoriia SSSR* no. 5 (1964), 106–11, based on K. Shelavin, *Rabochii klass i VKP(B) v fevralskoi revoliutsii* (Leningrad, 1927), p. 60.

41 S.A. Artemev, 'Sostav Petrogradskogo soveta v marte 1917 goda', *Istoriia SSSR* no. 5 (1964), 112–28.

42 Iu.S. Tokarev, *Petrogradskii sovet rabochikh i soldatskikh deputatov v marte-aprele 1917 g.* (Leningrad, 1976), pp. 119–25.

43 E.N. Burdzhalov, 'Nachalo vtoroi russkoi revoliutsii', *Uchenye zapiski Moskovskogo Gosudarstvennogo Pedagogicheskogo Instituta imeni V.I. Lenina* (Moscow, 1965), p. 139, where he takes issue with I.P. Leiberov, who had argued that the engineering workers were the spearhead of the revolution ('O revoliutsionnykh vystupleniiakh petrogradskogo proletariata v gody pervoi mirovoi voiny i fevralskoi revoliutsii', *Voprosy istorii*, no. 1 (1964), 63–77). Burdzhalov repeated his view in his book, *Vtoraia russkaia revoliutsiia: vosstanie v Petrograde* (Moscow, 1967), pp. 120–1.

44 Kh.M. Astrakhan, *Bolsheviki i ikh politicheskie protivniki v 1917 godu* (Leningrad, 1973), p. 73.

45 Znamenskii, 'Sovetskie istoriki', p. 287.

46 G.I. Zlokazov, *Petrogradskii sovet rabochikh i soldatskikh deputatov v period mirnogo razvitiia revoliutsii* (Moscow, 1969), p. 40. It is true that he somewhat undermines his case that Bolsheviks were *unanimously* elected by citing the Russkii Renault factory, where in fact one Bolshevik was elected out of two delegates. However, the point that these conditions were necessary for Bolsheviks to be elected at all can be taken.

47 Ibid., citing T. Kondratev, 'Vospominaniia o podpolnoi rabote v Petrograde', *Krasnaia letopis* 7 (1923), 69.

48 Burdzhalov, *Vtoraia russkaia revoliutsiia*, p. 406.

49 E.N. Burdzhalov, *Vtoraia russkaia revoliutsiia: Moskva, front, periferiia* (Moscow, 1971), p. 447.

50 Hasegawa, *February Revolution*, pp. 579. Hasegawa's analysis is a little more sophisticated than some Soviet writing in that he does admit the presence of SR and Menshevik agitators, as, of course, did Kaiurov.

Trotsky's view, as we have shown, was not that the revolution was led by lower-rank Bolshevik activists, but by workers trained over the years by the Bolshevik party. The distinction between these two groups lay behind the split at the party's Second Congress in 1903.

51 See also my 'The Divisions in the Bolshevik Party in March 1917', *Soviet Studies* 24 (1972), 61–76.

52 James White, 'The Sormovo-Nikolaev *zemliachestvo*', *passim*; Michael Melançon, 'Who Wrote What and When? Proclamations of the February Revolution in Petrograd, 23 February–1 March 1917', *Soviet Studies* 40 (1988), 479–500.

53 Hasegawa, *February Revolution*, pp. 215ff. Although he lists Iakovlev's article in his bibliography, he does not refer to it at all in connection with the dating of the revolution.

54 Ibid., p. 221.

17

THE LIBERTARIANS VINDICATED?
THE LIBERTARIAN VIEW OF
THE REVOLUTION IN
THE LIGHT OF RECENT WESTERN RESEARCH

EDWARD ACTON

W E are in the midst of a sea-change in the historiography of the Russian revolution. It has become increasingly difficult for specialists to subscribe to either of the two analytical frameworks in terms of which controversy over the revolution has long been conducted. Indeed, the past two decades have seen the gradual erosion both of the traditional Soviet approach, where the overriding preoccupation is with Bolshevik genius and the revolution as a process governed by universally applicable historical laws; and of the traditional liberal approach, where the revolution is treated as the sorry tale of an embryonic Western-style democracy aborted by total war and Bolshevik chicanery. The very bases of both approaches have been undermined by recent research analysing events 'from below' and examining in detail the mass organisations which sprang up in the course of 1917. Yet conventional wisdom – and non-specialist teaching – on the subject continues to be dominated by these two frameworks. Syntheses produced in both West and East, while including more caveats than those of a decade or two earlier, remain doggedly faithful to the basic approaches dominant in each. The dust may well have to settle before a compelling new synthesis, incorporating the insights of the past decade or so, can emerge. Yet until such a synthesis is developed, it will remain difficult for these insights to percolate beyond a narrow band of specialists.

A small step in that direction may be to draw into the mainstream of discussion a third, decidedly minority, tradition in the historiography: that derived from the 'libertarian' approach.[1] The libertarian view has generally been treated as beyond the pale. The one thing Bolshevik, Menshevik, liberal and conservative commentators could agree upon was the absurdity of the libertarians' view. Their interpretation has continued to be dismissed as the product of *petit-bourgeois* adventurism by Soviet historians and as utopian fantasy by most Western historians. In few academic institutions and history courses have they been regarded as being of sufficient importance to merit attention – or even representation in the library.[2] Yet, during the past decade, several libertarian themes have received a measure of confirmation from mainline historians whose ideological sympathies are neither obvious nor uniform and whose scholarship, despite some qualms about the sources on which it is based, commands all but universal respect. Indeed, in some respects the libertarian view is better placed to do justice to recent perspectives on the revolution than either its Soviet or liberal competitors.[3]

The driving force behind the libertarian understanding of 1917 is a sublime vision of human potential for social harmony and individual fulfilment. Given the chance, men and women are capable of and will aspire to a measure of creativity and mutual cooperation of which history has witnessed no more than the faintest inkling. The essential condition for realising this potential is the overthrow of all forms of oppression. And it is economic oppression, the exploitation of man by man, from which all other forms of oppression flow. The root of economic oppression, in the libertarian view, lies in the 'relations of production', in the way in which individuals and groups relate with one another in the process of producing wealth. The critical question, the acid test of socialism, is the distribution of power at the point of production. Wherever those who produce are subordinated to those who manage production, society will be marked by division and individuals will be subjected to humiliation and their potential stunted. But oppression can be overcome when the producers themselves manage production, when workers and peasants exercise self-management. There are no 'scientific' or historical laws guaranteeing that this potential will be realised: resistance to it – political, economic, psychological – is fierce; the necessary 'subjective' conditions, the self-conscious and collective will of the great majority of men and women, are no less crucial than an adequate level of production. But the human urge for liberty and self-affirmation is deeply rooted – and that urge has seldom found fuller expression than in the course of the Russian revolution.

The 'libertarian' view of the Russian revolution, inspired by this vision, was sketched out in the immediate aftermath of 1917 by anarchist activists. Much of their work was impressionistic and, in scholarly terms, decidedly lightweight. The best-known pioneering accounts – such as those of Volin, Maksimov, Berkman and Arshinov – were short on documentation and long on polemic.[4] Since the Second World War, however, and especially since the 1960s, many of the theses which they advanced have been taken up and refined. The emergence of the New Left in the West and of articulate dissent in Eastern Europe provided fertile soil for reconsideration of 1917 from a variety of anti-state socialist, though not necessarily anarchist, perspectives. Much of this work has remained on the fringes of academic respectability, developed in recondite leftist debate and rarefied journals. Black Rose Books of Quebec has contributed more than its fair share to the libertarian revival. Contributions from the far Left in France have tended to be at one remove from primary research. The work of Eastern European dissidents has proceeded at a high level of generalisation. Nevertheless, in these new studies written at greater distance from the revolution, the ideas of earlier libertarians have been developed with greater conceptual clarity and more attention to evidence.

The writers treated here as 'libertarian' do not adhere to one tightly knit pattern of thought. The differences that divide them are every bit as acute as those which divide the main body of Western historians who may broadly be labelled 'liberal'. Some draw their inspiration from post-war development studies; some would still recognise a certain allegiance to Marx while condemning the theory of Marxism–Leninism and the practice of régimes adhering to it; for others Marxism is the cardinal sin. But it is possible to identify a significant measure of common ground among them which amounts to a distinctive libertarian discourse. Here two central aspects of this discourse will be considered: the basic perspective from which the revolution is approached and the manner in which the 'failure' of the revolution is addressed.

In contrast to liberal and Soviet accounts, where the protagonists are the 'key' political figures and the 'vanguard party' respectively, libertarian accounts place the masses at the centre-stage of the revolution. Attention is focused not on Miliukov and Kerensky, Lenin and Trotsky but on the activity of ordinary men and women, anonymous peasants and workers, soldiers and sailors. The revolution 'was accomplished, not by any political party, but by the people themselves'.[5] For they were not enticed into revolt, not manipulated, brainwashed and bewitched by superior leaders. They chose. The goals for which they strove were their own. They responded only to what fulfilled their own aspirations; the rest they rejected. It was in this sense that not only February, but the whole social upheaval of 1917–18 was 'spontaneous' – unorchestrated, unplanned, but consciously willed, deliberately carried through by millions upon millions of ordinary people. The peasants sought to solve the 'agrarian question' in their own way and by themselves, while 'the autonomous action of the working class seeking totally to alter the conditions of its existence' was 'the most fundamental feature' of the period.[6] The overthrow of the Provisional Government in Petrograd in October amounted to little more than a reverberation of the mass revolt which provided the revolution with its momentum and direction, which *was* the revolution.

Moreover, the goals after which the masses strove were both lofty and rational. Protest which Bolshevik leaders dismissed as undisciplined and unreflecting, and which liberals and moderate socialists saw as mindless and destructive, libertarians hail as creative in the truest sense. The masses were motivated by something deeper than poverty, envy and the desire for revenge. They sought to assert their human dignity. They sought to overthrow that which oppressed, degraded, humiliated them. They sought to seize control over their own lives. Indeed, the upheaval of 1917 was the most vivid illustration of man's aspiration and potential for liberty in the full sense of the word. It was this aspiration, however simply and inarticulately expressed, which fuelled the rejection by workers, peasants and soldiers of the authority of Tsar, bourgeoisie and moderate socialists alike, the sustained assault upon the state and private property:

> The revolutionary masses by their own initiative began, long before the October days, to put into practice their social ideals. They took possession of the land, the factories, mines, mills and the tools of production. They got rid of the more hated and dangerous representatives of government and authority. In their grand revolutionary outburst they destroyed every form of political and economic oppression.[7]

That the goals of the masses were at once lofty and rational is borne out, in the libertarian view, by the nature of the challenge they mounted to political and economic oppression. At its height, the mass movement challenged the whole principle of authority and obedience, of hierarchy and subordination. It struck at the very roots of all forms of oppression: authoritarian relations at the point of production. During the revolution, the masses advanced from defence of their own interests against management and external authority towards full control over their own working lives, over the production process itself. Libertarian attention has been focused most closely upon the factory committees established during 1917 and 1918. Initially limited in their aims, the committees became increasingly assertive and interventionist. Their scope broadened throughout the period, moving from collective defence against the barbaric authoritarianism of Tsarist factory management towards fully fledged self-management. 'The shop and factory committees were the pioneers in labor control of industry, with the prospect of themselves, in the near future, managing the industries entire.'[8] For most workers, the factory-committee movement

> was not just a means of combating the economic sabotage of the ruling class or a correct tactical slogan . . . [but] was the expression of their deepest aspirations . . . Instinctively they sensed that who managed production would manage all aspects of social life.[9]

There was a parallel if less sophisticated movement on the land. The peasantry were determined to drive off the landlord and the government agent, to reintegrate the kulak and to establish the autonomy of the village commune. They were motivated not merely by economic desperation or the levelling instinct, but by a desire to build an egalitarian society imbued with their own values. In the countryside, the creative drive of peasant revolution was most fully developed under the umbrella of the Makhnovist movement in the Ukraine between 1918 and 1920. Here the peasantry asserted full control over their own lives in a network of freely organised, coordinated and disciplined communes. 'The movement of the revolutionary peasants became organised and unified, and realised ever more precisely its fundamental constructive tasks.'[10]

The masses' endeavours in town and countryside alike were rejected by those in authority; both were denounced as chimerical, romantic, recipes for economic chaos. In the libertarian view, however, it was not merely in moral and spiritual terms that their goals were rational. In economic terms, too, the endeavours of the masses were full of promise. There was bound to be economic dislocation in 1917–18. The war, the flight of capital, the social struggle made that inevitable. And no doubt workers and peasants made mistakes as they moved towards self-management. But the best hope of tackling the country's problems lay precisely in relying upon grass-roots initiative.

Freely elected factory committees were in the best position to judge the needs of their industries; to sustain the morale and self-discipline of their fellow-workers; and to find ways of overcoming the disastrous breakdown in trade between town and countryside.[11] Against the accusation, common at the time and reiterated ever since, that each factory committee was concerned only with its own plant, the libertarians point to the vigorous efforts the committees made to provide common guidelines, to cooperate, to coordinate their efforts. Self-management, the retention of power on the factory floor, they insist, by no means precluded the establishment of coordinated planning and distribution.[12] Likewise, peasant communes were in the best position to restore agriculture and respond to urban needs. What compounded the economic crisis was not the 'anarchy' of mass initiative, but its suppression. The restoration of authoritarian relationships in the factory from early in 1918 led to severe demoralisation among workers.[13] The use of force to extract grain from the village, and the establishment by the Bolsheviks of so-called 'Poor Peasant Committees' in 1918 to assist in the process, were equally counter-productive. The result was to alienate the peasantry, erect barriers between workers and peasants, and exacerbate the food shortage.[14] Indeed, it was only because the new Bolshevik régime's high-handed, repressive approach estranged and divided the masses that the Whites were able to remain in the field so long and the carnage and destruction of the Civil War reached the heights it did.[15] Far from being to blame for Russia's economic plight, the movement for self-management offered the only constructive way forward.[16]

A decade or two ago, it was easy to laugh this approach out of court. To treat Russian peasants, soldiers and workers as autonomous, to attribute to them concern for human dignity and the ability to respond rationally to the problems with which they were confronted, would have been generally regarded as sheer wishful-thinking. Yet willingness to take seriously the aspirations of the masses, to credit them with an independence, sense of direction and rationality of their own, has been central to the shift of perspective characteristic of much recent work on the revolution. It constitutes the major common premise behind Wildman's analysis of the soldiers' revolt, the studies of workers by Koenker, Smith and Mandel, and Wade's treatment of the Red Guards and workers' militias, to take just a few examples.[17] Progress has been made in breaking down the flabby concept of 'the masses': attention has been drawn to the different paths followed during the course of the revolution by skilled and unskilled workers, by peasants in the centre and those on the periphery. Yet the evaluation of the popular movement has been remarkably consistent with the libertarian position. Mandel's celebration of 'the developed political

consciousness and activism, the initiative and creativity, the deep and
genuine preoccupation with democracy and freedom' displayed by
Petrograd workers would have been music to the ears of Maksimov
and Berkman.[18] So would Getzler's conclusion that

> it was in its commune-like self-government that Red Kronstadt
> really came into its own, realising the radical, democratic and
> egalitarian aspirations of its garrison and working people, their
> insatiable appetite for social recognition, political activity and
> public debate, their pent-up yearning for education, integration
> and community.[19]

Volin and Arshinov would have been delighted by Shanin's presentation of the peasant movement during the 'dress rehearsal' of 1905–7:

> Every village proceeded throughout 1905–7 with its own never-
> ceasing debate . . . At the centre of this immense process of com-
> munication was not propaganda sent or brought from elsewhere,
> but rather a grandiose and spontaneous effort at political self-
> understanding and self-education by millions of illiterate and half-
> literate villagers. In an endless, slow, often clumsy and ill-
> informed and over-heated debate, masses of peasants looked at
> their life and environment anew and critically. They conceived
> and expressed what was often unthinkable until then: an image of
> a new world, a dream of justice, a demand for land and liberty.[20]

Their goals – land, bread, liberty and, in 1917, peace – were not
instilled into the masses by skilful propaganda: they welled up from
below. The moderate socialists who so quickly won allegiance in
soldiers' and local land and village committees, in trade unions and
soviets, were only able to retain their influence when they endorsed the
goals of their constituents. Bolshevik popularity among soldiers rose
not because they held out 'a new vision of the revolution', but rather
because they seemed to provide 'a more speedy and direct realisation
of the original one', an alternative path towards the masses' own
aims.[21]

Equally, the notion that determination to assert their dignity as
human beings was a central element in the motivation of the masses
has found a wide measure of corroboration. Heather Hogan's work on
metal-workers in the pre-revolutionary period has brought out this
concern for 'dignity issues'. The militancy of the skilled worker, in
particular, was intimately related to an increasingly conscious revolt
against the humiliation meted out by the Tsarist factory order, by the
violation 'of his self-respect in the most personal and humiliating of

ways'.[22] The motivation behind the initial selective purge of factory managers after February has been seen in precisely these terms. 'This was no elemental *bunt*, no anarchist rebellion against all authority, but a decisive rejection of unlimited, arbitrary power, experienced as an insult to the workers' self-respect.'[23] Equally, resentment at the indignities of Tsarist military discipline, symbolised by the familiar form of address used by officers speaking to the rank and file, has been underlined in examinations of both 1905–7 and 1917.[24] Reconsideration of the (very inadequate) evidence of social organisation under the Makhnovshchina in the Ukraine has pointed in the same direction.[25] And Shanin's picture of peasant aspirations stresses that their revolt was not solely about land, but about justice, humane treatment, an end to *proizvol*, 'about liberty, self-management and good order'.[26]

Recent studies of the factory-committee movement draw a more nuanced picture than that of the libertarians, and firmly reject the inflated claims occasionally made in early libertarian accounts about the influence of anarchist and syndicalist propaganda. But the two are closely compatible. The committees, which began to spring up as soon as the February revolution broke out, were established on the workers' own initiative. At first their concern was to curtail the authoritarian structure of the Tsarist factory, to halt the most direct assaults upon the dignity of workers, and to provide a collective mouthpiece for the advance of workers' interests. During the early weeks of the revolution, they entered into collective bargaining with their employers, showed great concern for good order, and seldom intervened directly in management.[27] Indeed factory committees were at first distinctly reluctant to take on the responsibility of running their enterprises. They were pragmatic, practical, in a sense defensive. 'The behaviour of Moscow's workers in 1917', comments Koenker, 'suggests a working class that was both highly rational in its responses to the political and economic pressure of 1917 and extremely patient as well.'[28] It was only as inflation ran out of control and as they confronted the threat of closures and unemployment that they began to intervene more directly in management. 'The policy of workers' control of production was first and foremost an attempt by factory committees to stem the tide of industrial chaos.'[29]

Moreover, from the start factory-committee activists showed acute awareness of the need for coordination. In the capital they were quick to convene a conference of factory committees, and they were among the earliest voices calling for central planning of the economy, proposing that it be based upon the directly elected factory-committee structure.[30] Equally, the notion that they were responsible for the economic chaos which engulfed the country has been rejected. For Smith, the expansion of workers' control was less a cause than a consequence of accelerating economic chaos.[31] According to Mandel, the very limited fall in employment in the capital between January and October 'was the major achievement of workers' control' and the positive impact of self-management in the Urals during the early months of Soviet power has been documented.[32]

The picture that emerges from recent portrayals, of a movement gradually broadening the scope of 'control', lends weight to the libertarian view. Rather than being the product of economically illiterate utopianism, the workers' vision of full-blown self-management hesitantly articulated after October was the product of experience and of the scale of economic catastrophe with which they were confronted. Smith's analysis traces the fusion of early concern to assert workers' dignity in the work-place with mounting pressure for direct intervention in management in order to keep the plant open:

> Throughout 1917 workers' control of industry had aimed, principally, to minimise capitalist disruption of industry, but it had never been concerned exclusively with that: it had also aimed to democratise relations of authority within the enterprise and to create new relations of production in which workers could display maximum initiative, responsibility and creativity.

The fusion led inexorably in the direction of self-management.[33]

Analysis of the economic rationality of the peasant movement has been less extensive. But attention has been drawn to both the initial restraint and the economic logic behind the shifting nature of peasant protest during 1917 – be it seizure of land, crops, timber or inventories.[34] Equally, the central thrust of the libertarian critique of the Bolshevik government's policy towards the peasantry – that the coercive methods used, and especially the experiment at forced grain-requisitioning through the Poor Peasant Committees, were profoundly counter-productive – has been widely endorsed. Bideleux's comparative study has drawn on a wide range of recent research to present a stimulating defence of the potential of village-based economic growth. Combining the work of Gregory and others on the economic progress of post-Emancipation peasant agriculture with evidence of the resilience of the commune and the family farm and limited scope of socio-economic differentiation in the village, he has provided fresh grounds for libertarian optimism about the economic promise of autonomous peasant agriculture.[35]

The second major feature of libertarian discourse is, as has been indicated, the manner in which it addresses the 'failure' of the revolution. The revolution failed, in the libertarian view, because the masses, for all their creative achievement, were unable to sustain their challenge to every form of authority. They lacked the experience, the firmly established organisations and the ideological clarity necessary to carry it through in the teeth of the most determined resistance. The constraints of the Tsarist era had stunted their ideological and organisational development. Their organisations 'had no historical tradition, no competence, no notion of their role, their task, their true mission'.[36] Even the factory-committee movement was 'unable to proclaim its own objectives (workers' self-management) in clear and positive terms'.[37] So they were inevitably 'taken in tow' by the political parties. During 1917 they had not the time to consolidate their own organisations, to entrench direct democracy and forestall bureaucratisation. Their challenge was sufficient to sweep away Tsarism and nobility, to dispossess the bourgeoisie and all but destroy the existing state. But they were unable to prevent the reassertion of authority in a guise less easy to expose than Tsarism or capitalism but no less oppressive: Bolshevism.

It is the Bolsheviks who bear the overriding responsibility for the débâcle. It was they who crushed the revolution. During 1917, the Bolsheviks succeeded in attracting a good measure of popular support. They adopted slogans that echoed the aspirations of the masses. They hailed the factory committees and workers' control (though not self-management), they championed the immediate transfer of the land to the peasants, an end to the war and traditional hierarchical authority in the army, and the dismantling of the bourgeois state. But the popular support they won did not guarantee the Bolsheviks victory. The primary allegiance of the masses was to their factory committees, their village assemblies, their soviets. What made it possible for the Bolsheviks to take advantage of the mass movement was superior organisation. Unlike the newly established representative bodies of peasants and workers, the party was strongly entrenched when the revolution broke out. Its centralised, disciplined organisation had the edge over the democratic organisations in the hands of the masses. 'Confronted with an "efficient", tightly-knit organisation of this kind ... it is scarcely surprising that the emerging factory committees were unable to carry the revolution to completion.'[38]

The party's espousal during 1917 of broadly libertarian aims had amounted, in fact, to conscious or unconscious demagoguery.[39] For Bolshevik ideology was permeated by élitism and authoritarianism.

Indeed, 'the fundamental characteristic of Bolshevik psychology was distrust of the masses, of the proletariat' – and to an even greater extent of the peasantry.[40] 'At heart the Bolsheviks had no faith in the people and their creative initiative.'[41] Behind the mystifying veil of revolutionary Marxism, they constituted 'the last attempt of bourgeois society to reassert its ordained division into leaders and led, and to maintain authoritarian social relations in all aspects of human life'.[42] They acted as the spokesmen not of the proletariat but of a new class: the intelligentsia.

In the libertarian view, together with the bourgeoisie and the proletariat, capitalism had bred a third class consisting of those 'who command knowledge which is generally recognised and rewarded (or punished) either for its technical application or for its ability to select and define general values and priorities'.[43] This new class embraced on the one hand the middle-ranking officers and bureaucrats of the old régime, and on the other the 'marginal intelligentsia' of Tsarist society. While these two strata were distinct, one working inside the imperial régime and the other in confrontation with it, their aim was the same. Both sought forceful economic modernisation of backward Russia, and both aspired to monopolise power over the distribution of wealth in the new society. Commanding no physical capital, they sought to establish their right to power and privilege on the grounds of their superior knowledge, their expertise. They sought a society based on 'reason' – their reason – where the surplus product of labour would be at the disposal not of idle capitalists and degenerate gentry – or, indeed, of labour itself – but of expert administrators.

Accordingly, during 1917, they looked askance at the seizure of power from below, at the dismantling of all forms of authority. Even those *intelligenty* – Socialist Revolutionaries (SRs), Mensheviks – who had been most eloquent in denouncing the old régime were appalled when the masses sought to resist their authority, to assert grass-roots control over their committees, their officials, their industrial and agricultural 'experts'. When the authority of tradition and property had been thoroughly dismantled, the intelligentsia sought through superior organisation and articulacy to draw a rigid line between manual and intellectual labour, and to re-establish the subordination of the former to the latter. And after the revolution the two strata coalesced to form a ruling class which repressed and exploited workers and peasants as brutally as did the capitalists of the West.

It was as spokesmen for this class that the Bolsheviks acted. Despite the working-class support which the party attracted, the separation between the Bolsheviks and the masses remained fundamental. 'The few Bolshevik cadres of working-class origin soon lost real contact with the class.' Those workers who supported it 'could not control the party. The leadership was firmly in the hands of professional revolutionaries.'[44] For them, it was enough that property be at the disposal of a centralised state which they themselves would run.[45] 'The professional revolutionaries who came to power in October 1917 were concerned to develop Russia's capitalist potential to the utmost, to carry the country farther and faster along the road than the feeble bourgeoisie.'[46] The tactical flexibility, authoritarian ideology and centralised organisation of the party made it the ideal vehicle for the imposition of the rule of the intelligentsia.

As soon as it was in a position to do so, the party moved to curtail self-management. It subordinated the factory committees to the trade unions, established rigid party control over the trade unions, and concentrated managerial power in the hands of a centralised state bureaucracy.[47] And once the state had asserted the right to appoint management from above, the division between officials and workers at the bench rapidly widened. At the same time, the new régime did all it could to gain control over the peasantry and to replace the free federative structures of the communes with hierarchical bodies directed by the party. The Bolsheviks brought to life Bakunin's prescient nightmare of the reign of scientific intelligence, 'the most oppressive, arrogant and scornful of all régimes'.[48]

Here, too, recent analysis has lent a considerable amount of support to the libertarian view. The failure of the factory committees, despite their progress in the direction of self-management, to develop their insights 'into a systematic strategy for socialism, alternative to that of Lenin and the majority of the Bolshevik leadership', has been recognised as a major weakness of the movement.[49] Koenker's study of the Moscow working class during the revolution identified precisely the weakness of its organisations as the Achilles' heel. Factory committees, trade unions and soviets sprang up in rich profusion, but they failed to keep pace with political developments and the growth of class consciousness. 'The organisational history of 1917 reveals the legacy of the relatively rapid formation of the Russian working class and the years of repression by the Tsarist political system. Perhaps a revolution teaches political and class consciousness in eight months', concludes Koenker, 'but organisational success took not just consciousness, but practice as well.'[50] The skilled, literate, articulate, self-confident echelons of the working class who led these organisations were in short supply, and the economic and military sequel to October drained the factory and the city of those there were. Weakly led, overlapping, competing working-class institutions failed to consolidate rank-and-file control and left a vacuum which the Bolshevik party filled.[51]

The evidence that suspicion between the intelligentsia and workers mounted during 1917 provides further grist for the libertarian mill. As pressure for soviet power and for plebeian control from below grew, there was a widening rift between intelligentsia and workers. Among the socialist intelligentsia, among technical specialists, civil servants and white-collar workers in general, there was increasing hostility towards the radicalism of the workers' demands.[52] After October there was considerable resistance from among white-collar workers, and tension between white- and blue-collar workers persisted. Moreover, few Western assessments of the outcome of the revolution would deny the restoration of managerial, technical and bureaucratic authority at the expense of self-management by workers and peasants alike, or the array of privileges which managers and officials came to enjoy.[53]

Analyses of Lenin's ideology, while recognising the ambivalence in his thought, have gone some way to confirming the libertarian thesis. Attention has been drawn to the emphasis he placed upon the level of the productive forces as the vital indicator of socialist potential, in contrast to the belated and intermittent interest he showed in the question of altering relations of production and workers' self-management; to his growing preoccupation with managerial and technical authority; to his condescending attitude towards the peasantry, his low regard for their capacity for initiative and organisation, his misconceived faith in fanning class war among them – and the direct impact this had upon the way in which he reacted to the grain crisis of 1918.[54]

Where the libertarian interpretation is most at odds with recent work is in its treatment of the Bolshevik party. In the first place, the description of the party in 1917 as essentially the instrument of the intelligentsia is no longer plausible: indeed, so profound was the transformation through which the party passed between February and October that it would be more accurate to regard it as being itself one of the mass organisations (re)created in the course of the revolution. The door to party membership was flung open. Numerically, the intelligentsia had long ceased to predominate: now they were swamped by worker recruits.[55] And the fierce hostility to the Bolsheviks evinced by most members of the intelligentsia makes it difficult to sustain the seductive libertarian thesis that in 1917 the party represented a new class of 'intellectuals'. Equally, the notion that before 1917 let alone during that year, the party operated as a tightly knit centralised body, on the model of *Chto delat?*, has been largely discredited.[56] Throughout 1917 and into 1918, the authority of the leadership was bucked and bucked again. The party was not a submissive instrument of Lenin's will but a vibrant, chaotic, largely democratic organisation. Over a host of issues, it was acutely divided – not least among those issues being the question of the factory committees themselves. It is no longer adequate to treat the fate of the committees after October in terms of a struggle between Bolsheviks and workers.[57] Party members were strongly represented among the leading lights of the factory-committee movement. During 1918, much of the pressure for firm state intervention arose from the committees themselves. And the increasingly desperate efforts by the committees to impose discipline amidst the hunger and economic breakdown of 1918 to 1920 went far towards alienating the rank and file.[58]

More generally, the libertarian approach anticipates the point at which the party came to dominate the political process. It underrates the fatal impact on local soviet democracy of precipitate military and industrial demobilisation, 'economic Balkanisation' and later civil war; the bitter internecine struggle over scarce resources which was engendered; and the contribution to the centralisation of power made by pressure from below.[59] In short, not unlike its liberal and Soviet rivals, the libertarian interpretation oversimplifies the sequel to the revolution by treating 'Bolsheviks' as a different species from other mortals.

Because of its polemical style, its sectarian associations and chiliastic overtones, the libertarian tradition has long been marginalised. Yet, to paraphrase Bacon, the origins of an historical approach do not determine its validity. By viewing the revolution from below; by emphasising the measure of autonomy, rationality and idealism in the mass movement; by drawing attention to the relative weakness of working-class organisation; by highlighting the 'productivism' in the thought of leading Bolsheviks; and by underlining the connection between the restoration of hierarchical relations at the point of production and the bureaucratisation of mass organisations, the tradition anticipates the findings of much new research. The rapprochement between the 'lunatic fringe' and mainline Western scholarship is interesting in itself. It also suggests that the libertarian tradition may offer a vantage point of as much value as those of its better-known rivals in our attempts to synthesise and grasp the implications of recent insights into the revolution.

NOTES

1 'Libertarian' is used here to denote the far Left of the political spectrum, rather than the far Right which has more recently laid claim to the label.

2 For two specialists publishing in the 1960s whose approach was in some respects sympathetic to the libertarians see P. Avrich, *The Russian Anarchists* (Princeton, 1967) and F. Kaplan, *Bolshevik Ideology* (London, 1969). J. Burbank, *Intelligentsia and Revolution. Russian Views of Bolshevism, 1917–1922* (Oxford, 1986), while presenting much interesting material on the anti-Bolshevik post-mortem, conforms to the generally dismissive attitude restricting analysis of the libertarian view to a brief consideration of Kropotkin.

3 Compare L. Schapiro, *The Russian Revolutions and the Origins of Present-Day Communism* (Hounslow, 1984) and P.A. Golub (ed.), *Istoricheskii opyt trekh rossiiskikh revoliutsii*, 3 vols. (Moscow, 1985–7) with C. Sirianni, *Workers' Control and Socialist Democracy. The Soviet Experience* (London, 1982), to date the most sophisticated treatment of the revolution from a broadly libertarian perspective.

4 Voline, *The Unknown Revolution 1917–1921* (Montreal, 1974); G.P. Maximoff, *The Guillotine at Work. Twenty Years of Terror in Russia* (Chicago, 1940); A. Berkman, *The Russian Tragedy* (Montreal, 1976); P. Arshinov, *A History of the Makhnovist Movement, 1918–1921* (Detroit, 1974).

5 Berkman, *Tragedy*, p. 13.

6 M. Brinton, *The Bolsheviks and Workers' Control* (Montreal, 1972), p. vii.

7 Berkman, *Tragedy*, pp. 36–7. Berkman was responsible for the translation of 'The Russian Revolution and the Communist Party' (1921), from which these comments are taken, but he attributed authorship to four Moscow anarchists.

8 Berkman, *Tragedy*, p. 58; Maximoff, *Guillotine*, pp. 348–51.

9 Brinton, *Bolsheviks*, p. 20.

10 Voline, *Revolution*, p. 569.

11 Voline, *Revolution*, pp. 289–301, 369,

12 Berkman, *Tragedy*, p. 58; Brinton, *Bolsheviks*, pp. 18–21. The issue of centralisation clearly touches a raw nerve but many libertarians would endorse Brinton's comment that: 'We doubt if there is any *intrinsic* merit in decentralisation ... The key question is whether the "centralised" apparatus is controlled from below (by elected and revocable delegates) or whether it separates itself from those on whose behalf it is allegedly acting' (Brinton, *Bolsheviks*, pp. 46–7).

13 Berkman, *Tragedy*, pp. 21–2, 58; Brinton, *Bolsheviks*, pp. 35, 47.

14 Voline, *Revolution*, pp. 250–1, 423–5; Maximoff, *Guillotine*, pp. 39–40, 67–71.

15 Voline, *Revolution*, p. 425; Maximoff, *Guillotine*, pp. 32–3.

16 Sirianni, *Workers' Control*, pp. 104–16; 185–97.

17 A.K. Wildman, *The End of the Russian Imperial Army: The Old Army and the Soldiers' Revolt (March–April, 1917)*, *The Road to Power and Peace* (Princeton, 1980, 1987); D. Koenker, *The Moscow Workers and the 1917 Revolution* (Princeton, 1981); S.A. Smith, *Red Petrograd. Revolution in the Factories 1917–18* (Cambridge, 1983); D. Mandel, *The Petrograd Workers and the Fall of the Old Régime* and *The Petrograd Workers and the Seizure of Soviet Power* (London, 1983, 1984); R.A. Wade, *Red Guards and Workers' Militias in the Russian Revolution* (Stanford, 1984).

18 Mandel, *Seizure*, p. 419,

19 I. Getzler, *Kronstadt 1917–1921: The Fate of a Soviet Democracy* (Cambridge, 1983), p. 248.

20 T. Shanin, *Russia, 1905–07. Revolution as a Moment of Truth. The Roots of Otherness: Russia's Turn of Century* (London, 1986), vol. II, pp. 130–1.

21 Wildman, *Soldiers' Revolt*, p. 379.

22 H. Hogan, 'Labor and Management in Conflict: The St Petersburg Metal-Working Industry, 1900–1914', Ph.D. dissertation, University of Michigan, 1981, p. 514.

23 Mandel, *Fall*, pp. 100, 12ff; Smith, *Red Petrograd*, pp. 40–1, 56–7.

24 J. Bushnell, *Mutiny amid Repression. Russian Soldiers in the Revolution of 1905–1906* (Bloomington, 1985), p. 102.

25 D. Dahlmann, 'Anarchism and the Makhno Movement', *Sbornik* 11 (1985), 14–16; see also M. Malet, *Nestor Makhno in the Russian Civil War* (London, 1982).

26 Shanin, *Russia*, p. 132.

27 Z. Galili y Garcia, 'The Menshevik Revolutionary Defensists and the Workers in the Russian Revolution of 1917', Ph.D. dissertation, Columbia University, 1982, pp. 147–8.

28 Koenker, *Moscow*, p. 359.

29 Smith, *Red Petrograd*, p. 146.

30 Smith, *Red Petrograd*, pp. 157–8.

31 Smith, *Red Petrograd*, p. 242.

32 Mandel, *Fall*, p. 216.

33 Smith, *Red Petrograd*, pp. 227, 149.

34 G. Gill, *Peasants and Government in the Russian Revolution* (London, 1979). Gill's approach to the *political* sophistication of the peasantry, stressing as he does their confusion, uncertainty and naïvety, conforms more closely to the traditional liberal view, pp. 31–3.

35 R. Bideleux, *Communism and Development* (London, 1985), pp. 12–18.

36 Voline, *Revolution*, p. 187.

37 Brinton, *Bolsheviks*, p. xiii.

38 Ibid.

39 Berkman, *Tragedy*, p. 37; Maximoff, *Guillotine*, pp. 21–5.

40 Berkman, *Tragedy*, p. 41.

41 Berkman, *Tragedy*, p. 16.

42 Brinton, *Bolsheviks*, p. 85.

43 G. Konrad and I. Szelenyi, *The Intellectuals on the Road to Class Power* (Brighton, 1979), p. 32. This theme in libertarian work derives from the Polish-born *intelligent*, Makhaev (Machajski), and indeed from Bakunin before him. Recent elaborations include R. Gombin, *The Radical Tradition. A Study in Modern Revolutionary Thought* (London, 1978).

44 Brinton, *Bolsheviks*, p. xii.

45 Konrad and Szelenyi, *Intellectuals*, p. 140.

46 Gombin, *Radical Tradition*, p. 27.

47 This is argued in some detail in Brinton, *Bolsheviks*.

48 *Archives Bakounine*, ed. A. Lehning (Leiden, 1967), vol. III, p. 148.

49 Smith, *Red Petrograd*, p. 261.

50 Koenker, *Moscow*, p. 365.

51 Ibid., pp. 354-5.

52 Mandel, *Fall*, pp. 237-40.

53 See K.E. Bailes, *Technology and Society under Lenin and Stalin. Origins of the Soviet Technical Intelligentsia, 1917–1941* (Princeton, 1978), pp. 19–66, for a discussion both of the technical intelligentsia's initial hostility towards the revolutionary upheaval – and specifically towards workers' control (p. 21) – and of their subsequent integration into the new state.

54 N. Harding, *Lenin's Political Thought. Theory and Practice in the Democratic and Socialist Revolutions* (London, 1983), vol. II, pp. 187–97, 209–19; P. Corrigan, H. Ramsay and D. Sayer, *Socialist Construction and Marxist Theory* (London, 1978), pp. 40–7; Smith, *Red Petrograd*, pp. 225–8.

55 R. Service, *The Bolshevik Party in Revolution. A Study in Organizational Change, 1917–1923* (London, 1979), pp. 42–7; W. Chase and J. Arch Getty, 'The Moscow Bolshevik cadres of 1917; a prosopographical analysis', *Russian History* 5 (1978), 84–105.

56 A. Rabinowitch, *The Bolsheviks Come to Power* (New York, 1976), pp. 310–14; Service, *Bolshevik party*, pp. 54–62.

57 Smith, *Red Petrograd*, pp. 149–50, 153–7.

58 On the fate of the factory committees, in addition to Mandel, *Seizure* and Smith, *Red Petrograd*, see the discussion in W.G. Rosenberg, 'Russian Labor and Bolshevik Power after October', *Slavic Review* 44 (1985), 205–38, and P.S. Flenley, 'Workers' Organizations in the Russian Metal Industry, February 1917–August 1918', Ph.D. dissertation, University of Birmingham, 1983.

59 In addition to J.L.H. Keep, *The Russian Revolution: A Study in Mass Mobilization* (London, 1976), see A. Rabinowitch, 'The Evolution of Local Soviets in Petrograd, November 1917–June 1918: The Case of the First City District Soviet', *Slavic Review* 46 (1987), 20–37, and the spate of recent doctoral dissertations which focus on the wider political repercussions of the economic crisis in 1918: L.T. Lih, 'Bread and Authority in

Russia: Food Supply and Revolutionary Politics, 1914–1921', Ph.D. dissertation, University of Princeton, 1981; T.J. Renehan, 'The Failure of Local Soviet Government, 1917–1918', Ph.D. dissertation, State University of New York, 1983; M.M. Helgesen, 'The Origins of the Party-State Monolith in Soviet Russia. Relations between the Soviets and Party Committees in the Central Provinces, Oct. 1917–March 1921', Ph.D. dissertation, State University of New York, 1980.

18

RUSSIAN MARXISM:
THEORY, ACTION AND OUTCOME

BARUCH KNEI-PAZ

THIS chapter is written in a somewhat unorthodox fashion. Although it is based on work that I have been doing for some years now,[1] it is not the result of any particular piece of research and does not purport to present specific 'findings', as this term is normally understood in historical scholarship. It is written from the perspective of a student of politics and social science interested in Russian Marxism and the Russian revolution of 1917 for the light they throw on political theory in general and the relationship between ideas and political action in particular. Its scope is very general (the somewhat overworked 'overview' is a word that springs to mind in this context, as does the even more suspicious 'reflections') and its claims are evaluative – though not in the simple normative sense – rather than merely descriptive since, amongst other things, they exploit the vantage point of historical hindsight. Apart from the fact that we all look at the past equipped with the knowledge of the present – can it be otherwise? – it is surely legitimate to analyse past political ideas and actions from the point of view of their outcomes and not only from that of declared intentions.

But beyond this, the claims made in this chapter are for the most part analytically asserted since, given the aims and structure of the paper, the assertive demeanour seems the most appropriate.[2] After all, more than seventy years after the event, it is perhaps not inappropriate to do some overall stocktaking of our theoretical knowledge as well – however uncertain it continues to be – of how 1917 came about, what it signified, and what it teaches us about such matters as modern social theory, ideology, political action and the historical results or consequences of all these.

Max Weber, it will be remembered, argued that the historian's or social scientist's understanding – *verstehen* – arises from his perception

406

of the meaning that historical actors have attributed to their actions. But as against this significance from the point of view of the actor, it was Weber himself who also sought the historical, sometimes unintended, even undesired, significance that emerges and is beyond the control of the actor even though he may himself, ironically, have contributed to it.[3] I have elsewhere endeavoured to analyse in some detail how such matters were linked in the case of the Russian revolution.[4] In what follows, however, I attempt to postulate certain far-ranging interpretative conclusions:

(1) Russian Marxism – like Marxism in general – and the Russian revolution of October 1917 were a twentieth-century species of a nineteenth-century genus: the symbiotic idea-action or theory-praxis construct, which became common enough in European intellectual circles around 1850, and which evolved in accordance with the precepts that man is the centre of all things, that he is the progenitor of his social world – including the cognitive means of both understanding and controlling it – and that this 'intellectual revolution' went hand-in-hand with a 'material revelation', namely, that history was inexorably moving in a direction of greater, even if still far from fulfilled, human liberation, equality and democratisation. Lest it be assumed that this interdependent joining of social theory (in effect social science) with political practice (in effect volitional intervention in history) was peculiarly Marxist, with its immediate Hegelian sources turned upside down, it should be noted that, *mutatis mutandis*, as an Enlightenment legacy it infiltrated the theory and politics of liberalism as well.

But there is no denying that it received its extreme, paradigmatic formulation in Marx's view of things. Of course, the conjoining of theory and practice at an abstract, epistemological level does not in itself decree what particular course of action is prescribed in a concrete conjunctural situation. The possible historical variables in any given situation are so manifold that they can only be decoded in the heat, so to speak, of action itself. No wonder that we are sometimes perplexed by Marx's own seemingly inconsistent, some would even say opportunistic, tactics as he reacted to changing empirical realities, whether before 1848 or between 1848 and 1850 or thereafter. But be that as it may, my point here is that Russian Marxism, and Bolshevism in particular of course, must in the first instance be understood in the light of the notion that the dichotomy between the comprehension of social phenomena and their transformation was no longer tenable, that, in fact, comprehension must necessarily culminate in domination

– in a manner not unlike that which had already occurred in the natural sciences where theoretical knowledge made possible both greater freedom from nature and *its* increasing subjugation to human intentions and purposes.

(2)   Nevertheless, it goes without saying, that not all Marxists made the connection between theory and action in the same uniform way. Such non-uniformity can hardly escape the notice of anyone who reads the texts in particular of Russian Marxism where the barricades over this matter were put up at an early stage and never came down. These texts abundantly reveal an uneasy methodological 'bedfellowship' between, on the one hand, the sociological proclivity and, on the other, the 'politological' – as I propose to use these terms.

This is not the same issue, referred to above, of what particular tactics are to be adopted in a given situation; for if that were all there was to it, we would be hard-pressed to explain the fundamental fissure in Russian Marxism between Mensheviks and Bolsheviks. At the same time, it would be a misrepresentation to perceive the two proclivities as parallel equivalents of the theory–action dichotomy since no Russian Marxists, not even the most 'patient' of Mensheviks, accepted this dichotomy in principle and such controversies as erupted were also reducible to practical articulations. If, however, we bear in mind that there is a difference between arguments over the *assessment* of practical possibilities as against those over the legitimacy of their perceived *consequences*, then, I think, we will get to the very real import of what admittedly, and on the face of it, looks like a mere 'academic' issue. To repeat, therefore, the sociological–'politological' division reflected an endemic tension that coloured the controversies and the mentalities of Russian Marxists from Plekhanov onwards. One should recall here that the uneasy relationship I am speaking of was already present in Marx – once again, the issue here is not particular tactics – as it must be in anyone who embraced so wholeheartedly the Enlightenment legacy.

The dilemma inherent in this legacy, as it crystallised in Marx, was twofold: first, how does one get from the historical–sociological analysis that material conditions determine the nature of human relations and social structures to the role of intentionality in these relations and structures, particularly if one theoretically attributes a subsidiary, dependent (or superstructure) function to politics? I only note in passing that in order to establish intentionality it is not enough to say, as Marx did, that men make their history: machines too 'make' things, yet we would not attribute intentions to them. Second, and as a corol-

lary to the preceding, is it always and necessarily the case that volitional intervention – purposeful political action – in the historical
process can have no distorting consequences in the *long-run* (never
mind the short-run) in the sense of engendering an otherwise ruled-out
future? I know, of course, that all this is a very complex matter, and
that much ink has been spilt to show that Marx did cope with these
questions.[5] But it is at best an open question whether, at a theoretical
level, Marx or any of his subsequent disciples resolved the dilemma I
have been discussing. I do not think that they did and I do not think
the project could be carried out.

Moreover, and much more to the point, it is clearly the case that
such Russian figures as Plekhanov and Martov, each in his own
agonising way, were in the end at best reluctant to make unequivocal
in practice what remained equivocal in theory. As against this,
however, it is precisely such an 'existential choice' that Lenin carried
out. (True, the Menshevik alternative is also an 'existential choice', in
the way that a non-decision is also a decision, but I am sure the reader
will appreciate the difference and I will in any case later revise this
tentative formulation.) Thus the Menshevik–Bolshevik split, as it
developed after 1903, takes the form of a schism between the 'sociologists' and the 'politologists' or – to forge the link I am seeking
between epistemological issues and the concrete politics that will
eventually emerge – as a schism between those who saw historical
sociology as a sufficient condition for change and those who saw it only
as a necessary, but insufficient, condition. To this one need only add
that attitudes or assessments at the level of tactics would follow logically in each case.

(3) All this may, perhaps, sound like a casuistic version of an old
story or a tortuously roundabout way of arriving at what many have
long claimed to know without the epistemological acrobatics – to wit,
that Lenin was simply interested in the seizure of power and his
Marxist convictions were merely so much grist for the revolutionary
mill. But this is emphatically *not* what I wish to argue. For if the matter
is looked at in the way I suggest, then, in fact, it behoves us to do away
once and for all with a question that for a long time cast its ubiquitous
shadow over the study of Russian Marxism: who were the real, the
genuine – whatever that may mean – Marxists: the Mensheviks or the
Bolsheviks?

Those who posed this question had, it seems, an axe to grind, a
propensity at any rate to characterise the Bolsheviks as Marxists in
name only – and thus usurpers – but, in reality, power-seekers with a

cynical, or at best a purely instrumental, attitude towards the integrity of Marxist theory.[6] If such a characterisation was once possible, even rampant, it can no longer be maintained with any credulity against the detailed and comprehensive textual re-interpretations of Lenin, Bukharin and that latter-day Bolshevik, Trotsky, which show only too clearly the seriousness of these men's historical–sociological sensibilities.[7]

Since it was Lenin who was always picked out for special treatment as an almost Machiavellian prince in Marxist disguise, it needs to be stressed that such treatment is possible only by ignoring or tendentiously misconstruing his writings. It is remarkable what a difference it makes if one looks at his political activities in the light of his writings rather than at his writings in the light of his activities, however oversimplified this formulation may be. That is why I make a distinction between the sociological and *politological, not* the political, for the term politological is meant to entail the epistemological basis of political action, not merely the crude reality of it.

If, therefore, the Menshevik–Bolshevik split is seen as a reflection of an unresolved, and perhaps unresolvable, dilemma in Marxist theory then both camps can claim at least equal legitimacy – though it is rather a different matter whether either is actually valid (I think not, but this is not the issue here since it is not their veracity that is at stake but rather the seriousness or conviction or persuasiveness with which both were put forward). At any rate, we are concerned not with the legitimacy of parenthood but the consequences of two plausible – or, at least, possible – choices; perhaps we should call them conscious mutations! It is not necessary to attribute to Lenin the view that 'politics is all', much less 'force is all' – to the exclusion, that is, of history, sociology, class struggle, objective constraints and so forth – as against the quite different view that politics is the *clinching* element making for the intentionality of necessary historical change (but imagine it, if I may make an abrupt shift of context, as a Beethoven-type coda which not only clinches matters but has some life and value of its own and wills, as it were, into being the musical structure that prefigured it, rather than a pre-Beethovenian coda which is only a perfunctory tail tacked on at the end and having no intrinsic interest).

Lenin's view of society and politics may thus be formulated in the following manner: history is pregnant with various possibilities – some will be still-born, others will be born so maimed as to die shortly after birth, still others will be born maimed but may live out a painful and unhappy life and others still may be born normal and healthy, though of these some will meet with a violent death. *Each* of these possibilities has its own historical logic and *all* are sociologically rooted in the society that gives birth to them. Which finally survives and triumphs is thus not only a question of politics but politics can have a clinching say in the matter. Hence, to recapitulate, for Lenin politics is not a necessary *and* sufficient condition for societal change, except where sociology – the objective historical conditions in the Marxist–Enlightenment sense – is *also* present as a necessary condition.

(4) Of course, none of this would be persuasive if it were to be demonstrated that Lenin's historical–sociological analysis of Russian society, even if serious in form, is so incoherent or inconsistent or wrong-headed in substantive content as to be in *this* sense merely a pretext for his politology, not to mention his politics. For the charge has often been made that however well-conceptualised, by no stretch of the imagination did Lenin's analysis make the case that Russia possessed those 'prerequisites' for the socialist revolution which Marxism enjoins. Even if, as argued in the previous section, there is no doubting the seriousness of Lenin's sociological toils, we still need an *a fortiori* claim about their empirical coherence. The charge of incoherence – and thus dishonesty? – is sometimes put in the form of the observation that he mercilessly both stretched and chopped the representation of Russian reality until he could force it into the proverbial Procrustean bed of Marxist historical materialism and then decreed that all was set or ripe for the clinching political blow.

A strong, very persuasive and admirably argued case against this charge has been made in recent years by Neil Harding in his study of Lenin's political thought.[8] I wish I could accept his account *in toto*, for it would serve my purposes here only too well. But since I disagree with him insofar as he makes too little of the peculiarly Russian–Jacobin elements also to be found in Lenin – about which presently – it would perhaps be unfair to recruit him in support of my argument. Nevertheless, his is surely a case to contend with for anyone making light of Lenin as an economic and social thinker.[9]

As for myself, I wish to propose merely the following two general reasons for treating Lenin as a Marxist of consistent and realistic intentions subscribing to the limitations that Russian society imposed on political objectives and revising those limitations only in the light of new empirical data. First, far from being impetuous for the sake, as it were, of political activism, his political prognosis was surprisingly moderate, even conservative; so much so that it grates against the stereotyped image. Thus, for example, until the First World War at least, and perhaps as late as the April theses of 1917, his view of the Russian future can only be described as ultra-orthodox and tediously schematic: he clung to the traditional theory of separate 'stages' which posited that Russia would first have to go through a 'bourgeois-democratic' revolutionary phase, even as he experimented with various formulas designed to radicalise this phase. Not Lenin but Trotsky was unorthodox, audacious and militant in the adaptation of Marxism to Russia debate; and Lenin disdainfully rebuffed Trotsky as having wild and dangerous ideas.

But it is true, by April 1917 there can be no doubt about Lenin's volte-face: the theses of that month were a radical departure in that Lenin now recognised the possibility of a direct, barely interrupted transition to a socialist seizure of power. It is difficult to repudiate the impression of opportunism that this quite sudden transformation in Lenin's position has always engendered.

However, and this is the second general reason in defence of Lenin's coherence, the opportunism is not simply political; it has a sociological–politological dimension as well. I risk the charge of special pleading but I believe that after February 1917 Lenin had fully come to grasp a twentieth-century phenomenon of vast historical implications, namely, that while backward societies such as Russia were indeed not yet ripe for socialism, neither could they confront their debilitating conditions through a retracing of the European 'democratic revolution'. The embryonic outlines of this thesis were hinted at in Lenin's earlier writings when he argued that a 'bourgeois-democratic' revolution in Russia would have to be carried out with the direct and leading participation of the workers, otherwise it would fail as a modernising revolution.[10] The international crisis precipitated by the First World War now convinced him that capitalist democracy was in any case collapsing everywhere and this made the possibilities of the immediate future in Russia all the more open.[11]

Like Trotsky – who had argued this since 1905 – Lenin now saw the dynamics of change (we would call it today modernisation) in back-ward or unevenly developed societies as generating unique sociological possibilities and thus entailing, indeed justifying, radical political action. At any rate, the 'bourgeois-democratic' future was no longer the most likely, certainly not the only, outcome *achievable*.

I stress the word 'achievable' at this point, with its connotation of goal or intention-oriented action, because, as I see it, while Lenin's argument was rooted in sociology, it was linked to the epistemic foundation of his politics, that is, to the issue of intentionality which I discussed earlier and to which he gave the 'clinching' interpretation of his politology. And it is, indeed, a historical fact that in the twentieth century predominantly agrarian, or backward, societies have rarely embraced, or 'achieved', the 'bourgeois–capitalist–democratic' model of development, and only too often have instead opted for the model first launched in October 1917 by Lenin – and Trotsky.

(5)   However, this is not yet the whole of the story, complicated enough though it may already be. Having attempted to make the case for the fundamental intelligibility of Lenin's theoretical system, there is still room, and need, to accommodate the view that the character of Bolshevism is *not* exhausted by the dilemmas of Marxism alone.[12] The assumption that all the difficulties of Bolshevism in power are to be attributed to the post-1917 situation – the survival of European capitalism, primarily, and the consequent isolation of the Soviet Union – seems to me to be only partly valid in that it concentrates on conjunctural factors alone, however massive these might have been.

To facilitate the intelligibility of what follows, I first remind the reader of the second aspect of the original Marxist–Enlightenment dilemma mentioned in section 2 above: can volitional intervention in the historical process distort the future in the long run from the perspective of the purpose or intention of the intervention? Seventy years and more after the event the obvious answer may be yes – whatever happens henceforth – but to give substance to the answer we need a specifically historical, a Russian-historical, explanation. I have already said enough to indicate unequivocally that I reject the simplistic view according to which the future was distorted because Lenin and his followers did not have Marxist-socialist intentions in the first place (this is the 'power-at-all-costs-in-Marxist-disguise' view). So the explanation has to take the form: why did things go wrong *despite* the best of Bolshevik intentions? The answer, to repeat, needs to be sought in the specifically Russian context.

In previously calling Lenin's politological choice an 'existential' one, I was, of course, not entirely accurate, especially as I then went on to argue for the coherence of this choice. If a choice were truly existential it would be arbitrary or so random as to be either inexplicable or, at best, explicable only in terms of the personal psychology of the chooser. As against this, a coherent choice is one which has a theoretical-cum-empirical structure of plausible persuasiveness. In this sense, I concluded, Lenin's 'choice' – that is, his resolution of the Marxist dilemma – was no less plausible than that of the Mensheviks. So much can be said for the purely Marxist context of the choice.

But even a coherent, theoretically sound choice has a cultural or historical context *as well* – which is to say, one cannot sever theoretical knowledge from the *sociology* of theoretical knowledge, as if the former were a purely cognitive world unto itself. Given that manifold and plausible theories are there for the picking, why is it that the theory–action nexus formulated by Lenin is so peculiar to Russia or similar societies (recall that this nexus was to be repeated, *mutatis mutandis*, in, for example, China) but virtually absent in the West where, in fact, the tendencies are the very opposite, as in Bernstein, Kautsky or Luxemburg, certainly before 1917.[13] Part of the answer has already been given: the peculiar circumstances of Russian history and society – uneven development creating radical possibilities – prompted what I have called Lenin's politology.

However, these same circumstances were also responsible for the peculiar character of Russian politics: it had, or could have, a degree of autonomy *vis-à-vis* society that was inconceivable, or at least structurally constrained, in Western, capitalist societies (except, perhaps, in moments of deep economic crisis in which case, however, it seemed to take a Fascist form). This degree of autonomy can be translated into one of two patterns of political behaviour: either that of quite remarkable mass action with its imaginative, 'progressive' notions of self-rule – witness the soviets of 1905 and of 1917;[14] or the no less remarkable, organisational action with its unique structure of decision and command – witness the Bolshevik party. Both patterns were ruled out in Western societies – Bolshevism got nowhere there, and commune-like institutions have made no more headway – but they were endemic to a society such as Russia because both testify to the extent to which *politics as intentional activity can outstrip the constraints of social resources and capabilities.*

It is at this juncture that the problem of political-action responsibility in terms of the legitimacy of perceived or imaginable *consequences* (see again section 2 above) enters the historical scene. The Mensheviks – and with them Trotsky until after February 1917 – were clearly inclined towards volitional *mass* action as the more legitimate, less future-distorting, alternative in the special circumstances of Russia; and they may be said to have attributed to Lenin, in our terminology, a strategy of volitional intervention that would so grossly outstrip societal resources and capabilities as either to culminate in total collapse or necessitate the perpetuation and constant enlargement of the original degree of political autonomy.[15]

Of course the Russian context is not everything; but the purely

Marxist conundrum is not the whole story either. If the case for the role of Russian 'Jacobinism' in Lenin's epistemological scheme of things is put in this, albeit sinuous, way, then I think it cannot be summarily dismissed – whatever Lenin's honest intentions and whatever the theoretical persuasiveness of his epistemology.

(6) And still we have not reached the end of the story; the problem of whether the Bolshevik revolution was doomed from the start by its own character or undermined by exogenous and contingent events has not been fully answered in section 5 above. There I argued that a certain kind of volitional intervention *can*, from the point of view of intended and expected outcomes, distort the future beyond recognition.

The objection that can be raised against this statement is that it isolates some aspect of Bolshevism as a cause of future consequences without proving that that aspect would have been active in *all* circumstances. If the external environment into which it was born – so the counter-argument goes – had been transformed as expected, then the so-called Jacobin elements of Bolshevism would have lain dormant, at most a phase of its past but irrelevant to its future. Since the European revolution had failed to materialise, the exigencies of *this* situation, not Jacobinism, forced Lenin and the Bolsheviks into creating the 'dictatorship of the proletariat' with all its attendant distortions of the socialist future.

Those who make this counter-argument then present us with the following tragic account of the degeneration of the Bolshevik revolution: having taken power and found themselves isolated in a hostile world, the Bolsheviks were forced back upon their impoverished resources – an economy shattered by Civil War, primitive industrial foundations, no development capital or only such as could be accumulated with difficulty from a now uncooperative peasantry, and a venal and incompetent bureaucracy incapable of administering society. In these ruinous conditions, the forces of Russian backwardness threatened to overpower the forces of modernisation. With no support in prospect from abroad, the Bolsheviks had only two alternatives: either to surrender power in exasperation or to drag Russia by the throat into the twentieth century. However reluctantly at first, Lenin, to be followed with a vengeance by Stalin, chose the second alternative, of course. And the – inevitable? – consequence was terror, untold human suffering, a new, ruthless bureaucracy now in control of everything and, through the state, mercilessly waging war against all segments of society.

The history of the October revolution thus told consists of two claims: first, that the initial 'deviation' (the creation of a dictatorial state and bureaucracy) is to be attributed to the non-materialisation of the European revolution (the exogenous factor); and, second, that the subsequent 'pathological' degeneration – Stalinism – is to be sought in the cruel logic of the internal situation (the endogenous factor).

These two claims are sometimes conflated, but they need not be. Let us begin with the first and meet it head-on by supposing (a) that the element of political autonomy – the Jacobinism previously attributed to Lenin – is a figment of my imagination, meaning that section 5 above has no basis in fact, and (b) that the prognosis of a European revolutionary conflagration in the wake of the First World War *has* materialised, as Lenin, Trotsky, Bukharin and others hoped or expected it would, meaning that workers' governments are in power in Berlin, Paris, even London, just as the Bolsheviks themselves come to power in Petrograd, or shortly thereafter. By granting these admittedly 'mind-boggling' suppositions, we can ask: what difference can *this* scenario make to the post-1917 future of the Soviet Union?

Such a counterfactual proposition is no doubt the stuff of which academic absurdities are made; but there is some method in the madness, that method which began by pursuing the epistemological underpinnings of Marxism in general and of Russian Marxism in particular. Recall that our point of departure was the Enlightenment nexus of theory and action, so intermeshed as to permit men the intentional creation of their future through the rationalisation of their intellectual capacities and material resources. Marx believed that this result could be realised only when the state, amongst other things, had been abolished. But we know better today. In retrospect, it now appears that to the extent that such intentionality and rationalisation were possible they were in large measure a consequence of the modern state and bureaucracy and of the necessities of the industrial economy in general. Far from becoming an irrational and restraining force upon the modern economy (as Marx thought), the state was instrumental rationality *par excellence* (as Weber thought, though he did not, for that reason, regard it as necessarily an object of unambivalent admiration). It was Weber too who accused Marx of fallaciously assuming that there was a necessary link between the state and the specifically class character of society. If, as Weber believed, these phenomena were not necessarily linked, then even a 'classless' society, or at any rate one without private property, committed to a modern, technological economy would be no less obligated to maintaining the state as a bureaucratic and rational instrument of human intentionality.[16]

To return now to our counterfactual scenario: even if there had been a revolution in Europe, Lenin's party, insofar as its declared aims were modernisation and socialism – the ultimate combination for the rationalisation of human life (so Marx and the Bolsheviks thought) – would have had no alternative but to enforce the state upon society, in a fashion not unlike the enforcement that actually took place starting from October 1917. The only difference would be that in our imaginary counterfactual scheme of things such enforcement would be carried out in conjunction with presumably similar efforts in Europe (Weber, in any case, certainly thought that a socialist Europe would expand the realm of the state, not confine it). And it is at best a moot point whether Europe in the wake of the First World War would have been in a position to assist the Soviet Union.

Was then the Marxist view of the function of the state simply a misunderstanding? It is tempting to conclude here that the trouble with Marx and with Lenin is that the one could not, and the other did not, read Weber.[17] But the latter did, after his own fashion, vindicate Weber in practice. It is even more tempting to conclude, therefore, that Leninism in power is the triumph of Weber over Marx – and that the Jacobin element in Leninism makes this triumph all the more complete.

(7)   It only remains to deal with the second claim referred to above, namely, that the post-Lenin degeneration of the Bolshevik revolution was dictated by the exigencies of the now exacerbated internal crisis, with the capitalist West once again in the picture as a historical given. Why it is that Stalin prevailed at the end of the 1920s, and not Trotsky or Bukharin or anyone else, is, of course, a question that can be answered only by a historical account of the events, personalities and processes of the period that followed Lenin's death (just as the coming to power of the Bolsheviks in October 1917 must be explicated in the context of *that* period).

But in conformity with the approach adopted in this chapter, it is not Stalin's attainment of power, but the significance of Stalinism as a system of rule, that concerns us here. Note, however, that the claim that Stalin was the unavoidable consequence of the aforementioned internal crisis can take two separate versions: the one is that, given the conditions then prevailing in the Soviet Union, Stalinism was the only possible system that could ensure the modernisation of Russian society; the other is that these conditions were so hopeless that they rendered modernisation, at any rate under a Soviet régime, impossible in the first place: if nothing could work, then Stalinism emerges as in effect the consequence of the futility of the Bolshevik revolution. In both cases, it is sometimes argued, *whoever* had come into power (and whatever his initial intentions) would have had no choice, sooner or later, but to become a 'Stalin'.

As to the first of these versions, it is sometimes conceded, however painfully, even by some of the most bitter enemies of Stalin. But what compelling reason is there to believe any longer that Stalinism *was* a system of modernisation, in view of what we know about the nature and outcomes of the Stalinist period? I argued in the previous section that Lenin was driven by the exigencies of *his* situation to become a Weberian *malgré lui* (though he did not realise this). But this was hardly the road which Stalin took. The latter's rule represented not the triumph of the – Weberian – bureaucratic, rationalised intentionality principle, but rather of its obverse: the principle of a largely subjective, and thus irrational, personal-political intentionality. We should not confuse the political exploitation of state and bureaucracy, as in Stalinism, with rule *by* state and bureaucracy, as in Weber's pure-type. The one is the hegemony of politics over bureaucracy, the other the hegemony of bureaucracy over politics. Neither is a prospect to be wished for, but the latter has the one redeeming feature that it functions instrumentally in accordance with some constant universal principles. This was not, to say the least, a characteristic of Stalinism.

If, in the case of Lenin, Jacobinism was still tempered by the rational objective of forging an instrumental state – an objective already entailing large measures of coercion – in the case of Stalin, political autonomy becomes severed from its rational underpinnings, and coercion turns into a way of life. If not from the outset then certainly by 1936 Stalin's system of rule had, surely, become a barrier to modernisation, not a means to it. Obsession with control over society engendered obsession with arbitrariness and the logical-empirical incompatibility of the two in turn engendered damage and atrophy on a monumental scale.[18] It could well be described as intentionality gone mad.

We can never know for certain, of course, whether, as against this, the alternatives propagated by others in the 1920s would have worked. The notion, however, that *nothing* could have worked, that Stalinism was the result of futility, the ultimate dénouement of the Bolshevik revolution and of Russian Marxism, is not an attractive one, intellectually or otherwise, particularly at a time when an attempt is once more being made to free the Soviet Union of the Stalinist legacy.

NOTES

1 See my *The Social and Political Thought of Leon Trotsky* (Oxford, 1978) and the forthcoming *Russian Marxism: From Ideas to Revolution*.

2 More detailed arguments may be found in the above forthcoming work.

3 See Max Weber, *The Theory of Social and Economic Organization* (Glencoe, 1964), esp. pp. 87ff.

4 See my 'Ideas, Political Intentions and Historical Consequences', in *Totalitarian Democracy and After* (Jerusalem, 1984), pp. 232–61.

5 For the most thoroughgoing attempt at this, see G.A. Cohen, *Karl Marx's Theory of History: A Defence* (Oxford, 1978).

6 Such a view is legion but the most sophisticated of its representatives was the late Leonard Schapiro, in various works too numerous to list but only too well known.

7 On Lenin, see Neil Harding, *Lenin's Political Thought*, 2 vols. (London, 1977 and 1981); on Bukharin, see Stephen Cohen, *Bukharin and the Bolshevik Revolution: A Political Biography, 1888–1938* (New York, 1975); on Trotsky, see B. Knei-Paz, *The Social and Political Thought of Leon Trotsky*.

8 See Harding, *Lenin's Political Thought*.

9 See also Robert Service, *Lenin: A Political Life*, vol. 1 (Bloomington, 1985), especially ch. 4.

10 Though he attributed, as always, a central role to the peasants as well.

11 The central text here is, of course, his *Imperialism, The Highest Stage of Capitalism*, which first appeared in 1916.

12 My argument here takes issue, as hinted previously, with the views of Harding; see, in particular, p. 327 of his second volume, *Lenin's Political Thought*.

13 The appearance, though very problematic assimilation of Leninist tendencies, thereafter can be attributed at first to the impact of the Bolshevik success in Russia and then, of course, to the Soviet influence over Western Communist parties.

14 Anyone doubting the seriousness, uniqueness and ingenuity of the soviets should consult the meticulous work done on this subject by Israel Getzler.

15 No one made a more penetrating analysis of this Bolshevik Jacobinism, as he called it, than Trotsky: see his *Nashi politicheskie zadachi* (Geneva, 1904). For the reasons which led him to join the Bolsheviks, see Knei-Paz, *The Social and Political Thought of Leon Trotsky*, pp. 225–33.

16 The central text for Weber's views on these matters is his *Economy and Society*, 2 vols. (Berkeley, 1978).

17 As far as I am aware there are only two or three references to Weber in

Lenin's writings and they are of no relevance to the issues discussed here. Lenin's *State and Revolution* is a work that would have profited immensely from a reading of Weber.

18 For a many-faceted discussion of the phenomenon of Stalinism, see Robert C. Tucker (ed.), *Stalinism: Essays in Historical Interpretation* (New York, 1977).

INDEX